Feminist Jurisprudence

New Feminist Perspective Series

General Editor: Rosemarie Tong, Davidson College

Claiming Reality: Phenomenology and Women's Experience
  by Louise Levesque-Lopman, Regis College

Evidence on Her Own Behalf: Women's Narrative as Theological Voice
  by Elizabeth Say, California State University, Northridge

Feminist Jurisprudence: The Difference Debate
  Edited by Leslie Friedman Goldstein, University of Delaware

Is Women's Philosophy Possible?
  by Nancy J. Holland, Hamline University

Manhood and Politics: A Feminist Reading in Political Theory
  by Wendy L. Brown, University of California, Santa Cruz

Rethinking Masculinity: Philosophical Explorations in Light of Feminism
  Edited by Larry May, Washington University, and Robert A. Strikwerda, Indiana University, Kokomo

Speaking from the Heart: A Feminist Perspective on Ethics
  by Rita C. Manning, San Jose State University

Toward a Feminist Epistemology
  by Jane Duran, University of California, Santa Barbara

Women, Militarism, and War: Essays in History, Politics, and Social Theory
  Edited by Jean Bethke Elshtain, Vanderbilt University, and Sheila Tobias, University of Arizona

Women, Sex and the Law
  by Rosemarie Tong, Davidson College

Feminist Jurisprudence

The Difference Debate

Edited, with an introduction by

Leslie Friedman Goldstein

Rowman & Littlefield Publishers, Inc.

ROWMAN & LITTLEFIELD PUBLISHERS, INC.

Published in the United States of America
by Rowman & Littlefield Publishers, Inc.
4720 Boston Way, Lanham, Maryland 20706

British Cataloging in Publication Information Available

Library of Congress Cataloging-in-Publication Data

Feminist jurisprudence : the difference debate / edited,
with an introduction by Leslie Friedman Goldstein.
p.   cm. — (New feminist perspectives series)
Includes bibliographical references and index.
1. Women—Legal status, laws, etc.—United States.   2. Sex
discrimination against women—Law and legislation—United
States.   3. Sex and law—United States.   4. Feminism—
United States.   5. Feminist theory.   I. Goldstein, Leslie
Friedman, 1945–   .   II. Series.
KF478.A5F46   1992
346.7301'34—dc20   92–7237   CIP
[347.306134]

ISBN 0–8476–7744–3 (cloth : alk. paper)
ISBN 0–8476–7745–1 (pbk. : alk. paper)

Printed in the United States of America

 The paper used in this publication meets the minimum requirements of
American National Standard for Information Sciences—Permanence of
Paper for Printed Library Materials, ANSI Z39.48–1984.

Contents

1
Introduction

Leslie Friedman Goldstein

This volume grew out of a panel at the September 1990 meeting of the American Political Science Association. The creation of that panel was a response to the burgeoning literature in feminist jurisprudence. Because reaction both on and off the panel was so enthusiastic, we concluded that it would be a good idea to draw the papers together into a single collection, supplemented and enriched by some of the leading examples of feminist jurisprudence from already published law review articles (Chapters 3 and 4), as well as by a paper (Chapter 8) on a legal issue that has become more prominent since 1990, that of fetal rights. The original panel discussants Prof. Richard Battistoni and Prof. Molly Shanley agreed to round out the collection with some concluding reflections on the book as a whole (in Chapter 9).

The compilation of reflections on and examples of feminist jurisprudence that comprise this book are unified by a shared concern with the legal significance of difference, that is, the difference between men and women. This question is at least as old as Plato's *Republic* but it has taken on a new urgency of late. That urgency became evident in 1987 with the public spectacle of feminist group pitted against feminist group in the chambers of the U.S. Supreme Court, disagreeing over whether it was legitimate for states to mandate a "special" benefit for women disabled by pregnancy (a disability leave of up to four months, depending on employee request and medical need).[1] The publicity generated by that case—*Cal Fed v. Guerra*—made clear that by the late 1980s the label *feminist* could no longer accurately predict a person's specific position on public policy affecting women. The pregnancy leave debate among feminists turned out to be only the tip of the iceberg; a whole slew of debates has been raging among feminist legal scholars during the past several years over not only a wide range of social policies but even such core questions as what it means to be a feminist or to employ a feminist methodology. This book is an attempt to introduce a wider range of readers to that debate. Although the participants in the debate all agree that law should be used to ameliorate the lot of women, disagreement is rampant over *how* to proceed with that amelioration. While individual scholars stake out a wide multiplicity of nuanced positions, the poles of the debate can be described as follows: One group insists that it is a fact that women now and for the foreseeable future (and, some would add, inevitably) are different from men not only in the lives they lead but also in what they value and how they think, and that law must be changed so that it will accommodate, make room for, and put a higher value (than heretofore) on woman's ways. The other group counters with the argument that such accommodation by the law functions in practice as a trap, and would lead women right back to the "pedestal as cage" position from which feminists for decades have been trying to free them.

This book introduces readers to the debate via Chapter 2, "Can This Marriage Be Saved? Feminist Public Policy and Feminist Jurisprudence"—an essay by this author that provides a detailed overview of the conflicts currently dividing scholars within the camp of feminist jurisprudence. After providing this overview, it tracks the evolution of those conflicts from the early, eclectic years of the modern feminist movement through legal and theoretical developments of the 1970s and 1980s. These developments included early impressive litigation successes experienced by proponents of formal legal equality, followed by increased rigidity on the part of those proponents, and then research by three important scholars whose work raised serious doubts about formal equality as a feminist strategy—Catharine MacKinnon, Lenore Weitzman, and Carol Gilligan. Finally, expanding on a typology developed by law professor Christine Littleton, the essay suggests a multi-pronged path out of the thicket of contemporary intrafeminist disputes.

That multipronged path attempts to take account of the fact that our society disadvantages women in a variety of ways. There are at least four different kinds of disadvantages faced by women: (1) They are penalized (as are men) when they fail to conform to the societal prescriptions for their gender (e.g., to wear skirts/dresses and delicate shoes in professional jobs). (2) When they do conform to the female gender role, as in performing housecare and childcare, the work women do is devalued. (3) They are discriminated against by virtue of being biologically female; this occurs both through measures of conscious sex discrimination and through institutionalized structures that are biased in favor of male physiology (as in university rules that strictly limit the years for publishing enough to earn tenure to those years which just happen to be, for women, their prime postdoc child-bearing years). (4) Finally, they are subordinated to men through sexual violence with such phenomena as rape, child molesting, pornography, and wife battering. A legal doctrine designed for rectifying one of these problems, if overly universalized, might be at best irrelevant for, and at worst detrimental to, another of them. The variegated range of contemporary feminist goals, this chapter concludes, can be attained only by policies that are in some cases sex conscious (as in making the workplace comfortable for pregnancy) and in other cases gender conscious (as in rectifying divorce settlements so they no longer systematically penalize the primary caretaker of the children).

Chapter 2 is followed by two of the outstanding examples of mutually opposed positions within feminist jurisprudence. The first of the pair —Chapter 3, "Deconstructing Gender" by law professor Joan C. Williams—is a tightly argued attack on what she calls "the feminism of difference." Her attack contests both the practical advisability of celebrating "women's culture" and the empirical validity of Carol Gilligan's influential assertion that women think about morality in terms different from those valued by men.[2] Professor Williams insists that, to the degree that Gilligan's portrayal is accurate, it "merely reflects the oppressive realities of the current gender system." Williams argues that, because this gender system produces the economic marginalization of women, the task of legal feminists ought to be the promotion of policies that will de-institutionalize in every possible way the correlation between gender roles and biological sex differences. The problem with the feminism of difference is that it functions with precisely the opposite effect, inevitably furthering the economic marginalization of women. She illustrates her claim with a trenchant analysis of the *EEOC v. Sears* sex discrimination case,[3] where feminism-of-difference arguments were turned against women with devastating effect. Finally, Williams argues that in terms of substantive reform the first priority of feminists ought to be the alteration of those aspects of the wage labor system that condemn women to poverty as a result of their role in reproduction and childcare. Her analysis indicates that (difference-oriented) arguments that further entrench childcare as peculiarly women's work have a retardant rather than progressive impact on such reform.

Chapter 4, "Prince Charming: Abstract Equality" by law professor Mary E. Becker, provides a correspondingly trenchant attack on the feminism that defends an abstract standard of legal equality for men and women. While Becker's essay does not specifically confront the arguments in Joan Williams's, the two pieces serve as a counterpoint to each other in this collection. With particular attention to alimony cases,[4] to the *Cal Fed* case, and to the Supreme Court decision in *Johnson v. Transportation Agency*[5] that upheld the legality of employers' affirmative action programs for women under Title VII,[6] Professor Becker argues that the women most likely to benefit from legal rules imposing equal treatment of men and women are a small elite—those few women who have managed to accumulate the achievements and the modes of behavior needed for success in a "man's world." Most women—those most influenced by the gender expectations of society—stand to suffer from the imposition of formally equal rules, both because the standard of what is needed to merit equal treatment is a standard constructed with stereotypical men in mind (e.g., male workers who have wives to care for their children) and because the judges who will be deciding what counts as "equal" will be mostly male and nonfeminist (as were the judges who upheld an award of only four years' alimony at an annual rate of 15 percent of her husband's salary to a woman who gave up a well-paying job when her first child was born and stayed out of the workforce—at her husband's insistence— for 20 years, serving in a variety of supportive roles for his successful career as a highly paid corporate executive). For these reasons, Professor Becker argues, feminists should openly champion compensatory policies for women disadvantaged by gender roles and by workforce rules constructed with attention to male rather than female physiology. She insists that piecemeal legislative change aiming at fairness for such women offers much more promise and harms fewer women than would a broad-based, judicially imposed requirement of formally equal treatment.

The ongoing difference debate between scholars like Joan Williams and Mary Becker is then reexamined in Chapter 5, "How Is Law Male? A Feminist Perspective on Constitutional Interpretation" by political scientist Judith Baer. She takes a closer look at the allegation, prominent among difference feminists, that law is derived from "predominantly male ways of knowing, thinking, and living" and is therefore "intrinsically destructive of women's interests." Upon reflection, Professor Baer concludes that much of what is considered female thinking—as in the kind typically done by mothers—includes a variety of the aspects of mental rigor widely viewed as masculine. Conversely, much of archetypically masculine reasoning—for example, that done by Supreme Court justices deciding legal cases—contains heavy doses of the attention to factual context and emotion-guided reaction (as in the shocks-the-conscience legal standard put forth by Justice Felix Frankfurter)[7] often associated with supposedly female thinking. Professor Baer concludes that judicial reasoning "does not maintain, in practice, a dichotomy between reason and emotion, between theory and experience, between the general and the individual" and that it is a profound mistake for feminists to reject legal reasoning as intrinsically "antifemale." Moreover, the judicial role in the American political scheme contains a number of elements that echo the feminine social role; these include the practical necessity for deference to and persuasion of more powerful others. And the negotiations engaged in by Supreme Court justices among themselves, like that stereotypically ascribed to women, has often included substantial doses of manipulation by appeal to emotion.

On the other hand, Professor Baer acknowledges that many legal and constitutional doctrines as they have in fact been developed do operate systematically to favor men's interests over women's. This, she explains, is not because law is per se male but rather because of the historic fact that law has been developed by men primarily for men. As women conscious of women's interests and willing to innovate in legal and constitutional doctrine move into influence within the legal and judicial profession, a feminist jurisprudence offers hope that American law could break free of its erstwhile male bias and promote a meaningful sexual equality, she concludes.

Each of the next three chapters in the volume provides an examination of a concrete policy issue with profound impact on women's lives: abortion policy, divorce policy, and fetal protection policy, respectively. Each of these policy explorations shows the impact of the new feminist jurisprudence, but the impact manifests itself in dramatically differing ways.

In Chapter 6, "Interpreting Abortion," Prof. Mark Graber's examination of the constitutionality of abortion regulation pays special heed to the advice of feminist law professor Catharine MacKinnon that a feminist jurisprudence ought to take a hard look at "what is, the meaning of what is, and the way what is, is enforced."[8] Indeed, he claims that his analysis of the abortion issue pays greater heed to this advice than does MacKinnon's own analysis. Graber argues that the proper starting point for considering the constitutionality of abortion restriction is an examination of the *actual* implementation of pre-*Roe*[9] abortion policy, with serious attention to the social consequences of that implementation. He insists that precisely this sort of enterprise is an important part of the reasoning appropriate for a broad range of issues in constitutional law. Professor Graber concludes that abstractions about privacy miss what should have been in *Roe* the dominant concern, namely, the constitutionality of a political practice he accurately describes as follows:

> First, the state passes various restrictions on abortion. Secondly, state officials permit physicians to perform abortions whenever their affluent friends wish to terminate their pregnancies, voice no objection when affluent women visit other states to have abortions, and wink at criminal abortions that maim and kill less affluent women.

This kind of careful look at public policy as it in fact affects the lives of real women is indeed what is being called for in many works of feminist jurisprudence, but it is worth noting that a social practice analysis of the sort Graber defends is compatible also with more mainstream jurisprudence. The Supreme Court itself, for instance, in *Furman v. Georgia*[10] decided that capital punishment *as practiced* in the United States was so arbitrary as to violate the due process clause.

Graber's examination of abortion as a social practice, while it may understate the degree to which even affluent women were burdened and harmed by abortion restrictions, does have the salutary effect of focusing attention on the unusual degree to which the implementation of abortion policy struck with arbitrary impact. One is hard pressed to come up with any illegal medical practice that physicians are tempted to perform for relatives, friends, and friends of friends with anything even remotely close to the frequency with which abortions were performed in the pre-*Roe* period. That fact may well tell us something important about the place of abortion in American culture—something that policymakers ignore at their peril.

Chapter 7, "Unsettling 'Woman': Competing Subjectivities in No-fault Divorce and Divorce Mediation," presents Prof. Lisa Bower's analysis of recent changes—both substantive and procedural—in the law of divorce. She focuses on the historic reform efforts of feminist legal scholar Herma Hill Kay, one of the early and influential advocates of no-fault divorce in California, which pioneered the no-fault movement that was to sweep the nation. While Professor Bower does not contradict the scholarly consensus that feminism as an organized political movement did not promote the no-fault reform in California, she does add a useful corrective to that consensus by zeroing in on the rhetoric of 1960s feminists and its depiction of traditional marriage as an institution oppressive to women. She argues persuasively that the 1960s feminist discourse, which aimed at restructuring marriage into an institution where woman could function as a coequal independent partner with as much right to personal fulfillment as her husband, influentially shaped public consciousness toward viewing divorce as a "potentially liberating experience." Her further analysis gives particular attention to the fact that competing conceptions of the subject *woman* were evident within feminist discourse as early as the 1960s. Bower's essay implicitly suggests that the conflicts Chapter 2 identifies within contemporary feminist jurisprudence have deeper historical and conceptual roots than is generally acknowledged.

Chapter 8, "Fetal Rights and Feminism" by Prof. Joseph Losco, takes a straightforward look at feminist debates over fetal protection policy. Following the theoretical framework suggested by Susan Behuniak-Long,[11] Losco groups feminist analysts of reproductive policy into two camps: radical and liberal. He then broadly outlines the postures of the two camps and proceeds to give a more detailed analysis of the liberal feminist arguments (and of their critics) since those are the ones that have been prominent within the specific arena of legal reform. While Losco does not proclaim himself to be a feminist, and while his essay examines the criticisms of feminist arguments as well as the arguments themselves, he ends up endorsing and developing a number of feminist positions. Notably, he endorses and develops further evidence for the argument put forth by legal feminists that the pattern of prosecutions of women for fetal abuse exhibits bias on the basis of sex, race, and class. Losco points to the growing body of scientific evidence of male parent contribution to preventable genetic defects, as well as to specific court cases where male partner involvement in causing harm to the fetus was ignored while solely the pregnant woman was prosecuted. Moreover, he cautions that the *Johnson Controls* decision[12]—hailed by many feminists as a victory—may backfire to women's detriment as corporations heed the decision in ways that guard themselves from liability for workplace harm to the fetus, "substantially increasing the liability of pregnant women in the long run." And finally, he endorses the argument that a judicial overturning of *Roe v. Wade,* while it would harm women in a number of ways, would also remove what has functioned as a major prop in the arsenal of pro-fetal-rights ethicists, namely, the claim that pregnant women, because they have freely chosen to continue the pregnancy to a live birth, have enforceable moral duties to their pre-born offspring.

The issue of difference permeates these three policy analyses, although with varying degrees of visibility. It is most prominent in the Bower treatment of changes in the law of divorce. Professor Bower centers her discussion on the competing ideas about what it means to be a woman; these ideas competed in the 1960s not only within the feminist camp, but even within the body of arguments put forth by individual feminists, such as Herma Hill Kay. The vision of woman as a nurturing, caring subject implied a special role for woman within the family structure, and that role entailed a certain degree of dependency. This particular vision would foster the maternal preference in child custody and a paternal duty of generous alimony and child support, to free up the mother for her nurturing role. On the other hand, the vision of woman as rational, capable, equal, and independent fostered ideas of egalitarian coparenting; easy no-fault divorce; joint custody after divorce; and divorce settlements that aimed at moving women quickly toward financial independence from the former spouse, with alimony only for limited periods and geared toward providing education and job training. Neither of these visions has entirely disappeared from feminist discourse or from aspects of the legal system. They continue in an unstable coexistence, competing for cultural dominance.

Although Professor Graber does not place it at the center of his discussion of the constitutionality of abortion restriction, he does contend that the issue of difference is the political fulcrum that divides anti-abortion activists from pro-choice activists. As Graber puts it, "this debate is over the meaning of sex equality." In his depiction, pro-choice women aim to minimize the societal effect of physiological sex differences by freeing women to subordinate their reproductive role to their career aspirations. Pro-life women, as he describes them, see such subordination as capitulation by women to male values, believe that the fulfillment of women lies in rearing children and loving and caring for husbands, and favor social policies that would place the same value on female as on male activities. Professor Graber drew these depictions from two studies of the politics of the abortion debate, those by Kristin Luker[13] and Faye Ginsburg.[14] While it would not be terribly surprising to learn from further studies that some abortion issue activists actually do care about such judicially emphasized concepts as privacy or the life of the fetus, the degree to which the difference debate seems to have permeated the grass-roots abortion debate is nonetheless striking.

While sex difference as such is not a prominent theme in Professor Losco's analysis of the fetal rights debate, his essay nonetheless clearly exposes a number of the ways in which physiological sex differences are socially constructed. As a physiological fact, the female carries the fetus in utero; the male does not. Still, our social policies have greatly exaggerated this difference by imposing fetus-protecting workplace restrictions on women, but not extending similarly cautious restrictions to gene-bearing male potential parents; by imposing criminal penalties on females who cause harm to their fetus, but not bothering to arrest or prosecute men whose behavior contributed to the identical harm; and by entertaining children's lawsuits against mothers, but not fathers, for behavior that caused birth defects. Moreover, the Losco essay reminds us that "the difference that difference makes"[15] varies dramatically by socioeconomic status. For instance, Losco describes studies showing that a slightly greater percentage of white women than black women indulge in illegal drugs; yet black women are nine and a half times more likely to be reported to state authorities for substance abuse than white women. This kind of discrepancy highlights the importance of the call increasingly found in works of feminist jurisprudence for paying more attention to the differences among various groups of women in order to rectify the variety of sex-related injustices faced by women.

The difference debate within feminist jurisprudence is not likely to end soon. This collection is offered in the hope that readers will be encouraged to join in the conversation.

Notes

1. *California Federal Savings and Loan v. Guerra*, 479 U.S. 272 (1987).

2. Carol Gilligan, *In a Different Voice* (Cambridge, Mass.: Harvard University Press, 1982).

3. *Equal Employment Opportunity Commission (EEOC) v. Sears, Roebuck and Company*, 628 F.Supp. 1264, aff'd. 839 F.2d 302.

4. *Orr v. Orr*, 440 U.S. 268 (1979); and *Otis v. Otis*, 299 N.W.2d 114 (Minn. 1980).

5. *Johnson v. Transportation Agency*, 480 U.S. 616 (1987).

6. Title VII of the Civil Rights Act, Public Law 88-352 (July 2, 1964), as amended; see 42 U.S.C. Secs. 2000e–2000e-17 (1982).

7. In the case *Rochin v. California*, 342 U.S. 165, 172 (1952).

8. Catharine MacKinnon, *Toward a Feminist Theory of the State* (Cambridge, Mass.: Harvard University Press, 1989), p. xii.

9. All references to *"Roe"* in this Introduction refer to *Roe v. Wade,* 410 U.S. 113 (1973).

10. *Furman v. Georgia,* 408 U.S. 238 (1972).

11. Susan Behuniak-Long, "Radical Conceptions: Reproductive Technologies and Feminist Theories," *Women and Politics* 10(3):39–64 (1990).

12. *United Automobile Workers (International Union, United Auto, Aerospace and Agricultural Workers of America, UAW, et al.) v. Johnson Controls,* 111 S.Ct. 1196, 498 U.S. — (1991).

13. Kristin Luker, *Abortion and the Politics of Motherhood* (Berkeley: University of California Press, 1984).

14. Faye Ginsburg, *Contested Lives: The Abortion Debate in an American Community* (Berkeley: University of California Press, 1989).

15. This evocative phrase was coined by Catharine MacKinnon and is repeated so often as to have become almost a slogan within feminist jurisprudence.

2

Can This Marriage Be Saved?
Feminist Public Policy and Feminist
Jurisprudence

Leslie Friedman Goldstein

In commonwealths, this controversy [over who should rule within the family, which arises because of the approximate natural equality of men and women] is decided by the civil law: and for the most part . . . *the sentence is in favor of the father; because for the most part commonwealths have been erected by the fathers,* not by the mothers of families.

Thomas Hobbes (emphasis added)[1]

I cannot see any purpose in calling any position in the debate between different feminist positions "anti-feminist." . . . We are also at a point at which feminists have no political unity.

Ellen DuBois, historian[2]

This chapter examines recent feminist jurisprudence, and observes that there is considerable discord in the house of feminist legal theory. The chapter documents disagreement among feminist jurists across a wide range of policy questions and underlying theoretical issues. It then tries to locate the sources of these conflicts by providing a political and theoretical genealogy of legal feminism.

The account begins with the observation that in its initial years the feminist movement adopted a multipronged and flexible approach for attacking women's subordination to men. One aspect of this approach—the call for formal legal equality—was enormously successful. That approach, however, left many problems unaddressed. With the nearly total success of formal equality, feminist energies were freed for other issues, and these took on increasing prominence. Moreover, three analysts (or architects of feminism, as we shall regard them later) began producing important limits to formal equality.

This essay indicates some of the lines of conflict produced by these newly important issues and theories. Next, it delineates four separate kinds of policy goals of American feminism, and concludes that these differing goals call forth differing legal approaches. Two of them will require sex-neutral (but gender-conscious) approaches, while two others will require sex-conscious policies. A single, all-encompassing approach is not capable of serving the variegated practical goals of the current feminist movement. Finally, the essay criticizes two dangers in current jurisprudential tendencies: (1) an oversimplified recourse to the research of Carol Gilligan, and (2) a kind of counterextreme of taking the deconstruction of the subject *woman* so far that nothing coherent remains of it, thus rendering a feminist political program impossible.

Discord in the House of Feminism, 1990

Feminist law professors have for the past couple of decades been attempting to cope with a reality acknowledged by Thomas Hobbes 350 years ago. Not only did government originate as a protection racket, but it originated as a *male* protection racket, set up by men for men. As was obvious to Hobbes and to other clear-eyed thinkers over the centuries, the systems of "civil law" have typically served men's interests at the expense of women's interests. The overwhelming male bias of these systems puts feminist lawyers and law professors in a difficult position. They are trying to fix a rigged system by means of the processes provided by that system.[3]

One partially successful strategy for alleviating the mistreatment of women—at least within the American legal system—has been to demand that the law be rendered more consistent with its own (wildly unfulfilled) promises regarding equality. Pursuing this strategy, the feminists of the 1960s and early 1970s focused attention on the equal protection clause of the Fourteenth Amendment and Congress's obligation to enforce it, as well as on Congress's duty "to establish justice" as promised in the Preamble to the Constitution. Antidiscrimination rules were adopted by Congress in the Equal Pay Act (1963), the Civil Rights Act (1964), Title IX (1972), and the Equal Credit Opportunity Act (1975). The Supreme Court became persuaded begin-

ning in November 1971 that the equal protection clause frowned on
sex discrimination in most circumstances.[4]

However, the limitations of this equality-based strategy became
apparent by the mid-1970s. In two cases involving the imposition of
economic disadvantages on women employees who give birth,[5] a
sharply divided all-male Supreme Court said, essentially, "This is not
sex discrimination. Giving birth is different from other life events (such
as illness or accidents). Therefore, it may be treated as different."
Although the Court's reasoning is easily mocked, there was nothing
illogical here. The problem was not logic. As many feminists have
since pointed out, the problem was that worker insurance systems—
like the legal and economic systems of which they are a part, and like
the labor unions that bargained or lobbied for the insurance systems—
were set up by men, for men. Thus, they insured all of the disabling
things that could happen to male workers: accidents, illnesses, and
even elective surgery. Naturally, they did not bother with the disabling
things that happened only to women workers: pregnancy and its
typically subsequent childbirth.

As this analysis has already revealed, one can *find* elements of
equality in experiences that are on the whole different. So some
feminists pursued the equality strategy in precisely that way, persuading Congress by 1978 that public policy should be guided by the
equality discoverable in the experience of incapacity to work as a
result of being *physically disabled* rather than by the differences
between childbirth and other disabilities (e.g., it is generally more fully
chosen than is "elective" surgery; it is a normal part of the life cycle,
etc.). The legislation that resulted from this campaign—the Pregnancy
Discrimination Act (PDA)—has since become the occasion of a much
publicized split among some feminist organizations and feminist attorneys. Following earlier sections in which it prohibits employment
discrimination "on the basis of sex," the act states:

> The terms . . . "on the basis of sex" include, but are not limited to,
> because of or on the basis of pregnancy, childbirth, or related medical
> conditions; and women affected by pregnancy, childbirth, or related
> medical conditions shall be treated the same for all employment-related
> purposes, including receipt of benefits under fringe benefit programs, as
> other persons not so affected but similar in their ability or inability to
> work, and nothing in section 2000e-2(h) of this title shall be interpreted to
> permit otherwise.[6]

The contending feminist groups divided specifically over the question whether state law may be permitted to diverge from the evident

"plain meaning" of the federal law in order to mandate employee leaves for workers incapacitated due to pregnancy and/or childbirth even when the state law does not mandate medically necessary leaves for nonpregnant workers. The group associated with the National Organization for Women (NOW) and a variety of other feminist organizations,[7] which group is most prominently led in the jurisprudential field by Prof. Wendy Williams, answered no. For the Supreme Court case *California Federal Savings and Loan v. Guerra*[8] their amici curiae briefs argued that, if the State of California wants to mandate leaves for workers disabled by pregnancy, it must honor the federal PDA by mandating leaves also to other disabled employees. The other group of feminists,[9] in a brief authored by Prof. Christine Littleton of the Coalition for Reproductive Equality in the Workplace, argued that employer provision of leave benefits to women disabled by pregnancy in fact operates to *equalize* employees' situation across sex lines: Just as male workers could become parents without fearing loss of employment, California's pregnancy leave requirement ensured that female workers, too, could face parenthood without that fear. Professor Littleton's version of nondiscrimination was accepted by the Court majority in the *Cal Fed* case, although Justice Thurgood Marshall also paid some lip service to the arguments of the NOW brief.[10]

While the specific pregnancy leave question was thus settled, the fissure among feminist legal theorists exhibited in the *Cal Fed* case extends, deeply and widely, to a range of public policy questions. In a political climate where a legislative mandate of sex-neutral parental leave faces the successful veto of President George Bush, should feminists work actively to try to get at least (non-sex-neutral) maternity leave mandated? Mary Becker, Sylvia Law, Christine Littleton, Herma Hill Kay, Ann Scales, Linda Krieger, and Patricia Cooney would say yes, while Wendy Williams, Nadine Taub, Deborah Rhode, and Joan Williams would say no.[11] Should laws make it possible for women to sue the producers of pornography when those women know their life chances have been negatively influenced by the pervasiveness of pornographic imagery that eroticizes the debasement, brutalization, and humiliation of women? Catharine MacKinnon, Ann Scales, Robin West, and Carrie Menkel-Meadow (with some reservations) say yes; Mary Dunlap, Deborah Rhode, and members of the Feminist Anti-censorship Task Force say no.[12] Is there something particularly female about the moral imperative that one should exhibit a sense of responsibility and care for others, and would the reform of our law to make it impose various duties of care for others entail the injecting of specifically female values into the law? Leslie Bender, Carrie Menkel-Meadow, Kenneth Karst, Lucinda Finley, Robin West, and Suzanna Sherry would say yes; Joan Williams, Cynthia Fuchs Epstein, and Wendy Williams would say no.[13] Should forcible rape laws be made sex neutral in their wording and enforcement? Mary Dunlap and Wendy Williams say yes, while Herma Hill Kay and Catharine MacKinnon say no.[14] Should statutory rape laws be made sex neutral in their wording and enforcement? Ann Scales, Nadine Taub, and Deborah Rhode say yes; Alison Jaggar says no.[15] Is the use of the "battered women syndrome" defense for women who kill their husbands or live-in partners[16] a development that marks feminist progress or regress? Lenore Walker would say progress; Elizabeth Schneider and Christine Littleton say regress.[17] In deciding child custody cases upon divorce, should the feminist jurist encourage a preference for the primary caretaker, who is generally the mother? Martha Fineman and Joan Williams argue yes; Deborah Rhode is critical of that solution, and leans toward a no.[18]

And beyond the widespread and deep schisms over concrete public policy, feminist theorists disagree on underlying basics as well. One legal theorist defines feminism as "a method, as the critique of objectivity";[19] another theorist of feminism insists that feminist epistemology offers a "stronger objectivity" than pre-feminist thinking has been able to attain.[20] Yet a third points out astutely that the frequent claim by feminist theorists, in law reviews and elsewhere, that the postmodern critique of objectivity is a feminist project fails to notice that the founders of this critique have all been privileged white male Europeans: Nietzsche, Heidegger, Wittgenstein, Saussure, Derrida, Foucault, and Lacan.[21] To put it mildly, their work is not noted for its feminist content.[22] Even at the level of explanation of the sources (and therefore potential malleability) of gender differences, the feminist legal theorists are divided. Robin West articulates a theory of biological essentialism to explain women's supposedly "different voice" and distinctive morality of nurturance, interpersonal responsibility, and trust,[23] whereas most feminist legal theorists attribute the same gender-linked characteristics to social conditioning—either to the female monopoly on childrearing[24] or to the vast array of societal incentives and disincentives structured to convince women they are born to serve.[25] These conflicting explanatory theories produce conflicting policy implications. For Robin West, the erotic charge of a bond with a more powerful, dominant Other resonates deeply with (many) women's authentic psychic needs and thus is something that feminists should

honor and foster;[26] for Catharine MacKinnon the eroticization by men
of their domination over women is *the* core of the problem that
feminists must attack.[27] Perhaps most basically of all, feminist legal
theorists are divided over the kind of society to which we should be
aspiring. As one law review article poses the question,

> Is "our" goal a world in which there is more respect for and reward of
> those traits, skills, and contributions traditionally associated with
> women? Or should we try to discourage these traits, skills, and contribu-
> tions so that women will be more like men? Feminists today are deeply
> divided on these issues.[28]

Can one identify any unifying structure at all, then, beneath all these
many fissures in the "many-gabled house" that is feminist jurisprudence?[29] Certainly one can at least say that this many-gabled house
does rest on a unitary foundation. All feminists share the commitment
to alleviate the systematic disadvantaging of women that goes on in all
known societies. The house of feminism then divides, however, into
widely disparate gables because feminists disagree even over what
constitutes (i.e., what would count as) the disadvantaging of women.
To envision the arrangement of these gables, it will be helpful to
provide a genealogy—political and theoretical—of the construction of
the many-gabled house of feminist legal theory.

The House That Feminists Built: Structure of the 1970s

In November 1967, the second annual conference of the National
Organization for Women laid out a blueprint for the initial structure of
feminist public policy with the NOW Bill of Rights.[30] Its planks were
as follows:

1. A federal Equal Rights Amendment
2. Enforcement of (existing) laws banning sex discrimination in
   employment
3. Maternity leave rights in employment and in Social Security
   benefits
4. Tax deductions for home and child care expenses of working
   parents
5. Childcare centers
6. Equal and unsegregated education

7. Equal job training opportunities and (living) allowances for women in poverty
8. Right of women to control their reproductive lives[31]

An analysis of this policy blueprint from the perspective of the wrongs it aimed to correct indicates that there were at least four different kinds of goals in the initial years of the modern feminist movement. First, planks 1, 2, 6, and the first half of 7 aim to give women formal equality of opportunity in the public economy. These take aim at the evil of discriminating on a group basis against individual women who qualify for jobs or education according to standards originally set for men. Second, planks 4 and 5 aim to liberate women from tasks imposed by gender ideology so as to free them to function effectively in the public economy.[32] Third, plank 3 aims to restructure the public economy in order to take women's reproductive physiology into account in a way that does not penalize women for being physically different from men. In aiming to restructure both women's lives and the public economy, all of these contain the core goal not of making women more like men (for whom the public economy, admittedly, was designed), but of *freeing* women from economic dependence on individual men.[33] It is worth emphasizing that the freedom from dependence on individual men did not entail the blind (to reality) abstraction *self-sufficiency*. As the planks about childcare centers, government subsidy of them through tax deductions, and government provision of decent living allowances for poor women[34] make clear, the modern women's movement understood from the start that women would need a societal support system if they were to get out from under dependence on individual men.[35]

The underlying theme of planks 1 through 7 was not rigid legal equality, then, although an end to sex discrimination did figure prominently in some of them.[36] Rather, the underlying theme of the original feminist platform of our time was an attack on women's subordination to men by means of the gender ideology of domesticity—the ideology that specified man as "head" and economic provider of the family and woman as supplier of sexual, domestic, and childcare service within the family. (This domesticity ideology was echoed in the public sphere; women's jobs tracked the wife/mother role: waitresses, secretaries, maids, nurses, nursery and elementary school teachers. And since women were not viewed as "providers," salaries for these jobs were kept low.)

Fourth and finally, one finds another kind of goal in the NOW Bill of

Rights. Plank 8, favoring reproductive freedom for women, implicitly swept much more broadly than the first seven. Reproductive freedom was a pressing issue for women in particular because of the sexual ideology[37] of our society. First of all, pregnancy out of wedlock was stigmatizing for females. Pregnant teenagers were routinely expelled from public schools, while the schools did nothing to penalize the fathers. Females could mitigate the stigma prior to the child's birth only by marriage, that is, by a public declaration that they belonged to one male. This stigma was part of a sexual double standard that distinguished "loose women" from "good girls": The loose ones were available for men's pleasure; the good ones, available to men for marriage and thus for assuring the reliability of a biological heir. Beyond the social stigma, pregnancy for a young woman meant either sole responsibility for caring for a helpless infant, or else marriage in which she would still have primary responsibility for the infant. Either way, the woman's education or career opportunities were severely disrupted. And even for married women, more children meant more childcare responsibilities.

One can imagine social arrangements in which control over one's reproductive life would not be such a pressing issue for women. For instance, instead of being stigmatized, childbirth might be socially honored—viewed, say, as risking one's life for the good of society, as going to war is viewed. Also imaginable might be a society in which the biological father or a societally run institution takes complete charge of the infant at birth. (I am not saying this is a desirable scenario, just that it is imaginable.) In such a society, where women who give birth would be viewed as public heroes and have zero responsibility for childcare, it is unlikely that abortion would be such a pressing women's issue.[38]

From this angle, the demand that women gain the right "to control their reproductive lives" reads as more about controlling the course of their lives than about the mere question of whether they reproduce. In this sense, the demand was implicitly attentive to a problem that was going to move much more into the spotlight in the decade of the 1980s, namely, the subordination of women to men by sexuality itself.

The original NOW policy package at the end of the 1960s, then, expressed a fairly consistent ideology. It said that the problem women faced was that the psychosocial expectations for women, which might be called "gender ideology," and the parallel expectations around reproduction, which might be called "sexual ideology," ended up pushing women into situations (read: traditional marriages) where they were utterly dependent on individual men for economic resources and social status and where they were expected to find fulfillment in promoting the flourishing of a small group of other people, namely, their husband and children. The kind of fulfillment that men have found in contributing to public life—by involvement in the public economy, in politics, in the public world of the arts, or in broad social issues— was denied to women by the prevailing gender ideology and by discrimination within the public sphere that reflected that ideology.[39] The NOW Bill of Rights called for public policies that would open up public life to women.

There is a sense in which the 1970s was a decade of massive success for feminist public policy and also a sense in which it was a tremendous failure. Thanks to feminism, at the level of public ideology, it became the norm for wives and mothers—even mothers of young children—to work outside the home, and it became socially acceptable to work in jobs not traditional for women. And contrary to what many people say, this shift was not simply a matter of economic need. What people "need" is very much influenced by ideology, by a sense of the appropriate. Husbands went from being ashamed of their wives' jobs (in the 1950s) to proud of them (in the 1980s). Women entered professional schools and the professions in unprecedented numbers. They even entered the last all-male bastions of the Ivy League (Yale, Princeton, Columbia, Dartmouth) and the military academies.

At the level of law there was enormous change, too. The Equal Rights Amendment garnered almost unanimous endorsement in Congress and ratification in 70 percent of the states, plus support by public opinion majorities in every state. Although the ERA did not become an official part of the Constitution, during the 1970s the Supreme Court did adopt something rather similar to it in constitutional doctrine interpreting the Fifth and Fourteenth Amendments.[40] Both Congress and the executive branch did adopt enforcement machinery for antidiscrimination laws, as well as the new antidiscrimination laws mentioned at the beginning of this chapter. And after four states had done so through legislative action in 1970, the U.S. Supreme Court legalized abortion nationwide in 1973.[41] (Feminists did not have only successes. By the late 1970s, states had begun to cut off Medicaid funding for abortions for the needy, and the Supreme Court permitted this;[42] but the legalizing of abortion had been a very dramatic policy success, and the number of abortions performed annually did not drop even after public funding was cut.)

At more local levels, feminists—besides attaining many state

ERAs—moved beyond the initial policy agenda by directing public attention to crimes directly involving sex or sexual violence. In response to feminist pressure, policymakers improved rape prosecution procedures by eliminating requirements that the victim's testimony be independently corroborated, by forbidding testimony about the irrelevant sexual history of the victim,[43] and by promoting the creation of special rape units in police departments, whose officers would be trained to be more sensitive to the needs of rape victims. Feminists also successfully urged more frequent prosecution of wife batterers, more issuance of restraining orders on batterers, and the creation of shelters for battered women and their children.[44] Feminists also called attention to the injustice in punishing (generally female) prostitutes but routinely ignoring their (almost always male) purchasers.[45] Also at the state and local level—in an effort to free women from what were viewed as the constraints of gender and/or sexual idology—in reforming divorce law, feminists successfully encouraged sex-neutral standards that awarded child custody either according to the "best interest of the child" or with a general preference for joint custody as a replacement for the earlier presumption favoring awards of young children to their mothers. Moreover, no-fault divorce laws were adopted all over the United States during this decade. Although these had not been a particular goal of the feminist movement, feminists had certainly not opposed such laws. The common wisdom by the late 1970s held that it was irrational for the government to insist couples had to come up with some "fault" of one party in order to obtain a divorce.

Childcare policy was another story. Largely in response to market forces—that is, because more mothers were in the job market—more day-care centers also opened up. But federal support for them was only token; the tax credit permitted for childcare covered only a small fraction of its cost. Free, publicly provided day care for the women at the bottom of the wage scale who really need it never became a widespread reality.[46]

The tremendous failure of the 1970s came not from any policy that feminists had implemented, but from the absence of action on certain fronts. Female wages for full-time workers remained less than two-thirds those of males by the end of the decade—largely because women still clustered in lower paying jobs, but also because women more often than men disrupted their years in the workforce for reasons related to having babies. Sometimes they lost their jobs involuntarily due to pregnancy-related disability, but sometimes they took time "off" to be with young children or switched to a less demanding job in order to have time with children. Profound changes involving divorce compounded the problem, making much more egregious the combination of the failure to attain a meaningful childcare policy and the absence of change in the earned income of women. There was a precipitous rise in the divorce rate between 1960 and 1980, and by 1980 Lenore Weitzman was publicly documenting the massive economic impact that divorce has on women.[47] She found that in California, on average, women experience a 73-percent lowering of their standard of living after divorce, while their ex-husbands experience a 42-percent rise.[48] From an economic standpoint, then, a strong argument could be made that, despite a decade of feminist legal change, women were worse off in 1980 than in 1970.

Meanwhile, apart from the question of policy accomplishments, the dominant legal ideology of the women's movement had shifted in the course of the decade. As indicated earlier, the decade had begun with a multipronged effort to undo the disadvantages suffered by women as a result of discrimination against them within the public sphere, discrimination that reflected the ideology of domesticity (i.e., women were supposed to find fulfillment as wife/mother while men found it as citizen/economic producer). While this effort had included a quest for the ERA, it had also included attention to women's particular needs— needs made "particular" to women because the workplace had been structured to exclude them and/or because of grossly imbalanced societal arrangements around reproduction. Even the leading proponents of the ERA in the early 1970s exhibited a flexibility regarding the norm of formal legal equality that was to be abandoned as the decade wore on. Early interpretations of the ERA by its feminist defenders acknowledged that the ERA would not forbid certain kinds of sex-differentiating legislation. These permitted differentiations fell into two categories:

1. Laws specifically dealing with differences of reproductive physiology were to be permitted. Examples of permissible sex differentiation itemized in official congressional reports and in the interpretation of the ERA authored by Ann E. Freedman and others (which interpretation was distributed by Rep. Martha Griffiths to every member of Congress and inserted into the *Congressional Record* by Sen. Birch Bayh) included laws "providing for payment of medical costs of childbearing,"[49] wet

nurses,[50] sperm donors,[51] prostitution (!),[52] rape,[53] and matters related to determinations of paternity.[54]

2. In addition, laws aimed at remedying "the effects of past discrimination" against women or at "dealing with the various economic and social conditions that underlie and support the present system of [gendered] inequality" were supposed to be permitted, according to leading ERA proponents.[55]

Despite this early acceptance of remedial legislation to compensate women for past discrimination both deliberate and structural, the ACLU Women's Rights Project—led by (now judge) Ruth Bader Ginsburg during the middle to late 1970s—argued against a number of statutes that the Supreme Court was to judge legitimate efforts to compensate women for past discrimination.[56] Similarly, despite repeated acknowledgment in the early 1970s that the equal rights principle did not require laws about rape to be sex neutral, by the end of the decade feminist attorneys like Wendy Williams were insisting that they did have to be.[57] And yet again, having acknowledged in the early 1970s that laws singling out the costs of childbearing would not violate the equal rights principle, feminist lawyers including Wendy Williams lobbied for the Pregnancy Discrimination Act with its statement that "women affected by pregnancy, childbirth, or related medical conditions, *shall be treated the same* for all employment related purposes . . . as other persons not so affected but similar in their ability or inability to work."[58] In short, by the end of the decade the norm that law must treat males and females *alike* in the sense of abstract formal equality appeared to have become increasingly reified among feminist jurists.

Moreover, this increasing rigidification of the norm of abstract formal equality, which required blindness to sex group in favor of a focus on individual traits and abilities,[59] by the end of the 1970s was appearing increasingly inappropriate for addressing the variety of wrongs against women to which feminists' attention was turning. Ironically, it was in large part the very success of the antidiscrimination (formal equality) approach during the 1970s, especially at the Supreme Court level,[60] that enabled feminists to turn to other kinds of disadvantages facing women.[61] A sex discrimination approach that requires formally equal treatment of similarly situated persons really had little to contribute to a wide range of policy problems that were to become dominant concerns of feminists in the 1980s:

1. discrimination against persons based not on sex but on failure to conform to prescribed gender role (e.g., men who wear earrings or women who wear no makeup)[62]
2. continuing inadequate enforcement of anti-rape statutes[63]
3. the dramatic undervaluing in the marketplace of work done by women (e.g., nursery school teachers' receiving considerably less pay than persons whose job it is to park cars and to "shovel ice into [a] chicken offal container," according to the federal government's 1975 *Dictionary of Occupational Titles*)[64]
4. continuing, inadequate provision for the safety of battered women and for sexually abused children[65]
5. the fostering of a public ideology that eroticizes the domination— both violent and nonviolent—of women[66]
6. the structuring of workplace rules around the assumption that workers are male, thus systematically disadvantaging female workers

Christine Littleton groups items 2, 3, 4 and 5 together as varying aspects of "sexual subordination," which she defines as "the devaluation . . . of anything associated with women or the identification of women with anything that is devalued."[67] While it is certainly true that individual acts of rape do express a devaluation of women, I would argue that there are important differences between issuing a low evaluation of the market value of kindergarten teachers and committing rape. These differences are sizable enough to warrant separate categories. Thus, besides *sex discrimination* (both the conscious no-women-need-apply variety and the institutionalized bias version, as in denying medical leaves for pregnancy) and *gender oppression*[68]—two of the three policy problems identified by Littleton—women face both *gender subordination* (the devaluing of the female social role) and *sexual subordination* (domination over women through sexuality, as expressed in sexual harassment and in nonviolent but objectifying pornography, or through sexualized violence—rape, wife battering, violent pornography, and adult male sexual abuse of female children.)[69] The significant variations in these four distinctive problems brought forth correspondingly variegated approaches in the feminist jurisprudence of the 1980s.

The Many Gables of 1980s Feminist Legal Theory

A number of works by feminists looking at law by the end of the 1970s implicitly drew attention to the increasing irrelevance of the nondiscrimination model of formal legal equality. As already indicated,[70] publications by Lenore Weitzman beginning in 1980 focused attention on the inadequacy of judges' understanding of the substantive meaning of "equality" in dividing property at divorce. In a germinal work that appeared in 1979,[71] Catharine MacKinnon argued that feminists needed to target the broader evil of women's subordinate status, rather than "discrimination"; they needed to shift their attention from "difference" of treatment to the systematic "inequality" accorded women. If societal structures are systematically disadvantaging women, then feminists need to alter those structures. In pursuit of that concern, MacKinnon by 1981 was turning her considerable talents to increasing the salience of pornography as an issue for feminist mobilization.[72] And Carol Gilligan in 1982 published *In a Different Voice,*[73] a work that looked not at law directly but at people's underlying understanding of morality, justice, and ethics. She argued that, when the dominant voices in academia (led by Lawrence Kohlberg in her specific research context) developed their theories of human psychological development, they ignored women subjects. Then they applied the male-oriented models to women and discovered that women did not measure up! She went back to the experimental drawing board with female subjects and came up with a theory that, while some women do think like men, many women discuss moral issues "in a different voice."[74] That is, they look at moral questions from a different perspective and thus come up with different kinds of answers. These answers are not "worse" or "less mature" than answers provided by typical males, but they are characteristically different—at least among white, middle-class women—and thus would tend to be undervalued if measured by the dominant male-oriented paradigm. It was not a big leap for female law professors to notice that law too has been structured with attention to males and that "legal discourse" seems to have a peculiarly male ring.[75]

In effect, the architects Weitzman, MacKinnon, and Gilligan laid out the models for the new and, arguably, somewhat mutually conflicting gables in the house of feminist legal theory. At this point the structural grounding of those conflicts can be laid bare.

Sex-neutral versus Gender-neutral versus Pro-women

Feminists addressing, for instance, the problems of divorced women—an issue that Lenore Weitzman successfully put on the public agenda—

eventually find themselves facing in differing directions. A number of factors contribute to the immiserization of women and their children upon divorce,[76] but one that was particularly targeted by some feminist jurists in the 1980s was the gender-neutral[77] approach to child custody awards. Martha Fineman pointed to an accumulating body of evidence that men use threats of child custody fights to extort lower "settlements" from their wives at the time of divorce.[78] Because of the newly prevalent gender-neutral child custody standards in law, men's economic advantages enable them to argue that they can provide the better home, and consequently they have a reasonable shot at obtaining custody.[79] Women have been far more likely to have been the primary caretaker of the children and thus are typically more strongly attached to them than the father is. This situation puts the mother in a weak bargaining position, rendering her liable to successful extortion. For that reason, Fineman and some others have argued for a move back from gender neutrality to a preference for the primary caretaker. In most cases this would be the mother.

Because a primary caretaker preference would in *impact,* if not in form, be heavily skewed toward women, certain feminist legal theorists have raised objections. As spokespersons for formal equality standards, Wendy Williams and Ann E. Freedman have argued that feminists should oppose laws that have a disparate impact on one sex unless such laws are justified by a truly compelling interest.[80] Pursuing this theoretical structure, Deborah Rhode has argued against the specific proposal of a primary caretaker preference, on the grounds that because of its blatantly disparate impact it could result in the further entrenchment of gender stereotypes.[81]

On the other hand, Joan Williams enters this debate by noting that there is a critical difference between a law that is gender neutral and one that is sex neutral.[82] A preference for the primary caretaker is not gender neutral, because that role is at the heart of our society's specification of the female gender role. Indeed, Joan Williams points out, no public policy that aims to correct the inequities involved in the devaluation of females and of the lives they live *could* be gender neutral; since women have been disadvantaged by gender in this society,[83] only legislation attentive—rather than blind—to gender can rectify the situation. The goal, says Joan Williams, cannot be gender-neutral legislation but *must* be sex-neutral legislation. Any man who has forgone the benefits of the male gender role by adopting the (female gender) role of primary caretaker should be permitted to benefit from whatever compensatory benefits law attaches to that role. A maternal preference in the law would not be sex neutral and thus would fail Joan Williams's test, but a primary caretaker preference *would* be sex neutral and therefore acceptable. She argues persuasively that laws working to unhinge sex from gender role serve the beneficial function of de-institutionalizing gender—a long-standing feminist policy goal.

In making this powerful argument, Joan Williams implicitly rejects the position against "disparate impact" held by Wendy Williams, Ann E. Freedman, and Deborah Rhode. In the context of laws that aim to undo women's subordinate status, disparate impact is not only acceptable; it is logically necessary. This is the force of Catharine MacKinnon's frequent counsel that feminists should not worry about "difference"; rather, the concern should be "the difference that difference makes." For law, however, to deal with child custody extortion by explicitly identifying females as the better parent for children—as a maternal preference would do—would unacceptably reify gender roles. A parallel can be drawn from the racial segregation context. It is unacceptably stigmatizing for government to force the races apart in public schools. In communities where the government never supported segregation, however, if neighborhood school boundaries happen to contain differing proportions of blacks and whites, that residential fact per se is not stigmatizing. Disparate impact alone does not strike with nearly the force that official government designation into separate categories does.

For a more feminist public policy, law should aspire toward all of the following goals: (1) to undo the societal disadvantaging of women that is structured around their reproductive function, *and* (2) to stop sexualized violence against women, *and* (3) to undo the devaluing of female gender roles, *and* (4) to free individuals from the constraints of gender roles.[84] The first of these requires a restructuring of workplace arrangements so they are not geared simply to male physiology. It no more discriminates against males to provide leave, or even paid leave, for pregnancy disability than it does to allow breastfeeding during breaks for firefighters.[85] The prior failure to adapt the workplace to women has not expressed neutrality; it has been a form of institutionalized sex bias, expressing an expectation of having only male workers. Explicit recognition of female reproductive physiology neither discriminates against men nor says all women must become mothers. It fosters the first goal without conflicting with the other three, and thus should be endorsed. The fear that such laws will foster the notion that all females per se are in need of protection makes no more sense than fear that a law requiring a protective plastic cup over the penis and testicles of varsity baseball catchers implies that all males need special protection. Similarly, regarding the second problem (sexualized violence), it does not discriminate against males if the sex crime by which they are violated is called "forcible sodomy" rather than "rape." It is a fact that different physiologies are involved, and the law does no harm in saying so. As for the third goal, the disadvantage heaped on women by the economic marginalization attached to their gender roles[86] can be rectified by laws aimed at those *roles*. Not just a primary caretaker preference fits this approach; so do sex-neutral parental leave policies and nurturing leave or days-off policies for care of the sick or elderly; and so does "comparable worth" or "pay equity" legislation. Avoiding tying these kinds of gender-oriented corrective legislation to a particular sex group can further the fourth task, of freeing men and women from the constraints of gender roles. To sum up the import of these four goals, sex-neutral (but not gender-neutral) legislation can ameliorate gender disadvantage while sex-conscious legislation makes more sense for making the world a safe and comfortable place for the female physiological structure. These goals and tactics are not necessarily mutually opposing. Mary Becker notes, for instance, that some states have implemented pregnancy disability leave (sex-conscious legislation) as a first step and then followed it up with (sex-neutral) parental leave legislation.[87]

Different Voice versus Postmodern Diversity versus (?) Feminism

Apart from specific policy goals, feminist jurisprudence in the 1980s exhibited an overwhelming fascination with Carol Gilligan's claims that women tend to speak about morality in a "different voice," a voice of care, connectedness, responsibility for others, and interpersonal contextuality in lieu of the characteristically male voice of universal rules, individual rights, abstract equality of persons, and hierarchically ordered values. As already noted, a common practice in 1980s feminist jurisprudence was to apply the Gilligan framework and to conclude that our legal system speaks in a male voice. From this conclusion was derived a common argument that, if feminism means an upgrading of female values, then feminism has transformative potential, because it promises to make our law more nurturant, more humane, and so on.[88]

This fashionable argument has already been subjected by other scholars to a number of devastating critiques. First, if the responsibility/care approach is not balanced by a sense of equality/justice, then the female voice becomes all too often the voice of the self-sacrificing victim: "me last, me least, me not at all."[89] Second, because these values are at the core of the gendered female role, the more one insists that they are true of women, the more one invites economic marginalization of women—since another core aspect of that role *is* economic marginalization.[90] Third, Carol Gilligan was studying an intellectually elite sample of white middle-class women. Gilligan herself has already admitted that her general characterization was not apt for high-achieving black women.[91] In other words, it has not been demonstrated that women universally share any particular psychological, mental, or moral traits.[92] It is true that Gilligan's descriptions in *In a Different Voice* rang true with many of us readers. But it is also true that we are ready to see the world in gendered ways; we have been raised to do so. When a man offers to carry a woman's heavy packages, is he being paternalistic and therefore asserting dominance, or is he being nurturant and therefore feminist? We see what we look for.

On the other hand, while the claim that women think differently from men is fraught with problems, the often allied claim that law is "male" in the sense that American legal systems were designed by men for men, and are generally geared to men's life experiences, is unexceptionable.[93] The raison d'être of legal feminism, in fact, is the effort to change legal structures so that they do justice to women's lived experiences, which are indeed, in this gendered world, different from men's experiences.[94] The extreme rigidification of the norm of formal equality in the 1970s begat a counterextreme in the tendency to claim that women, because they are female, think a certain way or believe certain things. But the excesses of that counterextreme should not blind reformers to the incontrovertible fact that legal systems were designed by men for men and therefore contain tendencies that feminists need to change.

In any case, one of the fruits of the critical reaction to the Gilliganesque claim that women speak in a different voice has been an increase of attention to the differences *among* women—differences of class, race, age, sexual orientation, able-bodiedness, ethnicity, and so on. At the very least, feminists now have a heightened consciousness of the importance of learning from one another, of listening to each other's diverse voices.[95]

In a strange twisting of this critique of the universalizing aspects of the different voice approach, or else by abstracting out of the approach the supposedly female focus on "context," some feminists have now begun claiming that a postmodern consciousness is what truly characterizes feminism. Besides being easily debunkable,[96] this claim carries a real political danger. The danger is that, if the concept of a fractured female subjectivity is taken too far[97]—if it goes beyond a moderate version that fosters a healthy respect for pluralism, to the point of deconstructing the subject *woman* so that there is nothing left of it[98]— what the postmodern turn will amount to is a recipe for feminist political paralysis. It should go without saying that without the subject *woman* there can be no feminist program.

Conclusions: Prospects for the 1990s

It should have been apparent from the start that, in a system of legal rules designed by men for men, the jurisprudential norm of formal legal equality would have been inadequate for eliminating the subordination of women. Indeed, the modern feminist movement began in the late 1960s with something of that awareness. The policy program of that era constituted a flexible, multipronged attack on several aspects of women's subordination to men—a subordination that is maintained by a variety of structures around both gender role and sexuality.

Through the decade of the 1970s that program was transformed in four important ways:

1. Through litigation and legislative lobbying, organized feminism was phenomenally successful in moving our society closer to the goal of formal legal equality across sex lines.
2. In part *because* of this success, feminists began to turn their attention toward kinds of policy goals that could not be reached by formal equality—for example, rape, wife battering, sexual harassment, pornography, and comparable worth.
3. By the end of the decade, the proponents of formal legal equality were interpreting it in a much more rigid way than at the beginning of the decade, that is, in a way that was much more closed to the idea that law might need to be adapted to women's particular needs.
4. Several factors together began to produce a visible feminization of poverty:
   a. the mushrooming in the divorce rate after 1960

   b. the continued clustering of women in jobs at the low end of the pay scale

   c. the fact that divorced women were ending up responsible for childcare and its costs, with divorce settlements producing large inequities to start with and then child support orders often going unenforced

Around 1980, three voices emerged that were to have a formative influence on the next decade of legal feminism. Lenore Weitzman perspicuously exposed the powerfully pro-male bias in formally equal judicial practices involving divorce settlements; Catharine MacKinnon convinced many legal scholars that the legal rectification of subordination *by means of sex* cannot possibly take place through laws that are neutral *as to sex;*[99] and Carol Gilligan convinced many jurists that males and females think about morality in characteristically different ways—and these jurists then concluded that, since law reflects the male way, feminists must transform the law to make it more consonant with the female way of thinking or the female "voice" of morality.

In attempting to adapt the powerful insights of these authors to the androcentric biases of our legal system, feminist jurists have wound up facing in mutually contradictory policy directions. This chapter has attempted to point in a conciliatory direction.

That conciliation among feminist legal scholars will require a recognition that—in addition to wanting to eradicate blatant discrimination against women—they aim at four different types of policy goals, two of which involve sexuality and two of which involve gender roles. Feminists aspire to end sexual violence against women and also to end the systematic disadvantaging of women that takes place via the societal institutions that structure reproductive practices. Sex-conscious policies are needed to attain these goals—a sex-conscious restructuring of the workplace to undo its androcentric assumptions, and a concerted attack on the crimes of sexual violation that women, specifically as women, confront.[100] By contrast, sex-conscious policies would be a bad idea for attacking the other two targets of the contemporary feminist movement: the devaluing specifically of the female gender role, and the constraining force of gender roles in general. These two targets call for gender-conscious but sex-neutral approaches, a number of which have already been developed in the feminist legal literature.

The next-to-last section of the chapter looked at the use and abuse of the research of Carol Gilligan. There really is no convincing evidence that there is such a thing as a universally female voice (and Gilligan concedes as much). The counterextreme to the overuniversalization of Gilligan is manifested in the postmodern uncovering of all the differences concealed in the unifying term *woman*. Both of these tendencies (the different voice argument and the critique of it) can have a salutary impact, if they cause the public to be attentive to the *many* voices that have heretofore been submerged or silenced in American society. On the other hand, if the postmodern impulse takes feminist theorists to the point of denying all coherence in the subject *woman,* then feminism will have reached a stage of political paralysis, for no political program can be launched on behalf of a nonexistent subject.

Notes

1. Thomas Hobbes, *Leviathan* (New York: Penguin, 1977) pt. II, ch. 20, p. 253.
2. Isabel Marcus, Paul Spiegelman, Ellen DuBois, Mary Dunlap, Carol Gilligan, Catharine MacKinnon, Carrie Menkel-Meadow, "Feminist Discourse, Moral Values, and the Law—A Conversation," 34 *Buffalo Law Review* 11, 85 (1985).
3. The strongest sense of discomfort with this problem appears in Carol Smart's *Feminism and the Power of Law* (New York: Routledge, 1989). Smart, a sociologist of law, depicts legal discourse as permeated by a "resistance to and denial of women's concerns." Her book aims primarily, she says, "to construct a warning to feminism to avoid the siren call of law" (p. 160).
4. An overview of these decisions is provided in Leslie Friedman Goldstein's "The Constitutional Status of Women: The Burger Court and the Sexual Revolution in American Law," *Law and Policy Quarterly* 3:5 (1981). The political background of these decisions is explored more fully in Leslie Friedman Goldstein's "Women as Litigants," in Beverly Blair Cook et al., *Women in the Judicial Process* (Washington, D.C.: American Political Science Association, 1988), pp. 40–49.
5. *Geduldig v. Aiello,* 417 U.S. 484 (June 1974); and *General Electric v. Gilbert,* 429 U.S. 125 (December 1976). For a different analysis of the relation between employer penalties and pregnancy, cf. *Cleveland Board of Education v. LaFleur,* 414 U.S. 632 (January 1974).
6. Pregnancy Discrimination Act, 42 U.S.C. Sec. 2000e(k).
7. For a list of the organizations, see Wendy Williams, "Notes from a First Generation," 1989 *University of Chicago Legal Forum* 99, at p. 101 n. 7.
8. *California Federal Savings and Loan v. Guerra,* 479 U.S. 272 (1987).
9. For a list of these organizations, see W. Williams, "Notes," p. 101, n.

6; and Mary Becker, "Prince Charming: Abstract Equality," in 1987, *Supreme Court Review* 201, at p. 203 n. 10—which is reprinted as Chapter 4 of this volume.

10. *Guerra,* 479 U.S. at 290–91.

11. Becker, "Prince Charming" (see Chapter 4 of this book); Sylvia Law, "Rethinking Sex and the Constitution," 132 *University of Pennsylvania Law Review* 1033 (1984); Christine Littleton, "Reconstructing Sexual Equality," 75 *California Law Review* 1270 (1987); Herma Hill Kay, "Equality and Difference: The Case of Pregnancy," 1 *Berkeley Women's Law Journal* 1 (1985); Ann Scales, "Towards a Feminist Jurisprudence," 56 *Indiana Law Journal* 375 (1981); Linda Krieger and Patricia Cooney, "The Miller-Wohl Controversy: Equal Treatment, Positive Action, and the Meaning of Women's Equality," 13 *Golden Gate Law Review* 513 (1983); Wendy Williams, "The Equality Crisis: Some Reflections on Culture, Courts, and Feminism," 7 *Women's Rights Law Reporter* 175 (1982), and "Equality's Riddle: Pregnancy and the Equal Treatment/Special Treatment Debate," 13 *NYU Review of Law and Social Change* 525 (1985); Nadine Taub, "From Parental Leaves to Nurturing Leaves," 13 *NYU Review of Law and Social Change* (1985) 381; Deborah Rhode, *Justice and Gender: Sex Discrimination and the Law* (Cambridge, Mass.: Harvard University Press, 1989), pp. 120–25; Joan Williams, "Deconstructing Gender," 87 *Michigan Law Review* 797 (1989), which is reprinted as Chapter 3 of this volume.

12. Catharine MacKinnon, *Feminism Unmodified* (Cambridge, Mass.: Harvard University Press, 1987); Ann Scales, "The Emergence of Feminist Jurisprudence," 95 *Yale Law Journal* 1373 (1986), where she does not specifically address pornography but endorses MacKinnon's general approach and indicates that feminists must oppose the "objectification which is at the heart of woman-loathing," at p. 1385; Robin West, "The Difference in Women's Hedonic Lives," 3 *Wisconsin Women's Law Journal* 81 (1987), at p. 83 n. 2; Carrie Menkel-Meadow in Marcus et al., "Feminist Discourse," pp. 78–79; Mary Dunlap in Marcus et al., "Feminist Discourse," pp. 30–32, 81–83; Rhode, *Justice and Gender,* pp. 270–73. The Feminist Anti-censorship Task Force presented an amicus curiae brief against the ordinance drafted by Catharine MacKinnon in *American Booksellers Association v. Hudnut,* 771 F.2d 323 (7th Cir. 1985) aff'd. sub. nom. *Hudnut v. American Booksellers Association,* 475 U.S. 1001 (1986).

13. Leslie Bender, "A Lawyer's Primer on Feminist Theory and Tort," 38 *Journal of Legal Education* 3 (1988); Carrie Menkel-Meadow, "Portia in a Different Voice: Speculations on a Women's Lawyering Process," 1 *Berkeley Women's Law Journal* 39 (1985); Kenneth Karst, "Women's Constitution," 1984 *Duke Law Journal* 447; Lucinda Finley, "Transcending Equality Theory," 86 *Columbia Law Review* 1118 (1986); Robin West, "Jurisprudence and Gender," 55 *University of Chicago Law Review* 1 (1988), and "Feminism, Critical Social Theory, and Law," 1989 *University of Chicago Legal Forum*

59, esp. pp. 80–81; Suzanna Sherry, "Civic Virtue and the Feminine Voice in Constitutional Adjudication," 72 *Virginia Law Review* 543 (1983); J. Williams, "Deconstructing Gender" (see Chapter 3 of this book); Cynthia Fuchs Epstein, *Deceptive Distinctions: Sex, Gender, and the Social Order* (New Haven, Conn.: Yale University Press, 1988), ch. 4; W. Williams, "Equality's Riddle."

14. Dunlap in Marcus et al., "Feminist Discourse," p. 30; W. Williams, "Notes," p. 110, and "Equality's Riddle," at n. 20; Herma Hill Kay, "Models of Equality," 1985 *University of Illinois Law Review* 39 (1985); Catharine MacKinnon, *Toward a Feminist Theory of the State* (Cambridge, Mass.: Harvard University Press, 1989), p. 245.

15. Scales, "Emergence," p. 1397 n. 126; Nadine Taub, "Book Review" (of *Sexual Harassment of Working Women* by Catharine MacKinnon), 80 *Columbia Law Review* 1686, 1691 (1980); Rhode, *Justice and Gender,* pp. 101–3, where she favors extension of the protection of statutory rape laws to both males and females, despite her acknowledgment that "gender neutrality may obscure factual asymmetries in sexual relationships"; Alison Jaggar, "Sexual Difference and Sexual Equality," in Deborah Rhode, ed., *Theoretical Perspectives on Sexual Differences* (New Haven, Conn.: Yale University Press, 1990), pp. 239–54, at pp. 243–44.

16. Lesbians, too, sometimes batter their partners. See Kerry Nobel, ed., *Naming the Violence* (Seattle, Wash.: Seal Press, 1986).

17. Lenore Walker, *Terrifying Love* (New York: Harper & Row, 1989), *The Battered Woman Syndrome* (New York: Springer, 1984), and *The Battered Women* (New York: Harper & Row, 1979); Elizabeth Schneider, "Describing and Changing: Women's Self Defense Work and the Problem of Expert Testimony on Battery," 9 *Women's Rights Law Reporter* 195 (1986); Christine Littleton, "Women's Experience and the Problem of Transition: Perspectives on Male Battering of Women," 1989 *University of Chicago Legal Forum* 23. Lenore Walker was trained as a psychologist and now devotes her career to serving as an expert witness in legal cases involving attacks by women on their batterers.

18. Martha Fineman, "Implementing Equality: Ideology, Contradiction and Social Change," 1983 *Wisconsin Law Review* 789, and "Dominant Discourse, Professional Language, and Legal Change in Child Custody Decisionmaking," 101 *Harvard Law Review* 727 (1988); Rhode, *Justice and Gender,* pp. 158–69; J. Williams, "Deconstructing Gender," pp. 839–40 (see Chapter 3 of this book).

19. Scales, "Emergence," p. 1373 n. 2.

20. Sandra Harding, *Whose Science? Whose Knowledge? Thinking from Women's Lives* (Ithaca, N.Y.: Cornell University Press, 1991), chs. 5–6. Sandra Harding is not a law professor but is a feminist epistemologist often cited in feminist legal theory articles. She was selected to deliver a plenary address at the Law and Society Association Convention of 1989.

21. J. Williams, "Deconstructing Gender," pp. 805–6 (see Chapter 3 of this

book). The names of Derrida, Foucault, and Lacan are my additions to her list.

22. For more general explorations of the relationship between feminism and postmodern epistemology, see Linda J. Nicholson, ed., *Feminism/Postmodernism* (New York: Routledge, 1990); and Rhode, *Theoretical Perspectives*.

23. West, "Jurisprudence and Gender," "Difference in Women's Hedonic Lives," and "Feminism, Critical Social Theory, and Law."

24. Many authors in feminist jurisprudence cite the combination of Nancy Chodorow, *The Reproduction of Mothering: Psychoanalysis and the Sociology of Gender* (Berkeley: University of California Press, 1978), and Dorothy Dinnerstein, *The Mermaid and the Minotaur: Sexual Arrangements and Human Malaise* (New York: Harper & Row, 1976).

25. MacKinnon, *Feminism Unmodified*, pp. 38–40; J. Williams, "Deconstructing Gender" (see Chapter 3 of this book).

26. West, "Women's Hedonic Lives."

27. This theme is omnipresent in MacKinnon's work.

28. Becker, "Prince Charming," p. 236 (see Chapter 4 of this book).

29. The metaphor comes from Judge Ruth Bader Ginsburg, who, in her career as an attorney for the Women's Rights Project of the ACLU, was one of the primary architects of that "house." See Ruth Bader Ginsburg and Barbara Flagg, "Some Reflections on the Feminist Legal Thought of the 1970's," 1989 *University of Chicago Legal Forum* 9, at p. 18.

30. I do not mean to imply that the NOW perspective had a monopoly in the initial period of the women's movement of the late twentieth century. There was a sizable other branch of the movement, a branch that focused more on cultural, psychosocial change, that saw itself as more radical and as aiming at "women's liberation" (a term that is no longer used in the post-Foucault 1990s) rather than merely "women's rights." I focus on NOW because it represented the dominant voice within the women's rights branch, which was the branch that concentrated on bringing about concrete political and legal change. See Jo Freeman, *The Politics of Women's Liberation* (New York: McKay, 1975).

31. Barbara Sinclair Deckard, *The Women's Movement* (New York: Harper & Row, 1979), p. 348, citing Judith Holes and Ellen Levine, *The Rebirth of Feminism* (Chicago: Quadrangle Books, 1971), p. 88.

32. The section of plank 4 that asks for government subsidy (via tax deduction) of the costs of "home care" illustrates most vividly the class bias of which the women's movement has been accused. Few women earn enough (and far fewer earned enough in 1967) to pay a third party to clean their house. On the other hand, government subsidy of domestic labor would raise its price and thus contribute to the professionalization of housecleaning (a phenomenon already well underway in 1990), which might in the long run help working-class women (who can obtain health insurance benefits, Social Security benefits, and collective bargaining benefits if they work in a large company—benefits often unavailable to the lone housecleaner).

33. I speak here of the NOW goals, not of individual feminist writers or works of the time, many of which—most notably Betty Friedan's *The Feminine Mystique* (New York: Dell, 1963)—sounded very much like they wanted women to become more like men. See Zillah Eisenstein's mea culpa on this score in her recent *The Female Body and the Law* (Berkeley: University of California Press, 1988), pp. 85–86, indicting not only her earlier self but also the early Betty Friedan, Alison Jaggar, and Juliet Mitchell.

34. This last did indicate a glimmering feminist awareness that feminists must aim to alleviate the disadvantages faced by *all* women, including the poor, and thus hints at the radical potential of the movement. But cf. note 32 above.

35. For a poignant account of the direness of this need, see Mary Ann Mason, *The Equality Trap* (New York: Simon & Schuster, 1988).

36. Planks 1, 2, 6, and 7.

37. I am using "gender ideology" to mean the ideology around sex-linked societally constructed role minus those aspects of the role that involve the reproductive process. When I say "sexual ideology," I refer to the ideology around the (also societally constructed) roles involving the reproductive process—what could be called the ideology around biological roles.

38. Cf. Judith Jarvis Thomson, "A Defense of Abortion," 1 *Philosophy and Public Affairs* 47 (1971), who writes as though the entire moral justification for women's right to abortion comes from the nine-month burden of carrying an embryo/fetus.

It is true that in 1967, as now, women could give up their newborns for adoption. But such behavior (despite pro-lifers' rhetoric and the deep gratitude of adoptive parents) is socially stigmatized. Especially if a woman is financially able to care for a child, such an action is viewed as cold and unnatural. No such stigma attaches to sperm donors or to men who make no effort to investigate whether their sex partners become pregnant.

39. This sentence sums up the message of Friedan, *Feminine Mystique*.

40. For a detailed argument to this effect, see Leslie Friedman Goldstein, "The ERA and the U.S. Supreme Court," 1 *Research in Law and Policy Studies* 145–61 (1987).

41. *Roe v. Wade*, 410 U.S. 113; and *Doe v. Bolton*, 410 U.S. 179 (both 1973).

42. *Beal v. Doe*, 432 U.S. 438; *Maher v. Roe*, 432 U.S. 464; *Poelker v. Doe*, 432 U.S. 519 (all 1977).

43. For a more detailed account, see Susette Talarico, "Women as Offenders and Victims in Criminal Justice," in Cook et al., *Women in Judicial Process*, pp. 36–37.

44. Sandra Wexler, "Battered Women and Public Policy," in Ellen Bonaparth, ed., *Women, Power, and Policy* (Elmsford, N.Y.: Pergamon, 1982), pp. 184–204.

45. Elizabeth Fry Moulds, "Women's Crime, Women's Justice," in Bonaparth, *Women, Power, Policy*, pp. 205–31, at pp. 223–25.

46. For an analysis of our still woefully inadequate childcare policy (or nonpolicy), see Rhode, *Justice and Gender*, pp. 128–31. For the politics surrounding childcare policy through the decade of the 1970s, see Jill Norgren, "In Search of a National Childcare Policy," 34 *Western Political Quarterly* 127 (1985).

47. Lenore Weitzman and Ruth B. Dixon, "The Alimony Myth: Does No-fault Divorce Make a Difference?" 14 *Family Law Quarterly* 141 (Fall 1980); Lenore Weitzman, "The Economics of Divorce: Social and Economic Consequences of Property, Alimony, and Child Support Awards," 28 *UCLA Law Review* 1181 (August 1981).

48. Lenore Weitzman, *The Divorce Revolution* (New York: Free Press, 1985). See also discussion in Joan Williams, "Deconstructing Gender," pp. 824–27 (see Chapter 3 of this book).

49. *Equal Rights 1970: Hearings in S.J. Res. 61 and S.J. Res. 231 before the Senate Committee on the Judiciary,* 91st Cong., 2d sess. 183, 299, 303 (1970); *Equal Rights for Men and Women 1971,* H.R. Rep. No. 92-359, 92d Cong., 1st sess. 7 (1971); *Equal Rights for Men and Women 1972,* S. Rep. No. 92-689, 92d Cong., 2d sess. 12, 16, 20 (1972); and Barbara Brown, Thomas Emerson, Gail Falk, and Ann Freedman, "The Equal Rights Amendment: A Constitutional Basis for Equal Rights for Women," 80 *Yale Law Journal* 871, 893–96 (1971).

50. Brown, Emerson, Falk, and Freedman, "Equal Rights Amendment," pp. 893–94.

51. Ibid.; and *Equal Rights 1970,* p. 299 (Emerson's testimony.)

52. *Equal Rights 1970,* p. 299 (Emerson's testimony); Citizen's Advisory Council on the Status of Women, *The Proposed Equal Rights Amendment to the Constitution* (Washington, D.C.: Government Printing Office, 1970), pp. 11, 13.

53. Citizen's Advisory Council *Proposed Equal Rights Amendment,* pp. 11, 13; *Equal Rights 1970,* p. 299 (Emerson's testimony); Brown, Emerson, Falk, and Freedman, "Equal Rights Amendment," p. 894; *Equal Rights for Men and Women 1972,* pp. 16, 20.

54. Brown, Emerson, Falk, and Freedman, "Equal Rights Amendment," p. 894.

55. Ibid, pp. 904–5.

56. *Kahn v. Shevin,* 416 U.S. 351 (1974), upheld Florida's $150 annual property tax break for widows, which was not available to widowers. *Schlesinger v. Ballard,* 419 U.S. 498 (1975), upheld an extra four years that the military permitted to women officers for attaining promotion before they would be fired for nonpromotion. (Robert Ballard was fired after nine years; women were permitted 13 years to try for promotion.) *Califano v. Webster,* 430 U.S. 313 (1977), permitted women retirees to eliminate certain low-earning years when calculating their Social Security benefits—permission that was not granted to male retirees. *Webster* was decided per curiam, so attorneys' names

are not in the *U.S. Reports,* but Karen O'Connor lists it as one of the Women's Rights Project cases. See Karen O'Connor, *Women's Organizations' Use of the Courts* (Lexington, Mass.: Lexington, 1980) pp. 97, 131–32.

57. W. Williams, "Notes," p. 110, and "Equality's Riddle," at n. 20.

58. See note 6 above; emphasis added.

59. Thus, the quintessential statements of formal equality requirements in the sex discrimination context appeared in the pension cases. Even though women *as a group* live longer than men, the prohibition on sex discrimination meant that women could not be grouped as women and had to receive (or pay) pension amounts each month that were equal to those of "similarly situated" individual males. See *Los Angeles Department of Water and Power v. Manhart,* 435 U.S. 702 (1978); and *Arizona Governing Committee v. Norris,* 463 U.S. 1073 (1983).

60. See citations in note 4 above.

61. See W. Williams, "Notes," for an elaboration of this point.

62. Christine Littleton has identified this as the problem of "gender oppression" in her "Equality and Feminist Legal Theory," 48 *University of Pittsburgh Law Review* 1043, 1045–46 (1987). See *Hopkins v. Price Waterhouse,* 109 S.Ct. 1775 (1989), for an instance of squeezing gender oppression into the rubric of "sex discrimination" for Title VII purposes.

63. See, e.g., Susan Estrich, *Real Rape* (Cambridge, Mass.: Harvard University Press, 1987).

64. Rhode, *Justice and Gender,* p. 170.

65. See, e.g., Littleton, "Women's Experience and Problem of Transition."

66. MacKinnon, *Feminism Unmodified* and *Toward a Feminist Theory of the State,* focuses particularly on this problem.

67. Littleton, "Equality and Feminist Legal Theory," pp. 1045–46.

68. Ibid. See note 62 above and the accompanying text.

69. Ibid.

70. See notes 47 and 48 and the accompanying text.

71. Catharine MacKinnon, *Sexual Harassment of Working Women* (Cambridge, Mass.: Harvard University Press, 1979), pp. 101–41.

72. MacKinnon, "Sex and Violence: A Perspective," in *Feminism Unmodified,* pp. 85–92—this was a speech by MacKinnon for a 1981 panel at the National Conference on Women and the Law. MacKinnon did not singlehandedly turn the spotlight on pornography, but she has been enormously important. In 1980, for instance, appeared the galvanizing collection of feminist antipornography essays *Take Back the Night,* edited by Laura Lederer (New York: Morrow Press, 1980).

73. Carol Gilligan, *In a Different Voice* (Cambridge, Mass.: Harvard University Press, 1982).

74. Carol Gilligan in Marcus et al., "Feminist Discourse." Gilligan provided a breakdown of who speaks in which "voice." If we shift from the voice metaphor to one of language, with males characteristically speaking the

language of rights and females characteristically speaking the language of care, her figures—derived from what she says at pp. 48–49—were as follows:

Males	**Females**
35% rights language only	
40% primarily rights language	18% primarily rights language
20% perfectly bilingual	20% perfectly bilingual
5% primarily care language	27% primarily care language
	35% care language only

Gilligan also noted there that the black females in her sample seemed more inclined to rights language than the white females did. This matches a finding by Carol Stack, "The Culture of Gender: Women and Men of Color," *Signs* 11:321 (1986).

It should be noted that a 1984 comprehensive review of 61 studies that did use the Lawrence Kohlberg paradigm to score moral reasoning for subjects of both sexes found *no* trend of higher scores for males. Lawrence Walker, "Sex Differences in the Development of Moral Reasoning: A Critical Review," 55 *Child Development* 667 (1984).

75. See the citations for Bender, Menkel-Meadow, Karst, Finley, West, and Sherry in note 13 above. But this was not news. See the Hobbes quotation at the beginning of this chapter. See also Lucinda Finley, "Breaking Women's Silence in Law: The Dilemma of the Gendered Nature of Legal Reasoning," 64 *Notre Dame Law Review* 886 (1989).

76. This immiserization was intensified in the early 1980s by a variety of cuts in poverty programs under the Reagan administration. See Eisenstein, *Female Body and the Law,* pp. 131–32.

77. I am using "gender" in this discussion of neutrality to refer to social role, whereas I am using "sex" to refer to the biological groups, male and female.

78. Fineman, "Implementing Equality" and "Dominant Discourse." Cf. discussion at Rhode, *Justice and Gender,* pp. 159–60.

79. According to Deborah Rhode, men win from a third to a half of all contested custody cases; see Rhode, *Justice and Gender,* p. 156. According to Joan Williams, they win from a half to two-thirds; J. Williams, "Deconstructing Gender" (see Chapter 3, note 161, of this book). Finally, "Why More Dads Are Getting the Kids," *Business Week,* November 28, 1988, p. 118, says that 68 percent of fathers win contested custody suits, and it cites Lenore Weitzman.

80. W. Williams, "Equality's Riddle," at n. 17 and accompanying text, quoting Ann E. Freedman's congressional testimony for a revived ERA in which Freedman specifically targeted laws about "primary breadwinners" for feminist opposition.

81. Rhode, *Justice and Gender,* pp. 157–61.

82. J. Williams, "Deconstructing Gender," pp. 837–41 (see Chapter 3 of this book).
83. See note 67 above and the accompanying text.
84. Ibid.
85. Jaggar, "Sexual Difference and Sexuality Equality," p. 253.
86. J. Williams, "Deconstructing Gender" (see Chapter 3 of this book), elaborates the link between female gender role and economic marginalization.
87. Becker, "Prince Charming," p. 218 and nn. 63–65 (see Chapter 4 of this book).
88. See the citations for Bender, Menkel-Meadow, Karst, Finley, West, and Sherry in note 13 above. See also Judith Resnik, "On the Bias: Feminist Reconsiderations of the Aspirations for Our Judges," 61 *Southern California Law Review* 1877 (1988), at pp. 1906–28.

For divergent political scientists' responses to this different voice trend, see Judith Baer, "Nasty Law; Nice Ladies," 11 *Women and Politics* 1–31 (1991), characterizing it as politically ill advised; and Gayle Binion, "Toward a Feminist Regrounding of Constitutional Law," 72 *Social Science Quarterly* 207 (June 1991), characterizing it as "progressive." See also J. Williams, "Deconstructing Gender," nn. 12, 17, commenting on the impact of Gilligan's work (see Chapter 3, notes 9 and 13, of this book).
89. This phrase comes from Wendy Williams commenting on her (and many of our) mother(s) approach to life. W. Williams, "Notes," p. 107 n. 19.
90. J. Williams, "Deconstructing Gender" (see Chapter 3 of this book); Christine Harrington and Janet Rifkin, "The Gender Organization of Mediation: Implications for the Feminization of Legal Practice," Institute for Legal Studies Working Papers, University of Wisconsin, 1988.
91. See note 74 above.
92. See Martha Minow, "Beyond Universality," 1989 *University of Chicago Legal Forum* 115, and "The Supreme Court 1986 Term—Foreword: Justice Engendered," 101 *Harvard Law Review* 10 (1987).
93. Much of Finley, "Breaking Women's Silence in Law," takes this other tack. And Becker, "Prince Charming" (see Chapter 4 of this book), fits completely within this genre.
94. The assertion that life experiences are profoundly conditioned by gender, and that those gendered conditions warrant political attention, is not incompatible with the understanding that the lived experience of genders is also permeated (and thus differentiated) by such categories as race and class. As Elizabeth Spelman puts it, "It is only if we pay attention to how we [women] differ that we come to an understanding of what we have in common." Elizabeth Spelman, *Inessential Woman* (Boston: Beacon Press, 1988), p. 113, see also pp. 131–32 and ch. 7.
95. See, for instance, the inclusion in the 1989 *University of Chicago Legal Forum* symposium on Feminism in the Law of Kimberle Crenshaw's essay on aspects of black female experience with law that would be unfamiliar to whites,

"Demarginalizing the Intersection of Race and Sex: A Black Feminist Critique of Antidiscrimination Doctrine, Feminist Theory, and Antiracist Politics," at p. 139. See also Minow, "Beyond Universality" and "Foreword"; also Judith Resnik, "Complex Feminist Conversations," 1989 *University of Chicago Legal Forum* 1, at pp. 6–7.

96. See notes 21 and 22 above and the accompanying text.

97. See Rhode, *Theoretical Perspectives,* for essays by various authors on this.

98. Karen Offen's essay, "Feminism and Sexual Differences in Historical Perspective," in ibid., pp. 13–20, particularly warns of this danger.

99. MacKinnon's usage of the term *sex* deliberately blurs the distinction between "sex" as a biological group (e.g., female humans) and "sex" as an activity (as in "having sex" with someone). This chapter has not followed her usage.

100. While it is true that individual men can be victims of sex crimes, in the case of men sex crimes do not function in a way that keeps them subordinated as a group. Women are chronically intimidated by fear of sexual violence. This fear makes them much more likely to want a male companion for (among other reasons) protection (from other males) and thus more likely to be willing to be subservient to the male companion they have chosen.

3

Deconstructing Gender

Joan C. Williams

I start out, as have many others, from the deep split among American feminists between "sameness" and "difference."[1] The driving force behind the mid-twentieth-century resurgence of American feminism was an insistence on the fundamental similarity of men and women and, hence, their essential equality. Betty Friedan comes to mind as an enormously influential housewife whose focus on men and women as individuals made her intensely hostile to gender stereotyping.[2]

Mid-century feminism, now often referred to somewhat derisively as "assimilationism," focused on providing opportunities to women in realms traditionally preserved for men.[3] In the 1980s two phenomena have shifted feminists' attention from assimilationists' focus on how individual women are *like* men to a focus on gender *differences,* on how women as a group differ from men as a group. The first is the feminization of poverty, which dramatizes the chronic and increasing economic vulnerability of women.[4] Feminists now realize that the assimilationists' traditional focus on gender neutrality may have rendered women more vulnerable to certain gender-related disabilities that have important economic consequences. The second phenomenon that plays a central role in the current feminist imagination is that of career women "choosing" to abandon or subordinate their careers so they can spend time with their small children.[5] These phenomena highlight the fact that deep-seated social differences continue to encourage men and women to make quite different "choices" with respect to work and family. Thus, sameness scholars are increasingly confronted by the existence of gender differences.

Do these challenges to assimilationism prove that we should stop trying to kid ourselves and admit the "real" differences between men and women, as the popular press drums into us day after day, and as

41

the "feminism of difference" appears to confirm?[6] Do such phenomena mean that feminists' traditional focus on gender neutrality is a bankrupt ideal? I will argue no on both counts, taking an approach quite different from that ordinarily taken by feminists on the sameness side of the spectrum. Sameness feminists usually have responded to the feminists of difference by reiterating their basic insight that individual men and women can be very similar. While true, this is not an adequate response to the basic insight of difference feminists: that gender exists, that men and women differ as groups. In this chapter, I try to speak to feminists of difference on their own terms. While I take gender seriously, I disagree with the description of gender provided by difference feminists.

I begin in Part I by challenging the widely influential description of gender advocated by Carol Gilligan. I suggest that Gilligan's description of "women's voice" is less a description of women's psychology than an attempt to attribute to women two influential critiques of contemporary Western culture. One is the critique of traditional Western epistemology. I argue that it is incorrect as a matter of intellectual history to claim, as have Gilligan and others, that the twentieth century's shift to a more contextualizing, antiformalist, and relativizing form of discourse constitutes a rejection of absolutist "male" epistemology in favor of "women's voice." The second critique Gilligan claims for women—the critique of possessive individualism—presents more subtle issues. Unlike the critique of traditional epistemology, the critique of possessive individualism *has* traditionally been associated with women. Gilligan's description of gender differences reclaims this critique for women through an updated version of the Victorian ideology of domesticity, whose attraction for modern feminists lies in its perceived potential "to transform our polity and its underlying assumptions [away] from the alienated world of atomistic competition."[7] This critique of individualism is one well worth exploring. But its power is undermined when modern feminists adopt domesticity's peculiarly domesticated version of the critique. The perils of modern domesticity become apparent in an analysis of the recent Title VII case of *Equal Employment Opportunity Commission (EEOC) v. Sears, Roebuck & Company*.[8] This case provides ample evidence of how domesticity's critique of possessive individualism serves to marginalize both women and the critique itself.

While Part I challenges the description of gender differences offered by Gilligan feminists, it does not deny the existence of gender differences. Gender differences do exist: that is, men *as a group* differ from women *as a group* not only on the basis of biological "sex" differences, but on the basis of social "gender" differences.[9] What I reject is Gilligan's description of gender differences, which I think is inaccurate and potentially destructive.

The chief strength of the feminism of difference is its challenge to what have been called "male norms." Part II demonstrates how these norms can be challenged without resort to domesticity. I begin from Catharine MacKinnon's description of gender as a system of power relations. While MacKinnon focuses on sexuality, I return to a more traditional topic: the relationship between work and family responsibilities. I argue that these issues are at the core of the contemporary gender system, which systematically enriches men at the expense of women and children. Problems such as the feminization of poverty stem in substantial part from a wage labor system premised on an ideal worker with no family responsibilities. Experiences since the late 1970s have shown that women can only enter the labor force without insisting on a redefinition of the ideal worker, at the expense of failing to meet the ideal.

Yet the gendered structure of wage labor is not being challenged. More astonishing, difference feminists celebrate a women's culture that encourages women to "choose" economic marginalization and celebrate that choice as a badge of virtue. The notion that women choose to become marginalized (nonideal) workers clouds the fact that all workers currently are limited to two unacceptable choices: the traditional male life pattern or women's traditional economic vulnerability. Wage labor does not have to be structured in this way. Changing it should be a central thrust of a feminist program.

In Part III, I continue to develop this alternative vision of gender. I first discuss the rejection by MacKinnon and others of the traditional feminist goal of gender neutrality. Its critics have argued that gender neutrality mandates a blindness to gender realities and so inhibits attempts to help women victimized by gender. I redefine the traditional goal, which in fact does not require neutrality, or blindness, with respect to gender, but rather advocates a consistent refusal to institutionalize a correlation between gender roles and biological sex differences. Thus redefined, the traditional goal has continuing validity, since institutionalizing a correlation between gender and sex necessarily reinforces gender stereotypes and the oppressive gender system as a whole. Moreover, the traditional goal does not preclude helping women disadvantaged by their adherence to gender roles, since such women can be protected in a sex-neutral fashion by protecting all people (regardless of biology) who are victimized by gender.

The chapter concludes by detailing the limitations of Gilligan's description of gender differences. This discussion responds to comments from some who have heard my analysis and then assumed that I cannot really be denying women's "different voice." I stress that, though I am not denying the existence of gender, I *am* denying the validity of the description of women's voice that Gilligan has provided. In particular I reject Gilligan's core claim that women are focused on relationships while men are not. To the extent this claim pinpoints actual gender differences, I argue it merely reflects the oppressive realities of the current gender system. Beyond that, Gilligan's claim is inaccurate and serves to perpetuate our traditional blindness to the ways in which men are nurturing and women are competitive and power seeking.

Part I:
The Feminism of Difference

The most influential source for the feminism of difference is Carol Gilligan's book in which she argues that women speak "in a different voice."[10] Women are portrayed as nurturers, defined by their relationships and focused on contextual thinking; men are depicted as abstract thinkers, defined by individual achievement. We should listen to women's "voice," argue Gilligan and her followers, because women's culture offers the basis for a transformation of our society, a transformation based on the womanly values of responsibility, connection, selflessness, and caring, rather than on separation, autonomy, and hierarchy.[11]

One reason why the feminism of difference has proved so persuasive is that it has claimed for women two of the central critiques of twentieth-century thought. In a strain of argument particularly popular in law reviews, feminists characterize traditional Western epistemology as male and identify the twentieth-century critique of that epistemology as an integral part of women's voice.[12] Gilligan and her followers also identify with women a critique of possessive individualism whose implications have been spelled out in *EEOC v. Sears*.

The New Epistemology as Women's Voice

Gilligan's description is often presented as a rediscovery of obvious differences between men and women we knew about all along.[13] In fact, even feminists of difference disagree about what are the "obvious" differences between men and women. Gilligan's description of women has been so widely adopted[14] that it is easy to overlook the fact that other feminists of difference have offered a sharply different version of women's true nature. Some radical feminists, more influential in the early 1980s than today, have espoused a view of women dramatically different from Gilligan's. Often using witch imagery, they stress women's intuition, their sexual power, and their alliance with deep forces of irrationality.[15]

This portrait of woman as id derives largely from the premodern stereotype of woman as the "weaker vessel."[16] Before the mid-eighteenth century, women were viewed not only as physically weaker than men; their intellectual and moral frailty meant they needed men's guidance to protect them from the human propensity for evil. Women's intense sexuality and their fundamental irrationality meant they were in need of outside control, because women in their weakness could be easily tempted. The darkest expression of the traditional view that women unsupervised quickly slipped into collusion with evil was the persecution (during some periods, massive in scale) of women as witches.[17]

This traditional stereotype of women crystallized after the early modern period into some traditional truths about women. As the philosophes of the Enlightenment celebrated logic and reason, women's intellectual inferiority came to be expressed as an inability to engage in rigorous abstract thinking. The Enlightenment also celebrated reason over emotion, and women's premodern alliance with the devil was transmuted into the view that women's limited ability for rational thought meant they were fundamentally emotional creatures.

These stereotypes have provided the link for many feminists of difference between women and the critique of traditional Western epistemology.[18] This critique, which I have elsewhere called "the new epistemology,"[19] consists of a broad and diverse intellectual movement that rejects a range of long-standing Western verities, some dating to the Enlightenment, and others all the way back to Plato. Perhaps the core element of the new epistemology is its rejection of an absolute truth accessible through rigorous logical manipulation of abstractions.[20] Feminists of difference have characterized the new epistemology with women's voice, noting that women traditionally have been thought to eschew abstraction for sensitivity to context, and to eschew logic for a faith in emotion and intuition as tools of thought.

On closer inspection, however, the traditional stereotype of women as overly emotional and incapable of rational, abstract thought is quite different from the critique proffered by the new epistemology: Feminists are being highly selective in the aspects of the traditional stereotype they choose to stress. It is true there are some similarities between the traditional stereotype of women and the new epistemology. Both share a sense of the limitations of pure logic and a faith in contextual thinking. But feminists of difference submerge the fact that the thinkers who have developed the new epistemology have, by and large, been cerebral and detached in the extreme. Neither they nor the new epistemology fits the traditional stereotype of women as too emotional for sustained rational thought. What the new epistemologists are talking about is a new kind of rationality—one not so closely tied to abstract transcendental truths, one that does not exclude as much of human experience as Western rationality traditionally has done. The ideal they propose represents a broadening of traditional intellectual life, whereas the traditional caricature of women as emotional and irrational represents a formal marginalization of those characteristics of human personality that the Western tradition has devalued.[21]

Thus, this attempt to rehabilitate traditional stereotypes as "women's voice," and to associate women's voice with the new epistemology, fails to come to terms with the extent to which the gender stereotypes were designed to marginalize women. These stereotypes no doubt articulated some values shunted aside by Western culture. But the circumstances of their birth mean they presented a challenge to predominant Western values that was designed to fail, and to marginalize women in the process.

At a simpler level, the attempt to claim the new epistemology for women is unconvincing simply because the new epistemology has been developed largely by men. These include philosophers from Friedrich Nietzsche and the American pragmatists to Martin Heidegger and Ludwig Wittgenstein, all of whom helped develop the movement's critique of absolutes. Important figures in developing the new epistemology's view of truths as necessarily partial and contextual include the fathers of post-Newtonian physics (Albert Einstein and Max Planck), the linguists Benjamin Whorf and Ferdinand de Saussure, and Wittgenstein, who rejected the "picture theory"—that Truth is an objective picture of reality—in favor of the view that a multiplicity of truths exists as an integral part of culture and context.

Note that all these scholars, and most others who were seminal in articulating the basic outlook of the new epistemology, are male. This history is no news to relational feminists, who regularly cite Wittgenstein and others as sources of inspiration.[22] In what sense, then, is this vast epistemological shift "feminist" or even "feminine"? The simple answer is that the new epistemology is not in any meaningful way "women's voice."

Women's Voice and the Critique of Possessive Individualism

The traditional stereotype of women, designed to justify women's subservience in a society that saw hierarchies as natural and desirable, came during the course of the eighteenth century to seem inconsistent with the emerging political philosophy of liberalism, which held all men as equal.[23] Gradually a new gender ideology—the ideology of domesticity—developed, in which women continued to be viewed as weaker than men physically and intellectually, but were newly extolled as more moral than men.[24]

The Feminism of Difference as a Resurgence of Domesticity

Gilligan echoes domesticity's "discovery" of women's higher morality. Unlike the Victorians, Gilligan does not argue explicitly that women's morality is of a higher order; she articulates her ideal as a "dialectic mixture" of the male and female "voices." Yet commentators have noted the striking resemblance between Gilligan's ideal morality and her description of female emotional maturity.[25] An emotionally mature woman, it seems, will reach Gilligan's ideal moral state automatically, while men will attain it only through a fundamental restructuring of their gender identity.

A close analysis of the traits Gilligan attributes to women suggests that she and other scholars who share her view of women offer domesticity with a difference. These "relational feminists,"[26] as they have been aptly called, reclaim the compliments of Victorian gender ideology while rejecting its insults. Thus, relational feminists agree with the Victorians that women are more nurturing than men ("focused on relationships"), less tied to the questionable virtues of capitalism, and ultimately more moral than men. But they disagree with the Victorians' view that women are also more passive than men, less competent, more timid, and naturally demure.

Relational feminism has had a pervasive impact on women's history, and it is a historian of women who has best illustrated its relation to the ideology of domesticity. One of the major achievements of relational feminism in women's history is Suzanne Lebsock's subtle and persuasive study of a small Virginia town before the Civil War. In *The Free Women of Petersburg*,[27] Lebsock summarizes her conclusions about women's values in the pre–Civil War period as follows:

> [H]ere, in one list, are the documentable components of a women's value system. Women, more than men, noticed and responded to the needs and merits of particular persons. This showed in their tendency to reward favorite slaves and to distribute their property unevenly among their heirs. It also showed in their ability to make independent judgments about their own fitness to administer estates. Women were particularly sensitive to the interests of other women and to their precarious economic position; this was demonstrated in favoritism toward female heirs and in the establishment of separate estates. As their real estate and credit transactions suggest, women wanted financial security for themselves as well as for others. Beyond that they were not as ego-invested as were men in the control of wealth. Our list grows a bit longer if we add the more ambiguous evidence derived from women's vanguard action in providing relief to the poor and in promoting religion. Women as a group were more invested than were men in Christian communities and the life of the spirit. And in their efforts to give assistance to the poor, both personalism and regard for other women surfaced again; the poor were mainly women and children, most of whom cannot have "deserved" their poverty.
>
> The people who wrote the antebellum period's popular literature have been trying to tell us all along that women were different from men, better than men in some respects. Perhaps it is time we took their message more seriously.[28]

Lebsock's book, published shortly after Gilligan's, comes to some strikingly similar conclusions. Both authors conclude that women are more focused on relationships than are men, and both suggest that women's is a higher morality. But Lebsock differs from Gilligan, and from most other relational feminists, in her awareness that she is reclaiming stereotypes from domesticity. Unlike scholars who have glossed over the Victorians' negative characterizations of women, Lebsock confronts them directly, and her conclusions are instructive. She asserts that women were not uniformly inept; many were active and competent as executors of their husbands' estates. Nor were they passive as investors—only risk averse. When it comes to the positive attributes of Victorian gender stereotypes, Lebsock's conclusions differ. She concludes that women were characterized by a "personal-ism" that made them more sensitive to slaves, the poor, and vulnerability in other women, less involved in capitalist values, and (consequently?) more moral than men.

Lebsock thus rejects the insults of Victorian gender ideology but embraces those elements complimentary to women. So do most feminists of difference, though few make their selectivity so clear. Moreover, relational feminists often seem unaware of their own selectivity. "Perhaps it is time we took [the antebellum] message more seriously," Lebsock argues, forgetting the half of the antebellum message she rejects. In this she is joined by the majority of relational feminists.[29]

Given the decision to rehabilitate domesticity's gender stereotypes, it is not surprising that relational feminists choose domesticity's compliments over its insults. But this veils the deeper question: Why return to domesticity at all?

In answer, let us start with a telling exchange between Carol Gilligan and Catharine MacKinnon in the 1984 "conversation" held at the Buffalo School of Law.[30] In a discussion of Jake, Gilligan's typical male, and Amy, her typical female, Gilligan argued that her goal was to assimilate Amy's voice into the mainstream of society. MacKinnon responded that Amy needed to develop a new voice that "would articulate what she cannot now, because his foot is on her throat." Gilligan's Amy, said MacKinnon, "is articulating the feminine. And you are calling it hers. That's what I find infuriating." "No," replied Gilligan, "I am saying she is articulating a set of values which are very positive."[31]

Note Gilligan's assumption that, because what she has found is "very positive," she cannot have found "the feminine," that is, conventional gender stereotypes derived from domesticity. MacKinnon is right that what Gilligan has found is femininity; Gilligan is right that there is something positive there.

Domesticity as a Critique of Possessive Individualism[32]

The conventional wisdom among the sameness contingent[33] is that relational feminists in their celebration of women's voice are simply basking in self-congratulation. I think this misses the mark. Relational feminists' interest in the feminine stems from its transformative potential.[34] Relational feminists find enshrined in domesticity "female" values that, they believe, will enable women to achieve equality not by buying into the male world on male terms, but by transforming the world in women's image. Thus Kathy Ferguson in *The Feminist Case against Bureaucracy* asserts that feminist theory "can provide for a reconceptualization of some of the most basic terms of political life."[35] Carrie Menkel-Meadow, a leading disciple of Gilligan within the legal community, hopes to restructure the legal system to express the values of "Portia's" voice.[36] Robin West recommends a new focus on connectedness and intimacy.[37] Other relational feminists go further and argue that women's voice is the best hope for the future of the planet. But Suzanne Lebsock, as usual, says it best: "If we find that all along women have managed to create and sustain countercultures, then the chances increase that as women come to power, a more humane social order will indeed come with them."[38]

For all these feminists, this "more humane social order" entails a new ethic of care[39] based on a focus on relationships, not competition; on negotiation, not combat; on community, not individual self-interest.[40] "What is needed," concludes the early and influential difference feminist Elizabeth Wolgast, "is another model. . . . We need a model that acknowledges . . . other kinds of interest than self-interest."[41] A more recent legal feminist echoes this thought, noting his aspiration "to transform our polity and its underlying assumptions from the alienated world of atomistic competition to an interconnected world of mutual cooperation."[42] The model being rejected is possessive individualism.

If we examine the transformation proposed by relational feminists, we uncover a critique of this model that dates back to the original version of domesticity. Historians have long known that domestic ideology presented a challenge to the capitalist mainstream of American society. Said Daniel Scott Smith in 1973:

> Instead of postulating woman as an atom in competitive society, [the Victorians] viewed women as a person in the context of relationships with others. By defining the family as a community, this ideology allowed women to engage in something of a critique of male, materialistic, market society and simultaneously proceed to seize power within the family.[43]

In 1977, historian Nancy Cott worked out in detail the way domesticity functioned as an internal critique of capitalism. She linked the invention of domestic ideology with changes in work patterns that accompanied the industrial revolution. Cott argued that domesticity developed in conjunction with the shift from traditional "task-oriented" work, which mixed labor and leisure, to modern "time-disciplined" wage labor, which isolates work both temporally and geographically from family life. She argued that domestic ideology set up the home as a haven from the heartless world of nineteenth-century capitalism.

In accentuating the split between "work" and "home" and proposing the latter as a place of salvation, the canon of domesticity tacitly acknowledged the capacity of modern work to desecrate the human spirit. Authors of domestic literature, especially the female authors, denigrated business and politics as arenas of selfishness, exertion, embarrassment, and degradation of soul. These rhetoricians suggested what Marx's analysis of alienated labor in the 1840s would assert, that "the worker . . . feels at ease only outside work, and during work he is outside himself. He is at home when he is not working and when he is working he is not at home." The canon of domesticity embodied a protest against that advance of exploitation and pecuniary values.[44]

Cott's description of domesticity as a *"cri de coeur* against modern work relations" suggests that domesticity has from the beginning functioned as an internal critique of Western capitalism.[45] Gilligan and her followers carry on this tradition in their visions of the future that extol connection, cooperation, and community (the "values of the web") and aspire to overcome competition and self-interest.[46]

Gilligan picks up not only domesticity's claim that women offer an alternative to capitalism, but also its stereotype of men as capitalists par excellence. "For men," Gilligan asserts, "the moral imperative appears . . . as an injunction to respect the rights of others and thus to protect from interference the rights to life and self-fulfillment."[47] By labeling as "male" the "morality of rights and noninterference," Gilligan links men with the liberal ideology that underlies American capitalism.[48] Gilligan also attributes to men the liberal premise that the world is one of "people standing alone,"[49] arguing, in effect, that men accept liberalism's vision of society as a set of preconstituted individuals who choose to associate for limited purposes. Hence Jake, Gilligan's typical male, is "concerned with limiting interference" and places a high value on separation and autonomy.[50] Gilligan associates the male voice with the pursuit of self-interest, and therefore with capitalism's central tenet that this pursuit will benefit society as a whole.[51]

Relational feminism is better understood as a critique of possessive individualism than as a description of what men and women are actually like. Gilligan herself acknowledges this when she refuses to associate her voices with males and females.[52] Yet Gilligan appears not to heed her own warnings on this point, for in the remainder of her book she invariably associates men with one voice and women with the other, and often makes sweeping statements about the way men and women "are."[53] Gilligan's inconsistent signals about whether she is talking about women or the feminine have left relational feminism with the potential to be used as a weapon against women. As evidence of this, I next turn to the *Sears* case, a clear example of the perils of modern domesticity.

EEOC v. Sears: The Perils of Modern Domesticity

In *EEOC v. Sears, Roebuck & Company,* Sears argued successfully that women were underrepresented in its relatively high-paying commission sales positions not because Sears had discriminated against them, but because women lacked "interest" in commission sales. Sears used the language of relational feminism to support its core argument that women's focus on relationships at home and at work makes them choose to sacrifice worldly advancement in favor of a supportive work environment and limited hours that accommodate their devotion to family.[54] An unmistakable undertone is Sears's subtle intimation that women's sacrifice is limited, since their "different voice" makes the fast track unappealing. Women's "ethic of care" enables them to rise above the fray, so they are not truly hurt when they are excluded from high-powered, competitive jobs in commission sales.[55]

The brilliance of Sears's lawyers lies in their success in enshrining gender stereotypes at the core of Title VII.[56] *Sears* provides a dramatic illustration of the power of relational feminism to provide a respectable academic language in which to dignify traditional stereotypes. The case holds the potential to transform Title VII law in a way that pits gender discrimination plaintiffs against stereotypes in a battle the stereotypes are designed to win, for in effect *Sears* establishes a legal assumption that all women fit gender stereotypes and imposes on plaintiffs a burden to disprove that assumption as part of their prima facie case.

Understanding the potential impact of *Sears* requires some background in Title VII law. The usual focus of a Title VII class action lawsuit is on statistics comparing the proportion of women in a given job category with the proportion of women in the relevant labor market. Statistics are direct proof that a facially neutral hiring policy has a disparate impact on a group protected under Title VII.[57] Statistics also are evidence of intent, as is illustrated by the "billiard ball" example. Say one begins with a barrel containing 50 black and 50 white billiard balls. If balls were removed in a random fashion, one would expect half black and half white balls to be chosen. The further the results are from a 50/50 split, the greater the likelihood that some other factor is at work. Because defendants who discriminate are rarely open about it, the law helps plaintiffs through a presumption that the "other factor" involved is discrimination. Thus, courts have required only that evidence of a statistically significant disparity be presented by a plaintiff to establish a prima facie case of discrimination.[58] Thereafter, the burden shifts to the defendant to articulate some nondiscriminatory reason for the disparity documented.[59]

In contrast to courts prior to *Sears,* both the trial and appellate *Sears* courts required the EEOC to prove not only statistical disparities, but also men's and women's "equal interest."[60] Under *Sears,* therefore, a class of gender discrimination plaintiffs cannot prove their prima facie case simply by proving a disparity between the proportion of women in the relevant labor market and the proportion of women in the jobs at issue. Instead they have the additional burden of establishing that women are equally "interested" in the jobs at issue.

Sears based its argument, first, on testimony of managers, one of whom made the now famous claim that women did not want commission sales jobs because such salesmen were required to work outside the store and women do not like to go out when "it's snowing or raining or whatever."[61] The managers' testimony was bolstered by a sociologist who testified about a survey of Sears employees,[62] by a writer on women's issues,[63] and by historian Rosalind Rosenberg, who cited Gilligan and other relational feminists to support her assertion that the EEOC's "assumption that women and men have identical interests and aspirations regarding work is incorrect. Historically, men and women have had different interests, goals and aspirations regarding work."[64]

To support this statement, Rosenberg offered portraits of men and women that closely echoed Gilligan's. Women she depicted as "humane and nurturing," focused on relationships, and averse to capitalist virtues such as competition.[65] Again echoing Gilligan, she painted men as competitive and motivated by self-interest—possessive individualists par excellence.

Sears proceeded to use against women the gender stereotypes rehabilitated by relational feminism.[66] The implication of Sears's successful use of domesticity's insults is that relational feminists delude themselves if they think they can rehabilitate domesticity's compliments without its insults. To relational feminists, the key point of domesticity may be women's higher morality; to Sears managers, it was that women are weak and dependent, delicate and passive.

A closer look at the trial transcript dramatizes the power of these stereotypes once unleashed, for it shows how Sears systematically used stereotypes to override information about the desires and the aspirations of actual women. The most obvious example of this occurs in the testimony of Joan Haworth, Sears's major statistical witness, who argued that even female applicants who appeared to be interested in commission sales were, in fact, not interested. When the EEOC challenged this statement, Haworth chose three applications that indicated background and experience in commission sales and explained how she knew none was truly interested.[67] The EEOC located two of the three women Haworth discussed, both of whom testified they had in fact been seeking jobs in commission sales.[68] The trial judge glossed over this rebuttal in his opinion.[69]

Sears also systematically discounted interests expressed by female applicants in "male" jobs such as auto sales. Haworth, who argued that those applicants were puffing up their interest, guarded against this by "normalizing" the scores of female applicants. Her methodology functioned to ensure that sales applicants who indicated interest in working both in "male" areas such as auto sales and in "female" areas such as the baby department had their "male" interests systematically discounted.[70]

Sears's attorneys had help from the trial judge in policing gender stereotypes.[71] Judge John A. Nordberg, a Reagan appointee, played an active role in shaping the evidence to support his eventual holdings that women lack interest in "male" jobs. Whenever EEOC witnesses made statements about women's commitment to the home and their lack of commitment to wage labor that contradicted gender stereotypes, Nordberg insisted they specify the precise percentage of women whose interests diverged from those of women in general (i.e., from gender stereotypes). Here is one example from the testimony of historian Alice Kessler-Harris, who countered Rosenberg's testimony by arguing that women generally have taken higher paying jobs when they became available, despite the mandates of domesticity.

Could I just interrupt for one second, Dr. Harris, or Kessler-Harris. This is what I have said to others, and if you had sat through all the testimony, you would understand the reason for my saying this. One of the difficulties in analyzing and dealing with the evidence in the case is a tendency of witnesses to use the phrase "men and women" as though it is 100 percent of men or 100 percent of women. I think that the testimony makes it clear that there are a range of personalities, interests, experiences, achievements, and everything in both sexes. . . . And what this case in a sense is getting down to, because of the statistical nature of the case, is percentages. It would be very helpful to me during the course of your testimony to try to quantify the percentage or the proportion or possible number that you are dealing with in any particular thing that you say. I [know] it is hard, because you are, in a sense, seeking to generalize. But it makes it very difficult when it is asserted that either women so and so or men so and so, when we all know that it isn't 100 percent correct.[72]

Judge Nordberg repeated the same point as a constant refrain to the testimony of EEOC witnesses. Women behave like this, they testified. What percentage? Nordberg asked again and again.[73] When Sears witnesses made generalized statements about women that *confirmed* stereotypes derived from domesticity, Nordberg's concern for quantification evaporated. I found no instance in which Nordberg felt the need for this type of quantification from Sears witnesses.[74] Nordberg's opinion shows why: He adopted the argument advanced by Sears (through Rosalind Rosenberg) that women who do not fit conventional stereotypes are a marginal group of (uppity?) college women. No statistical evidence supported this assertion.[75]

Nordberg's insistence on quantification in effect required plaintiffs to specify the precise percentage of women interested in nontraditional jobs such as commission sales. By not requiring Sears to provide equivalent proof of the specific percentage of women who *fit* gender stereotypes, the *Sears* district court opinion in effect establishes a legal presumption that all women fit gender stereotypes. The Seventh Circuit opinion wholeheartedly adopted this approach.[76]

Sears's doctrinal innovation clashes at a fundamental level with the thrust of Title VII. *Sears* allows information about *gender*, about women *as a group*, to be used to establish a legal presumption about individual plaintiffs consolidated into a class. This is inappropriate because Title VII is designed to protect women who do not fit gender stereotypes, who want to work as physicists, or in auto sales. Title VII's underlying goal is to protect women who want nontraditional work. Establishing a legal presumption that every class of female plaintiffs conforms to gender stereotypes frustrates this goal.

Sears is thus inconsistent with the underlying goal of Title VII and should be overruled. From a theoretical standpoint, *Sears* shows the power of gender stereotypes to overshadow evidence about actual women. *Sears* also shows how relational feminism's critique of possessive individualism serves to marginalize both women and the critique itself.

Unlike the critique of capitalism from traditional radical discourse, domesticity's critique does not compel its followers to confront capitalist practice and to change it. Instead, an abiding tenet of domesticity is that women's aversion to capitalist virtues makes them "choose" home and family. This is an argument that encourages women to "choose" economic marginalization and celebrate that choice as a badge of virtue. This analysis of domesticity as an ideology designed to enlist women in their own oppression will be more fully developed later. For now the important thing is how Sears mobilized domesticity's critique of possessive individualism against women.

Once can see how domesticity's compliments add up to its critique: Women reject crass competition; they favor a friendly, cooperative, working environment over mere material advancement; they value their commitments to family over career success.[77] Sears's argument demonstrates how domesticity's critique of possessive individualism rests on a claim that women are psychologically unsuited to the economic mainstream. All Sears did was pick this up and use it to argue that women are psychologically unsuited to work in commission sales.

Sears thus illustrates how domesticity's gendered critique of possessive individualism functions to marginalize the women who espouse it. It also shows that domesticity's power derives from its ability to make arguments about women's "choice" vaguely complimentary instead of clearly insulting. When defendants prior to *Sears* tried to mobilize the interest argument, they met with little success because their "interest" arguments so clearly mobilized racist or sexist insults. For example, the assertion in a 1976 race discrimination case that blacks lacked interest in law enforcement evidently smacked too much of a claim that blacks are lazy and shiftless, or inherently not law abiding.[78] In another case, the defendant's argument that women did not need the vocational training available to men since women choose unskilled jobs anyway also struck a jarring note.[79] In both cases, the interest argument evidently struck the courts as a blatant attempt to use against minorities the insulting stereotypes to which they traditionally have been subjected. Sears's lawyers succeeded because they used against women not the insults but the compliments of domesticity. Once the interest argument was linked with women's *virtues*, the trial judge and the conservative Seventh Circuit found it easier to frame complimentary holdings asserting that women choose their relative poverty, while framing their argument as a paean to female virtue.[80]

If *Sears* contains some disturbing messages for relational feminists, it also contains a comforting one: that by giving up domesticity's critique of possessive individualism, they are abandoning a singularly ineffective critique. A key source of the attraction of "women's voice" for feminists and other progressive thinkers is that, in a society where radicals have had trouble being taken seriously, relational feminism offers a critique of capitalism that avoids the perceived stridency of traditional radical discourse. It is Marxism you can take home to mother. But, as *Sears* shows, this strength is also a weakness, for what domesticity offers is a singularly "domesticated" critique that accepts the notion that anyone who rejects the values of contemporary capitalism freely chooses to eschew the spoils of capitalist endeavor. As traditional radical discourse makes clear, the whole point of critiquing capitalism is to challenge the way in which wealth is created and distributed. Domesticity's critique is designed to evade the central issue of whether society should be transformed.

Concluding Remarks on the Feminism of Difference

Lebsock offered a balanced assessment of relational feminism when she noted that the "emphasis on gender differences has great promise and great strategic risks. The risks derive from the difficulty we have in thinking in genuinely egalitarian terms. . . . The promise lies farther off."[81] With *Sears*, the risks associated with relational feminism have been played out. Moreover, I have argued that the promise of relational feminism—its critique of possessive individualism—is fundamentally flawed. Plenty of less dangerous, nongendered critiques exist to help progressives in their search for words against the resurgence of classical economic liberalism: The ongoing fascination with republicanism offers a possible alternative.[82] Neither this approach, nor traditional radical discourse—nor, for that matter, standard New Deal rhetoric— holds the pitfalls of relational feminism.[83] Instead of rehabilitating inherently loaded stereotypes, contemporary feminists should follow through domesticity's insights into the gendered structure of American capitalism to their logical conclusion. This following section begins that process.

Part II:
Challenging the Gendered Structure of Wage Labor

The challenge to "male norms" offered by the feminism of difference is comprised of two quite different elements. The first is the critique of "male" behavior and values, which in essence is the critique of possessive individualism. A second element is the critique of men's traditional life patterns. Like the first, this second critique has traditionally been linked with domesticity, but it need not be. In this section, I present an analysis that challenges the desirability of men's traditional life patterns without linking the critique to domestic ideology.

A rejection of men's traditional life patterns entails a fundamental challenge to the structure of wage labor. In articulating such a challenge, I begin from Catharine MacKinnon's analysis of gender as a system of power relations.[84] While I disagree with many of MacKinnon's conclusions, her initial premise is a powerful one: that inequalities of power are the core feature of the gender system as we know it. MacKinnon and her followers have explored the implications of this insight primarily in the context of sexuality. Here I turn to a more conventional topic, and analyze the Western wage labor system as a system of power relations that leaves women economically and socially vulnerable.

Western wage labor is premised on an ideal worker with no childcare responsibilities.[85] In this system men and women workers are allocated very different roles. Men are raised to believe they have the right and the responsibility to perform as ideal workers.[86] Husbands as a group therefore do far less childcare, and earn far more, than their wives. Women are raised with complementary assumptions. They generally feel that they are entitled to the pleasure of spending time with their small children. Moreover, even upon their return to work, the conventional wisdom is that women's work commitment should be defined to accommodate continuing childcare responsibilities.[87]

This gender system results in the impoverishment of women, since it leads mothers systematically to "choose" against performing as ideal workers in order to ensure that their children receive high-quality care. The phenomena that comprise the gender system today are often noted, but the way the system functions as a coherent whole remains largely hidden.[88] The following analysis will show how the impoverishment of women upon divorce, the feminization of poverty, and to some extent the wage gap between men and women are all parts of a dynamic that leads to the systematic impoverishment of women.

Before the industrial revolution, both men and women engaged in economic production; and though women were viewed as inferior, a certain fluidity existed between men's and women's roles.[89] This situation changed with the shift from task-oriented to time-disciplined labor in the late eighteenth century. By the nineteenth century, men's and women's roles were sharply differentiated. Under the new gender system, married women ordinarily experienced utter financial dependence on their husbands, though a divorceless society protected wives from destitution so long as they stayed with their husbands and—perhaps more to the point—their husbands stayed with them.

This gendered division of labor had a certain logic during the colonial era, when the average white woman got pregnant once every 24 months and had an average of more than seven live births.[90] In addition, childbirth was hazardous and frequently incapacitated women for substantial periods.[91] Moreover, married women played a vital role in production of food, clothing, and other household goods.[92] Under these conditions the blanket assumption that married women were not suitable for lifelong careers of time-disciplined labor may not have been far from the truth.

Since colonial times, domestic production has virtually ended, childbirth has become safer, and birthrates have fallen precipitously,[93] yet the structure of wage labor remains unchanged. Meanwhile, divorce rates have risen at an astonishing rate. In 1870, 8 percent of marriages ended in divorce; today 48 percent of all marriages do, and half of all American children will experience family disruption by age 18.[94] This has created a new dynamic within the traditional gender system that makes the system more repressive than at any other time in its history.[95] In contexts where women are keeping their side of the gender bargain by "choosing" to marginalize themselves economically in order to allow their husbands to perform as ideal workers, many men no longer are honoring their commitment to support their mates and children. Divorced men in massive numbers pay little or no alimony or child support.[96] Under these conditions, women's choice to eschew "ideal worker" status for the sake of their children often leads to impoverishment of their children as well as themselves.[97]

The impoverishment of previously married women parallels the pattern among single mothers. With the breakdown of sexual taboos, increasing numbers of mothers are never married to the fathers of their children. These unwed fathers tend to play even less of a role in financial support of their children than do divorced fathers.[98]

The wage gap, a third crucial factor in the feminization of poverty, also appears to stem in part from the gendered distribution of wage labor and childcare responsibility.[99] Economists employing "human capital" theory have argued that the wage gap is attributable not to discrimination, but to women's choices.[100] One study has estimated that roughly half of the wage gap between men and women is attributable to factors that, on inspection, relate to women's childcare responsibilities. These factors include differences in work experience, work continuity, and ability to work full time and during illnesses of the worker or other family members.[101] (Note that, even were we to agree that women choose disproportionate childcare responsibilities, human capital theorists themselves implicitly acknowledge that such choices cannot account for all of the wage gap. Their own estimates leave 55% of the wage gap unexplained. This percentage may reflect discrimination.)[102]

In fact, both discrimination against women and women's "choices" must be seen as elements of an integrated system of power relations that systematically disadvantages women. The impoverishment of women that results has been well documented.[103] Researchers consistently have documented a sharp fall in mothers' economic position, and a sharp rise in fathers', after divorce.[104] Statistics on the feminization of poverty also are well known. Three out of every five people with incomes below the poverty line are women.[105] Three-fourths of all black families below the poverty line are headed by women.[106] Two out of every three poor elderly people are women.[107] Almost one in three female-headed households is poor; only about one in eighteen male-headed households is.[108] The average income of female-headed families is less than half that of male-headed families. Moreover, families composed of women and children are ten times more likely to stay poor than are families where a male is present.[109]

The feminization of poverty reflects the way the gendered labor system invented at the time of the industrial revolution has adapted to modern conditions. In a world where many more women than ever before are raising children without significant financial assistance from men, the gender system has taken on a more repressive dynamic than at any time since its invention.

Why is this so difficult to see? In large part because of the ideology that women's disadvantaged position results from choices made by women themselves. Alexis de Tocqueville offered an early version of this argument over a century ago.

In America, a woman loses her independence forever in the bonds of matrimony. While there is less constraint on girls there than anywhere else, a wife submits to stricter obligations. For the former, her father's house is a home of freedom and pleasure; for the latter, her husband's is almost a cloister. . . . [Yet, the American woman] herself has freely accepted the yoke. She suffers her new state bravely, for she has chosen it.[110]

The modern form of this argument is the contemporary celebration of women who either subordinate their careers or abandon them altogether because they "know their own priorities." "[A] woman shouldn't have to apologize for her priorities," said Betty Friedan in a recent interview on "sequencing," that is, women dropping out of professional life for the period when their children are young.[111] News articles on sequencing seem invariably to point to women such as Jeane J. Kirkpatrick, Sandra Day O'Connor, and D.C. Circuit Chief Judge Patricia Wald, each of whom took from five to fifteen years off to stay home with young children.[112] Only occasionally do these articles note that such women are the exception.[113] I suspect most women would take years off their careers if they could be guaranteed that upon their return they could become an ambassador to the United Nations, a Supreme Court justice, or a D.C. Circuit Court judge—just as many men (and women) would take time off for a stint as an artist, a carpenter, or a ski bum if they could be offered the same assurance. But most sequencers are not so lucky. In the words of one company executive, "From a total career standpoint, anyone has to realize the realities of a big hiatus in their career—that it is certainly going to slow it down."[114] (And this executive worked for a company that is actively seeking to hire reentering women. What do the executives of companies say who refuse to hire such women?)

There is growing evidence that a career hiatus, at least in some professions, does not merely slow women down, but places them permanently in a second-class, relatively low paid "mommy track."[115] This development has received particular attention in the law. One recent article notes the "frightening possibility" that law firms will evolve into institutions "top-heavy with men and childless women, supported by a pink-collar ghetto of mommy-lawyers," often with permanent associate status.[116]

The professional who removes herself from the fast track is only part of the syndrome by which women systematically "choose" economic marginalization. Probably the more important aspect of the phenomenon is the tendency among women to select jobs that will allow them to fulfill their "family responsibilities," even if such jobs pay less and offer less opportunity for advancement.[117]

These two phenomena are an integral part of the economic marginalization of women. Decoded, the current talk about women's priorities is a translation into new language of domesticity's old argument that women's values lead them to make different choices. The persistence of this classic argument makes it imperative for feminists to analyze why the argument has abiding persuasiveness. The approach most useful to an analysis of women's "choice" is Antonio Gramsci's concept of cultural hegemony.[118] Gramsci painted a complex picture of how the dominant culture rules with the consent of the governed by shaping a "hegemony" of values, norms, perceptions, and beliefs that "helps mark the boundaries of permissible discourse, discourages the clarification of social alternatives, and makes it difficult for the dispossessed to locate the source of their unease, let alone remedy it."[119]

Gramsci's thought suggests that feminists can approach women's culture as a system of cultural hegemony. Marxist feminists have long argued that domesticity is a capitalist tool to privatize the costs of workers at the expense of women for the benefit of the employers.[120] Gramsci's analysis offers needed subtlety by focusing on the complexities surrounding women's consent. For Gramsci consent is a complex state fraught with ambiguities, a " 'contradictory consciousness' mixing approbation and apathy, resistance and resignation."[121]

Gramsci's analysis of consent suggests that feminists must come to terms with the ways in which women's culture has served to enlist women's support in perpetuating existing power relations. As historian T. J. Jackson Lears has expressed it,

> The idea that less powerful folk may be unwitting accomplices in the maintenance of existing inequalities runs counter to much of the social and cultural historiography of the last fifteen years, which has stressed the autonomy and vitality of subordinate cultures. Discovering nearly inexhaustible resources for resistance to domination, many social historians have been reluctant to acknowledge the possibility that their subjects may have been muddled by assimilation to the dominant culture—perhaps even to the point of believing and behaving against their own best interests.[122]

Women's historians and other feminists have illustrated this reluctance. In their effort to do justice to the dignity of women, they resoundingly rejected the image of women as victims, and instead have celebrated women's "nearly inexhaustible resources for resistance."[123] Now that this refusal to see women as victims has been transposed into a blame-the-victim argument through the rhetoric of choice, there is an acute need for a more balanced view of women's culture. A balanced perspective could be achieved by synthesizing two distinct periods of women's history that thus far have remained remarkably resistant to such synthesis.

Before the mid-1970s, many women's historians concentrated on documenting how domesticity cramped women's lives.[124] This early focus on how domesticity oppressed women was replaced after 1975 by a revisionist movement initiated by Carroll Smith-Rosenberg's influential article entitled *The Female World of Love and Ritual: Relations between Women in Nineteenth-century America.*[125] Smith-Rosenberg's article began a celebration of nineteenth-century women's culture, as historians explored the close emotional ties as well as the empowering aspects of women's separate sphere.[126] This literature, which developed simultaneously with Gilligan's feminism and echoed its celebration of women's different voice, takes on new meaning when it is combined with the earlier literature documenting the oppressive aspects of nineteenth-century women's culture. To put it bluntly, women's rich emotional relationships in their disempowered sphere and the seductive compliments of domesticity—in particular, the notion that women were more moral than men[127]—encouraged women to choose their own repression. This analysis need not deny the positive elements of women's culture. But it does dramatize the need to assess how domesticity seeks to enlist women in their own oppression, and the extent to which it does so successfully. *Sears* showed how traditionalist judges can use women's culture against women. The more troubling point is that women use it against themselves, every time a woman "chooses" to subordinate her career "for the good of the family" and congratulates herself on that choice as a mature assessment of her own "priorities."[128]

Feminists need to arm women to resist the argument that women's economic marginalization is the product of their own choice. Challenging this argument should be easy, since, in fact, in our deeply gendered system men and women face very different choices indeed. Whereas women, in order to be ideal workers, have to choose not to fulfill their "family responsibilities," men do not.[129] The question women ask themselves is this: Should I make professional sacrifices for the good of my children? In order for the wife's choice to be equivalent to her husband's, first, she would have to be in a position to ask herself whether or not she would choose to be an ideal worker if her husband would choose to stay home with the children. Second, she would have to pose the question in a context where powerful social norms were telling her he was peculiarly suited to raising children. When we speak of women's "choices" to subordinate their careers, we are so blinded by gender prescriptions that we can forget that the husband's decision to be an ideal worker rests on the assumption that his wife will choose not to be one in order to allow him that privilege. This is true whether the wife eschews a career altogether or whether (in the modern pattern) she merely subordinates her career to childcare responsibilities.[130] The point is that the husband is doing neither.[131] Women know that if *they* do not sacrifice *no one* will, whereas men assume that if *they* do not *women* will.

Thus women do not enjoy the same choices as men. But the underlying point is a deeper one: that society is structured so that everyone, regardless of sex, is limited to two unacceptable choices— men's traditional life patterns or economic marginality. Under the current structure of wage labor, people are limited to being ideal workers, which leaves them with inadequate time to devote to parenting, and being primary parents condemned to relative poverty (if they are single parents) or economic vulnerability (if they are currently married to an ideal worker). Wage labor does not have to be structured in this way.

The increasing onerousness of the gender system makes a challenge to the structure of wage labor a priority of the highest order. Moreover, a historic opportunity exists for a challenge: the current revolution in wage labor itself.

The revolution is not that women work; women have always worked.[132] The change is that the majority of *mothers* now engage in wage labor.[133] In 1890, only 2.5 percent of married white women did so;[134] but 59 percent of married women do today, including 51 percent of those with children under three, and 54 percent of those with children under six.[135] Not only have married women gone out to work, but the social taboos against such work—a crucial policing mechanism of domestic ideology—also are disappearing.[136] The shift in the traditional assumption that mothers will not work outside the home is encapsulated in the recent welfare reforms.[137]

This massive shift in the gendered distribution of wage labor has produced intense pressures to challenge the assumption that the ideal worker has no childcare responsibilities. But this pressure is being evaded by a cultural decision to resolve the conflicts between home and work where they have always been resolved: on the backs of women. In the nineteenth century, married women "chose" total economic dependence in order to fulfill family responsibilities.[138] Today, many women with children continue to make choices that marginalize them economically in order to fulfill those same responsibilities, through part-time work, "sequencing," the "mommy track," or "women's work."[139] In each case, the career patterns that accommodate women's childcare responsibilities often are ones that hurt women's earning potential.

Day care, widely assumed to be the key to incorporating mothers into the labor force,[140] is part of the emerging gender system that reinforces women's traditional condemnation to the margins of economic life, for even mothers with day care cannot truly perform as ideal workers. The ideal worker is one who can work a minimum of 40 hours a week and has no career interruptions (such as time out for childbirth, infant care, or care of the sick)[141] and who can do the things required for "normal" career advancement—which frequently include the ability to work overtime and the willingness to travel and (for white-collar jobs) to be transferred to a different city. Employers are taught they can expect this, but mothers cannot fulfill this career profile even with most types of day care. The single exception may be the mother with a full-time housekeeper—a solution available only to the relatively rich.[142]

The childcare options available to the great bulk of workers often require someone to take time from work when the child or the caregiver is sick or for other appointments that must take place during business hours.[143] Moreover, many day-care centers and many family-care situations offer sharply limited hours that do not accommodate many employers' requirements for overtime work.[144] So long as mothers systematically take up the slack, the traditional gender system will not change; mothers will remain at the margins of economic life. And 85 percent of all working women are likely to become mothers during their working years.[145]

Women can work without insisting on a redefinition of the ideal worker, but most can do so only at the cost of failing to fulfill the ideal. What we are seeing today in the absence of a sustained challenge to the ideal worker template, is the adjustment of the gender system to new conditions in a way that ensures women's continued relegation to the margins of economic life. We are living through a reinvention of the gender system, when we as feminists should be proposing a paradigm shift[146] that entails a redesign of wage labor to take parenting activities into account. There are three basic options for changing the status quo. One is for each individual woman to rebel against the traditional demand that she sacrifice in order for her husband to be an ideal worker. But what will that mean: that *she* will become the ideal worker and he will play the supportive role? This is an alternative most men would find unthinkable because they are socially conditioned to believe that the option to be an ideal worker is their birthright. Most women, moreover, would find this option unattractive because society has nourished in them the belief that it is their birthright to be able to take time off the grind and enjoy their children while they are small.

A second alternative is for both men and women to give a little, so that they share the family responsibilities that preclude ideal worker status. But then neither husband nor wife functions as an ideal worker—a risky strategy in an age of economic uncertainty.[147]

The third and only remaining alternative is to challenge the structure of wage labor. Since the current structure, and the gender system of which it is a part, increasingly condemn women to poverty, this should be at the core of a feminist program.[148]

Such a program would build on many reforms that currently exist. These include programs such as day care, flex-time, and four-day workweeks,[149] organized labor contracts that provide for unconditional personal days that can be used for care of sick children,[150] as well as paid maternity leave (for the physical disability associated with childbirth) and parental leave.[151] More sweeping proposals are those offered by noted childcare specialists Benjamin Spock and Penelope Leach,[152] and by noted economist Heidi Hartmann, who advocates a six-hour workday for all workers.[153]

Feminists' goal must be to redesign wage labor to take account of reproduction. Such a goal today seems utopian—but then the eight-hour workday seemed utopian in the mid-nineteenth century.[154] The notion that the wage labor system should take account of the human life cycle has always faced the argument that such "private costs" as aging or raising children are of no concern to employers. Even in the United States, this view has been successfully challenged: Old age is now acknowledged as a reality, and wage labor expectations have been modified accordingly. That, too, once seemed a utopian goal.[155] But expectations change; hegemony is never complete. Feminists should begin to work both toward cultural change and toward the kind of small, incremental steps that will gradually modify the wage labor system to acknowledge the reality of society's reproductive needs.

Part III:
Refocusing the Debate

This section pursues two themes that will be crucial in refocusing the debate within feminism away from the destructive battle between sameness and difference, toward a deeper understanding of gender as a system of power relations. I first argue that, despite the force of Catharine MacKinnon's insight that gender involves disparities of power, her rejection of the traditional feminist ideal of gender neutrality rests on misconceptions about this traditional goal, whose core aim is to oppose rules that institutionalize a correlation between gender and sex. Thus the traditional goal is not one of gender blindness; the goal instead is to deinstitutionalize gender—a long and arduous process that requires us to see through the seductive descriptions of men and women offered by domesticity. I conclude the chapter by aruging that, to the extent these descriptions offer an accurate description of gender differences, they merely reflect the realities of the oppressive gender system. Beyond that, the description is unconvincing.

From Gender Neutrality to Deinstitutionalizing Gender

Sameness feminists' focus on the similarities between individual men and individual women led them to advocate "gender-neutral" categories that do not rely on gender stereotypes to differentiate between men and women. Recent feminists have challenged the traditional goal of gender neutrality on the grounds that it mandates a blindness to gender that has left women in a worse position than they were before the mid-twentieth-century challenge to gender roles.

This argument has been made in two different ways. Scholars such as Martha Fineman have argued that liberal feminists' insistence on gender neutrality in the formulation of "no-fault" divorce laws has led to courts' willful blindness to the ways in which marriage systematically helps men's, and hurts women's, careers.[156] Catharine MacKinnon has generalized this argument. She argues that because women are systematically disadvantaged by their sex, properly designed remedial measures can legitimately be framed by reference to sex.[157]

MacKinnon's "inequality approach" would allow for separate standards for men and women so long as "the policy or practice in question [does not] integrally contribute[] to the maintenance of an underclass or a deprived position because of gender status."[158] In its strongest form, her argument asks: Why let liberal feminists' taboo against differential treatment of women eliminate the most effective solution to inequality?

This debate is graced by a core truth and massive confusion. The core truth is that an insistence on gender neutrality, by definition, precludes protection for women victimized by gender.

The confusion stems from the use of the term *gender neutrality*. One *could* argue that problems created by the gendered structure of wage labor, or other aspects of the gender system, should not be remedied through the use of categories that identify the protected group by reference to the gender roles that have disadvantaged them. For example, one could argue that workers whose careers were disadvantaged by choices in favor of childcare should not be given the additional support they need to "catch up" with their former spouses, on the grounds that the group protected inevitably would be mostly female, and this could reinforce the stereotype that women need special protections. Yet I know of few feminists who would make this argument, which would be the position of someone committed to gender neutrality.

Traditionally, feminists have insisted not on a blindness to gender, but on opposition to the traditional correlation between sex and gender. MacKinnon's crucial divergence is that she accepts the use of sex as a proxy for gender. Thus MacKinnon sees nothing inherently objectionable about protecting workers who have given up ideal worker status due to childcare responsibilities by offering protections to *women*.[159] Her inequality approach allows disadvantages produced by *gender* to be remedied by reference to *sex*. This is in effect an acceptance and a reinforcement of the societal presumption that the social role of primary caretaker is necessarily correlated with possession of a vagina.

MacKinnon's approach without a doubt would serve to reinforce and to legitimize gender stereotypes that are an integral part of the increasingly oppressive gender system. Let us focus on a specific example. Scholars have found that the abolition of the maternal presumption in child custody decisions has had two deleterious impacts on women.[160] First, in the 90 percent of the cases where mothers (up until very recently) have received custody,[161] mothers often find themselves bargaining away financial claims in exchange for custody of the children. Even if the father does not want custody, his lawyer often will advise him to claim it in order to have a bargaining chip with which to bargain down his wife's financial claims. Second, the abolition of the maternal preference has created situations where a father who wants custody often wins even if he was not the primary caretaker prior to the divorce—on the grounds that he can offer the children a better life because he is richer than his former wife. In these circumstances, the ironic result of a mother's sacrifice of ideal worker status for the sake of her children is that she ultimately loses the children.

While these results are no doubt infuriating, do they merit a return to a maternal presumption, as MacKinnon's approach seems to imply? No. The deconstruction of gender, by highlighting the chronic and increasing oppressiveness of the gender system, demonstrates the undesirability of the inequality approach, which would reinforce the gender system in both a symbolic way and a practical one. On a symbolic level, the inequality approach would reinforce and legitimize the traditional assumption that childrearing is "naturally" the province of women. MacKinnon's rule also would reinforce gender mandates in a very concrete way. Say a father chose to give up ideal worker status in order to undertake primary childcare responsibility. MacKinnon's rule fails to help him, because the rule is framed in terms of biology, not gender. The result: a strong message to fathers that they should not deviate from established gender roles. MacKinnon's rule operates to reinforce the gender system.

What we need, then, is a rule that avoids the traditional correlation between gender and sex, a rule that is *sex*- but not *gender*-neutral. The traditional goal, properly understood, is really one of *sex* neutrality or, more descriptively, one of deinstitutionalizing gender.[162] It entails a systematic refusal to institutionalize gender in any form. This approach mandates not an enforced blindness to gender, but rather a refusal to reinforce the traditional assumption that adherence to gender roles flows naturally from biological sex. Reinforcing that assumption reinforces the grip of the gender system as a whole.

For an example that highlights the distinction between gender neutrality and deinstitutionalization, let us return to our "divorce revolution" example. It is grossly unfair for courts suddenly to pretend that gender roles within marriage do not exist once a couple enters the courtroom, and the deinstitutionalization of gender does not require it. What is needed is not a gender-neutral rule, but one that avoids the traditional shorthand of addressing gender by reference to sex.

This analysis shows that the traditional commitment, which is really one to deinstitutionalizing gender rather than to gender neutrality, need not preclude rules that protect people victimized by gender. People disadvantaged by gender can be protected by properly naming the group: in this case, not mothers, but anyone who has eschewed ideal worker status to fulfill childcare responsibilities.[163] One court, motivated to clear thinking by a legislature opposed to rules that addressed gender disabilities by reference to sex, has actually framed child custody rules in this way.[164]

The traditional goal is misstated by the term *gender neutrality.* The core feminist goal is not one of pretending gender does not exist. Instead, it is to deinstitutionalize the gendered structure of our society. There is no reason why people disadvantaged by gender need to be suddenly disowned. The deconstruction of gender allows us to protect them by reference to their social roles instead of their genitals.

Deconstructing Difference

How can this be done? Certainly the hardest task in the process of deconstructing gender is to begin the long and arduous process of seeing through the descriptions of men and women offered by domesticity. Feminists need to explain exactly how the traditional descriptions of men and women are false. This is a job for social scientists, for a new Carol Gilligan in reverse, someone who can focus the massive literature on sex stereotyping in a way that dramatizes that Gilligan is talking about metaphors, not actual people.[165] Nonetheless, I offer some thoughts on Gilligan's central imagery: that women are focused on relationships while men are not. As I see it, to the extent this is true, it is merely a restatement of male and female gender roles under the current system. Beyond that, it is unconvincing.

This is perhaps easiest to see from Gilligan's description of men as empty vessels of capitalist virtues—competitive and individualistic and espousing liberal ideology to justify this approach to life. Gilligan's description has an element of truth as a description of *gender.* It captures men's sense of entitlement to ideal worker status and their gendered choice in favor of their careers when presented with the dichotomy society sets up between childcare responsibilities and being a "responsible" worker.

Similarly, Gilligan's central claim that women are more focused on relationships reflects gender verities. It is true in the sense that women's lives are shaped by the needs of their children and their husbands—but this is just a restatement of the gender system that has traditionally defined women's social existence in terms of their husbands' need to eliminate childcare and other reponsibilities that detract from their ability to function as ideal workers. And when we speak of women's focus on relationships with *men,* we also reflect the underlying reality that the only alternative to marriage for most women—

certainly for most mothers—has traditionally been poverty, a state of affairs that continues in force to this day.[166]

The kernel of truth in Gilligan's "voices," then, is that Gilligan provides a description of gender differences related to men's and women's different roles with respect to wage labor and childcare under the current gender regime. Yet we see these true gender differences through glasses framed by an ideology that distorts our vision. To break free of traditional gender ideology, we need at the simplest level to see how men nurture people and relationships and how women are competitive and powerful. This is a task in which we as feminists will meet considerable resistance, both from inside and outside the feminist movement.

Our difficulty in seeing men's nurturing side stems in part from the word *nurture*. Although its broadest definition is "the act of promoting development or growth,"[167] the word derives from nursing a baby, and still has overtones of "something only a mother can do." Yet men are involved in all kinds of relationships in which they promote another's development in a caring way: as fathers, as mentors, as camp counselors, as Boy Scout leaders. These relationships may have a somewhat different emotional style and tone than do those of women, and often occur in somewhat different contexts; that is the gender difference.[168] But a blanket assertion that women are nurturing while men are not reflects more ideology than reality.

So does the related claim that women's voice involves a focus on relationships that is lacking in men. Men focus on relationships, too. How they can be said not to do so in a culture that deifies romantic love as much as ours does has always mystified me. Perhaps part of what resonates in the claim that men do not focus on relationships is that men *as a group* tend to have a different style than do women: Whereas women tend to associate intimacy with self-disclosure, men tend not to.[169] This may be why women forget about the role that relationships play in men's lives, from work relationships, to solidarity based on spectator sports, to time spent "out with the boys."[170] These relationships may not look intimate to women, but they often are important to men.

Ideology not only veils men's needy side; it also veils the competitive nature of many women who want power as avidly as men. "Feminists have long been fiercely critical of male power games, yet we have often ignored or concealed our own conflicts over money, control, position, and recognition. . . . It is time to end the silence."[171] The first step, as the authors of this statement note, is to acknowledge the existence of competition in women's lives. Women's desire for control may be exercised in running "a tight ship" on a small income, in tying children to apron strings, or in nagging husbands—the classic powerplays of the powerless.[172] Note how these examples tend to deprecate women's desire for power. These are the stereotypes that come to mind because they confirm the ideology that "real" women don't need power. These are ways women's yearning for power has been used as evidence against them, as evidence they are not worthy as wives, as mothers, or as women. Feminists' taboo against competition has only reinforced the traditional view that real women don't need power.[173] Yet women's traditional roles always have required them to be able to wield power with self-confidence and subtlety. Other cultures recognize that dealing with a two year old is one of the great recurring power struggles in the cycle of human life. But not ours. We are too wrapped up in viewing childrearing as nurturing, as something opposed by its nature to authoritative wielding of power, to see that nurturing involves a sophisticated use of power in a hierarchical relationship. The differences between being a boss and a mother in this regard are differences in degree as well as in kind.

Moving ever closer to the bone, we need to reassess the role of power in relationships based on romantic love. The notion that a marriage involves complex ongoing negotiations over power may seem shocking. But if we truly are committed to a deconstruction of traditional gender verities, we need to stop blinding ourselves to nurturing outside the home and to power negotiations within it.[174]

Conclusion

The first message of this chapter is that feminists uncomfortable with relational feminism cannot be satisfied with their conventional response: "When we get a voice, we don't all say the same thing."[175] The traditional focus on how individuals diverge from gender stereotypes fails to come to terms with gender similarities of women as a group. I have tried to present an alternative response. By taking gender seriously, I have reached conclusions very different from those of the relational feminists. I have not argued that gender differences do not exist; only that relational feminists have misdescribed them.

Relational feminism, I have argued, can best be understood as encompassing two critiques: the critique of possessive individualism and the critique of absolutes. Both are better stated in nongendered terms, though for different reasons. Feminists are simply incorrect when they claim the critique of absolutes as women's voice, since that critique has been developed by men, and its ideal is different from the traditional stereotype of women as emotional and illogical.

Relational feminism's linkage of women to the critique of possessive individualism is trickier. If all relational feminists claim is that elite white men are disproportionately likely to buy more completely into the ideology that controls access to wealth, then in one sense this is true. I would take it on faith that a higher proportion of elite white males buy into possessive individualism than do black males, working-class and poor males, or women of all groups. Indeed, in the past 20 years writers have documented that these marginalized groups have developed their own cultures incorporating critiques of mainstream culture.[176] "One very important difference between white people and black people is that white people think you are your work," a black informant told an anthropologist in the 1970s. "Now a black person has more sense than that."[177] Marginalized groups necessarily have maintained a more critical perspective on possessive individualism in general, and the value of wage labor in particular, than did white males who had most to gain by taking the culture's dominant ideology seriously.[178] Moreover, the attitude of white women toward wage labor reflects their unique relationship with it. Traditionally, married white women—even many working-class women—had a relationship to wage labor that only a very few leisured men have ever had: These women viewed wage labor as something that had to prove its worth in their lives, because the option not to work remained open to them psychologically (if, at times, not economically).

Fewer blacks and women have made the virtues of possessive individualism a central part of their self-definition, and this is a powerful force for social change. But blacks as a group and women as a group have these insights not because they are an abiding part of "the" black family or of women's "voice." These are insights black culture and women's culture bring from their history of exclusion. We want to preserve the insights but abandon the marginalization that produced them, to become part of a mainstream that learns from our experience. The *Sears* case shows how these insights' transformative potential can easily backfire if the critiques can be marginalized as constitutive of a semipermanent part of the black or female personality.

Relational feminists help diffuse the transformative potential of the critique of possessive individualism by championing a gendered version of that critique. The simple answer is that they should not say they are talking about women if they admit they aren't. Once they admit they are talking about *gender*, they have to come to terms with domesticity's hegemonic role in enlisting women in their own oppression.

The approach of deconstructing gender requires women to give up their claims to special virtue. But it offers ample compensation. It highlights the fact that women will be vulnerable until we redesign the social ecology, starting with a challenge to the current structure of wage labor. The current structure may not have been irrational in the eighteenth century, but it is irrational today. Challenging it today should be at the core of a feminist program.

The message that women's position will remain fundamentally unchanged until labor is restructured is both a hopeful and a depressing one. It is depressing because it shows that women will remain economically vulnerable in the absence of fundamental societal change.[179] Yet it is hopeful because, if we heed it, we may be able to unite as feminists to seize the opportunity offered by mothers' entry into the workforce, instead of frittering it away rediscovering traditional (and inaccurate) descriptions of gender differences.

Notes

1. A wide range of scholars has identified the task of resolving this split as the major challenge for modern feminism. See, e.g., Alcoff, *Cultural Feminism versus Post-structuralism*, 13 SIGNS: J. WOMEN CULTURE & SOCY. 405 (1988); Kerber, *Separate Spheres, Female Worlds, Woman's Place: The Rhetoric of Women's History*, 75 J. AM. HIST. 9 (1988); Boris, *Looking at Women's Historians Looking at "Difference,"* 3 WIS. WOMEN'S L.J. 213 (1987); Littleton, *Reconstructing Sexual Equality*, 75 CALIF. L. REV. 1279 (1987); Scott, *Deconstructing Equality versus Difference: Or, the Uses of Post-structuralist Theory for Feminism*, 14 FEM. STUD. 33 (1988); West, *Jurisprudence and Gender*, 55 U. CHI. L. REV. 1 (1988); Minow, *Rights of One's Own* (book review), 98 HARV. L. REV. 1084 (1985). Christine Littleton offers an especially interesting and insightful analysis of how various groups of legal feminists are distributed across "sameness" and "difference." See Littleton, supra. at pp. 1292–1301. Robin West implicitly discounts "sameness" feminists by omitting them from her description of feminist thought. See West, supra, at pp. 13–15. This position is necessarily entailed in West's search for "a jurisprudence built upon feminist insights into women's true nature," at pp. 3–4, a formulation that shows the influence of her biological essentialism, at pp. 2–3.

It is worth noting that the perception that sameness and difference themes are necessarily in opposition is relatively recent. During the debate over suffrage, sameness and difference arguments were used "in the same breath by the same people, with no perception of conflict." Letter from Suzanne Lebsock to author (November 29, 1988, on file with author). Why these themes came to be perceived as conflicting and whether this modern tendency should be perpetuated are important questions for contemporary theorists. I am grateful to Suzanne Lebsock for this point.

2. B. FRIEDAN, THE FEMININE MYSTIQUE (New York: Dell, 1963). For a discussion of the breadth of the resurgence of feminism in the 1960s, see J. SOCHEN, ed., THE NEW FEMINISM IN TWENTIETH-CENTURY AMERICA (Lexington, Mass: Heath, 1971). It should be noted that Friedan has substantially changed her focus. See B. FRIEDAN, THE SECOND STAGE (New York: Summit Books, 1981), pp. 38–41, 83–87.

3. See, e.g., Wasserstrom, *Racism, Sexism, and Preferential Treatment: An Approach to the Topics,* 24 UCLA L. REV. 581, 606 (1977). Wasserstrom's comparison of sex to eye color is often criticized by feminists of difference, who argue that something would be lost if sex were treated as a factor as irrelevant as eye color. See, e.g., E. WOLGAST, EQUALITY AND THE RIGHTS OF WOMEN (Ithaca, N.Y.: Cornell University Press, 1980), pp. 22–23; Finley, *Transcending Equality Theory: A Way out of the Maternity and the Workplace Debate,* 86 COLUM. L. REV. 1118, 1139 (1986); Littleton, *Reconstructing Sexual Equality,* at p. 1291.

4. For a classic article, see Pearce, *Welfare Is Not for Women: Toward a Model of Advocacy to Meet the Needs of Woman in Poverty,* 19 CLEARING-HOUSE REV. 412, 413–14 (1985).

5. See A. CARDOZO, SEQUENCING (New York: Atheneum, 1986); Rimer, *Sequencing: Putting Careers on Hold,* New York Times, September 23, 1988, p. A21, col. 1; Hickey, *The Dilemma of Having It All,* WASH. LAW., May/June 1988, p. 38; Fierst, *Careers and Kids,* Ms. MAGAZINE, May 1988, p. 62; Kantrowitz, *A Mother's Choice,* NEWSWEEK, March 31, 1988, p. 46; WOLGAST, EQUALITY, at p. 156.

6. See, e.g., Barber, *Beyond the Feminist Mystique,* NEW REPUBLIC, July 11, 1983, p. 26, passim; Friedan, *How to Get the Women's Movement Moving Again,* New York Times Magazine, November 3, 1985, p. 26; Salholz, *Feminism's Identity Crisis,* NEWSWEEK, March 31, 1986, p. 58; Brubach, *Men Will Be Men,* ATLANTIC MONTHLY, April 1983, pp. 118, 124; Ciulla, *Corporate Leadership: Try a Little Tenderness,* PSYCHOLOGY TODAY, March 1986, p. 74; Lubin, *Superwomen of the Financial World,* WORKING WOMAN, September 1984, pp. 161, 166; Gilligan, *Why Should a Woman Be More like a Man?* PSYCHOLOGY TODAY, June 1982, p. 68; Hickey, *Dilemma,* passim; see also responses published under the title of *Parenting & the Law,* WASH. LAW., September/October 1988, p. 46; D. KIRP, M. YUDOF & M. FRANKS, GENDER JUSTICE (Chicago: University of Chicago Press, 1986), p. 113; cf. FRIEDAN, SECOND STAGE, at p. 86.

7. Comments of Paul J. Spiegelman in *James McCormick Mitchell Lecture: Feminist Discourse, Moral Values, and the Law—A Conversation, 34* BUFFALO L. REV. 11, 36 (1985), hereinafter *A Conversation*.

8. *Equal Employment Opportunity Commission (EEOC) v. Sears, Roebuck & Company*, 628 F.Supp. 1264 (N.D. Ill. 1986), aff'd. 839 F.2d 302 (7th Cir. 1988).

9. Some influential feminists have denied the importance of the distinction between sex and gender by arguing in effect that most (or all) of the important differences between men and women are biological as opposed to social. See, e.g., WOLGAST, EQUALITY, at p. 26. Perhaps the most influential author to take this position currently is Robin West. See West, *Jurisprudence*, at pp. 2–3. West stands by her claim that the behavior differences between men and women are biological, not social, even when in the last pages of her article she modifies her "separation" thesis with an admission that men as well as women are focused on connection as well as separation. To me this suggests that a focus on connection is not determined by biology (i.e., sex) but by socialization (i.e., gender). West, however, assumes that if men are "connective," there must be a biological reason; she attributes their connectivity to the fact of men's attachment to their mothers through the umbilical cord. Are we to conclude that women are more "connective" than men because, whereas men spend only nine months biologically connected to another human being, women who become mothers spend another nine months for each child they bear—more if they nurse and we count nursing as connective (as West does)? Are adoptive mothers then less connective than biological mothers?

West's biological determinism, in addition to singling out biological mothers who nurse as the ideal life form, leads her to the somewhat strange assertion that one of the unique connective experiences for women is sexual intercourse. Whom are they connected to? Are not men by definition also connected? And in what sense is menstruation "connection," as West claims?

West does not seem to realize that she is dealing not with biology, but with metaphor. She uses metaphors drawn from human experience to argue that experiences (notably childbirth) lead human beings to certain values—notably "connectivity." Isn't that true only if those people interpret the biological experiences West discusses in the same way she does? Pregnancy indeed represents an opportunity for human beings to recognize the beauty of their connections with others. Indeed, for me, one of the unadvertised beauties of pregnancy was the opportunity to feel a connection not only with the baby, but with the human community at large. Pregnancy, I kept saying, is like hitchhiking. It brings out the best in people, their most caring and communal side. But the point is that women can interpret this aspect of pregnancy (and all others) differently; many professional women interpret strangers' demonstrations of their sense that they too "own" a pregnant woman's tummy as invasive and demeaning. Moreover, women themselves sometimes experience pregnancies (particularly unwanted ones) as invasive. Nonetheless, some of the most influential feminists of difference have shared West's biological determinism.

10. C. GILLIGAN, IN A DIFFERENT VOICE (Cambridge, Mass.: Harvard University Press, 1982), pp. 24–63. Gilligan is only the most famous of the scholars who have defined gender in psychological terms. Her findings parallel, and presumably were influenced by, the work of Jean Baker Miller; see J. B. MILLER, TOWARD A NEW PSYCHOLOGY OF WOMEN, 2d ed. (Boston: Beacon Press, 1986). See also N. CHODOROW, THE REPRODUCTION OF MOTHERING: PSYCHOANALYSIS AND THE SOCIOLOGY OF GENDER (Berkeley: University of California Press, 1978). All three authors focus in different ways on "connectedness" as a crucial (if not *the* crucial) gender difference. See GILLIGAN, supra, at pp. 8–9; MILLER, supra, at pp. 83, 148 n. 1; CHODOROW, supra, at pp. 90–91, 167–70, 178–79. But only Chodorow seems clearly to recognize that what she is talking about is the psychological construction of gender and its costs for women, at pp. 213–19.

It is important to place Gilligan's work into historical context. Though I take issue with her conclusions about women's voice, I endorse her fundamental motivation, namely, to reverse the previous practice of ignoring women altogether, or treating any differences between men and women as reflecting women's inadequacy. Gilligan's primary contribution was to articulate a modern challenge to "male norms."

11. See GILLIGAN, DIFFERENT VOICE, at pp. 19–21, 64–66, 70–71, 82–83.

12. See, e.g., Scales, *The Emergence of Feminist Jurisprudence: An Essay,* 95 YALE L.J. 1373 (1986); Matsuda, *Liberal Jurisprudence and Abstracted Visions of Human Nature: A Feminist Critique of Rawls' Theory of Justice,* 16 N. MEX. L. REV. 613 (1986); Kornhauser, *The Rhetoric of the Anti–Progressive Income Tax Movement: A Typical Male Reaction,* 86 MICH. L. REV. 465 (1987); Areen, *A Need for Caring* (book review), 86 MICH. L. REV. 1067, 1073 (1988).

13. Feminists of difference often set up a rhetorical structure in which their willingness to admit "real" differences is contrasted with the ideological commitment of assimilationists to deny them. See, e.g., KIRP, YUDOF & FRANKS, GENDER JUSTICE, at p. 113.

14. Gilligan's work has spawned a huge literature. "[T]he very name *Gilligan* has become a buzzword in both academic and feminist circles." Watstein, *Psychology,* 4 WOMEN'S ANNUAL 167, 178 (1984). Some examples: in psychology, M. F. BELENKY, B. MCVICKER CLINCHY, N. R. GOLDBERGER & J. M. TARULE, WOMEN'S WAYS OF KNOWING (New York: Basic Books, 1986), pp. xi, 7–8; Lyons, *Two Perspectives: On Self, Relationships, and Morality,* 53 HARV. EDUC. REV. 125 (1983); Sassen, *Success Anxiety in Women: A Constructivist Interpretation of Its Source and Its Significance,* 50 HARV. EDUC. REV. 13, 18 (1980); in social theory: K. FERGUSON, THE FEMINIST CASE AGAINST BUREAUCRACY (Philadelphia: Temple University Press, 1984), pp. 159–60; in ethical theory: N. NODDINGS, CARING (Berkeley:

78 Chapter Three

University of California Press, 1984); in literary criticism: S. O'BRIEN, WILLA CATHER: THE EMERGING VOICE (New York: Oxford University Press, 1987); in the media: Van Gelder, *Carol Gilligan: Leader for a Different Kind of Future*, Ms. MAGAZINE, January 1984, p. 37 (Gilligan was *Ms. Magazine's* "Woman of the Year"); Shreve, *Viva la Difference*, in MacNeil/Lehrer Newshour, June 21, 1988, p. 15 (of transcript); in the law: Areen, *Need for Caring*; Finley, *Transcending Equality Theory*, at pp. 1118, 1154, 1158, 1161, 1166–67; Karst, *Woman's Constitution*, 1984 DUKE L.J. 447, 480–508; Kornhauser, *Rhetoric*, at 507–18; Menkel-Meadow, *Portia in a Different Voice: Speculations on a Women's Lawyering Process*, 1 BERK. WOMEN'S L.J. 39, 41–42 (1985); Minow, *Rights for the Next Generation: A Feminist Approach to Children's Rights*, 9 HARV. WOMEN'S L.J. 1, 15 n. 37 (1986); Rifkin, *Mediation from a Feminist Perspective: Promise & Problems*, 2 LAW & INEQUALITY: J. THEORY & PRAC. 21, 24 n. 14 (1984); Scales, *Emergence*, at p. 1374; Schneider, *The Dialectic of Rights and Politics: Perspectives from the Women's Movement*, 61 NYU L. REV. 589, 613–18 (1986); Spiegelman, *Court-ordered Hiring Quotas after Stotts: A Narrative on the Role of the Moralities of the Web and the Ladder in Employment Discrimination Doctrine*, 20 HARV. C.R.–C.L. L. REV. 339, 342 (1985). The grip of Gilligan's description on legal scholars is such that an editor of one women's law review to which this article was submitted indicated she had never before seen an article that disagreed with Gilligan; telephone conversation with Carrie Newkirk, article editor of the BERKELEY WOMEN'S LAW JOURNAL on September 20, 1988. Perhaps Elizabeth Schneider's thoughtful footnote may mark the beginning of a less deferential approach to Gilligan's work; see Schneider, supra, at p. 616 n. 140.

15. See, e.g., M. DALY, PURE LUST (Boston: Beacon Press, 1984), pp. xii, 4–7; M. DALY, GYN/ECOLOGY (Boston: Beacon Press, 1978), pp. 220–22. The French feminists combine elements of domesticity with elements of this earlier image of women. See, e.g., L. IRIGARAY, THIS SEX WHICH IS NOT ONE (Ithaca, N.Y.: Cornell University Press, 1985), pp. 29, 208–11.

16. For an introduction, see A. FRASER, THE WEAKER VESSEL (New York: Random House, 1984), pp. 1–6; N. COTT, THE BONDS OF WOMANHOOD: "WOMAN'S SPHERE" IN NEW ENGLAND, 1780–1835 (New Haven, Conn.: Yale University Press, 1977), pp. 201–4.

17. C. KARLSEN, THE DEVIL IN THE SHAPE OF A WOMAN (New York: Random House, 1987), pp. 154–81; J. DEMOS, ENTERTAINING SATAN (New York: Oxford University Press, 1982), pp. 60–64, 197–209, 394–95; J. KLAITS, SERVANTS OF SATAN (Bloomington: Indiana University Press, 1985), pp. 51–59; G. R. QUAIFE, WANTON WENCHES AND WAYWARD WIVES (New Brunswick, N.J.: Rutgers University Press, 1979), pp. 14–15, 182–83; L. ULRICH, GOOD WIVES (New York: Random House, 1980), pp. 96–99, 106–12; Bloch, *Untangling the Roots of Modern Sex Roles: A Survey of Four Centuries of Change*, 4 SIGNS: J. WOMEN CULTURE & SOCY. 237, 240–41 (1978); Demos, *Husbands and Wives*, reprinted in J. FRIEDMAN & W. SHADE, OUR AMERICAN

SISTERS: WOMEN IN AMERICAN LIFE AND THOUGHT (Lexington, Mass.: Heath, 1982), pp. 41–42. Pre-nineteenth-century women also had a very different relationship to commerce (which itself was not yet capitalistic). See Ulrich, *Housewife and Gadder: Themes of Self-sufficiency and Community in Eighteenth-century New England,* in C. GRONEMAN & M. B. NORTON, eds., TO TOIL THE LIVELONG DAY (Ithaca, N.Y.: Cornell University Press, 1987).

18. See generally A. JAGGAR, FEMINIST POLITICS AND HUMAN NATURE (Totowa, N.J.: Rowman & Allanheld, 1983), pp. 364–84; E. LANGLAND & W. GOVE, eds., A FEMINIST PERSPECTIVE IN THE ACADEMY (Chicago: University of Chicago Press, 1981); S. HARDING, THE SCIENCE QUESTION IN FEMINISM (Ithaca, N.Y.: Cornell University Press, 1986); C. MCMILLAN, WOMEN, REASON, AND NATURE (Princeton, N.J.: Princeton University Press, 1982); Vickers, *Memoirs of an Ontological Exile: The Methodological Rebellions of Feminist Research,* in G. GINN & A. MILES, eds., FEMINISM IN CANADA: FROM PRESSURE TO POLITICS (Cheektowaga, N.Y.: Black Rose Books, 1982).

19. See Williams, *Critical Legal Studies: The Death of Transcendence and the Rise of the New Langdells,* 62 NYU L. REV. 429 (1987).

20. Ibid., at pp. 432–34.

21. The most sophisticated of the feminist scholars who link traditional rationalism with males is the historian of science (a scientist herself) Evelyn Fox Keller. See E. F. KELLER, REFLECTIONS ON GENDER AND SCIENCE (New Haven, Conn.: Yale University Press, 1985), pp. 61–65. Keller convincingly argues that the ideology of science developed as part and parcel of a new gender system in the early modern era. But this does not establish, as she and others seem to assume, that the new epistemology (which is a critique of that system of science in the sense that science has built upon the tenets of traditional epistemology) is "female" in any meaningful sense.

22. See, e.g., Scales, *Emergence,* at p. 1374 n. 3.

23. See Bloch, *Untangling the Roots,* at p. 241 (hierarchy as natural); L. KERBER, WOMEN OF THE REPUBLIC: INTELLECT AND IDEOLOGY IN REVOLUTIONARY AMERICA (Chapel Hill: University of North Carolina Press, 1980), pp. 13–15. Kerber describes the initial accommodation between liberalism and gender in the concept of republican motherhood, at pp. 265–88.

24. See Baker, *The Domestication of Politics: Women and American Political Society, 1780–1920,* 89 AM. HIST. REV. 620 (1984); COTT, BONDS OF WOMANHOOD; Bloch, *Untangling the Roots,* at pp. 249–50. This description is an oversimplification. Domesticity changed the image of white middle-class women, but the older stereotype lived on. It continued to be applied to lower-class women, to black women, and to white middle-class women who violated the code of female behavior mandated by domesticity. These themes are astutely explored in Hall, *"The Mind That Burns in Each Body": Women, Rape and Racial Violence,* and Peiss, *"Charity Girls" and City Pleasures: Historical Notes on Working-class Sexuality, 1880–1920,* in A. SNITOW, C. STANSELL & S. THOMPSON, eds., POWERS OF DESIRE (New York: Monthly Review Press, 1983).

25. See Auerbach, Blum, Smith & Williams, *Commentary on Gilligan's* In A Different Voice, 11 FEM. STUD. 149, 156–59 (1985); see also Ehrenreich, *Accidental Suicide* (book review), ATLANTIC, October 1986, pp. 98, 100 (Gilligan's work being used "to re-open the old case for women's absolute moral superiority"); Kerber, *Some Cautionary Words for Historians*, 11 SIGNS: J. WOMEN CULTURE & SOCY. 304, 309 (1986).

26. Offen, *Defining Feminism: A Comparative Approach*, 14 SIGNS: J. WOMEN CULTURE & SOCY. 119, 135 (1988).

27. S. LEBSOCK, THE FREE WOMEN OF PETERSBURG: STATUS AND CULTURE IN A SOUTHERN TOWN, 1784–1860 (New York: Norton, 1984). Lebsock won the prestigious Bancroft prize for this work.

28. Ibid., at pp. 142–43.

29. The one Victorian compliment that relational feminists have rejected is the view of women as passionless. The classic study of the different cultural meaning of asexuality is Cott, *Passionlessness: An Interpretation of Victorian Sexual Ideology, 1790–1850*, in N. COTT & E. PLECK, A HERITAGE OF HER OWN (New York: Simon & Schuster, 1979).

30. Conversation between Carol Gilligan and Catharine MacKinnon, Mitchell Lecture Series, State University of New York at Buffalo School of Law, November 20, 1984, reprinted in *A Conversation*, at p. 11.

31. Ibid.

32. The term *possessive individualism* comes from C. B. MACPHERSON, THE POLITICAL THEORY OF POSSESSIVE INDIVIDUALISM (New York: Oxford University Press, 1962), pp. 3, 263–64. The term refers to the liberal premises that society consists of market relations, and that freedom means freedom from any relations with others except those relations the individual enters voluntarily with a view to his own self-interest.

33. I don't mean to imply that MacKinnon is one of the sameness contingent. She is not. See C. MACKINNON, *Difference and Dominance: On Sex Discrimination*, in FEMINISM UNMODIFIED (Cambridge, Mass.: Harvard University Press, 1987), pp. 33–45. The relationship between MacKinnon's viewpoint and relational feminism is aptly capsulized by Robin West. See West, *Jurisprudence*, at p. 15.

34. Although Gilligan herself sends mixed messages—see the text accompanying notes 52 and 53 below—her recent comments show that she diverges from many of her followers in a significant way on the issues of the transformative potential of women's voice. She has from the beginning acknowledged that both men and women face challenges, though they are different ones, in achieving emotional maturity. Men need to appreciate relationships while women need to realize that a caring and nuturing outlook should include their own, as well as others', needs. See *A Conversation*, at pp. 35, 45–46.

35. FERGUSON, FEMINIST CASE, at p. 166; see also Spiegelman, *Court-ordered Hiring Quotas*, at pp. 422–24. Gilligan herself believes that many current institutions would benefit from hearing women's voice. See, e.g.,

comments by Carol Gilligan in *A Conversation*, at p. 63. In other contexts, though, she has acknowledged MacKinnon's charge that women's voice is the "voice of the victim," as, for example, when she argued in IN A DIFFERENT VOICE that women need to have more respect for their own autonomy. See GILLIGAN, DIFFERENT VOICE, at pp. 151–74; see also comments by Catharine MacKinnon in *A Conversation*, at pp. 27.

36. Menkel-Meadow, *Portia,* at p. 43. Other commentators have argued that law is male. See, e.g., Rifkin, *Toward a Theory of Law and Patriarchy*, 3 HARV. WOMEN'S L.J. 83 (1980); Polan, *Toward a Theory of Law and Patriarchy*, in D. KAIRYS, ed., THE POLITICS OF LAW (New York: Pantheon, 1982), p. 294. The view of law as male comes up repeatedly in some feminist contexts. For an intelligent protest, see F. Olsen, "The Sex of Law," 1984, unpublished paper given to the Section on Women and the Law, American Association of Law Schools Annual Meeting, January 6, 1985. MacKinnon appears to agree with the characterization of law as male. See MacKinnon, *Feminism, Marxism, Method and the State: Toward Feminist Jurisprudence*, 8 SIGNS: J. WOMEN CULTURE & SOCY. 635, 645 (1983).

37. See West, *Jurisprudence*, at p. 65.

38. S. LEBSOCK, FREE WOMEN, at p. 144. Lebsock's claims are modest: "This is a hopeful vision," she continues, "but not necessarily a utopian one; we may be talking about the realm of small improvement." Other feminists are more openly utopian. An example is Rep. Patricia Schroeder's statement that "doing something about women's poverty won't make the gender gap disappear. Women will still worry that unless we change the old caveman rules, we will all be blown up"; O'Reilly, *Getting a Gender Message,* Time, July 25, 1983, p. 12. Other feminists are more aggressive in their claims for the transformative potential of women's voice. See, e.g., West, *Jurisprudence*, at p. 65.

39. See NODDINGS, CARING, passim; Areen, *Need for Caring*.

40. See, e.g., Karst, *Woman's Constitution*, at pp. 486–95; Menkel-Meadow, *Portia,* at pp. 50–55; GILLIGAN, DIFFERENT VOICE, at p. 29; West, *Jurisprudence*, at p. 37. West makes it explicit that she sees feminism as the way out of liberalism (within which category she includes critical legal studies, as the "unofficial story"). How feminists differ from critical legal scholars in their yearning for a vision of community and connection she makes less clear.

41. WOLGAST, EQUALITY, at p. 156.

42. Comments of Paul J. Spiegelman in *A Conversation*, at p. 36.

43. Smith, *Family Limitation, Sexual Control, and Domestic Feminism in Victorian America*, in COTT & PLECK, A HERITAGE OF HER OWN, at pp. 222, 238–39. Cf. CHODOROW, REPRODUCTION OF MOTHERING, at p. 213.

44. COTT, BONDS OF WOMANHOOD, at pp. 67–68; see also C. LASCH, HAVEN IN A HEARTLESS WORLD: THE FAMILY BESIEGED (New York: Basic Books, 1977).

45. COTT, BONDS OF WOMANHOOD, at p. 70; see also Baker, *Domestication of Politics*, at p. 620.

46. GILLIGAN, DIFFERENT VOICE, at pp. 17, 62–63.
47. Ibid., at p. 100.
48. Ibid., at p. 22.
49. Ibid., at p. 29.
50. Ibid., at p. 38.
51. Ibid., at pp. 35, 79.
52. Ibid., at p. 2. This is a standard disclaimer. S :e, e.g., Karst, *Woman's Constitution*, at p. 483; Menkel-Meadow, *Portia*, at p. 41. But the disclaimer does not solve the underlying problem. Even if one accepts that these descriptions accurately describe gender differences (which I do not; see the text accompanying notes 164–73), neither Gilligan nor her followers explain why men and women whose behavior does not adhere to gender stereotypes should be denied the dignity of being "real" men or "real" women (which they are when those with a "different voice" are systematically referred to as "women" and those with the other voice are systematically referred to as "men"). Although I suspect Gilligan herself might blanch at the practice, some relational feminists explicitly police the stereotype of women they advocate, by calling "male-identified" any feminist who disagrees with their characterization of women. For a polite example, see Littleton, *Reconstructing Sexual Equality,* at p. 1280. This kind of gender-policing epithet, parallel to the Victorian use of the word *unladylike,* makes explicit the assumption that women who do not speak in "women's voice" are somehow not real women. Note also that part of the power of the modern epithet *male-identified* is its assertion that a woman without "women's voice" is a man. This insult reflects a gender system that, first, mandates correlation of behavior patterns with genitals and, second, consequently admits of only two (consistently dichotomous) behavior patterns.

There is evidence Gilligan is becoming increasingly uneasy about her claim that women's voice is gendered. See the comments of Paul J. Spiegelman in *A Conversation,* at p. 48. In fact, Gilligan has acknowledged that an equal proportion of women focus on the "justice" and on the "care" perspective. The ethic of care thus does not characterize all—or even most—women's approach. Nonetheless, virtually no men focus on the care perspective. Evidently the situation is far more complex than Gilligan's initial hypothesis of two dichotomous voices suggests. See Carol Gilligan, *Moral Orientation and Moral Development,* in E. F. KITTAY and D. T. MEYERS, eds., WOMEN IN MORAL THEORY (Lanham, Md.: Rowman & Allanheld, 1987), p. 21.

53. Nel Noddings is more successful than most relational feminists at following through her statement that the "caring" ethics she advocates is available, and in fact practiced, by both men and women. See NODDINGS, CARING, at p. 2.

54. This argument was made most clearly through the testimony of Rosalind Rosenberg; Offer of Proof concerning the Testimony of Dr. Rosalind Rosenberg, at paras. 11, 16–22, *EEOC v. Sears* (No. 79-C-4373), and see case

numbers at note 8 above. Sears's testimony at times made it seem that all women prefer part-time work.

55. See ibid. at paras. 16–22. Another Title VII defendant successfully used a similar interest argument in *Equal Employment Opportunity Commission v. General Telephone Company of Northwest,* 40 Fair Empl. Prac. Cas. (BNA) 1533 (W.D. Wash. 1985), affd. 45 Fair Empl. Prac. Cas. (BNA) 1888 (9th Cir. 1988) (unpublished opinion).

56. See 42 U.S.C., secs. 2000e–2000e-17 (1982).

57. I'm simplifying for clarity. In individual cases, of course, what the relevant labor market is can be a subject of hot contention. See D. BALDUS & J. COLE, STATISTICAL PROOF OF DISCRIMINATION (Colorado Springs, Colo.: Shepard's/McGraw-Hill, 1980), pp. 44–49, 102–41.

58. For a good general discussion, see Boardman & Vining, *The Role of Probative Statistics in Employment Discrimination Cases,* 46 LAW & CONTEMP. PROBS. (Autumn 1983), p. 189; for an advanced discussion, see BALDUS & COLE, STATISTICAL PROOF, at pp. 26–31, 290–93.

59. See BALDUS & COLE, STATISTICAL PROOF, at p. 27.

60. See *EEOC v. Sears,* 628 F.Supp. at 1305–15; 839 F.2d at 320–21.

61. Trial Transcript at 8439, Testimony of Ray Graham, *EEOC v. Sears* (No. 79-C-4373). Graham, Sears's corporate director of equal opportunity, repeatedly expressed the opinion that some jobs (hardware, for example) have "natural appeal" for men, at 8435, while others (draperies) are "a natural" for women, at 8432. His assessments were based on assertions that women are averse to competition, at 8433, and pressure, at 8434–35.

62. See *EEOC v. Sears,* 628 F.Supp. at 1308–13.

63. Ibid., 628 F.Supp. at 1307.

64. Offer of Proof concerning Testimony of Rosenberg, at para. 1, *EEOC v. Sears* (No. 79-C-4373).

65. Ibid., at paras. 16–22.

66. Some thoughtful comments on drafts of this chapter have suggested that all *Sears* proves is that relational feminism can be misused. I disagree. The fact that stereotypes drawn from relational feminism can so successfully be used against women suggests, to me, their inherent limitations (namely, that they were designed to be used against women), not that Rosenberg and the trial judge, John A. Nordberg, distorted Gilligan's imagery. I want to stress that my charge that Gilligan's description of gender is inaccurate and potentially harmful does not mean that I think feminists should stop exploring gender differences (see the text accompanying notes 164–73); it means only that our explorations should break free from the grip of verities derived from domestic ideology.

In addition to using domesticity's compliments against women, Sears also subtly mobilized the insults that are an integral part of the traditional stereotypes. Rosenberg notes women's traditional association with dependence; *EEOC v. Sears* (No. 79-C-4373), at para. 17; Ray Graham's testimony is pervaded by notions of women as weak—ibid., Trial Transcript at 8425–26, 8436—delicate, at 8425, 8439, and vulnerable, at 8435, 8438. Other managers also stressed women's sexual vulnerability; see ibid., Offer of Proof concerning the Testimony of Thomas Biczak, at para. 26, and Offer of Proof concerning the Testimony of Daniel Mihalovich, at para. 12.

67. Ibid., Trial Transcript at 14626–29, Testimony of Joan Haworth. Haworth was analyzing applications that provided a single box marked "sales" for applicants to check, without a breakdown into commission and noncommission sales. The EEOC's analysis incorporated the assumption that female applicants who checked sales and had background and experience in commission sales were interested in commission sales positions. Sears challenged this assumption by putting Haworth on the stand to testify that such women were not in fact interested in commission sales.

68. One of these women stated, "[C]ommission sales is exactly what I was looking for and was the reason I came to Sears and put in an application." Ibid., Written Testimony of Lura L. Nader at 1. See also ibid., Written Testimony of Alice Howland at 4.

69. Judge Nordberg's opinion discounted these witnesses' testimony on the ground that the EEOC had not proven that they were discriminated against. *EEOC v. Sears*, 628 F.Supp. at 1318. This of course was not the purpose for which these witnesses' testimony was submitted.

70. This arose in Sears's lawyers' analysis of Sears's Applicant Interview Guides (AIGs), in which applicants were asked to rate their interest in selling various categories of items from 1 to 5 in terms of interest, experience, and skill. In Judge Nordberg's words, "The scores were normalized to take into account that some applicants might inflate their scores to increase their chances of being hired." Ibid., 628 F.Supp. at 1322. Normalization is a commonly used statistical technique, but two of EEOC's experts testified they had never seen it used as Dr. Haworth used it.

The normalization procedure only registered the applicant in a category if the applicant gave herself a rating for each of the three dimensions (interest, skill, and experience) that was 125% of her average rating for that dimension on all other AIG activities. For example, if an individual rated herself 4 for each of interest, experience, and skill in home improvement, this rating would be counted only if her average rating for all other activities covered by the AIGs was not greater than 3.2 for each of interest, experience, and skill. This procedure penalized people with varied interests and experience. It was therefore likely to penalize women with interest or experience in nontraditional work unless those women both disclaimed interest in and had never done traditional women's work. Thus, women's interest in nontraditional work was systematically discounted. Consequently, a woman who had held a low-paying sales position of the type in which women retail workers are disproportionately concentrated would be likely to have any interest she expressed, or experience she had, in commission sales discounted. Since men are less likely to have experience or interest in (lower paying) women's work, their interest in higher paying jobs traditionally held by men was much less likely to be discounted. Compare Judge Nordberg's analysis, ibid., 628 F.Supp. at 1322 n. 79, with Brief of the Equal Employment Opportunity Commission as Appellant, *EEOC v. Sears*, 839 F.2d at 41–42.

71. Sears also had help from the EEOC. The agency's decision not to provide testimony from victims of discrimination made it much easier for Sears to make general arguments on the basis of stereotypes. The EEOC's position is that, if it had provided witnesses, the trial judge would have discounted their testimony on the grounds that the witnesses were too few in number or were otherwise unrepresentative of the nationwide class. Brief of the Equal Employment Opportunity Commission as Appellant, *EEOC v. Sears*, 839 F.2d at 151–53. However, the testimony of live women interested in nontraditional jobs might have made it more awkward for the courts to accept Sears's assertions about women's interests. Maybe not, of course; see notes 66 and 67 above. But the existence of victim testimony so labeled would at the least have required the Seventh Circuit to write its opinion differently. It relied heavily on the lack of testimony from "real" victims. See *EEOC v. Sears*, 839 F.2d at 310–12.

72. Trial Transcript at 16501–2, *EEOC v. Sears* (No. 79-C-4373).

73. For example, Nordberg repeated this point to Alice Kessler-Harris six times. Ibid., Trial Transcript, passim.

74. I have not read the entire 19,000-page transcript. However, I note that Nordberg never pressed Sears's complementary witness Rosalind Rosenberg to attach a percentage to her claims about women, although those claims often were as unqualified as Kessler-Harris's, or more so. To Rosenberg, Nordberg stressed the need to qualify her statements by designating the time period to which they applied. Ibid., Trial Transcript at 10374–76. That objection was much easier to meet; it is easier for a historian to limit generalized statements to a given century than to specify what precise percentage of women during a given period wanted nontraditional jobs (or otherwise diverged from women's traditional roles).

75. See *EEOC v. Sears*, 628 F.Supp. at 1314–15; Offer of Proof concerning Testimony of Rosenberg, at para. 23, *EEOC v. Sears* (No. 79-C-4373).

76. See *EEOC v. Sears*, 839 F.2d at 320–21.

77. Compare the Offer of Proof concerning Testimony of Rosenberg, at paras. 19(c) and 20(a) (women reject competitiveness) *and* para. 19(a) ("Women tend to be more interested than men in the cooperative, social aspects of the work situation.") *with* para. 10 ("Even as they have entered the labor force in increasing numbers, women have retained their historic commitment to the home."), *EEOC v. Sears* (No. 79-C-4373).

78. *Castro v. Beecher*, 334 F.Supp. 930, 936 (D. Mass. 1971).

79. *Glover v. Johnson*, 478 F.Supp. 1075, 1086–88 (E.D. Mich. 1979), affd. sub nom. *Cornish v. Johnson*, 774 F.2d 1161 (6th Cir. 1985), cert. denied, 478 U.S. 1020 (1986).

80. See *EEOC v. Sears*, 628 F.Supp. at 1307–8; 839 F.2d at 320–21.
81. LEBSOCK, FREE WOMEN, at p. 144.
82. See, e.g., Sunstein, *Interest Groups in American Public Law*, 38 STAN. L. REV. 29 (1985); Michelman, *The Supreme Court, 1985 Term—Foreword: Traces of Self-government*, 100 HARV. L. REV. 3 (1986); Sherry, *Civic Virtue and the Feminine Voice in Constitutional Adjudication*, 72 VA. L. REV. 543 (1983); Horwitz, *Republicanism and Liberalism in American Constitutional Thought*, 29 WM. & MARY L. REV. 57 (1987); Forbath, *The Ambiguities of Free Labor: Labor and the Law in the Gilded Age*, WIS. L. REV. 767 (1985). For critiques of possessive individualism not framed in gendered terms, see R. BELLAH, R. MADSEN, W. SULLIVAN, A. SWIDLER & S. TIPTON, HABITS OF THE HEART: INDIVIDUALISM AND COMMITMENT IN AMERICAN LIFE (Berkeley: University of California Press, 1985), pp. 275–96; Cornell, *Toward a Modern/Postmodern Reconstruction of Ethics*, 133 U. PA. L. REV. 291 (1985); Gottlieb, *Relationism: Legal Theory for a Relational Society*, 50 U. CHI. L. REV. 567 (1983); Lynd, *Communal Rights*, 62 TEXAS L. REV. 1417 (1984); Simon, *The Invention and Reinvention of Welfare Rights*, 44 MD. L. REV. 1 (1985); Sparer, *Fundamental Human Rights, Legal Entitlements, and the Social Struggle: A Friendly Critique of the Critical Legal Studies Movement*, 36 STAN L. REV. 509 (1984). I find it particularly disturbing when feminists cite ungendered critiques and characterize them as "feminine." See, e.g., Sherry, supra at pp. 543–44. Indeed, Hendrik Hartog has argued that, to the extent republicanism is gendered, it is patriarchal. See Hartog remarks in a round-table discussion on The Constitution, Republicanism, and Women in the New Nation, at the Seventeenth Annual Meeting of the American Society for Legal History, October 23–24, 1987. The only overlap I can see between Sherry's description of republicanism and that of the "feminine voice" is that both constitute critiques of liberal individualism. This overlap does not make republicanism feminine. See also Schneider, *Dialectic*, at pp. 612–13 (discussing parallels between feminist theory and Sparer's nongendered critiques of capitalism).

83. See Tronto, *Beyond Gender Difference to a Theory of Care*, 12 SIGNS: J. WOMEN CULTURE & SOCY. 644 (1987).

84. See, e.g., C. MACKINNON, SEXUAL HARASSMENT OF WORKING WOMEN: A CASE OF SEX DISCRIMINATION (Cambridge, Mass.: Harvard University Press, 1979), pp. 92, 101–29, 215–21; MACKINNON, FEMINISM UNMODIFIED, at pp. 32–42.

85. I would like to thank Ann Freedman for insights and encouragement in developing this argument, of which she has a somewhat different version. Mary Joe Frug has articulated the core insight that Western wage labor assumes a worker with no childcare responsibilities, in her seminal study, Frug, *Securing Job Equality for Women: Labor Market Hostility to Working Mothers*, 59 BU L. REV. 55 (1979).

Note that I am not arguing that I have provided a full explanation of gender dynamics. Other commentators have analyzed other parts of the gender system—notably Catharine MacKinnon in her work on the social construction of sexuality. See MACKINNON, *Difference and Dominance,* at pp. 85–92.

Scholars outside the law—notably Zillah Eisenstein—also have developed analyses that overlap with the one presented here. See Z. EISENSTEIN, THE RADICAL FUTURE OF LIBERAL FEMINISM (Boston: Northeastern University Press, 1981); Eisenstein, *The Sexual Politics of the New Right: Understanding the "Crisis of Liberalism" for the 1980s,* 7 SIGNS: J. WOMEN CULTURE & SOCY. 567 (1982). Although Eisenstein's analysis is insightful, I question her assumption that a change in the structure of wage labor necessarily entails a wholesale abandonment of liberalism and capitalism. Wage labor could be restructured to eliminate the conflict between wage labor and reproduction while leaving intact the basic premise of decentralized production fueled by "private" capital. Moreover, while I recognize that one approach to redefining the ideal worker is to redefine liberalism's demarcation between the public and private spheres by making childcare a state responsibility, in my view this approach fails to address the fact that an eight- to ten-hour workday often does not leave enough time for effective parenting.

86. I do not mean that all men choose to be ideal workers, just that men as a group generally feel it is their right to be ideal workers if they so choose. Individual variation remains important. Some men do decide to scale back their career aspirations in order to spend more time with their families.

87. Although in the text I focus on childcare, women also shoulder a disproportionate share of the housework. See Burros, *Women: Out of the House But Not out of the Kitchen,* New York Times, February 24, 1988, p. A1, col. 1.

88. What I describe here are only the most recent developments of a long-standing pattern. See Hartmann, *The Family as the Locus of Gender, Class, and Political Struggle: The Example of Housework,* 6 SIGNS: J. WOMEN CULTURE & SOCY. 366, 371–73 (1981).

89. See ULRICH, GOOD WIVES, at pp. 14–50. Actually, as Ulrich explains, while women could perform male activities so long as they were acting under the supervision and authority of their husbands, men did not similarly cross over and perform women's activities. This is the classic pattern, today best illustrated by patterns of dress: It is easier to persuade the dominant group to share its privileges with the subservient group than it is to persuade the dominant group to threaten its status by adopting behaviors associated with subservience. In short, real women may wear tuxedos, but real men do not wear high heels.

90. The first figure is for women in New England. See *New England: The Little Commonwealth,* in E. PLECK & E. ROTHMAN, eds., THE LEGACIES BOOK: A COMPANION VOLUME TO THE AUDIOCOURSE *LEGACIES: A HISTORY OF WOMEN AND THE FAMILY IN AMERICA, 1607–1870* (Mill Valley, Calif.: Business Media Resources, 1987), p. 32. The second figure is for all American

white women. See J. LEAVITT, BROUGHT TO BED (New York: Oxford University Press, 1986), p. 14; Smith, *Family Limitation*, at p. 226. Leavitt points out that the standard statistic refers to live births, which implies a substantially greater number of pregnancies to account for stillbirths and miscarriages.

91. See LEAVITT, BROUGHT TO BED, at pp. 13–35.

92. See Gordon & Buhle, *Sex and Class in Colonial and Nineteenth-century America*, in B. CARROLL, ed., LIBERATING WOMEN'S HISTORY (Champaign: University of Illinois, 1976), pp. 279–84. The development of a market economy worked to disrupt household production by the end of the eighteenth century. Ibid., at p. 283. See also H. R. HAYS, THE DANGEROUS SEX, 2d ed. (New York: Putnam, 1972), p. 270.

93. See Smith, *Family Limitation*, at pp. 226–27.

94. L. WEITZMAN, THE DIVORCE REVOLUTION (New York: Free Press, 1985), p. 215; U.S. DEPARTMENT OF COMMERCE, BUREAU OF THE CENSUS, STATISTICAL ABSTRACT OF THE UNITED STATES, 108th ed., Supp. (Washington, D.C.: Government Printing Office, 1988); U.S. DEPARTMENT OF COMMERCE AND LABOR, BUREAU OF THE CENSUS, MARRIAGE AND DIVORCE: 1867–1906 (Washington, D.C.: Government Printing Office, 1909), p. 13.

95. See T. ARENDELL, MOTHERS AND DIVORCE (Berkeley: University of California, 1986), pp. 150–60 (comprehensive look at the gender bias in divorce). It should be emphasized again that the gender system has always served to transfer wealth from women to men; the developments discussed here are only the most recent. See Hartmann, *The Unhappy Marriage of Marxism and Feminism: Towards a More Progressive Union*, in L. SARGENT, ed., WOMEN AND REVOLUTION (Boston: South End Press, 1981), pp. 15–19.

96. WEITZMAN, DIVORCE REVOLUTION, at pp. 143–83, 262–322; Pearce, *Welfare Is Not for Women*, at pp. 413–14.

97. The impoverishment of middle- and working-class women upon divorce is a tragedy with striking potential for changing cultural norms, as women come to realize that they need to be empowered to perform as ideal workers to protect not only their own futures, but those of their children. "Legislation can only go so far," said New York family court judge Emily Jane Goodman. "No divorce reform will be successful until women have economic independence. Women need to concentrate on being financially independent before, during and after marriage." Blair, *Women Who Divorce: Are They Getting a Fair Deal?* WOMAN'S DAY, May 27, 1986, pp. 36, 45.

98. Unwed fathers are almost as likely to pay formal child-support awards, but the annual awards are much lower in amount ($1,147 compared to $2,538). Moreover, many fewer never-married mothers than divorced mothers are granted child support awards (19% compared to 82%). U.S. DEPARTMENT OF COMMERCE, BUREAU OF THE CENSUS, CHILD SUPPORT AND ALIMONY, ADVANCED DATA FROM MARCH–APRIL 1986, Current Population Surveys, Series P-23, No. 152 (Washington, D.C.: Government Printing Office, August 1987). Note that experts caution that formal child-support awards are not a good

indicator of responsibility among fathers, since they do not count informal gifts of money and nonmonetary help, such as childcare. Author's conversation with Gina Adams, Children's Defense Fund, August 25, 1988; CHILDREN'S DEFENSE FUND, ADOLESCENT AND YOUNG ADULT FATHERS (Washington, D.C.: Children's Defense Fund, May 1988).

99. See M. BLAXALL & B. REAGAN, eds., WOMEN AND THE WORKPLACE: THE IMPLICATIONS OF OCCUPATIONAL SEGREGATION (Chicago: University of Chicago Press, 1976); B. RESKIN, ed., SEX SEGREGATION IN THE WORKPLACE: TRENDS, EXPLANATIONS, REMEDIES (Washington, D.C.: National Academy Press, 1984); Beller, *Occupational Segregation and the Earnings Gap,* in COMMISSION ON CIVIL RIGHTS, COMPARABLE WORTH: ISSUE FOR THE 80'S (Washington, D.C.: GPO, 1984), pp. 23–33; Burns, *Apologia for the Status Quo* (book review), 74 GEO. L. J. 1791, 1798 (1986); Frug, *Securing Job Equality,* at pp. 57–61; Kingston, *Women in the Law Say Path Is Limited by Mommy-Track,* New York Times, August 7, 1988, p. A1, col. 5 (professional jobs "off the fast track").

100. See C. LLOYD & B. NIEMI, THE ECONOMICS OF SEX DIFFERENTIALS (New York: Columbia University Press, 1979), pp. 88–150; Polachek, *Discontinuous Labor Force Participation and Its Effect on Women's Market Earnings,* in C. LLOYD, ed., SEX, DISCRIMINATION, AND THE DIVISION OF LABOR (New York: Columbia University Press, 1975), p. 90; see also B. BERGMANN, THE ECONOMIC EMERGENCE OF WOMEN (New York: Basic Books, 1986), p. 25 (criticizing these theories).

101. See LLOYD & NIEMI, ECONOMICS OF SEX DIFFERENTIALS, at pp. 79–80.

102. See ibid., at pp. 204–5. See also R. TSUCHIGANE & N. DODGE, ECONOMIC DISCRIMINATION AGAINST WOMEN IN THE UNITED STATES (Lexington, Mass: Lexington Books, 1974), pp. 35–40.

103. See WEITZMAN, DIVORCE REVOLUTION, at pp. 337–56; see also R. EISLER, DISSOLUTION: NO-FAULT DIVORCE, MARRIAGE, AND THE FUTURE OF WOMEN (New York: McGraw-Hill, 1977), pp. 20–54; Levin, *Virtue Does Not Have Its Reward for Women in California,* 61 WOMEN LAW. J. 55, 57 (1975); Prager, *Shifting Perspectives on Marital Property Law,* in B. THORNE & M. YABLOM, eds., RETHINKING THE FAMILY: SOME FEMINIST QUESTIONS (Detroit, Mich.: Longman, 1982), pp. 111, 123. Betty Friedan has played a role in popularizing the issue. See, e.g., B. FRIEDAN, IT CHANGED MY LIFE (New York: Dell, 1976), pp. 325–26; Friedan, "How to Get," at p. 98.

104. Weitzman, *Divorce Revolution,* at pp. 337–56 (divorced men's standard of living rises an average of 42%, while divorced women's falls an average of 73%, in the year following divorce). See also Burtless, *Comments on Income for the Single Parent: Child Support, Work, and Welfare,* in C. BROWN & J. PECHMAN, eds., GENDER IN THE WORKPLACE (Washington, D.C.: Brookings Institution, 1987), p. 263; Blair, *Women Who Divorce,* at p. 36. For a list of other studies on the economic impact of divorce on women, see J. B. Singer,

Divorce Reform and Gender Justice, 67 N.C.L. REV., 1103, 1104 (1989) ("Virtually all . . . studies have found that no-fault divorce is financially devastating for women and the minor children of the households.")

105. Eisenstein, *Sexual Politics*, as reprinted in N. O. KEOHANE, M. E. RISALDO & B. GELPI, eds., FEMINIST THEORY: A CRITIQUE OF IDEOLOGY (Chicago: University of Chicago Press, 1981), p. 77.

106. Pearce, *Welfare*, at p. 413.

107. Eisenstein, *Sexual Politics*, as reprinted in FEMINIST THEORY, at p. 91.

108. Figures for households not headed by females are from the National Advisory Council in Economic Opportunity study, which reported that 39% of all female-headed households live under the poverty line. See Blair, *Women Who Divorce*, at p. 40.

109. Pearce, *Welfare*, at p. 413.

110. A. DE TOCQUEVILLE, DEMOCRACY IN AMERICA, J. Mayer & M. Lerner, eds. (New York: Harper & Row, 1966), p. 568.

111. See Rimer, *Sequencing*.

112. See, e.g., Fierst, *Careers*, pp. 62–63; Rimer, *Sequencing*.

113. See, e.g., Rimer, *Sequencing*. See also Torry, *Female Lawyers Face Persistent Bias, ABA Told*, Washington Post, August 9, 1988, pp. A1, A4 ("women are not increasing their representation among partnerships, judgeships and tenured law faculty positions in nearly the percentages their numbers and class rank indicate" in part due to the fact "they are forced to sacrifice career advancement . . . to have children").

114. Rimer, *Sequencing*. See also sources cited in notes 99–102 above.

115. See Kingston, *Women in the Law;* Hickey, *Dilemma*, at p. 59.

116. Hickey, *Dilemma*, at p. 59.

117. See Fuchs, *Sex Differences in Economic Well-being*, SCIENCE, April 26, 1986, pp. 459, 462–63; Frug, *Securing Job Equality*, at pp. 55–59; K. GERSON, HARD CHOICES: HOW WOMEN DECIDE ABOUT WORK, CAREER, AND MOTHERHOOD (Berkeley: University of California Press, 1985), pp. 91–122; P. BLUMSTEIN & P. SCHWARTZ, AMERICAN COUPLES: MONEY, WORK, SEX (New York: Morrow, 1983), pp. 325–26; S. HEWLETT, A LESSER LIFE: THE MYTH OF WOMEN'S LIBERATION IN AMERICA (New York: Warner Books, 1986), pp. 18–47; INSTITUTE FOR WOMEN'S POLICY RESEARCH, UNNECESSARY LOSSES, executive summary, 1988, p. 10 (new mothers' annual earnings and hours of employment are lower than those of women without babies).

118. Good introductions to Gramsci are A. GRAMSCI, SELECTIONS FROM THE PRISON NOTEBOOKS, Q. Hoare & G. Smith, eds. & trans. (New York: International Publishers, 1971); W. ADAMSON, HEGEMONY AND REVOLUTION: A STUDY OF ANTONIO GRAMSCI'S POLITICAL AND CULTURAL THEORY (Berkeley: University of California, 1980); J. CAMMETT, ANTONIO GRAMSCI AND THE ORIGINS OF ITALIAN COMMUNISM (Stanford, Calif.: Stanford University Press, 1967); A. DAVIDSON, ANTONIO GRAMSCI: TOWARDS AN INTELLECTUAL BIOGRAPHY (Atlantic Highlands, N.J.: Humanities Press, 1977); J. FEMIA, GRAM-

SCI'S POLITICAL THOUGHT (New York: Oxford University Press, 1981); T. NEMETH, GRAMSCI'S PHILOSOPHY: A CRITICAL STUDY (Brighton, Sussex, England: Harvester Press, and Atlantic Highlands, N.J.: Humanities Press, 1980).

119. Lears, *The Concept of Cultural Hegemony: Problems and Possibilities*, 90, 20 AM. HIST. REV. 567, 569–70 (1985).

120. This has long been noted by Marxists. See, e.g., Hartmann, *Unhappy Marriage*, at p. 28; see also Harding, *What Is the Real Material Base of Patriarchy and Capital?* in SARGENT, WOMEN AND REVOLUTION, at p. 130.

121. Lears, *Concept of Cultural Hegemony*, at p. 570.

122. Ibid., at p. 573 (footnote omitted).

123. Ibid.

124. See, e.g., Welter, *The Cult of True Womanhood: 1820–1860*, 18 AM. Q. 151, 152 (1966). A sampling of other representative works: Faragher & Stansell, *Women and Their Families on the Overland Trail to California and Oregon, 1842–1867*, 2 FEM. STUD. 150 (1975); Smith-Rosenberg, *The Hysterical Woman: Sex Roles and Role Conflict in 19th-Century America*, 39 SOC. RES. 652 (1972); Wood, *The "Scribbling Women" and Fanny Fern: Why Women Wrote*, 23 AM. Q. 3 (1971). Welter and other contemporary writers of women's history were directly influenced by Betty Friedan's *The Feminist Mystique*. See Kerber, *Separate Spheres*, at p. 11. Kerber offers an astute reassessment of women's history designed to move beyond the stages I discuss here.

125. Smith-Rosenberg, *The Female World of Love and Ritual: Relations between Women in Nineteenth-century America*, reprinted in COTT & PLECK, A HERITAGE OF HER OWN, at p. 311.

126. See Kerber, *Separate Spheres*, at pp. 14–15.

127. It should be noted that the notion women are more moral than men offered women real power in the nineteenth century—something I would argue it does not do today. See Ginzberg, *"Moral Suasion Is Moral Balderdash": Women, Politics, and Social Activism in the 1850s*, 73 J. AM. HIST. 601 (1986).

128. I do not mean to imply that all women who take primary childcare responsibility at the expense of their ability to be ideal workers do so because they are persuaded by domesticity's reassurance that their choice places them on a higher moral plane. Many no doubt settle for part-time work or make other trade-offs with the sense that they are making the best of a bad bargain through a temporary expedient not desirable but inevitable under the circumstances. Yet my sense is that the societal message that women are inherently more nurturing and self-sacrificing, and less competitive and ambitious, often plays a role in helping persuade women that what is inevitable is also "natural" and desirable.

129. This is the case primarily because, despite the entry of large numbers of mothers into the workplace, most fathers have not taken on significantly more home responsibilities. Thus their wives are left trying to perform as ideal

workers *and* to provide the support services their husbands require in order to perform as ideal workers. See C. TAEUBER & V. VALDISERA, WOMEN IN THE AMERICAN ECONOMY, U.S. Dept. of Commerce, Bureau of the Census, Current Population Reports, Series P-23, No. 146 (Washington, D.C.: Government Printing Office, 1986), pp. 7–8. As many news articles testify, this is impossible. See, e.g., Hickey, *Dilemma,* at pp. 40–45; Salholz, *Feminism's Identity Crisis.*

130. In a recent Gallup poll, 28% of working and 57% of nonworking mothers said they had quit work since having children; 43% of working and 37% of nonworking mothers said they had changed jobs or hours to spend more time with family; 35% of working and 45% of nonworking mothers said they had cut back on career goals. Kantrowitz, Witherspoon, Burgower, Weathers & Huck, *A Mother's Choice,* NEWSWEEK, March 31, 1986, pp. 46, 51.

131. The power of gender is such that even where the husband's job has the flexibility to accommodate substantial childcare responsibilities, whereas the wife's job does not, the wife often ends up making professional sacrifices to shoulder a disproportionate burden of the childcare. For example, when the husband is an academic and the wife works in a law firm, the wife nonetheless often jeopardizes her chances for partnership by working part-time in order to take primary childcare responsibility. See Kingston. *Women in the Law,* at p. 1.

132. See A. KESSLER-HARRIS, WOMEN HAVE ALWAYS WORKED (New York: Feminist Press at the City University of New York, 1981); A. KESSLER-HARRIS, OUT TO WORK (New York: Oxford University Press, 1982). Kessler-Harris's title illustrates the difficulty of trying to be consistent about not referring to wage labor as "work"—a usage that implies that women's traditional activities, from bearing children to housework, are leisure.

133. *Working Mother Is Now Norm, Study Shows,* New York Times, June 16, 1988, p. A19.

134. Smith, *Family Limitation,* at p. 225. Married black women have always worked outside the home in greater numbers. See J. JONES, LABOR OF LOVE, LABOR OF SORROW (New York: Random House, 1985), pp. 6–8. Moreover, the figure for white women has been challenged—see, e.g., Bose, *Devaluing Women's Work: The Undercount of Women's Employment in 1900 and 1980,* in WOMEN AND WORK RESEARCH GROUP, ed., HIDDEN ASPECTS OF WOMEN'S WORK (New York: Praeger, 1987), p. 95—as have the presumptions that generate it; see Turbin, *Beyond Conventional Wisdom: Women's Wage Work, Household Economic Contribution, and Labor Activism in a Mid-Nineteenth Century Working-class Community,* in GRONEMAN & NORTON, TOIL LIVELONG DAY, at pp. 47, 54–56.

135. U.S. DEPARTMENT OF COMMERCE, BUREAU OF THE CENSUS, STATISTICAL ABSTRACT OF THE UNITED STATES (Washington, D.C.: Government Printing Office, 1987), p. 383. The equivalent figures for 1970 were 40%, 26%,

and 31%. BERGMANN, ECONOMIC EMERGENCE, at p. 25. Women's labor-force participation in their prime child-raising years (ages 25–34) increased from 34.4% to 63.8% between 1954 and 1979. "Between 1950 and 1978, the labor participation rates of mothers with children under six more than tripled, rising from 14 percent to 44 percent"; Law, *Women, Work, Welfare, and the Preservation of Patriarchy,* 131 U. PA. L. REV. 1249, 1254 (1983). The percentage of married women with children under one who worked outside the home more than doubled between 1970 and 1985. See Kay, *Equality and Difference: A Perspective on No-fault Divorce and Its Aftermath,* 56 U. CIN. L. REV. 1, 18 n. 66 (1987).

136. BERGMANN, ECONOMIC EMERGENCE, at pp. 3–4; BLUMSTEIN & SCHWARTZ, AMERICAN COUPLES, at pp. 117–27 (suggesting ambivalence on the issue).

137. See Stevens, *The Welfare Consensus,* New York Times, June 22, 1988, p. 4, col. 5.

138. Professions often enforced women's "choice" with formal rules that required married women to discontinue work. See, e.g., M. ROSSITER, WOMEN SCIENTISTS IN AMERICA (Baltimore: Johns Hopkins University Press, 1982), pp. 15–16 (about a promising female physics professor who was forced to resign by Barnard in 1906, upon becoming engaged; her career ended, although her engagement did not ultimately result in marriage).

139. See H. KAHNE, RECONCEIVING PART-TIME WORK (Totowa, N.J.: Rowman & Allanheld, 1985), pp. 24–60; S. SHARPE, DOUBLE IDENTITY: THE LIVES OF WORKING MOTHERS (Harmondsworth, Middlesex, England, and New York: Penguin Books, 1984), pp. 54–63; Kingston, *Women in the Law,* at p. 1; Rimer, *Sequencing;* Hickey, *Dilemma,* at p. 59. See also sources cited at note 117 above. The ten leading occupations of women are ones in which it is relatively easy for workers to leave and reenter. See Marshall & Paulin, *Employment and Earnings of Women: Historical Perspective,* in K. KOZIARRA ET AL., WORKING WOMEN: PAST, PRESENT, FUTURE (Washington, D.C.: BNA Books, 1987), pp. 10, 24.

140. See, e.g., Rossi, *Equality between the Sexes: An Immodest Proposal,* 93 DAEDALUS 607, 630 (1964); R. SIDEL, WOMEN AND CHILDREN LAST: THE PLIGHT OF POOR WOMEN IN AFFLUENT AMERICA (New York: Viking Penguin, 1980), p. 131. Rossi has changed her view, and has turned to sociobiology to support her new argument that women are "naturally" more suited to "mothering." Rossi, *A Biosocial Perspective on Parenting,* DAEDALUS 1, 4–5 (Spring 1977); Rossi, *Gender and Parenthood,* 49 AM. SOC. REV. 1, 9 (1984).

I do not mean to sound negative about day care, which is an inevitable (and probably desirable) part of a total solution. My only point is that day care by itself is a solution that reinforces the marginalization of women.

141. See Taub, *From Parental Leaves to Nurturing Leaves,* 13 NYU REV. L. & SOC. CHANGE 381–84 (1984/85).

142. In Washington, D.C.—admittedly an inflated market—the average

price for a full-time nanny is $225–$250 per week, according to estimates by nanny services. See Shannon in the WASHINGTONIAN, October 1988, p. 171. They place the range from $150 per week to $350 per week, in addition to a fee of between $300 and $1,200 due to the nanny agency as a finder's fee, at pp. 171–72.

143. Many employees' sick leave policies do not allow them to take sick leave to care for sick children, and many states' licensing laws do not allow children with communicable diseases to be in day care. Even where licensing requirements do not forbid it, most centers (for obvious reasons) have policies forbidding sick children to attend. Author's telephone conversation with Barbara Reisman, Child Care Action Campaign, on December 16, 1988.

144. Many centers have policies charging parents $1 per minute for each minute they are late. Although this is understandable from the viewpoint of the childcare workers, it imposes a burden on parents whose employers require them to work overtime. These include not only professional workers, but others. For example, postal workers are required by collective bargaining agreement to work up to two hours overtime with no advance notice. Author's telephone conversation with Barbara Reisman, Child Care Action Campaign, on December 16, 1988. See D. BELL, D. DOLAN, D. GOLDMAN, B. HENSLER, A. HOFFMAN, N. KOLBAN, B. REISMAN, N. B. TRUE, J. WINEMAN & M. FRANK, BARGAINING FOR FAMILY BENEFITS: A UNION MEMBER'S GUIDE (Washington, D.C.: AFL/Coalition of Labor Union Women, 1985).

145. S. KAMERMAN, A. KAHN & P. KINGSTON, MATERNITY POLICIES AND WORKING WOMEN (New York: Columbia University Press 1983), p. 5.

146. Cf. Kerber, *Separate Spheres*, at p. 27.

147. Both these options are doomed politically, as is any political strategy that attempts to gain equality for women by insisting men share women's traditional disabilities. This strategy has been tried before, with notably unsuccessful results. An example is the Victorian attempt to eliminate the sexual double standard by insisting that men join them in adhering to the sexual purity expected of women. Modern reformers have been careful to disassociate advancements for women from sacrifices for men. For example, the Equal Pay Act requires that salary disparities be remedied by raising women's salaries, not lowering men's; see Equal Pay Act, 77 Stat. 56 (1963), codified as amended at 29 U.S.C., sec. 206(d) (1982), and discussed in *Corning Glass Works v. Brennan,* 417 U.S. 188, 190–91, 195–204 (1974).

In addition, it is likely that men face even greater career difficulties than women when they demand accommodation of childcare responsibilities. See Project, *Law Firms and Lawyers with Children: An Empirical Analysis of Family/Work Conflict,* 34 STAN. L. REV. 1263, 1300 (1982).

148. For an examination of various policy approaches, see Frug, *Securing Job Equality,* at pp. 61–103; Taub, *Parental Leaves,* passim. (Taub contends that various sorts of work leaves should be available for caretaking responsibilities other than parental ones, at pp. 383–84.) To the extent to which

employers are changing job expectations to accommodate childcare responsibilities, these changes are commonly thought of as special accommodations to women. See, e.g., Collins, *Wooing Workers in the 90's: New Role for Family Benefits*, New York Times, July 20, 1988, p. A1. This will not change until feminists challenge the assumption that men, but not mothers, are entitled to perform as ideal workers simply because of their sex. Moreover, some evidence exists that such "accommodations to women" are occurring primarily in underpaid "women's jobs." See Brown & Peckman, *Introduction*, in GENDER IN WORKPLACE, p. 8.

149. See Collins, *Wooing Workers*, at pp. A1, A14. This article, based on research from a nonprofit group, notes that companies will have to offer "family benefits" in coming years in order to attract workers, since two-thirds of all new entrants into the workforce will be women. The same organization reports that 3,500 companies offer some form of childcare support.

150. See generally COALITION OF LABOR UNION WOMEN, BARGAINING.

151. See Collins, *Wooing Workers*, at p. A14. Parental leave bills introduced in the 100th Congress were not enacted into law. H.R. 925, 100th Cong., 2d sess., 1988 (Family and Medical Leave Act); S. 2488, 100th Cong., 2d sess., 1988 (Parental and Medical Leave Act).

152. "Go after our industries!" advises Doctor Spock. He recommends more flexibility in hours, six-hour workdays, and subsidized day care. Both Penelope Leach, a psychology Ph.D., and Dr. T. Barry Brazelton believe that current trends have potentially adverse psychological consequences for today's families. Brazelton has stressed the need for improved pay for day-care workers; Leach advocates extensive paid maternity leave (6 months) and part-time work by both parents (next 18 months). See *Work and Families*, WASHINGTON PARENT, November 1988, pp. 1, 3, 5 (report of a panel discussion in Boston, April 1988). See also Brazelton, *Stress for Families Today*, INFANT MENTAL HEALTH J., Spring 1988, p. 65.

153. See Hartmann, *Achieving Economic Equity for Women*, in M. RASKIN & C. HARTMAN, eds., WINNING AMERICA: IDEAS AND LEADERSHIP FOR THE 1990s (Boston: South End Press, 1988), p. 99.

154. "In 1840, the average work week in the United States was 78 hours." Frug, *Securing Job Equality*, at p. 97 n. 248, citing Northrup, *The Reduction in Hours*, in C. DANKERT, F. MANN & H. NORTHRUP, eds., HOURS OF WORK (New York: Harper & Row, 1965).

155. See A. EPSTEIN, THE CHALLENGE OF THE AGED (Salem, N.H.: Ayer, 1976), p. vii; see also C. MEYER, SOCIAL SECURITY: A CRITIQUE OF RADICAL REFORM PROSPECTS (New York: Free Press, 1987), p. 9.

156. Fineman, *Implementing Equality: Ideology, Contradiction and Social Change*, 1983 WIS. L. REV. 789, 791; Levin, *Virtue*, at p. 55. See also Finley, *Transcending Equality Theory*, at pp. 1148–63.

157. MACKINNON, SEXUAL HARASSMENT, at pp. 100–41, discussing *Phillips v. Martin Marietta Corporation*, 400 U.S. 542 (1971); MACKINNON, FEMINISM UNMODIFIED, at pp. 35–36.

158. MacKinnon, Sexual Harassment, at p. 117. See Taub, Book Review, 80 Colum. L. Rev. 1686 (1980).

159. MacKinnon, Sexual Harassment, at pp. 122–24.

160. See Polikoff, *Why Mothers Are Losing: A Brief Analysis of Criteria Used in Child Custody Determinations,* 7 Women's Rts. L. Rep. 235 (1982); Weitzman, Divorce Revolution, at pp. 217, 310–18.

161. See Polikoff, *Why Mothers Are Losing,* at p. 236. Fathers now win an estimated one-half to two-thirds of all custody battles. See Salholz, *Feminism's Identity Crisis,* at p. 59.

162. Experts agree. See Polikoff, *Why Mothers Are Losing,* at p. 237. See also Kay, *Equality and Difference,* at pp. 24, 79.

The term *deinstitutionalizing gender* is Alison Jaggar's. Jaggar, *On Sexual Equality,* 84 Ethics 275, 276 (1975). Jaggar's position appears to have changed. See Jaggar, Feminist Politics, at p. 148.

163. Of course, most of those protected will be women, and that in itself will reinforce the notion that women "are really different but we're not allowed to say so."

Though this is a drawback of sex-neutral standards, it does not obviate the need for them. Such statements are useful because they address pressing social issues without bowing to a central tenet of gender ideology—namely, that gender roles are necessarily correlated with biology—and without penalizing men who choose to play gender roles ordinarily assigned to females.

Nonetheless, sex-neutral standards designed to address gender-produced disabilities have very real limitations: They no doubt will tend to reinforce the connection between biology and gender in people's minds. This limitation simply highlights the need to link short-term solutions, such as sex-neutral protections for those disadvantaged by gender, with a long-term strategy challenging basic tenets of the gender system as a whole.

164. See *Garska v. McCoy,* 278 S.E.2d 357, 360–63 (W.Va. 1981), cited in Williams, *The Equality Crisis: Some Reflections on Culture, Courts, and Feminism,* 7 Women's Rts. L. Rep. 175, 190 n. 80 (1982).

165. For a recent survey of studies on sex differences, see I. Frieze, J. Parsons, P. Johnson, D. Ruble & G. Zellman, Women and Sex Roles: A Social Psychological Perspective (New York: Norton, 1978), pp. 45–68. For a readily accessible survey of the literature, see Taub, *Keeping Women in Their Place: Stereotyping Per Se as a Form of Employment Discrimination,* 21 B.C. L. Rev. 345, 349–61 (1980).

Although this is not the place to do it, it is also time to bring up out of the footnotes law reviews' treatment of the numerous and cogent critiques of Gilligan's methodology and conclusions. See, e.g., Auerbach, Blum, Smith & Williams, *Commentary;* Broughton, *Women's Rationality and Men's Virtues: A Critique of Gender Dualism in Gilligan's Theory of Moral Development,* 50 Soc. Res. 597 (1983); Flanagan & Adler, *Impartiality and Particularity,* 50 Soc. Res. 576 (1983); Kerber, Greeno, Maccoby, Luria, Stack & Gilligan, *On*

In a Different Voice: *An Interdisciplinary Forum,* 11 SIGNS: J. WOMEN CUL-
TURE & SOCY. 304 (1986); Nails, *Social-scientific Sexism: Gilligan's Mismea-
sure of Man,* 50 SOC. RES. 643 (1983). The interesting thing from a cultural
standpoint is how little impact these critiques have made on the widespread
acceptance of Gilligan's theories.

166. See MACKINNON, *Difference and Dominance,* at p. 39. MacKinnon
has begun the task of diffusing the "naturalness" of gender stereotypes about
women.

167. See WILLIAM MORRIS, ed., THE AMERICAN HERITAGE DICTIONARY
(Boston: Houghton Mifflin, 1970).

168. See WOLGAST, EQUALITY, at p. 129 ("The kind of nurturing given may
be sex-differentiated, then, while nurturing is not."). Nonetheless, feminists
of difference often tend to assume that nurturing belongs to women in the
sense that it is part of "women's voice." See, e.g., Auerbach, Blum, Smith &
Williams, *Commentary,* at p. 158.

169. See Rubin & Shenker, *Friendship, Proximity, and Self-disclosure,* 46
J. PERSONALITY 1–22 (1978).

170. The irony is that, as recently as 20 years ago, male bonding was
celebrated. Perhaps the celebration of women's culture can be viewed as a
response by women who as youngsters were informed (as I was) that women
were too petty and competitive to enjoy the kind of deep and lasting friendships
males experienced. See E. L. RANELAGH, MEN ON WOMEN (London: Quartet,
1985).

171. V. MINER & H. LONGINO, eds., COMPETITION: A FEMINIST TABOO?
(New York: Feminist Press at the City University of New York, 1987), p. 1.

172. Literature provides a rich source of examples of men as nurturers and
women as power hungry, for those of us who are not sociologists. See, e.g., P.
ROSE, PARALLEL LIVES: FIVE VICTORIAN MARRIAGES (New York: Knopf,
1983), pp. 8–9.

173. Ibid.

174. For an insightful analysis, see ibid. We need also to become more self-
conscious about how ideological influences make our interpretations highly
selective. Note that we hear incessantly that ten-year-old girls establish best
friend relationships whereas boys band together for games. See, e.g., GILLI-
GAN, DIFFERENT VOICE, at pp. 9–11; Maccoby, *Social Groupings in Child-
hood: Their Relationship to Prosocial and Antisocial Behavior in Boys and
Girls,* in D. OLWENS, J. BLOCK & M. RADKE-YARROW, eds., DEVELOPMENT
OF ANTISOCIAL AND PROSOCIAL BEHAVIOR: RESEARCH, THEORIES, AND IS-
SUES (San Diego, Calif.: Academic Press, 1986); Shreve, *Viva,* at p. 15.
Maccoby's study is cited to prove that women focus on relationships whereas
men focus on competition—an interpretation that ignores the important bonding that occurs in team sports as well as the intensely competitive jockeying
that accompanies the school-age battle for desirable "best friends."

175. Comments of Ellen DuBois in *A Conversation,* at p. 73.

176. See, e.g., Janeway, *Women and the Uses of Power,* in H. EISENSTEIN & A. JARDINE, eds., THE FUTURE OF DIFFERENCE (New Brunswick, N.J.: Rutgers University Press, 1985).

177. J. L. GWALTNEY, DRYLONGSOUL: A SELF-PORTRAIT OF BLACK AMERICA (New York: Random House, 1981), pp. 173–74, quoted in S. Harley, "When Your Work Is Not Who You Are": The Development of a Working-class Consciousness among Afro-American Women, Paper given at the Conference on Women in the Progressive Era, sponsored by the American Historical Association in conjunction with the National Museum of American History, Washington, D.C., March 10–12, 1988.

178. See generally T. RABB & R. ROTBERG, eds., THE NEW HISTORY: THE 1980S AND BEYOND: STUDY IN INTERDISCIPLINARY HISTORY (Princeton, N.J.: Princeton University Press, 1982).

179. Feminists have long realized that "[a]chieving sex-based equality requires a social movement for transformation of the family, child-rearing arrangements, the economy, the wage labor market, and human consciousness." Law, *Rethinking Sex and the Constitution,* 132 U. PA. L. REV. 955, 956 (1984).

4
Prince Charming: Abstract Equality

Mary E. Becker

Most lawyers, scholars, and judges interested in changing the relative status of women and men assume that there is an appropriate general or abstract standard of equality, which should be applied by judges. The debate centers on what standard is most appropriate and how to apply it. Throughout the 1970s, most participants agreed that formal equality was the most appropriate general standard,[1] though the more flexible disparate-impact standard should perhaps be available in some employment cases. Today, these are the two dominant legal standards. The standard of formal equality is applied in constitutional cases under the equal protection clause of the Fourteenth Amendment. And in Title VII cases, involving discrimination in employment, formal equality is augmented by disparate impact, which is available in some cases.

In the 1980s, feminists became increasingly critical of these two legal standards.[2] Within the feminist community, a consensus seems to be developing that formal equality is inadequate. Some feminists have proposed alternatives.[3]

This debate has, however, assumed a questionable proposition: that a single general standard of equality should be adopted and applied.[4] Rather than attempting to find one abstract standard to solve women's problems, we should identify objectionable aspects of particular situations and argue for particular changes in the appropriate forum, which will often be the legislature. Any general, or abstract, approach is unlikely to effect much real change without seriously risking worsening the situation of many women, especially ordinary mothers and wives. Three cases from the 1986 U.S. Supreme Court term serve to illustrate these points: *California Federal Savings and Loan Association v. Guerra*,[5] *Johnson v. Transportation Agency*,[6] and *Wimberly v. Labor and Industrial Relations Commission of Missouri*.[7]

Contemporary Legal Standards of Equality

I begin with *Guerra* and *Johnson*. In *Guerra*, the question was the legality of a California statute requiring employers to give workers disabled by childbirth (but not workers otherwise disabled) up to four months unpaid leave. The case arose when Lillian Garland sought to resume working as a receptionist after taking a two-month leave following the birth of her daughter. Her employer told her that her old job had been filled and that there were no similar positions available. Garland was unable to find another job immediately and, because of her unemployment, she lost her apartment and eventually custody of her daughter.[8] When Garland sought to enforce her statutory right before the California Department of Fair Employment and Housing, her former employer, Cal Fed, brought an action in federal district court seeking a declaration that the California statute was inconsistent with and preempted by Title VII.

The feminist community divided sharply on whether employers should be required to give unpaid leave to workers disabled by pregnancy. NOW, the ACLU's Womens' Rights Project, and a number of other feminist organizations (hereinafter NOW et al.), argued against permitting states to require disability leaves only for pregnancy.[9] Other feminist groups argued that such statutes should be permissible despite their violation of formal equality.[10] The Supreme Court agreed, and ruled that the California statute guaranteeing jobs only to women disabled by pregnancy was permissible despite Title VII's ban on sex and pregnancy discrimination.[11]

In *Johnson*, the question was the legality of an affirmative action plan for women in promotions to a position previously held only by men. The Santa Clara County Transit District Board of Supervisors adopted an affirmative action plan for the County Transportation Agency in December 1978. The plan authorized the agency to consider sex as one factor in deciding which of several qualified applicants to promote to traditionally male job classifications. A year later, in December 1979, the agency announced a road-dispatcher opening. Dispatchers assign road crews, equipment, and materials, and maintain records of road maintenance jobs. Twelve employees applied for this promotion, including Paul Johnson and Diane Joyce. Joyce was the first woman ever to be a road maintenance worker. She was the only woman in a force of 110 road maintenance workers at the time of the promotion, and the promotion requirements included at least four years of dispatch or road maintenance work. No woman had previously been road dispatcher—a skilled craft position—nor had any woman ever held any of the 238 skilled craft positions at the agency. Joyce and six men were certified as eligible for promotion after an interview by a two-person board. This board scored applicants on their interview performance. Johnson received a 75, Joyce a 73. (A score over 70 was required to be deemed eligible for the promotion.)

Thereafter, three agency supervisors conducted a second interview. One of these supervisors had been Joyce's supervisor when she began work as a road maintenance worker. He had issued her coveralls (routinely issued to the men) only after she had ruined her clothes on several occasions, complained several times, and finally filed a grievance. Another member of this panel described Joyce as a "rebel-rousing [*sic*], skirt-wearing person."[12] This member scheduled the interview (apparently deliberately)[13] so as to conflict with Joyce's disaster preparedness class. The three-man panel recommended that Johnson be given the promotion.

James Graebner, the director of the agency, was authorized to make the final selection of the new road dispatcher from among those eligible. Graebner, consistent with the recommendation of the agency's affirmative action coordinator,[14] promoted Joyce. Women's groups unanimously argued that this affirmative action was permissible under Title VII, and the Supreme Court agreed.[15]

Formal Equality

Both cases were rightly decided. Yet both are inconsistent with the established standard of formal equality. *Johnson* is obviously inconsistent. There, the Court allowed the employer to treat similarly situated women and men differently, by giving women a "thumb on the scale" in promotion decisions.

The inconsistency of *Guerra* (the pregnancy leave case) and formal equality is more subtle. At first glance, formal equality might seem consistent with the result in *Guerra* (upholding the statute treating workers disabled by pregnancy differently from other workers). This statute does not violate formal equality for sex-based classifications; it classifies on the basis of pregnancy, not on the basis of sex. Title VII was, however, amended specifically to reject this kind of reasoning.[16] As amended, it provides that discrimination on the basis of sex includes discrimination "on the basis of pregnancy, childbirth, or related medical conditions; and women affected by pregnancy, childbirth, or related medical conditions shall be treated the same for all employment-related purposes . . . as other persons not so affected but similar in their ability or inability to work.''[17]

The language of the amended statute indicates that Congress considered pregnant women similar to others who were equal in their ability or inability to work. From this perspective, the outcome in *Guerra* is inconsistent with a standard of formal equality for Title VII: Similarly situated pregnant women and other individuals are treated differently under the California statute. Only those temporarily disabled by pregnancy have any right to a leave of absence; those unable to work for reasons unrelated to pregnancy can be fired.

The Inadequacy of Formal Equality

These cases illustrate a number of problems with formal equality. First, as the discussion above illustrates, the question of who is similarly situated is hardly susceptible to answer by objective, value-free analysis.[18] There is, for example, a sense in which disabled pregnant workers are similar to other workers disabled for similar periods. From another perspective, it seems strange to consider women and men similarly situated with respect to pregnancy-related disabilities since only women are physically disabled by the onset of parenthood. Which perspective seems appropriate depends on the particular issue and on one's perspective and values.[19] As this example illustrates, formal equality is not capable of discerning discrimination against pregnant people. This, in itself, is a major failing.

As another example of the subjectivity inherent in identifying those similarly situated, consider *Johnson*. Giving Joyce an edge over Johnson at the end of the promotion process is affirmative action only if Johnson and Joyce were similarly situated. If they were not similarly situated, it would not violate formal equality to treat them differently. The notion that they might have been similarly situated is fanciful. Their prior employment experiences were not similar even when they had identical titles. For Joyce, work as the only female road maintenance worker would have involved a constant struggle, including dealing with hazing and harassment. Johnson was one of the boys. It is, however, likely that many male decision makers would neither see what Joyce went through nor appreciate that her unique experiences might be qualifications for promotion. They would be more likely to consider Johnson better qualified because, as road dispatcher, Joyce will probably continue to have problems operating in a male world.

To date, standards have not been developed to identify the appropriate perspective from which to decide whether groups or individuals are similarly situated. Typically, judges simply note, in a conclusory fashion, that A and B are (or are not) similarly situated, as though the point was obvious and noncontroversial.[20] In the absence of appropriate standards, women are not likely to be served well by a formal equality standard applied by predominantly male judges on the basis of their subjective values and perspectives.

Second, under formal equality, women who are perceived to be like men are entitled to be treated like men.[21] This "nondiscrimination" rule is not neutral with respect to sex; it is androcentric.[22] Women cannot use formal equality to challenge workplace rules and practices that fit well with men's life-styles, needs, and experiences but less well with women's. Formal equality is not violated by workplace rules under which—as happened in *Guerra*—a new mother loses her job and custody of her daughter because she was the parent who was pregnant. Similarly, when the next Lillian Garland returns to work at Cal Fed following her statutorily guaranteed pregnancy leave, her employer can ignore that she is primarily responsible for the care of her daughter. Such results are not sex neutral. As Catharine MacKinnon puts it, "day one of taking gender into account" was the day the job was structured with the expectation that its occupant would have no childcare responsibilities.[23]

Let me put the same point in another way. Formal equality uses (or misuses)[24] Aristotle's notion of distributive justice to define equality and discrimination. Aristotle defined distributive justice as treating similarly situated people similarly.[25] Formal equality defines equality as treating similarly situated individuals similarly. Conversely, discrimination is treating differently individuals who are actually similarly situated. But discrimination is not necessarily the opposite of distributive justice. Discrimination and distributive justice might be quite unrelated things. If discrimination encompasses women's experiences of subordination, then there is more to discrimination than treating differently individuals who are similarly situated: "[I]t is not only lies and blindness that have kept women down. It is as much the social creation of differences, and the transformation of differences into social advantages and disadvantages upon which inequality can rationally be predicated."[26]

Discrimination consists of repeatedly turning real or perceived differences into socially constructed disadvantages for women and socially constructed advantages for men. For example, the fact that only women are disabled by pregnancy does not mean that a policy, like Cal Fed's, under which new mothers (but not new fathers) lose their job is not discriminatory. Indeed, it is precisely because only women are disabled by pregnancy that a facially neutral policy like Cal Fed's is part of the system that has kept women subordinate to, because economically dependent on, men.[27]

The fact that only women are disabled by pregnancy does not even explain why women lose their jobs because of the onset of parenthood. The actual difference between the ability of women and men to work at the onset of parenthood need not be transformed into this socially created disadvantage for women. Imagine, for example, the socially constructed advantages women could be given as compensation for (and to facilitate) bearing and rearing children. Statutes could give mothers preferences in employment like those given veterans in many states. Large employers could give mothers extended leaves while their children are young, just as they gave male inductees extended leaves for military service during the draft. Women who care for their children rather than participating full time or at full speed in the wage labor market could be given Social Security credits in their own accounts for their contributions to the future rather than having only very contingent claims as their husbands' dependents.[28]

Third, formal equality is based on a counterfactual assumption; because of this assumption formal equality will, in practice, actually mean inequality. Formal equality assumes that it is possible to ignore an individual's sex. Both common sense and empirical data suggest that we cannot and do not ignore sex in dealing with an individual.[29] Moreover, the empirical data indicate that the routine and unconscious differential treatment of individual women and men tends to dampen ratings of women's competence and potential relative to the ratings of men.[30] To the extent that we cannot treat similarly situated women and men the same, formal equality can mask real, though perhaps unconscious, discrimination.

Johnson illustrates this point. The promotion interviews were conducted entirely by men, who had never promoted a woman to that position before, nor any similar position. One of the interviewers regarded Joyce as a "rebel-rousing [*sic*], skirt-wearing person."[31] Another interviewer had been her first supervisor as a road maintenance worker, the one who issued her work overalls only after she filed a grievance. Those interviews cannot have been precisely equal opportunities for both Joyce and Johnson. In the absence of the affirmative action plan challenged in *Johnson,* it is most unlikely that

Joyce would have had a promotion opportunity equal to Johnson's. Yet, after a two-day trial, the district court found that the agency had never discriminated on the basis of sex.[32]

A two-day trial could not possibly have afforded a factual basis for concluding that an employer with 238 skilled craft workers and no woman ever in such a position (and one woman out of 110 road maintenance workers) had never discriminated on the basis of sex. Even after the passage of Title VII, women were routinely and overtly excluded from skilled craft positions by both unions and employers. Yet the incredible finding—that the agency had never discriminated on the basis of sex in hiring skilled craftsmen (as the workers were doubtless originally described)—was not overruled by either reviewing court.

A comparison of *Johnson* and *Steelworkers v. Weber*[33] suggests that systemic discrimination on the basis of sex may be less visible to judges enforcing Title VII than is discrimination on the basis of race. Prior to the affirmative action plan at issue in *Weber*, 1.83 percent (five out of 275) of the skilled craft workers were blacks in Kaiser's plant where *Weber* arose. (Compare zero women out of approximately 238 at the agency prior to the affirmative action plan at issue in *Johnson*.) In *Weber*, the Court reversed the two lower court decisions holding Kaiser's plan illegal and noted that "[j]udicial findings of exclusion from crafts on racial grounds are so numerous as to make such exclusion a proper subject for judicial notice."[34] Women, too, have been traditionally, explicitly, and routinely excluded from crafts,[35] but—unlike the exclusion of blacks that was judicially noticed in *Weber*—women's exclusion was apparently invisible to all the judges deciding *Johnson*. Justice Antonin Scalia relied heavily on the district court's finding that the Santa Clara County Transportation Agency had never discriminated on the basis of sex, and apparently believed it. None of the justices dismissed the finding as incredible and necessarily lacking a factual basis after a two-day trial.[36] Judges can say no woman was ever discriminated against, but saying it cannot make it true.

Justice Scalia would probably respond that even if road maintenance and skilled craft positions had always been open to women, and even if the agency had advertised for women, it is likely that there would never have been a woman actually interested in either position prior to Joyce. This point brings out another problem with formal equality as a solution to sexual inequality. Systemic discrimination against women is often so effective that no woman will apply for a traditionally male job. Perhaps some women do prefer lower paying women's jobs. But some may think that the job is only nominally open to them.[37] Others may dread the harassment likely to be experienced in breaking into male jobs—especially blue-collar ones.[38] There is no effective remedy for such harassment. Perhaps women have been socialized not to consider rough outdoor jobs, but could be interested with a little encouragement. Formal equality ignores all these problems. As long as the job is open to women, so that there is no discrimination by this decision maker today, formal equality is satisfied. Formal equality is often inconsistent with the only means available for overcoming discrimination, whether by co-workers or by our educational system and socialization practices or by the employer's own practices (past or present, conscious or unconscious): taking "affirmative" steps to encourage and facilitate women's entry into traditionally male spheres.

The affirmative action exception to formal equality, both under the equal protection clause of the Fourteenth Amendment and Title VII, alleviates these problems at least a little. In *Johnson*, for example, the Court allowed Joyce's employer to compensate, albeit roughly and indirectly, for the fact that Joyce and Johnson did not have the same opportunities or experiences. Affirmative action is troubling because the word *affirmative* implies that, in its absence, women and men would have had equal opportunities. In *Johnson*, "affirmative" conveys the unrealistic notion that, had there been no thumb on the scale for Joyce at the very end of the promotion procedure, Johnson and Joyce would have had equal employment opportunities at Santa Clara County Transportation Agency.

Another problem with affirmative action is that it is only an exception—a basis for permitting employers to undertake some appropriate but voluntary acts to alleviate the problems faced by women like Joyce. It does not supplement formal equality by offering an alternative model of discrimination for plaintiffs to use in challenging the status quo. Only the disparate impact strand of Title VII offers plaintiffs such an alternative.

In sum, formal equality—even with an exception for affirmative action—cannot be expected to transform society by equalizing the status of women and men. In the context of employment, it only opens men's jobs to women on the terms and conditions worked out for men. Further, under formal equality, it is likely that the differences in treatment of women and men will often be invisible to the extent that the differences consist of preferential treatment of men. More specifically, it is likely that a man will appear better qualified when there is no relevant difference between a woman and a man or when the woman is marginally better qualified. And it is likely that a woman's unique qualifications (because of her experiences as a woman) will not be visible, let alone regarded as qualifications.

The Case for Formal Equality, despite Its Inadequacy

Despite these flaws, formal equality has an advantage. At least when women are perceived as similar to men, formal equality can be used effectively to challenge rules or requirements expressly restricting entry to privileged male occupations. Throughout the 1970s and early 1980s, feminists arguing for legal change—either before courts or in pushing for the ERA and other legislative reforms—relied primarily on the concept of formal equality.[39] Because of these efforts, many laws, rules, and practices limiting women's opportunities have been eliminated.[40]

As a result of this experience, a number of feminists continue to insist on strict formal equality.[41] In *Guerra*, NOW et al. filed briefs arguing that California could not require its employers to give unpaid leaves only to women disabled by pregnancy and not to other workers disabled for similar periods. In those briefs, and in the general debate on the issue posed by *Guerra*, these feminists made three major points. First, they argued that "special" treatment of women is dangerous and reinforces traditional sex roles. Special treatment has been used to burden as well as to benefit; consider the protectionist legislation of earlier eras. By requiring that pregnant workers be treated like the most similar nonpregnant workers, these feminists would guard against judges' and employers' biases and stereotypes of pregnant women.[42] Maternity leaves (even if nominally for periods of disability) inevitably become childcare leaves. By insisting that parental leaves, if available, are available to both parents, these feminists seek to change the traditional assignment of childcare responsibilities primarily to mothers.[43] Second, these feminists have argued that, by treating pregnant workers like the most similarly situated nonpregnant workers, we can emphasize what is common about human experience.[44] They argue that special treatment will unnecessarily alienate women and co-workers who actually have common concerns, such as adequate leave policies for all disabled workers. Third, these feminists concede that formal equality in itself cannot always effect needed change, but maintain that sex-neutral parental leave legislation is the best way to achieve such change in law.[45]

The Case against Formal Equality

There are a number of problems with these arguments. First, NOW et al.'s arguments in *Guerra* are undermined by their own position in *Johnson* (the affirmative action case). Despite their vehement objections to special treatment in *Guerra*, in *Johnson* these groups favor affirmative action. Affirmative action—deliberately giving Joyce a "thumb on the scale" at the end of the decision-making process—is as much a form of special treatment as is the pregnancy disability statute at issue in *Guerra*. Affirmative action, perhaps even more than the pregnancy disability statute at issue in *Guerra*, divides workers from each other and makes men resentful.[46] Yet, in the affirmative action cases, NOW et al. did not consider it so dangerous that it should always be avoided as a solution to women's problems.[47]

Second, the problem with formal equality is not simply that it is incapable of radically changing society or of ensuring that similarly situated women and men are treated similarly. Formal equality has actually hurt many women. Formal equality is likely to help most, and hurt least, professional women who either have no children or who hire other women to care for their children and are able to compete with men on men's terms. These women have tended to control the women's movement. And it is likely to hurt most mothers and wives who are not well-paid professionals.[48]

Despite the failure of the ERA campaign, formal equality has been implemented wholly or partially, directly and indirectly, through legislation and judicial changes in many ways.[49] Because of this trend, women have lost many of the traditional sex-based rules that gave them some measure of financial security and protection. For example, consider the effect on women of the shift from the traditional maternal preference in child custody disputes. During the 1960s, judges assumed that it was in the best interest of a child of tender years to give custody to its mother.[50] Many jurisdictions have either eliminated this presumption[51] or replaced it with a presumption in favor of joint custody,[52] thus giving a bargaining chip to fathers in negotiations with mothers. Because mothers seem to want custody much more than fathers,[53] the result of giving this bargaining chip to fathers is that mothers who desperately want custody offer economic concessions to settle the custody issue rather than submitting it to a judge.[54]

The gender-neutral custody rules adopted to date have not effected any radical restructuring of parenting roles. Instead, these rules may have contributed to the further economic impoverishment of divorced women and their children. The poverty of divorced women and their children (relative to men)[55] is not, of course, entirely attributable to the move away from the maternal presumption. There are no estimates of the effect of movement away from the maternal preference on the postdivorce economic status of women and children. The point is only that notions of formal equality have had a negative economic effect on a group that is not in a good position to bear the cost of social change.

In calculating child or spousal support at the time of divorce, which will typically be paid (if it is paid)[56] by the father to the custodial mother, judges today often assume that the ex-homemaker will find a good-paying job.[57] After all, Title VII and the Equal Pay Act ban wage discrimination; women and men are equal. But full-time female workers continue to earn substantially less than full-time male workers, and a woman who has no recent wagework experience is likely to have difficulty finding even a decent woman's job. If she is the custodian of small children, as is typically the case when there are small children at the time of the divorce, she cannot enter the workforce unless she either neglects her children or earns a great deal so that she is able to pay for childcare. Here, too, treating women and men as though they were equal when, in fact, they are not has worsened the postdivorce economic position of women and children—especially those women (and their children) who are most in need because they are least like men.

Traditionally, during marriage, husbands had a duty to support their wives (and not vice versa). That duty has never been directly enforceable by wives during marriage,[58] but wives' creditors were sometimes able to enforce the duty.[59] In recent cases, in pursuit of formal equality, some judges have imposed a duty on all women to support their husbands, a duty enforceable by creditors.[60] As a result, a widow who has been a homemaker all her life may find, after her husband's expensive final illness, that she is personally liable for his hospital expenses. Ordinary wives are, however, less likely than their husbands to be economically capable of supporting their spouses, especially at age 65 or over when the husband dies. Again, treating women and men as though they are similarly situated when they are not hurts many women.

NOW would respond that sex-neutral legislation is the way to solve these problems. And one can imagine sex-neutral rules that would probably be acceptable solutions to most of these issues. But acceptable sex-neutral rules have not been widely adopted in any of these areas. Consider, for example, the appropriate standard for child custody at divorce. The traditional standard, giving an explicit preference to mothers at least during "tender years," created an explicit distinction on the basis of sex and reinforced traditional stereotypes of mothers as the nurturing parent. This standard is not ideal. Under it, for example, mothers were less likely even to consider whether they actually wanted custody, let alone to decide against custody without guilt, than they would have been under a less loaded standard. A gender-neutral rule could lessen these problems. If the new rule awarded custody to the parent likely to want custody most—for example, to the primary caretaker provided only that she were fit—the gender-neutral rule would not significantly affect the bargaining process. Of the many jurisdictions moving from a maternal preference to a gender-neutral rule, however, very few have adopted a rule preferring the parent who has been primary caretaker.[61] In the real world, there is nothing to ensure that the gender-neutral "solution" to an unnecessarily and inappropriately sex-based classification will not further weaken women's economic position.

In *Guerra* itself, the choice was not between a sex-based rule giving leave only to women disabled because of pregnancy and the ideal parental-leave rule advocated by NOW when lobbying before Congress. Nor was the choice between a sex-based rule giving leave only to women disabled because of pregnancy and a rule giving all workers leaves for disabilities of up to four months, though in its brief NOW argued that the leave policy be extended to all workers.[62] Instead, the choice was between having no statutorily guaranteed leave for new parents and having leaves at least for women disabled by pregnancy. In other Western industrialized nations, where parenting leaves of one kind or another have been legally mandated for some time, regulation began in the form of maternity leaves. The trend, however, is to expand the policies to parental leaves.[63] Four jurisdictions in this country have adopted parental leave policies, and two of them began with maternity leave policies.[64] Eleven other jurisdictions have maternity leave policies.[65] These states may, in the future, follow the European trend and extend the benefit to include paternity leave.

A number of the decisions hailed as giant steps for women have hurt rather than helped many women by banning sex-based legislative classifications. And some of the Supreme Court cases striking explicitly sex-based classifications as impermissible forms of discrimination seem shockingly irrelevant to discrimination in the real world. *Orr v. Orr*[66] and *Otis v. Otis*[67] illustrate these points.

In *Orr*, the Supreme Court held that state statutes could not constitutionally provide for alimony to be paid by some husbands to some wives. The Court explained that permissible sex-neutral legislation would either deny alimony to both men and women or extend it to both on the same terms. It postulated two reasons for alimony: (1) because the recipient is needy; and (2) because women were discriminated against during marriage. Both purposes could be served by holding individualized hearings, the Court concluded.

Statutes imposing alimony obligations only on some husbands are hardly the linchpin of systemic discrimination on the basis of sex.[68] Far more important, by any measure, are sex-neutral statutes giving employment preferences to veterans[69] and statutes, rules, and practices that result in the ex-husband's receiving the lion's share of the financial security (including old-age security) accumulated during the ordinary marriage.[70] Yet of these policies, formal equality captures only the relatively trivial case of alimony imposed only on men. Such statutes are less than ideal; they reinforce notions that women are dependents because they are women. But they are not of much importance in the systemic subordination of women.[71]

More importantly, *Orr v. Orr* has hurt ordinary mothers and wives. Since 1960, there has been a decrease in alimony awarded even to full-time long-term homemakers.[72] It is likely that *Orr v. Orr* (and the notion of formal equality that both produced it and was reinforced by it) have contributed to this decline. In *Orr v. Orr*, the Court could imagine only two reasons for awarding alimony: a needy recipient, and as compensation for discrimination in marriage. The Court never did explain what it meant by the latter, rather nebulous, concept.[73] The other reason is need. Need is not, in itself, a very compelling reason for postdivorce payments to an ex-spouse. Far more compelling reasons were ignored entirely by the Court.

Consider *Otis v. Otis*, which was decided a year after *Orr* by the Supreme Court of Minnesota. The Otis marriage had lasted more than 20 years. The trial judge ordered the husband (who earned over $120,000 a year as a vice-president of Control Data) to pay his ex-wife alimony for four years (at an average of $1,500 per month). Ms. Otis had quit her job as an executive secretary when her son was born "in order to fulfill the expected role of wife and hostess for a rising and successful business executive."[74] She played an important role in her husband's career. For example, before his last promotion she too was interviewed. When the board of directors met in Greece for a week in 1977, she was the official hostess. She had wanted to return to work a number of years previously, but her husband said he was "not going

to have any wife of mine pound a typewriter."[75] When she was awarded
only short-term alimony, she was 45 years old and had been out of the
workplace for approximately 20 years. The Supreme Court of Minnesota upheld the award of the trial court because, it explained, postdivorce transfer payments are based on need and Ms. Otis should be
able to "rehabilitate" herself within four years.

Ms. Otis's need—in and of itself—is the weakest imaginable reason
for awarding her postdivorce transfer payments. Her current need
reflects her investment in her husband's career—an investment from
which he will continue to profit. Her need reflects the reliance loss she
sustained by not working in order to raise their son and further her
husband's career (and in order to avoid embarrassing him by typing).
Having relied so substantially for so long, she cannot now, at 45,
recover what she would have had if she had put her own career first.
Her needs should be met because a reasonable term of their arrangement—with its traditional division of labor—was that, in exchange for
her reliance in engaging exclusively in nonwage domestic production
and reproduction and contributing to his career rather than her own,
she would receive a reasonable share of the profit brought in by her
husband's career and a reasonable share of the financial security
accumulated for their old age.[76]

NOW might argue that ideal sex-neutral postdivorce rules can be
imagined. There are, of course, other possible approaches besides
tying alimony to sex (thus reinforcing stereotypical notions about
women's dependency) and ignoring the lifelong economic effects of
the division of labor within marriage. *Otis v. Otis* is not, however,
unusual. Ideal rules have not been developed to replace sex-linked
alimony.[77] Instead, judges have stressed the weakest of reasons for
ordering one spouse to make postdivorce income transfers to the other
spouse.

Orr v. Orr is not, of course, solely responsible for cases like *Otis v.
Otis*. *Orr v. Orr* reflects and reinforces notions of formal equality that
have eliminated such notions as that ex-wives should receive alimony
because they are women. Judges, like the justices in *Orr v. Orr*, have
been unable to think of any very good alternative reasons for awarding
anyone alimony. Many—probably most—judges, like the justices in
Orr v. Orr, have been unable to come up with anything more compelling than simple need. As a result, alimony (even when awarded) tends
to be for relatively short periods of time (typically two to four years)
and designed only to allow the ex-wife to become self-supporting. In
the past, alimony was more often awarded permanently, that is, until

the ex-wife remarried or either spouse died.[78] This change has not been good for most women—especially women who, like Ms. Orr, were homemakers for 20 years or more. Many women would have been better off if feminists had argued for needed economic rights and greater economic security for women (in recognition of their domestic production and reproduction) rather than for strict formal equality in family law matters.

NOW, or someone else, might argue that women have been hurt just about as much as possible under strict formal equality. They should therefore try at least to get its benefits, having paid the price. There are, however, still some sex-specific rules, statutes, and practices. These are still, at least arguably, permissible because we have not yet adopted strict formal equality as the appropriate standard. Further movement toward a formal equality standard would jeopardize such classifications. For example, a few jurisdictions retain a weakened form of the maternal preference;[79] even in those jurisdictions in which it has been formally changed, individual judges continue to use it in actually deciding cases.[80] Public schools still have separate sports programs for girls and women.[81] In many jurisdictions, unwed fathers who have never lived with or supported a child cannot take a newborn away from its mother or interfere with her decision to let the child be adopted.[82] In a few jurisdictions, the obligation of husbands to support their spouses has not been extended to wives.[83] In many jurisdictions, clubs for women only are permissible.[84] All these rules, and others, would be threatened by further movement toward formal equality.[85]

In addition, formal equality has yet to permeate effectively our entire culture. Women can, therefore, be harmed by increased acceptance of formal equality in the surrounding culture. For example, even in the jurisdictions that have formally abolished the maternal custody preference, individual judges deciding individual cases often—consciously or unconsciously—consider mothers the more appropriate custodian for a child of tender years. Similarly, some judges deciding postdivorce economic issues recognize that most women cannot earn as much as men. Despite the fact that courts regard protectionist legislation as preempted by Title VII,[86] some women working in factories continue to enjoy some of the advantages (such as limits on what they can be required to lift) initially implemented through protectionist legislation.[87] Such results might become more tenuous in a world with greater stress on formal equality. As this suggests, the real-world negative effects of formal equality are difficult to see, let alone predict.

In the end, there are two distinct kinds of problems associated with formal equality. One is that formal equality cannot be the basis for implementing the kinds of changes that must be made if the status of women and men is to be equalized. The other is that the limited changes effected by formal equality will often hurt many women—especially ordinary mothers and wives.

Formal equality is dangerous for women in a way in which it is not dangerous for other minority groups. Few, if any, traditional racially explicit classifications ever had either the purpose or overall effect of benefiting a racial minority. There is, for example, no racial analogy to the maternal preference standard in custody disputes, no traditional racial classification that, despite its reinforcement of a stereotype, also gave a racial minority a better bargaining position in negotiations with nonminorities than would race-neutral rules. Because the legal system has protected women better than it has protected other minorities (though not, of course, as well as it has protected men), formal equality is dangerous for women in a unique way.

The trend, throughout law, is strongly toward strict formal equality. There is, at the same time, another legally accepted model of discrimination, a model available for Title VII cases: disparate impact.

Disparate Impact

Under Title VII, a plaintiff can use disparate impact to challenge a practice or requirement that disproportionately disqualifies women from employment opportunities.[88] For example, under Title VII, women can challenge height and weight requirements on the ground that such requirements are likely to disqualify more women than men.

Some feminist students and litigators have argued that disparate impact should be generally available as a basis for challenging discriminatory policies and practices.[89] There are, however, a number of limitations that prevent disparate impact from being a solution to the problems of formal equality. In order to use disparate impact, one has to have a perspective and some basis for comparison. For example, when disparate impact is used to challenge a height and weight requirement, one looks to see whether more female than male applicants fail to qualify because of the height and weight requirements. One assumes that, in the absence of the challenged requirement, women and men would qualify in proportion to their numbers in the applicant pool.[90] One can therefore compare the actual pass (or qualifying) rate and the assumed pass rate (i.e., the proportion of women in the pool) to see whether the test or requirement has a disparate impact.

In other settings, there is no single reference for comparison. Even assuming a basis for comparison, often one can imagine many solutions that could be implemented by various defendants. Consider, for example, *Wimberly v. Labor and Industrial Relations Commission of Missouri*, a third case from the 1986 U.S. Supreme Court term and one factually much like *Guerra* except that it arose in Missouri, which had no statute analogous to California's. Like Garland, Linda Wimberly was not rehired after her pregnancy leave because there were no suitable openings. She filed a claim for unemployment benefits with the Missouri Division of Employment Security. The agency denied her claim because, under Missouri law, unemployment benefits were never available to a claimant who "left his work voluntarily without good cause attributable to his work or his employer." Wimberly challenged the decision, arguing that the Missouri ruled violated a federal requirement that states not deny unemployment compensation claims "solely on the basis of pregnancy or termination of pregnancy."[91] The Supreme Court unanimously held that Missouri law was consistent with the federal requirement since Missouri did not deny claims solely on the ground the employee quit because of pregnancy. Instead, Missouri denied claims like Wimberly's on the more general ground that unemployment compensation was available only to workers who quit their jobs for work-related reasons. But the Missouri law can be viewed as having a disparate impact on pregnant workers relative to other possible policies. Under the Missouri plan, workers who lost their jobs because of pregnancy and childbirth are never eligible for unemployment compensation. A policy extending unemployment benefits to all workers—once able to work again—who lost their jobs because of physical disability (lasting up to four months) would not have so negative an impact on new mothers.[92]

No court is likely to recognize a disparate impact claim in Wimberly's situation;[93] the claim, the remedy, the proper defendant, are all too indeterminate. One solution has just been suggested: to order the Labor and Industrial Relations Commission of Missouri to extend benefits to all workers who lost their jobs because of short-term disabilities lasting four months or less. Alternatively, the commission could be ordered to extend coverage only to women disabled because of pregnancy or only to individuals who lost their jobs because of a disability lasting two months or less. Or Wimberly's employer could be ordered to reinstate her after her period of disability; that too would eliminate some of the disparate impact of the Missouri policy. Alternatively, Wimberly's employer could be ordered to give leaves to all workers disabled up to two months (or up to four months or up to six weeks) or to give leaves to all new parents. Indeed, although one can imagine more desirable policies, any disparate impact on pregnant workers would be eliminated by ordering all Missouri employers to require that every man in Missouri take an (unpaid) paternal leave when his child is born, equal to the length of time the mother of his child is disabled by childbirth.

As another example, consider the argument, made by the State of California in its brief in *Guerra*, that the state statute was permissible because an employer's failure to give at least four months' disability leave for pregnancy would necessarily have a disparate impact on pregnant workers.[94] The ACLU Women's Project in their amicus brief in *Guerra* responds that "[i]n fact, the average number of days lost from work due to disability, including childbirth and illness during pregnancy, is remarkably similar for men and women workers."[95] The ACLU Women's Project cites evidence that "men workers experience an average of 4.9 days of work loss due to illness or injury per year while women experience 5.1 days per year."[96] Men lose more days of work from all injuries than women do because, among other things, men tend to work at more dangerous jobs and suffer more job-related disability. In their amicus brief, the California Women Lawyers et al. respond that this is the wrong comparison. One needs to ask whether disability leaves inadequate for most pregnancies (the average length of pregnancy disability may be six weeks) have a disparate impact on women. The fact that women have an average of 5.1 days of disability a year and men an average of 4.9 days a year is irrelevant to the question of whether the lack of leaves adequate for most pregnancies has a disparate impact on women.[97]

If the question is whether a no-leave policy has a disparate impact on women, then there is a sense in which each of these litigants is right. There is no one perspective from which to judge disparate impact on women in this situation.[98] In addition, changes could be made by a number of different entities; disparate impact does not give a court any guidance about who is a proper defendant. At least to date, even supposedly activist judges have not been willing to develop standards for choosing among various policies to be implemented by various defendants.

There is another problem with disparate impact. Like formal equality, disparate impact refers to male performance levels. Women are, at most, entitled to succeed at men's rates.[99] This antidiscrimination rule (like formal equality) has a male reference point; it is not neutral with respect to sex. Disparate impact cannot, for example, afford a basis for challenging promotion requirements designed by and for men as long as women, by dint of whatever efforts are necessary given their typically greater domestic responsibilities[100] and other disadvantages, are nevertheless as successful as men.

Only a few feminists (other than litigators) have argued for a disparate impact standard in contexts outside hiring or promotion requirements.[101] Instead, most feminists disenchanted with contemporary standards of equality have tried to develop alternatives.

Feminist Alternatives

For purposes of this discussion, feminist alternatives may be put under three headings: first, Catharine MacKinnon's inequality approach;[102] second, Christine Littleton's acceptance approach;[103] and third, formal equality with limited special treatment.[104] Some feminists have suggested other approaches to equality in recent years but have not elaborated judicially enforceable standards. Instead, they have primarily attempted to expand the kinds of arguments that might be made to employers and legislators.[105] This discussion is limited to judicially enforceable feminist approaches.[106]

The Inequality Approach

The inequality approach, developed by MacKinnon in the 1970s, is a powerful and influential model, as well as being itself a devastating critique of formal equality. The inequality model begins with the seemingly obvious observation that when we use the word *discrimination*, we are referring to "systematic disadvantagement of social groups."[107] As already noted, formal equality assumes that distinctions based on relevant differences are not discriminatory. But systemic discrimination consists primarily of turning differences, real or perceived, into socially constructed disadvantages for women and socially constructed advantages for men.

MacKinnon refuses, therefore, to focus on the rationalizations for distinctions that, however "reasonable," are part of the systemic subordination of women to men. Instead, she focuses on whether a

particular practice or rule "participates in the systemic social deprivation of one sex because of sex. The only question for litigation is
whether the policy or practice in question integrally contributes to the
maintenance of an underclass or a deprived position because of gender
status."[108]

At least one feminist, Ann Scales, has argued for MacKinnon's
inequality standard as a general, judicially enforceable approach to
discrimination.[109] Although MacKinnon describes the question to be
litigated as whether a practice or policy contributes to women's subordinate status, it is unlikely that MacKinnon understands inequality
as a general judicially enforceable standard for challenging any practice
or policy that contributes to the subordination of women.[110]

Despite Scales's optimism, the inequality approach is not a general
solution to the problems raised by formal equality and disparate
impact. Typically, a policy or practice contributes to women's subordinate status because of its interaction with other policies, practices,
and social mores. Typically, one can imagine many changes to the
status quo, implemented by many different entities, that would result
in less systematic subordination of women. Inequality's question to be
litigated does not identify either the appropriate defendant or the
appropriate change. Each of the points made in the earlier discussion
of disparate impact and pregnancy policies could be made again here.

As an example, consider whether the inequality standard would be
violated when a worker disabled by pregnancy is fired. Her employer
fires all workers disabled for more than two weeks for reasons that are
not work related. Such a policy contributes to the subordination of
women, by tending to make them dependent on men after childbirth.
But even giving the worker an unpaid leave of absence during pregnancy-related disability tends to contribute to the subordination of
women, by tending to make them dependent on men while temporarily
disabled by pregnancy. There are a number of ways in which these
policies could be changed so as to make women more independent.
Employers could be required to give women leaves for pregnancy-
related disabilities with full pay. Alternatively, employers could be
required to give women unpaid leaves, and state unemployment compensation systems could be changed to give women unemployment
compensation during the period of pregnancy-related disability. Or
employers could be required to give all new parents a period of paid
leave for six months. Alternatively, employers could be required to
give new parents six months of unpaid leave, and some new state-

mandated insurance system could provide financial benefits to parents taking such leaves.

Identifying current policies as contributing to the subordinate status of women simply does not identify a single defendant or one appropriate change. Like disparate impact, inequality as a general standard is simply too indeterminate to expect judges to use it in the foreseeable future.[111]

The Acceptance Standard

Christine Littleton suggests that judges apply equality in terms of an acceptance standard. She identifies men's power to determine what is of value as an essential element of the inequality of the sexes. She proposes to "rescue equality" by "making sex difference not make a difference in equality, by making difference 'costless' (or at least cost less)."[112] In applying an acceptance standard, judges would make difference cost less by equalizing the resources (money, status, and access to decision making) allocated on the basis of "gendered complements."[113]

For example, under Littleton's acceptance standard, comparable worth would be appropriate in disputes about pay because male and female job categories should be paid equally. In other contexts, acceptance would be implemented by "inventing complementary structures containing female norms."[114] For example, an employer with a job-related height requirement (tending disproportionately to disqualify women relative to men) would be required to restructure the job (or offer equal job opportunities) to accommodate the disqualified women.[115] In the context of pregnancy, Littleton would require that, in the workplace, "money, status, and opportunity for advancement flow equally to the womb-donating woman and the sperm-donating man."[116] Littleton argues that motherhood and military service could be established as gendered complements; this would mean "requiring the government to pay mothers the same low wages and generous benefits as most soldiers."[117] Littleton suggests that this could "mean encouraging the use of motherhood [like the use of military service today] as an unofficial prerequisite for governmental office."[118]

Littleton's standard adds another level of indeterminacy to disparate impact analysis. In addition to eliminating those policies and practices that have a disparate impact on women in terms of money, status, or access to decision making, judges must initially identify appropriate gendered complements.

Consider a worker who stops working when her first child is born, works on a part-time basis at low-paying jobs intermittently for the next ten years, and then resumes full-time work when her youngest child enters first grade. It is unrealistic to think that judges can or will order changes equalizing her and her husband's (or the average man's?) access to money, status, and decision making. What is the gendered complement for the various stages of her life? Should she receive soldier's pay (what rank?) and benefits until her youngest child is 18? Even after the youngest is 18, she will probably continue to receive lower wages because she took time off from wagework to care for her children. After 20 years of motherhood, should she be entitled to military retirement benefits? Although Littleton's acceptance standard suggests arguments that might be made to legislatures, it is unrealistic to think that judges will be willing to implement so nebulous a standard.

Formal Equality with Limited Special Treatment

Through the early 1980s, the current feminist movement relied primarily on formal equality in pressing for change both in courts and in other arenas. In recent years, a number of feminists have argued that formal equality should be qualified by allowing for policies treating women differently from men in very limited circumstances centering on the biological fact that only women bear children.[119] These feminists would uphold the California statute challenged in *Guerra*, since women are given special treatment only when—on the level of physical reality— they are situated differently from men: They are disabled by pregnancy.

This approach can be criticized both by those who would never permit special treatment (other than affirmative action) and by those who think special treatment in such limited circumstances too narrow a standard. (I have already summarized and responded to the objections of the first group, feminists like Wendy Williams and the leadership of the National Organization of Women, who argue for strict formal equality with no exceptions other than affirmative action.) Special treatment in such limited circumstances does not go very far toward rectifying the many—and I think devastating—reasons for rejecting formal equality, reasons already discussed in detail. If special treatment is permissible only when warranted by physical biological differences, then the standard remains one of formal equality in almost all instances, augmented by special treatment only in the most narrow of circumstances.

Formal equality augmented by such limited special treatment will not effect nearly enough beneficial change and will often result in change detrimental to most women. Few of the criticisms of formal equality elaborated above were limited to the use of formal equality when there is actually a biological difference. Even with an exception for biological differences, formal equality affords no basis for challenging rules that structure the workplace to fit men's life experiences and needs, but not women's. This limited exception does nothing to correct the male bias inevitable in a standard of formal equality applied mostly by men. It still accepts actual or perceived differences as justifications for further differential treatment. The exception does not help make visible the discrimination that is often invisible under a standard of formal equality.

Most importantly, the limited exception for differential treatment based on biological differences will not preclude the use of formal equality though the result may be to further disadvantage many ordinary mothers and wives. True, under this standard, a court would not overrule a statute giving women pregnancy leaves. But courts would continue to strike down the maternal preference in custody, and judges would tend increasingly (in a world with greater acceptance of formal equality) to regard fathers as equally appropriate custodians of young children and to regard mothers as equally capable of supporting children financially.

An Impossible Dream?

We use equality to refer to a number of things, including both of these: (1) the situation in an ideal (nonsexist) world, and (2) a legal standard to be applied by judges (based either in the Constitution or in a statute such as Title VII). Hopefully, (2) should be a means to get from this world to the ideal world imagined in (1).

We cannot, today, know what an "ideal" world with equality between the sexes would look like, let alone how best to get there. This is another difference between race and sex. With race, we can at least imagine a world in which blacks and whites are equal. We can imagine a world in which race is no more important than eye color. We cannot so easily imagine a world in which women and men are equal or in which sex would matter no more than eye color. Most of us would not want to live in a world in which sex was no more important or relevant than eye color. Perhaps equality could occur in a world in which sex still matters, but in different ways from the ways in which it matters in this world. Few of us can imagine what that world might look like.

For those including myself who think that, whatever it might look like, a reasonably ideal world would look rather different from this one, formal equality must be rejected. Formal equality is not capable of producing enough change in the status quo, and is likely to impose significant costs on those women most in need of change because most unlike men.

Perhaps formal equality's proponents regard harm to some women (especially ordinary mothers and wives) as a justifiable cost of effecting social change. If the economic position of ordinary women (especially after divorce, an ever present danger today) becomes tenuous enough, fewer women will be willing to fulfill traditional roles or (as is often the case) attempt to combine traditional roles and some (often limited) wagework. As a result of greater insecurity, more women will work (even while their children are small), will consider their own jobs as important as their husbands', and will refuse to be primarily responsible for either childcare or other domestic duties. Also, if their chances of having postdivorce custody are no greater than their husbands', they will invest less in their children during marriage, thus equalizing fathers' and mothers' investments in raising children.

There are, however, a number of problems with such justifications for formal equality. First, formal equality tends to help most the exceptional professional women, with the costs borne by another group. The elite who lead the feminist movement should be reluctant to press for change they consider desirable when it means imposing its costs on other women.

Second, it is likely that a majority of women would consider this formal equality "solution" unacceptable. It is, for example, unlikely that most women would want to be only as involved with children as their husbands. Perhaps this is the result of their socialization, and a form of false consciousness about their own best interests. We should, however, be reluctant to use false consciousness as the basis for ignoring women's desires. One important aspect of women's subordination has been that others have defined who women are and what they want. Feminists have generally stressed the importance of listening to what women say, rather than dictating what women should say and feel.

Most women might prefer other means to other ends. True, one way of effecting change is to make traditional roles (even when combined with limited employment) too risky. But one could, instead, improve the position of ordinary women by making women's traditional roles less risky, empowering women by making them less dependent on men. Is "our" goal a world in which there is more respect for and reward of those traits, skills, and contributions traditionally associated with women? Or should we try to discourage these traits, skills, and contributions so that women will be more like men? Feminists today are deeply divided on these issues[120] and, were it possible to ask all women for their views, they too would have vastly different responses. Formal equality should be rejected because it takes one particular approach to a number of complicated questions about which women disagree vehemently.

Third, our young people continue to have different expectations about their futures—and different futures—depending on their sex.[121] As long as we continue producing girls and boys with different expectations, it is fundamentally unfair to treat women, once they are grown, as though they were like men in order to foster change. Change could be more effectively and fairly fostered by changing socialization than by making motherhood, childcare, and domestic work riskier through implementation of strict formal equality.

Fourth, if—as feminists have suggested—women tend (more than men) to define themselves in terms of others,[122] it may be very unrealistic to think that women will respond to increased insecurity by taking steps in their own individual self-interest despite harms to the interests of those closest to them. Yet increased risks associated with traditional roles will effect an appropriate level of change only if women act in their individual self-interest.

Fifth, making traditional roles more costly as a means of effecting change assumes that women will assess correctly the risk associated with traditional roles given the probability of divorce. Although some women (especially remarried women) seem to take the risk of divorce into account in making decisions about wagework versus full- or part-time homemaking, many women (especially women who have never been divorced) seem irrationally confident that divorce will not happen to them.

For all these reasons, as well as the reasons stated earlier, formal equality should not be regarded as the solution to women's problems and should not be too rigidly applied in challenges to sex-based classifications. To date, we have not developed any workable and satisfactory general alternative to formal equality, any alternative that judges would be willing to use and that would effect significant change. The remaining question is whether we should continue to seek another general standard for equality, or substitute therefor, as a solution to women's problems.

It is not feasible to prove an abstract negative: that we cannot possibly imagine a workable satisfactory general standard of equality (or substitute therefor) to replace formal equality and to be applied by judges. That may, however, be the case. I suspect it is, at least for the foreseeable future.

Current Standards, Institutional Concerns, and Change

Any standard capable of effecting real change would have to be based on a notion of both the desired end and the appropriate means. If we do not know what equality is, we cannot know where we are going nor how to get there. How, then, can we give judges a standard of equality that will ensure our arrival? Women do not form a homogeneous group with widely shared beliefs on these issues. Instead, women form a large group of very different people with vastly different interests and concerns. I suspect that, for the foreseeable future, any abstract standard capable of effecting real change would implement one subgroup's notion of equality, with the risk that other subgroups would bear most of the cost.

The Constitutional Standard

Even if we could imagine a satisfactory general standard capable of effecting real change, we should be hesitant about adopting it as a constitutional standard to be enforced by judges, at least for the foreseeable future. Judges are, and are likely to remain for the foreseeable future, mostly older and relatively conservative males. They are powerful members of the established order. One cannot realistically expect them to use a general abstract standard to implement much real change in the relative status of women and men. More importantly, as the experience with formal equality suggests, one must worry that an abstract standard will be implemented in ways that will hurt women.

Harmful decisions are then enshrined as part of constitutional law and difficult to change.

A flexible constitutional standard, allowing a fair amount of leeway to legislatures—rather than a rigid one like formal equality—is, of course, dangerous. Under a flexible standard, a legislature may enact legislation that expressly discriminates between women and men in a way detrimental to women, and the Constitution would afford no reliable basis for striking the statute. But formal equality illustrates that using an abstract standard to overrule legislation creating distinctions between women and men is also dangerous. Under such a standard, courts can replace standards distinguishing between women and men with sex-neutral standards that worsen the position of many women (especially ordinary mothers and wives), because women and men are not similarly situated.

The current constitutional standard, although it has gone a ways toward formal equality, is still fairly flexible. I would suggest that it has gone too far already; we should not push for further movement toward either strict formal equality for sex-based classifications (analogous to the standard for racial classifications) or for any alternative general standard as a constitutional matter.

I do not mean to suggest that feminists should be content with the current constitutional standard. That standard is seriously flawed, and it may be possible to fashion concrete refinements that make it more effective while retaining some flexibility. We should not, however, expect even a refined constitutional standard to solve all, or even many, of women's problems.

For example, MacKinnon suggests one possible refinement to the current constitutional standard. Women might be better off were the current constitutional standard modified so that, instead of permitting express distinctions between women and men based on reasonable differences, express distinctions would be permitted only when they would pass muster under MacKinnon's inequality standard. Judges would decide whether a distinction between women and men was part of the system subordinating women.[123] One could not expect to see any radical restructuring of society with a standard that would only examine express classifications to see if they contribute to the subordination of women. This refinement might, nevertheless, be better than the current standard; it might be less dangerous to entrust the question of whether an express classification contributes to the subordination of women to judges than for judges to continue to uphold express distinctions based on sex whenever supported by a difference perceived as relevant. Thus, for example, were *Johnson* (the affirmative action case) a constitutional challenge to an affirmative action plan designed to increase the number of women in traditionally male jobs, a court could use a refined equal protection standard to uphold it, because such a plan is much more likely to empower women than it is to contribute to their subordination; the alternative to affirmative action is not sex-neutral treatment, but invisible discrimination in favor of men.

Other refinements might be possible. For example, it might be possible to expand equal protection coverage of sex discrimination to include other distinctions that are typically elements of the systematic subordination of women though not distinctions expressly between the sexes. Thus, for example, a court could recognize pregnant/nonpregnant as a classification as suspect as male/female, since distinctions based on pregnancy have traditionally been used to subordinate women. A statute like that in *Guerra* (requiring disability leaves for only pregnant persons) could then be challenged under the equal protection clause of the Fourteenth Amendment.

Such a statute should, under the refinement suggested above, pass constitutional muster. The statute would be permissible because not part of the systematic subordination of women. Granted, the statute reinforces stereotypical notions connecting mothers, more than fathers, with small infants. And equality may be difficult—perhaps impossible—to achieve as long as only women are the primary caretakers of young infants.[124] The stereotype that mothers care for infants remains, nevertheless, overwhelmingly accurate. Ideally, a statute would provide for temporary leave for any new mother or father. But we do not live in an ideal world. We must choose, for the time being in California at least, between letting employers deny all employees short-term disability leaves and requiring that employers give workers disabled by pregnancy up to four months' disability leave. Women—who are, after all, the only parents temporarily out of commission because of the onset of parenthood and who are primarily responsible for the care and feeding of newborns in the vast majority of relationships[125]—are less dependent on men under the California statute than they would be under employer policies such as those of Cal Fed. A major part of the systematic subordination of women has consisted of giving them few options other than relying on men for financial security after having children. This statute empowers women by facilitating the combination of motherhood and wagework.

I would not, however, expect even an improved Fourteenth Amendment standard to offer a remedy whenever women are in fact subordinated by a rule, policy, or practice.

The Title VII Standard: Johnson *and* Guerra

Title VII should also be interpreted as a fairly flexible standard, allowing for some distinctions on the basis of sex in at least some instances, as in both *Johnson* and *Guerra*.

In *Johnson*, the question was whether an employer's voluntary affirmative action plan—which took sex into account in promoting Joyce to a position previously held only by men—was a form of sex discrimination barred by Title VII.[126] Had the Court never decided an affirmative action case, this would have been a difficult question of statutory construction.[127] Justice William J. Brennan was, however, able to rely on *Steelworkers v. Weber*[128] in writing the opinion of the Court upholding Joyce's promotion as a permissible form of affirmative action.

Justice Brennan began by specifying the three *Weber* criteria for a permissible voluntary affirmative action plan: (1) The plan must remedy a " 'manifest imbalance' that reflect[s] underrepresentation of women in 'traditionally segregated job categories.' "[129] (2) It must not trammel "the rights of male employees or create[ ] an absolute bar to their advancement."[130] (3) It must be "intended to *attain* a balanced work force, not to maintain one."[131] Justice Brennan found the first requirement satisfied because women were underrepresented at the transportation agency in those areas in which "women have not been traditionally employed in significant numbers."[132] Specifically, he noted that none of the 238 skilled craft positions was held by a woman and that "[a] plethora of proof is hardly necessary to show that women are generally underrepresented in such positions and that strong social pressures weigh against their participation."[133] (In *Weber*, in contrast, five out of 273 skilled craft positions had been held by blacks at Kaiser's Gramercy plant prior to the affirmative action plan.)[134] Both blacks and women have traditionally been excluded from skilled crafts. At the end of World War II, for example, many women were fired from traditionally male—and often skilled—jobs to make room for returning soldiers.

Next, Justice Brennan found that the plan did not trammel on the rights of male employees because it did not close any employment opportunities categorically to men and because it set only rather modest goals once fully implemented. True, the initial plan created, as a long-term goal, a workforce in which major job classifications mirrored the available workforce. But the plan required the formulation of annual short-term goals in light of a number of factors, such as the number of openings during the coming year and the percentage of women and minorities in the local workforce qualified for the position. At the time Joyce was promoted over Johnson in 1980, no annual goal had been established for skilled craft positions. But, as Justice Brennan noted, the agency's plan emphasized "that the long-term goals were not to be taken as guides for actual hiring decisions."[135] Instead, "supervisors were to consider a host of practical factors in seeking to meet affirmative action objectives, including the fact that in some job categories women were not qualified in numbers comparable to their representation in the labor force."[136] Graebner, the person who made the decision to promote Joyce over Johnson, testified thus: "I tried to look at the whole picture, the combination of her qualifications and Mr. Johnson's qualifications, their test scores, their expertise, their background, affirmative action matters, things like that. . . . I believe it was a combination of all those."[137]

Justice Brennan also noted, though in the margin, that the plan had not in fact trammeled the rights of male employees. Of the 111 new skilled craft positions filled at the agency between 1978 and 1982, "105, or almost 95%, went to men."[138] Indeed, when the agency first set a numerical goal for hiring women into skilled crafts (for the year 1982) that goal was a modest 5.4 percent of new hires (three out of 55).[139] Certainly the effort to bring women into skilled crafts in *Johnson* was much more restrained than the effort at issue in *Weber*, where the employer established a skilled craft training program and filled half the trainee positions with blacks.

Finally, Justice Brennan discussed whether the agency's plan was intended to attain a balanced workforce or to maintain one. The plan did not have any explicit termination date; it could have been better drafted. Justice Brennan refused to invalidate the plan for this reason, however, concluding that the absence of an explicit end date was understandable given the agency's flexible approach, which, as the evidence just cited suggests (with its modest goals), was not expected to yield immediate success. Given the glacial speed of the plan—under which only three women were, for example, to be among the 55 skilled workers hired in 1982—the failure to specify an end date was irrelevant to anything that might happen during this century, and entirely understandable.

Although *Johnson* was a fairly straightforward application of *Weber*, it was the first time that the Supreme Court actually upheld an affirmative action plan in the context of sex. As discussed earlier, however, there is little reason to distinguish between *Johnson* and *Weber* in terms of the need for "affirmative" action if women (like blacks) are ever to enjoy equal employment opportunity. Women, like blacks, have traditionally been excluded from the skilled crafts and are likely to be significantly underrepresented in the foreseeable future even with affirmative action.[140]

Guerra does not represent quite so straightforward an application of *Weber*. The California statute gave pregnant workers a permanent preference. The U.S. Supreme Court nevertheless upheld the California statute on a *Weber*-like rationale. Justice Thurgood Marshall, speaking for the Court, reasoned that Congress, in requiring that employers treat pregnant workers like other workers similar in their ability to do the job, intended to create a floor below which treatment of pregnant workers could not drop, but that Congress did not intend to create a ceiling above which beneficial treatment could not rise.[141] The California statute was therefore permissible because it "promotes equal employment opportunity," which was, after all, Congress's purpose in enacting Title VII.[142]

Although the preference permitted for pregnant workers in *Guerra* is permanent, this extension of *Weber*'s rationale[143] is easily justified in the context of sex. *Weber* allows, in order to achieve equality, some preference as long as a minority group is substantially underrepresented in a position from which it has traditionally been excluded. In general, once a minority group successfully integrates a traditionally closed position, it should (we hope) be possible for members of the minority group to continue to enjoy access, for a number of reasons.[144] Women face an additional problem, however. It is not just that some jobs have been formally or informally closed to women. Another access problem (inter alia) is that rules and practices have been structured with the expectation that workers would not be new mothers. This problem is not solved simply by hiring women in appropriate numbers. It can only be solved by changing workplace policies and practices so that it is easier for women to combine wagework and reproduction. *Weber* should, therefore, be extended to allow statutes that guarantee pregnant workers their jobs during pregnancy-related disability.

Guerra and *Johnson* suggest two ways in which Title VII's apparently absolute ban on sex discrimination should be construed so as to permit some distinctions based on sex. Perhaps, in the future, additional refinements will also be suggested for Title VII—refinements that will make it a more effective means to achieving equality between the sexes. *Johnson* and *Guerra* might not be sufficient to promote real equality.

Certainly, as of today, the statute—despite the flexibility afforded by *Guerra* and *Johnson*—is inadequate as the solution to women's problems in achieving equality in the wage labor market. It does not afford any way to challenge much of what needs to be challenged. For example, the statute (like the Constitution) does not provide a means for women to challenge the use of employment requirements and standards that are well adapted to male life-styles and poorly adapted to female life-styles. Nor does it provide a means of challenging the undervaluation of jobs traditionally performed by women.[145]

Change through the Political Process

Since it is unlikely that we will be able to imagine one abstract standard capable of providing an effective means for resolving all such problems, much change in the legal system must occur (if it is to occur at all) as a result of legislative change—often, piecemeal legislative change. This "solution" will not, however, be easy.

A responsive political process would seem an ideal forum for resolving women's conflicting visions of equality and how to get there. There are other advantages to legislative forums. One can make all kinds of arguments. Effective arguments need not be traditional arguments. Disparate impact arguments can be effective in this setting and need a label no more esoteric than the simple word *fairness*. A legislature can choose which of many policies to modify to effect a desired change. Unlike a court, a legislature can choose the appropriate "defendant." Specific legislative reform—such as changing the Social Security system so that homemakers receive credits in their own accounts for their contributions (based, perhaps, on their husbands' wages)—is often the only way to effect needed changes. Only a legislature will do the kind of detailed tinkering necessary to implement many of the changes needed if the legal system is to be as responsive to women's needs as it is to men's. Many needed changes simply cannot and will not be ordered by a court pursuant to an abstract standard of equality. A final advantage of the legislative forum is that legislatures can experiment with various approaches more easily than courts. It may not always be apparent whether a certain change would be desirable or not. Or a change, desirable at one time, may become obsolete or undesirable at another. It is easier for legislatures than for courts to take different approaches at different times.

Unfortunately, it is not going to be easy to change the status of women through the legislative process, for two major reasons. The first is that the political process itself is not responsive to women, in part because women are not a homogeneous group. A number of factors make it difficult for women to operate as a cohesive political force: Women are geographically dispersed; women are members of different classes; women identify with male interests because of relationships that are often only temporary; women are still raised to consider the home (rather than the public arena) their special sphere of interest; women still do not enter politics in proportion to their numbers in the population; women tend (more than men) to define themselves in terms of the interests of others (their husbands and children), and may therefore be less likely than other groups to push for their own interests in the legislative arena; women tend to have less time and money (than men) to spend lobbying; legislatures are still predominantly male enclaves and not, one imagines, much easier for individual women to break into, or to effect change within, than the all-male road maintenance gang on which Joyce worked. In addition, many issues of special concern to women are state-law issues, and many state legislatures are very conservative—even hostile—to "women's lib," a label likely to taint any change designed to equalize the status of women and men.

The second major problem is that, even when women succeed in effecting legislative change, the new laws will be more or less general and will typically require judicial implementation. Judges may fail fully to implement the desired change. To some extent, this problem can be avoided by careful drafting and detailed legislative history. But, to be effective, the groups interested in change must continue to monitor the situation after the desired legislation is enacted and, when necessary, begin another round of lobbying for additional legislative reform.

Legislative change—especially piecemeal legislative change—is not a miraculous solution. If, however, for the foreseeable future, it is the only solution to many of women's problems with the current legal structure, surely it is better to face squarely that fact and attempt to implement piecemeal legislative change than to continue striving to implement some vague and abstract standard of equality that will effect too little good and too much harm.

Conclusion

To date, we have not discovered any abstract standard of equality (or substitute therefor) with the potential for real change. Formal equality (with and without limited exceptions when there are biological differences)—the leading contender as the general standard—can effect only limited change. It cannot, for example, ensure that jobs are structured so that female workers and male workers are equally able to combine wagework and parenthood. Nor can it ensure that Social Security, unemployment compensation, and other safety nets are structured so as to provide for women's financial security as well as they provide for men's. Moreover, women—especially ordinary mothers and wives—have been harmed by the changes effected to date by the movement toward formal equality. Further movement in that direction could bring additional harm. Any other satisfactory and workable general standard to be applied by judges is as yet unimagined and likely to be so for the foreseeable future.

Women do not share a single vision of equality or one view of how to get there from here. Women are not a homogeneous group with homogeneous values, concerns, and interests. Were the legislative process more responsive to women, it would be a good forum for women to resolve their conflicting interests and visions of equality. Unfortunately, it is unresponsive, and certainly far from ideal. Nevertheless, piecemeal legislative change, especially in the area of economic rights, is likely to be more effective in improving the lives of many women than is the development of any abstract standard of equality.

Notes

1. See, e.g., Ginsburg, "Sexual Equality under the Fourteenth and Equal Rights Amendments," 1979 *Wash. U. L. Q.* 161; Ginsburg, "Gender and the Constitution," 44 *U. Cin. L. Rev.* 1 (1975); Ginsburg, "Sex and Unequal Protection: Men and Women as Victims," 11 *J. Fam. L.* 347 (1971); Cole, "Strategies of Difference: Litigating for Women's Rights in a Man's World," 2 *L. & Inequality* 33 (1984); Brown, Emerson, Falk & Freedman, "The Equal Rights Amendment: A Constitutional Basis for Equal Rights for Women," 80 *Yale L. J.* 871 (1971).

2. In addition to the sources cited in note 3 below, see Rhode, "Justice, Gender, and the Justices," in Crites & Hepperle, eds., *Women, the Courts, and Equality* (Newberry Park, Calif.: Sage, 1987), pp. 13, 18–19; Finley,

"Transcending Equality Theory: A Way out of the Maternity and the Workplace Debate," 86 *Col. L. Rev.* 1118 (1986). Other feminists have presented more general critiques of liberalism. See Jaggar, *Feminist Politics and Human Nature* (Totowa, N.J.: Rowman & Allanheld, 1983), pp. 27–48, 173–203; Elshtain, *Public Man, Private Woman* (Princeton, N.J.: Princeton University Press, 1981); Wolgast, *Equality and the Rights of Women* (Ithaca, N.Y.: Cornell University Press, 1980).

3. See MacKinnon, *Sexual Harassment of Working Women* (Cambridge, Mass.: Harvard University Press, 1979); Littleton, "Rethinking Sexual Equality," 75 *Calif. L. Rev.* 201 (1987); Scales, "The Emergence of a Feminist Jurisprudence: An Essay," 95 *Yale L. J.* 1373 (1986); Kay, "Models of Equality," 1985 *Univ. Ill. L. Rev.* 39; Kay, "Equality and Difference: The Case of Pregnancy," 1 *Berkeley Women's L. J.* 1 (1985); Law, "Rethinking Sex and the Constitution," 132 *U. Penn. L. Rev.* 955 (1984). See also Wolgast, *Equality* (suggesting some ways in which the standard of equality might be improved but not suggesting any one developed equality standard); "Note," 95 *Harv. L. Rev.* 487 (1981) (similar); Freedman, "Sex Equality, Sex Differences, and the Supreme Court," 92 *Yale L. J.* 913 (1983) (similar).

4. For a somewhat similar analysis, see Krieger & Cooney, "The Miller-Wohl Controversy: Equal Treatment, Positive Action and the Meaning of Women's Equality," 13 *Golden Gate Univ. L. Rev.* 513 (1983).

5. *California Federal Savings and Loan Association v. Guerra*, 479 U.S. 272 (1987).

6. *Johnson v. Transportation Agency*, 480 U.S. 616 (1987).

7. *Wimberly v. Labor and Industrial Relations Commission of Missouri*, 479 U.S. 511 (1987).

8. See "Garland's Bouquet," *Time*, January 26, 1987, p. 14.

9. See *Guerra*, Brief Amici Curiae of the National Organization for Women (and six other signatories), and Brief of the American Civil Liberties Union (and four other signatories). Both briefs argued that the Supreme Court should extend the statutory benefit to all workers disabled for four months or less.

10. See, e.g., *Guerra*, Brief Amici Curiae of Coalition for Reproductive Equality in the Workplace; Betty Friedan; International Ladies' Garment Worker's Union, AFL–CIO; 9 to 5; National Association of Working Women; Planned Parenthood Federation of America, Inc., California School Employees Association; American Federation of State, County, and Municipal Employees, District Council 36; California Federation of Teachers; Coalition of Labor Union Women, Los Angeles Chapter (and 30 other signatories).

11. Only Justice Antonin Scalia declined to reach the merits of the Title VII issue; his concurrence in the judgment rested on preemption grounds. Chief Justice William Rehnquist and Justices Byron White and Lewis Powell dissented.

12. *Johnson*, 480 U.S. at 624 n. 5.

13. See ibid.

14. Joyce contacted the county affirmative action officer prior to the second interview because she was understandably worried about receiving a fair review. Under the terms of the agency's affirmative action plan, the affirmative action coordinator was responsible for keeping the director informed of opportunities for the agency to accomplish the plan objectives, which included achieving "a statistically measurable yearly improvement in hiring, training, and promotion of minorities and women throughout the Agency in all major job classifications where they are underrepresented." *Johnson*, 480 U.S. at 621 (quoting plan).

15. Rehnquist, C.J., White & Scalia, JJ., dissenting.

16. In *General Electric Company v. Gilbert*, 429 U.S. 125 (1976), the Court had held that Title VII's ban on sex discrimination was not violated by an employer's health plan that covered all medical treatment except treatment related to pregnancy. The Court concluded that a distinction between pregnant and nonpregnant persons was not a distinction on the basis of sex. In response, Congress enacted the Pregnancy Discrimination Act of 1978, which defines sex discrimination to include distinctions based on pregnancy, childbirth, or related medical conditions. According to the reports of both houses on the Pregnancy Discrimination Act, Congress considered the approach in *Gilbert* inconsistent with a proper understanding of Title VII's nondiscrimination mandate. See Amending Title VII, Civil Rights Act of 1964, Sen. Rep. No. 95-331, 95th Cong., 1st sess. 2–3 (1978); Prohibition of Sex Discrimination Based on Pregnancy, H.R. Rep. No. 95-948, 95th Cong., 2d sess. 2–3 (1978). In *Geduldig v. Aiello*, 417 U.S. 484 (1974) (challenge to state disability insurance system that specifically excluded pregnancy from list of compensable disabilities), the Supreme Court held that classifications based on pregnancy are not equivalent to classifications based on sex for purposes of equal protection analysis. *Geduldig* remains good law in constitutional cases.

17. Pregnancy Discrimination Act of 1978, 42 U.S.C., sec. 2000e(k).

18. See Scales, "Emergence," at p. 1377; Minow, "The Supreme Court 1986 Term—Foreword: Justice Engendered," 101 *Harv. L. Rev.* 10, 40–45 (1987).

19. See *Gilbert*; *Geduldig*. In other contexts, even prior to Congress's overruling *Gilbert* with the Pregnancy Discrimination Act of 1978 (see note 16 above), the Court perceived special treatment of pregnancy as a form of sex discrimination. See *Nashville Gas Company v. Satty*, 434 U.S. 136 (1977).

20. For an extreme example of this problem, see *Rostker v. Goldberg*, 453 U.S. 57 (1981) (upholding registration only of young men for military service because women were not allowed in combat; men and women were not, therefore, similarly situated).

21. See MacKinnon, *Sexual Harassment*, pp. 144–46.

22. For discussions of the chimera of neutrality, see McConnell, "Neutrality under the Religion Clauses," 81 *Nw. U. L. Rev.* 146 (1986); Minow, "Supreme Court 1986 Term—Foreword," at p. 10; Sunstein, "Lochner's Legacy," 87 *Colum. L. Rev.* 873 (1987).

23. MacKinnon, *Feminism Unmodified* (Cambridge, Mass.: Harvard University Press, 1987), p. 37.

24. Aristotle also pointed out that it is unjust to treat similarly people who are not similarly situated. See *Nichomachean Ethics*, Ross trans. (Oxford, England: Oxford University Press, 1925), V(3), p. 112. Under formal equality, the result is that women are often treated like men though they are not similarly situated. In addition, Aristotle advocated the use of practical, rather than abstract, reason in attempting to identify the good for humans. *Nichomachean Ethics*, I(3), pp. 2–5.

25. Ibid., V(3), at pp. 112–14.

26. MacKinnon, *Sexual Harassment*, at p. 105.

27. Although men may sustain as many or more disabilities on the average than women, such disabilities are less likely to lead to parallel male economic dependence on women. Men are likely to sustain more work-related disabilities (because men tend to have more physically hazardous jobs). But work-related disabilities tend to be compensated by workers' compensation systems. Men who sustain them are not, therefore, entirely dependent economically on women. In addition, although Social Security never affords disability coverage to women temporarily disabled by pregnancy, it often affords disability coverage to workers who sustain other disabilities.

28. Women who care for children (full or part time) could be protected by accounting changes; one need not impose additional taxes on families. During marriage, half of the wages of each spouse could be credited directly to the Social Security account of the other spouse. See Supplementary Statement by Commissioners Ball, Keys, Kirkland, Moynihan, and Pepper, from the Report of the National Commission on Social Security Reform (1983), statement (2), pp. 5–7.

29. In addition to the sources cited in note 30 below, see, e.g., Buczek, "A Promising Measure of Sex Bias: The Incidental Memory Task," 10 *Psychology of Women Q.* 127 (1986); Schulman & Hoskins, "Perceiving the Male versus the Female Face," 10 *Psychology of Women Q.* 141 (1986); Deutsch, LeBaron & Fryer, "What Is in a Smile," 11 *Psychology of Women Q.* 341 (1987).

30. See, e.g., McArthur, "Social Judgment Biases in Comparable Worth Analysis," in Hartmann, ed., *Comparable Worth: New Directions for Research* (Washington, D.C.: National Academy Press, 1985), pp. 53, 55–64; Gerdes & Garber, "Sex Bias in Hiring: Effects of Job Demands and Applicant Competence," 9 *Sex Roles* 307 (1983); Francesco & Hakel, "Gender and Sex as Determinates of Hireability of Applicants for Gender-typed Jobs," 5 *Psychology of Women Q.* 747 (1981); Plake, Murphy-Berman, Derscheid, Gerber, Miller, Speth & Tomes, "Access Decisions by Personnel Directors: Subtle Forms of Sex Bias in Hiring," 11 *Psychology of Women Q.* 255 (1987); Francesco, "Gender and Sex as Detriments of Hireability of Applicants for Gender-typed Jobs," 5 *Psychology of Women Q.* 747 (1981).

31. See note 12 above.

32. See *Johnson v. Transportation Agency*, Santa Clara County, California, No. C-81-1218-WAI (SJ) (N.D. Calif., July 23, 1982).

33. *Steelworkers v. Weber*, 443 U.S. 193 (1979).

34. Ibid., at 198 n. 1.

35. See generally Falk, "Women and Unions: A Historical View," 1 *Women's Rights L. Reptr.* 54 (1973).

36. The finding may be partly attributable to collusion between the plaintiff Johnson and the defendant employer. Neither would have wanted to give a court a basis for finding that there had been discrimination against women. The courts upholding the affirmative action plan (the Ninth Circuit and the U.S. Supreme Court) could have decided the case without any finding on whether there had ever been discrimination against women. That would seem the more prudent course in the absence of an adequate basis for finding such a fact.

37. Women often presume that blue-collar jobs are not open to them, but are interested if information is presented in a form indicating that the employer is interested in hiring women. See Roos & Reskin, "Institutional Factors Contributing to Sex Segregation in the Workplace," in Reskin, ed., *Sex Segregation in the Workplace: Trends, Explanations, Remedies* (Washington, D.C.: National Academy Press, 1984), 237–38, 241, 245; Walshok, *Blue Collar Women* (New York: Anchor Books, 1981), pp. 155–70. See also note 140 below.

38. See, e.g., Roos & Reskin, "Institutional Factors," at pp. 228–32, 239–40, 259–60.

39. See, e.g., Ginsburg, "Gender and Constitution"; Brief of the American Civil Liberties Union, Amicus Curiae, filed in *Orr v. Orr* (see note 66 below); Brown, Emerson, Falk & Freedman, "Equal Rights Amendment"; Cowan, "Women's Rights through Litigation: An Examination of the American Civil Liberties Union Women's Rights Project, 1971–1976," 8 *Colum. Human Rights L. Rev.* 373 (1976); Mansbridge, *Why We Lost the ERA* (Chicago: University of Chicago Press, 1986).

40. See, e.g., *Davis v. Passman*, 442 U.S. 228 (1979); *Phillips v. Martin Marietta Corporation*, 400 U.S. 542 (1971); *Hishon v. King & Spaulding*, 457 U.S. 69 (1984).

41. See, e.g., Williams, "Equality's Riddle: Pregnancy & the Equal Treatment/Special Treatment Debate," 13 *NYU Rev. of L. & Social Change* 325 (1985); Williams, "The Equality Crises: Some Reflections on Culture, Courts, and Feminism," 7 *Women's Rights L. Rep.* 175 (1983).

42. See, e.g., Williams, "Equality Crises," at pp. 196–97; *Guerra*, Brief of American Civil Liberties Union, at pp. 10–35.

43. Williams, "Equality's Riddle," at pp. 353–56; Williams, "Equality Crises," at pp. 195–96.

44. Williams, "Equality's Riddle," at p. 326; Williams, "Equality Crises," at p. 196.

45. Williams, "Equality's Riddle," at pp. 374–80.

46. See "The Supreme Court Puts the Mike in Diane Joyce's Hands, Giving Feminists a Major Victory," *People*, April 13, 1987, pp. 49, 53 (quoting Johnson on whether affirmative action should be used in promotion decision: "You should work for what you get, and if you work, you should get it.").

47. See *Johnson*, Brief Amici Curiae of NOW Legal Defense and Education Fund et al.

48. See Woloch, *Women and the American Experience* (New York: Knopf, 1984), p. 384 (describing criticisms of the ERA movement in the 1920s); Rothman, *Woman's Proper Place: A History of Changing Ideals and Places, 1870 to the Present* (New York: Basic Books, 1978), p. 160; Hewlett, *A Lesser Life* (New York: Warner Books, 1986), esp. pp. 202–3.

49. The ERA would not, necessarily, have to be interpreted as a formal equality standard; see MacKinnon in "Excerpts from MacKinnon/Schlafly Debate," 1 *L. & Inequality* 341, 341 (1983). Nevertheless, the ERA was widely understood as incorporating a formal equality standard. See, e.g., Brown, Emerson, Falk & Freedman, "Equal Rights Amendment"; Ginsburg, "Sexual Equality."

50. For a description of the traditional rule, see, e.g., Clark, *The Law of Domestic Relations in the United States* (St. Paul, Minn.: West Publishing, 1968), sec. 17.4 at pp. 584–85.

51. See, e.g., *Ex Parte Devine*, 398 So.2d 686 (1981) (maternal presumption unconstitutional under U.S. Supreme Court decisions; court notes presumption has been eliminated in Alaska, Arizona, California, Colorado, Connecticut, Delaware, Georgia, Hawaii, Illinois, Indiana, Iowa, Maine, Massachusetts, Michigan, Nebraska, New York, North Carolina, Ohio, Texas, and Washington and rendered questionable in Kansas, Oregon, Pennsylvania, and Vermont); Horowitz & Davidson, eds., *Legal Rights of Children* (Colorado Springs, Colo.: Shepard's/McGraw-Hill, 1984), sec. 6.03, p. 236.

52. See, e.g., West's Ann. Cal. Civ. Code, sec. 4600.5 (creating presumption of joint custody on application of either parent); Horowitz & Davidson, *Legal Rights of Children*, sec. 6.05, at pp. 239–42; Schulman & Pitt, "Second Thoughts on Joint Child Custody: Analysis of Legislation and Its Implications for Women and Children," 12 *Golden Gate Univ. L. Rev.* 539, 545 (1982) (as of March 1982, 24 states have some form of joint custody statute). Although joint custody can refer to joint physical custody, more often in practice it means simply joint legal custody (both parents having the right to make decisions about education, medical care, etc.). See Schulman & Pitt, supra, at pp. 542–43. For discussions of problems with joint custody, see., e.g., ibid.,; Adler & Chambers, "The Folly of Joint Custody," 1 *Family Advocate* 6 (1978).

53. See, e.g., Weitzman, *The Marriage Contract* (New York: Free Press, 1981), pp. 105–6 & 105n.

54. See Schulmann & Pitt, "Second Thoughts," as reprinted in Folberg, ed., *Joint Custody and Shared Parenting* (New York: Guilford Press, 1984),

p. 209; Scott & Derdeyn, "Rethinking Joint Custody," 45 *Ohio St. L. J.* 455, 478 & n. 106 (1981); Pearson & Ring, "Judicial Decision-making in Contested Custody Cases," 21 *J. Fam. L.* 703, 719 (1982); Neely, "The Primary Caretaker Parent Rule: Child Custody and the Dynamics of Greed," 3 *Yale L. & Pol. Rev.* 168 (1984).

55. See Weitzman, *The Divorce Revolution* (New York: Free Press, 1985), p. xii; Espenshade, "The Economic Consequences of Divorce," *J. of Marriage & Fam.* 615 (August 1979); Women's Research & Education Institute, Congressional Caucus for Women, *The American Woman: A Report in Depth* (New York: Norton, 1987), pp. 78–82 (citing surveys).

56. Only 4 million women (out of 8.7 million living with children of absent fathers) were to receive child support from fathers in 1983. Of those due payments, half received (about 2 million) the full amount due. About a quarter (1 million) received nothing, and an approximately equal number received a partial payment. See U.S. Bureau of the Census, *Child Support and Alimony: 1983*, Current Population Reports, Special Studies, Series P-23, No. 141 (Washington, D.C.: Government Printing Office, July 1985). The *New York Times* reported that the average payment for child support dropped 12.4% from 1983 to 1985. See "Average Child Support Payment Drops by 12%," *New York Times*, August 23, 1987, sec. 1, p. 26. Because of recent federal legislation, women should be receiving more of what is awarded than in the past. See Child Support Enforcement Amendments of 1984, 98 Stat. 1305 (August 16, 1984).

57. See, e.g., Weitzman, *Divorce Revolution*, at pp. 188–89.

58. See, e.g., *McGuire v. McGuire*, 157 Neb. 226, 59 N.W.2d 336 (1953).

59. See, e.g., *Sharpe Furniture, Incorporated v. Buckstaff*, 99 Wis.2d 114, 299 N.W.2d 219 (1980).

60. See, e.g., *Jersey Shore Medical Center v. Estate of Baum*, 84 N.J.2d 137, 417 A.2d 1003 (1980) (rule to be applied in future cases).

61. See *Garska v. McCoy*, 278 S.E.2d 357 (1981). In most jurisdictions, the identity of the primary caretaker is only one of many factors considered; see, e.g., *Pusey v. Pusey*, Utah. Sup. Ct. No. 20365 (August 18, 1987).

62. NOW might have preferred the extension of the California statute to all workers, but the Supreme Court was not likely to extend that kind of state statute in the way advocated by NOW, despite its alternative holding to that effect in *Guerra*. See Becker, "Barriers Facing Women in the Wage-labor Market and the Need for Additional Remedies: A Reply to Fischel & Lazear," 53 *U. Chi. L. Rev.* 934, 942–43 (1986). In addition, even if the Court had extended the statute, the California legislature would have been free to repeal it. Further, other legislatures could not, in the future, enact maternal leave statutes unless willing to give short-term disability leaves to all workers.

63. Seventy-five countries—including every industrialized country except the United States—have some form of maternal or paternal leave. See Kamerman, Kahn & Kingston, *Maternity Policies and Working Women* (New York:

Columbia University Press, 1983), pp. 15 & 16–22, table 1.3; Hewlitt, *Lesser Life*, pp. 96–100 & 167–74. Sweden adopted the first (and still most generous) parental leave policy in 1975. Hewlitt, *Lesser Life*, at p. 96; International Labor Office, *Maternity Benefits in the Eighties: An ILO Global Survey (1964–1984)* (Geneva: ILO, 1985), pp. 18–22. As of 1984, five additional countries (Norway, Denmark, Italy, France, and Portugal) within the European Economic Community had adopted some form of paternity leave in addition to maternity leave. ILO, *Maternity Benefits*.

64. The four states are Connecticut, Minnesota, Oregon, and Rhode Island. See *Pregnancy and Employment: The Complete Handbook on Discrimination, Maternity Leave, and Health and Safety* (Washington, D.C.: BNA Books, 1987), pp. 98, 102, 104–6. Of these, two began with maternity leave policies— Connecticut and Oregon. See ibid., at pp. 98 & 104. The Connecticut parental leave statute covers only state employees. Ibid., at p. 98.

65. Five states have statutes guaranteeing maternity leaves: California, Iowa, Massachusetts, Montana, and Tennessee. Ibid., at pp. 96, 100–101, 105. Six states have regulations guaranteeing maternity leaves: Colorado, Hawaii, Illinois, Kansas, New Hampshire, and Washington. See ibid., at pp. 97, 100–101, 103, 105–6.

66. *Orr v. Orr*, 440 U.S. 268 (1979).

67. *Otis v. Otis*, 299 N.W.2d 114 (Minn. 1980).

68. As of 1978, only 14.3% of divorced women had been awarded any alimony. See U.S. Bureau of the Census, *Child Support and Alimony*, at p. 4, table E.

69. Such statutes violate neither the Constitution nor Title VII. See *Personnel Administrator of Massachusetts v. Feeney*, 442 U.S. 256 (1979) (veterans' preference does not violate equal protection clause though women are effectively excluded from top levels of state government); 42 U.S.C., sec. 2000e-11 (exempting veterans' preference statutes from preemption by Title VII).

70. The financial security accumulated during the marriage includes the present earning power and future earning potential (to the extent accumulated during the marriage) as well as tangible and intangible pension rights and Social Security credits. Women who are dependent because of their specialization in domestic production and reproduction are not awarded half of these assets. See, e.g., *Umber v. Umber*, 591 P.2d 299 (1979) (Social Security Act preempts distribution to wife of part of Social Security account accumulated in husband's name though both worked in family drugstore but Social Security contributions were paid only into husband's account); 42 U.S.C., sec. 402(b) (during life of wage-earner ex-husband, divorced spouse receives, at most, 50 cents for every dollar of benefits he is entitled to receive). When a wife is given a share of a pension, she is sometimes "bought out," i.e., given cash or other disposable assets to offset the pension rights given the husband. See, e.g., Weitzman, *Divorce Revolution*, at pp. 120–21; *In re Marriage of Gillmore*, 29 Cal. 3rd 1, 174 Cal. Rptr. 493, 629 P.2d 1 (1981).

71. See note 70 above and Weitzman, *Divorce Revolution*, at pp. 143–45. Even under a statute imposing equivalent obligations on ex-wives and ex-husbands, very few wives are going to be ordered to pay alimony because, inter alia, women usually have custody of the children and earn less than ex-husbands.

72. See Weitzman, *Divorce Revolution*, at pp. 143–83 (based on California statistics).

73. The Court did suggest that individualized hearings could be held on whether "the institution of marriage did discriminate against" a particular woman, but gave no clue as to what a hearing would actually investigate. *Orr*, 440 U.S. at 281. Because of problems of perspective and bias, women might be better off with sex-based rules than with individualized hearings.

74. *Otis*, 299 N.W.2d at 118 (Otis, J., dissenting).

75. Ibid.

76. In *Otis*, the court divided approximately equally the property accumulated during the marriage except that it also awarded Mr. Otis all of his vested pension plan. The court does not attach any specific value to that plan.

77. Ordinary women may also be hurt by discretionary rules—rules requiring judges to find an appropriate basis for awarding alimony in a particular case—rather than alimony awarded on the basis of sex, since bias may affect individual decisions. This problem has been ignored by the Supreme Court, which seems unable to perceive any cost—other than administrative—associated with individualized hearings. Cf. *In re Marriage of Hitchcock*, 265 N.W.2d 599 (1978) (wife unsuccessfully tries to repudiate divorce settlement reached after trial judge had made statements indicating that he would award her little as her share of husband's business; among other things, the judge compared her "interest in her husband's business to his own wife's interest in his retirement fund should they be divorced" with the implication that neither wife should receive a share of the specified asset).

78. If alimony is basically a form of expectation-reliance (contract) damages for the needy traditional wife when a marriage breaks up, it should not necessarily terminate entirely with her remarriage. Thus, I do not mean to suggest that traditional rules could not be improved upon.

79. See, e.g., *Pellegrin v. Pellegrin*, 478 S.2d 306 (Miss. 1985) (error to award custody to mothers solely on the basis of children's tender years); *In re Marriage of Kershner*, 400 So.2d 126 (Fla. 1981) (dictum: where all other factors are equal, custody of children of tender years should go to mother).

80. See Weitzman, *Divorce Revolution*, at pp. 235–36; *Report of the New York Task Force on Women in the Courts* (New York: Unified Court System, Office of Court Administration, 1986), pp. 162–65.

81. Cf. *Vorchheimer v. School District of Philadelphia*, 532 F.2d 880 (3rd Cir. 1976) (equal protection clause challenge to "separate-but-equal" public high schools for boys and girls), aff'd by an equally divided Court, 430 U.S. 703 (1977).

82. See Krause, *Child Support in America* (Charlottesville, Va.: Michie, 1981), pp. 139–52. The trend is, however, contra. "Modern" judges tend to equalize the status of new fathers and new mothers despite the obvious disparity between their contributions to, and involvement with, the newborn. See, e.g., *Collinsworth v. O'Connell*, No. BQ-305 (Fla. 1st Dist. 1987); *In re Baby Girl Eason*, No. 44709 (Ga. 1987).

83. See, e.g., *Schilling v. Bedford County Memorial Hospital*, 303 S.E.2d 905 (Va. 1983) (abolishing support duty); *Marshfield Clinic v. Discher*, 314 N.W.2d 326 (Wis. 1982) (retaining traditional doctrine with qualification that wives are ordinarily responsible for their own necessities).

84. See Rhode, "Association and Assimilation," 81 *Nw. U. L. Rev.* 107, 115 (1986).

85. Perhaps such distinctions are already unconstitutional. The Supreme Court has not, however, decided cases squarely on these points. It can at least be argued that the Court might allow these distinctions to survive their middle-tier scrutiny applied in sex discrimination cases.

86. See, e.g., *Rosenfeld v. Southern Pacific Company*, 44 F.2d 1219 (1971).

87. See Hewlett, *Lesser Life*, at pp. 202–3; cf. Bielby & Baron, "Undoing Job Discrimination: Job Integration and Comparable Worth," in Bose & Spitze, eds., *Ingredients for Women's Employment Policy* (Albany: SUNY Press, 1987), pp. 211, 221–22 (discussing continuing job segregation by sex; authors stress "the tendency for organizational arrangements to be inert in the absence of profound environmental shocks").

88. See *Griggs v. Duke Power Company*, 401 U.S. 424 (1971) (race case).

89. See Williams, "Equality's Riddle," at pp. 364–65, 372–74; Stone, "Comparable Worth in the Wake of *AFSCME v. State of Washington*," 1 *Berkeley Women's L. J.* 78 (1986) (arguing for comparable worth as a form of disparate impact); Siegel, "Employment Equality under the Pregnancy Discrimination Act of 1978," 94 *Yale L. J.* 929 (1985) (arguing for general availability of disparate impact under Pregnancy Discrimination Act); *Guerra*, Brief of State of California at 14–21.

90. See *Dothard v. Rawlinson*, 433 U.S. 206 (1977) (height and weight requirements are impermissible because of disparate impact on women; employer must test directly for strength).

91. This provision applies to states participating in the federal–state unemployment compensation program and is codified at 26 U.S.C., sec. 3304(a)(12) (1982).

92. One can, of course, imagine other policies that would also be preferable from the perspective of pregnant workers, e.g., a plan that considered all reasonable quits (including pregnancy) as covered by the plan.

93. Wimberly did not frame her claim in terms of disparate impact. Instead, she argued that the federal provision mandated "preferential treatment for women who leave work because of pregnancy." *Wimberly*, 479 U.S. at 516. Something like disparate impact has, however, been recognized in the context

of the free exercise clause. States must extend unemployment benefits to workers who are fired for refusing to work on their Sabbath. See *Sherbert v. Verner*, 374 U.S. 398 (1963); *Hobbie v. Unemployment Appeals Commission of Florida*, 480 U.S. 136 (1987).

94. See *Guerra*, Brief of California at 14–21.

95. See *Guerra*, Brief of ACLU et al. at 25.

96. Ibid. at 26.

97. See *Guerra*, Brief of California Women Lawyers et al.—see note 10 above—at 12–13. On the other hand, workers who sustain work-related disabilities are less likely (than workers disabled by pregnancy) to lose their jobs. Employers are usually anxious to avoid charges that employees were fired in retaliation for filing a work-related disability claim and are anxious to do everything possible to limit the size of the claim. Both these purposes are served by allowing the worker to return to work at the earliest possible date. Indeed, California prohibits employers from terminating employees because of work-related disabilities. Cal. Labor Code, sec. 132a, cited in *Guerra*, Brief of California at 18–19 n. 16.

98. Because Title VII specifically defines sex discrimination as including discrimination on the basis of pregnancy, perhaps the disparate impact question in this Title VII case should focus on whether a no-leave policy has a disparate impact on pregnant workers, rather than women workers. The State of California argued that the appropriate focus was pregnant workers. See *Guerra*, Brief of California at 14–22, esp. n. 16 at 18–19. The ACLU considered the appropriate focus women workers, not pregnant workers. See *Guerra*, Brief of ACLU et al. at 23–35.

99. Cf. MacKinnon, *Sexual Harassment*, at pp. 145–46 (noting that inequality is buried in standards—such as the height and weight standard at issue in *Dothard*, which was actually average male height and weight; see note 90 above).

100. Even in families in which both spouses work, women are primarily responsible for domestic tasks. See, e.g., Blumstein & Schwartz, *American Couples* (New York: Morrow, 1983), pp. 144–46; Gilbert, *Men in Dual Career Families: Present Realities and Future Prospects* (Hillsdale, N.J.: L. Earlbaum Associates, 1985), pp. 60–90; Pleck, "Men's Family Work: Three Perspectives and Some New Data," 28 *Family Coordinator* 481 (1979).

101. See sources cited in note 89 above.

102. See, e.g., MacKinnon, *Sexual Harassment*, esp. at pp. 101–41; MacKinnon, *Feminism Unmodified*, esp. at pp. 32–45.

103. Littleton, "Reconstructing Sexual Equality," 75 *Cal. L. Rev.* 201 (1987).

104. See Kay, "Models of Equality"; Law, "Rethinking Sex and Constitution"; Kay, "Equality and Difference." Ann Scales also advocated this approach in an early article—see Scales, "Towards a Feminist Jurisprudence," 56 *Ind. L. J.* 375 (1981)—but in more recent work has advocated MacKinnon's inequality approach. See Scales, "Emergence."

105. Finley, "Transcending Equality Theory"; Wolgast, *Equality*.
106. I do not discuss the "choice" standard advocated by Kirp, Yudof, and Franks in *Gender Justice* (Chicago: University of Chicago Press, 1986). As Lucinda Finley points out in her review, the choice approach is a reformulation of conventional liberalism. See Finley, "Choice and Freedom: Elusive Issues in the Search for Gender Justice," 96 *Yale L. J.* 914 (1987).
107. MacKinnon, *Sexual Harassment*, at p. 116.
108. Ibid., at p. 117.
109. See Scales, "Emergence."
110. Certainly, MacKinnon has not taken such an approach. In *Sexual Harassment*, she used her inequality approach in arguing that policies of sexual harassment that explicitly treat women and men differently are forms of sex discrimination because they contribute to the inequality of women. But in her attempts to have pornography recognized as a form of sex discrimination, she has used inequality analysis as a basis for arguing for legislative change, rather than as a judicially enforceable abstract standard of equality capable, in itself, of affording a remedy for such discrimination.
111. For a similar analysis, see Law, "Rethinking Sex and Constitution," at pp. 1005–6.
112. Littleton, "Reconstructing Sexual Equality," at pp. 238–43.
113. Ibid., at pp. 244, 253.
114. Ibid., at p. 248.
115. Ibid. (No remedy would be available under Title VII, as currently interpreted, for the policy described in the text, because the height requirement is job related.)
116. Ibid.
117. Ibid., at p. 251.
118. Ibid., at pp. 251–52 n. 260 (by changing media treatment of female political candidates and by establishing preferences for employment similar to those granted veterans).
119. See Scales, "Towards Feminist Jurisprudence" (women should be regarded as having rights different from men only with respect to sex-specific conditions that are completely unique to women, i.e., pregnancy and breast feeding); Law, "Rethinking Sex and Constitution"; Kay, "Equality and Difference"; Kay, "Models of Equality." In a 1986 article, Scales moved from the limited-special-treatment view to share MacKinnon's dominance (or inequality) approach. See Scales, "Emergence," esp. at p. 1381 n. 46.
120. There is a great deal of controversy even among those who would identify with the word *feminist* about how and why women are different from men, the causes of any differences, and what changes to the current order are desirable. As Jane Flax has pointed out, "Feminist discourse is full of contradictory and irreconcilable conceptions of the nature of our social relations, of men and women and the worth and character of stereotypically masculine and feminine activities." Flax, "Postmodernism and Gender Relations in Feminist

Theory," 12 *Signs* 621, 638 (1987). See also Gerson, "Emerging Social Divisions among Women: Implications for Welfare State Politics," 15 *Politics & Society* 213 (1986/87); Rosenfelt & Stacey, "Second Thoughts on the Second Wave," 13 *Feminist Studies* 341 (1987).

121. See, e.g., Marini, "Sex Differences in the Determination of Adolescent Aspirations: A Review of Research," 4 *Sex Roles* 723 (1978); Marini & Greenberger, "Sex Differences in Occupational Aspirations and Expectations," 5 *Sociology of Work and Occupations* 147 (1978); Lyson, "Race and Sex Differences in Sex Role Attitudes of Southern College Students," 10 *Psychology of Women Q.* 421 (1986); Waite, Haggstrom & Kanouse, "Changes in the Employment Activities of New Parents," 50 *Am. Soc. Rev.* 263 (1985).

122. See, e.g., Chodorow, *The Reproduction of Mothering* (Berkeley: University of California Press, 1978).

123. Granted, it is not always easy to distinguish benefits (empowerment) from burdens (disempowerment), and women may be hurt if burdens are judged benefits. In addition, as has been noted repeatedly here, often a policy helps some women and hurts others. On the other hand, as the affirmative action cases illustrate well, it is not always impossible to judge that it is likely a certain policy benefits more women than it hurts. This standard might work out to be much like that proposed by Suzanna Sherry in "Selective Judicial Activism in the Equal Protection Context: Democracy, Distrust, and Deconstruction," 73 *Georgetown L. J.* 89 (1984) (only disfavored classes should be able to bring equal protection challenges).

124. Several feminists have suggested that, as long as women are the primary caretakers of young children, we will have difficulty relating to women as individuals. See, e.g., Chodorow, *Reproduction of Mothering*; Dinnerstein, *The Mermaid and the Minotaur* (New York: Harper & Row, 1976).

125. See, e.g., Gilbert, *Men in Dual Career Couples*, at pp. 60–90; Pleck, "Men's Family Work."

126. Although the defendant was a public employer, Johnson did not use the Fourteenth Amendment to challenge the affirmative action plan. Perhaps he did not use equal protection because, in the context of sex, an equal protection challenge might have been even weaker than the Title VII challenge. Cf. *Kahn v. Shevin*, 416 U.S. 351 (1974) (upholding a Florida statute giving property tax preference to widows but not to widowers). Because he did not challenge the agency's affirmative action plan on equal protection grounds, the Court did not reach the equal protection standard for permissible affirmative action. See *Johnson*, 480 at 628 n. 6. That standard might, of course, be different for sex and race.

127. See Meltzer, "The *Weber* Case: The Judicial Abrogation of the Antidiscrimination Standard in Employment," 47 *U. Chi. L. Rev.* 423 (1980).

128. See note 33 above.

129. *Johnson*, 480 U.S. at 631.

130. *Johnson*, 480 U.S. at 637–38.

131. Ibid. at 639.

132. Ibid. at 634 (quoting plan).

133. Ibid. at 634 & n. 12 (quoting appellate decision below). Justice Scalia, at 1467, would have interpreted *Weber* as allowing affirmative action only as a remedy for an employer's own past discrimination. He relied heavily on the district court's finding that the agency had not discriminated on the basis of sex.

134. *Weber*, 443 U.S. at 198.

135. *Johnson*, 480 at 636.

136. Ibid.

137. Quoted in ibid. at 625. In his dissent, Justice Scalia stresses that Johnson would have received the promotion rather than Joyce but for the affirmative action plan. Sex was therefore the determinative factor in this case. Ibid. at 663–64. It is of course true that, under any affirmative action plan having any effect, some decisions will come out differently because of sex or race.

138. Ibid. at 638–39 n. 15.

139. Ibid.

140. It is often suggested that women do not want traditionally male skilled-craft jobs. The evidence suggests, however, that women are interested in such jobs if they think that such jobs are actually open to them. See, e.g., Walshok, *Blue Collar Women*. And see note 37 above.

141. The ACLU Women's Project had argued that the California statute, like protectionist legislation in an earlier era, would "reinforce[ ] stereotypical attitudes [toward pregnancy and women's biological nature] which threaten women's employment status in subtle but significant ways." *Guerra*, Brief of ACLU et al. at 18 and generally at 11–23. Justice Marshall, speaking for the Court, rejected this argument, noting that "unlike protective labor legislation prevalent earlier in this century, [the California statute] does not reflect archaic or stereotypical notions about pregnancy and the abilities of pregnant workers" because it covers only the "period of *actual physical disability*." *Guerra*, 479 U.S. at 290 (emphasis in original).

142. *Guerra*, 479 U.S. at 290. As an alternative ground for decision, Justice Marshall noted that, even if Title VII banned leave policies giving preferential treatment to pregnant workers, California employers could obey both Title VII and the California statute by offering leaves to all workers disabled for up to four months.

143. This is not to suggest that *Guerra* should be labeled an "affirmative action case." As discussed earlier, "affirmative" action is misleading. In his opinion, Justice Marshall did not refer to the California statute as a form of affirmative action. Instead, he stressed that the effect of the California policy was to equalize the situation of working women and men since, "by 'taking pregnancy into account,' California's pregnancy disability leave statute allows women, as well as men, to have families without losing their jobs." *Guerra*, 479 U.S. at 289. Cf. *Guerra*, 479 U.S. at 294 ("preferential treatment," per Stevens, J.).

144. For example, those hiring will no longer have unconscious expectations that members of the excluded minority group are uninterested in the position or not competent to hold it. In addition, the "old boy" hiring network should be operating to bring in members of the minority group once they are represented in the job in sufficient numbers.

145. See, e.g., Becker, "Barriers Facing Women."

5

How Is Law Male?
A Feminist Perspective on
Constitutional Interpretation

Judith A. Baer

This chapter applies to constitutional law some of the arguments developed in recent feminist critiques of conventional scholarship. I discuss a number of ways in which law can be said to have a male bias, and assess the validity of these assertions by examining various primary and secondary sources on constitutional adjudication. I argue that, while constitutional law is not male biased in its method, certain modes of interpretation reinforce the male dominance that has characterized this discipline. Finally, I suggest ways to recreate constitutional theory so that it can be part of a woman-centered jurisprudence.

We can fairly say of American constitutional law what a Jesuit scholar once said of Latin, one of its ancestor languages: For years, it was "spoken and written . . . with totally negligible exceptions only by males" (Ong, 1972, p. 615). The original Constitution and its most important amendments are documents written and ratified exclusively by males selected for this task by other males. Constitution applying, like constitution making, has been an enterprise conducted by males responsible to other males. Judges—"those who apply the law to particular cases" (*Marbury v. Madison*, 1803, p. 175)—have been male, as have the practitioners, scholars, and students who engage in this enterprise. Men have written the Constitution, enacted the laws in pursuance thereof, brought the cases challenging the laws, argued the cases, written the opinions that dispose of the cases, and criticized the opinions that settle the cases that challenge the laws that refer to the Constitution that men wrote.

The exceptions to the generalization are no longer negligible, including, as they do, roughly half the nation's law students, growing numbers of jurists and judges, and even a U.S. Supreme Court justice. However, an observation that Evelyn Fox Keller has made about medicine holds also for law and, indeed, for other disciplines: "It is understood how readily women, or any 'outsiders' for that matter, come to internalize the concerns and values of a world to which they aspire to belong" (1987, p. 234). Women who come to the enterprise of constitutional interpretation work within a male tradition. The "heavenly chorus" of jurisprudence has not only sung, to paraphrase E. E. Schattschneider, "with a strong upper-class accent" (1960, p. 35); it has sung on the bass clef. Law has been a male activity. It is now a male activity in which both men and women engage.

In this respect, law does not differ much from scholarship in general. The observations I have just made about law also hold for such disciplines as philosophy, history, psychology, and political science. They were all male preserves until recently. The women in these professions, like women in law, are participating in an activity developed, regulated, once monopolized, and still dominated by males. Perhaps the most important development is that in all these professions, including law, women are unmasking and challenging male biases and constructing women-centered scholarship.

One way in which the male history of these disciplines has been manifest is, not surprisingly, through overt sexism. Constitutional law has plenty of examples of this phenomenon, from Congress's failure to take demands for women suffrage seriously during Reconstruction through the patronizing protectionism of *Muller v. Oregon* to Justice Harry Blackmun's assertion that a teenage girl who had had sexual intercourse only after being repeatedly struck "appears not to have been an unwilling participant."[1] Beliefs like these—that men are superior to women, that sex differences make women unfit for full citizenship, or that violence against women does not force them to act against their will—have never been shared by all men; nor, for that matter, have all women rejected these male supremacist notions. But the male-dominated environment in which these ideas took root did not provoke serious challenges to these received truths.

Feminist legal scholars have devoted considerable time and energy to exposing this kind of blatant sexism (e.g., Baer, 1978; Kanowitz, 1969; Law, 1984; MacKinnon, 1987 and 1989; Murray and Eastwood, 1965; Rhode, 1990; Sachs and Wilson, 1979; Taub and Schneider, 1982). These efforts, and the continuing integration of women into the profession, have changed and are still changing law's ideology. There is still much male supremacist doctrine to expose, and new threats to gender equality arise all the time. Consider, for example, the current "fetal protection" movement (see *United Automobile Workers v. Johnson Controls*, 1991). But the tasks of feminist scholarship are not limited to identifying sexist opinions and doctrines.

A growing number of feminist jurists, like their counterparts in other disciplines, assert that the pervasive maleness of their field has shaped it in ways that go far beyond ideology. These authors hold that law, derived from predominantly male ways of knowing, thinking, and living, is intrinsically destructive of women's interests, wholly or in part, whether or not it is overtly sexist (e.g., Bartlett, 1990; "Feminist Discourse," 1985; Finley, 1986; MacKinnon, 1989; Scales, 1986; Schneider, 1986; West, 1988).

The purpose of this chapter is to inquire whether, how, and to what extent this masculine bias characterizes constitutional law. I have divided this inquiry into three parts. First, I ask whether constitutional interpretation can be described as an inherently male type of intellectual activity. Second, I examine the political context in which constitutional interpretation takes place to evaluate the gendered nature of that activity. Third, I examine the existing modes, methods, and techniques of interpretation to see whether they introduce male bias into the enterprise.

Constitutional Thinking . . .

Whatever else constitutional interpretation is, it is thought. It is reason—a facility often viewed as inherently masculine, so much so that some radical feminists distrust reason on the grounds that it is an instrument for female oppression, for patriarchy's "gang rape of minds as well as bodies" (Daly, 1973, p. 9; see also Griffin, 1978). The author of the following passage indicates, through her pronouns, that she does not accept this ascription of gender to the intellect. A thinker "engages in a discipline. That is, she asks certain questions rather than others; she establishes criteria for the truth, adequacy, and relevance of proposed answers; and she cares about the findings she makes and can act on" (Ruddick, 1983, p. 214). This description of thought comes from an essay about *maternal* thinking. Constitutional interpretation has something in common with an activity in which women have always engaged.

But certainly, constitutional thinking is a different *kind* of activity from maternal thinking. A logical starting point for explaining the activity that is constitutional interpretation is the fact that it is indisputably a type of legal reasoning. The scholarly literature contains numerous definitions and descriptions of legal reasoning: Among the best known characterizations are "the processes of analogy, discrimination, and deduction" (Holmes, 1897, p. 22), "reasoning by example" (Levi, 1949, p. 1), and a "blend of case facts, prior law, social background facts, and moral values" (Carter, 1988, p. 4).

What questions, criteria, and rules distinguish constitutional interpretation from other modes of intellectual activity? One way of illustrating this field's particular standards and distinctions is to examine an instance of doctrine in the making: *Cruzan v. Missouri*, the U.S. Supreme Court's first "right to die" case. The constitutional issue in this case was whether the parents of 32-year-old Nancy Cruzan, who had been in a "persistent vegetative state" for six years as the result of an automobile accident, had the right to decide to discontinue life-sustaining treatment for her.

Cruzan had been kept alive by tube feedings since an automobile accident in 1983. Before her accident, she had once told friends that she would not want to be kept alive in such a condition. But when Lester and Joyce Cruzan asked the hospital to stop feeding her, administrators refused to grant this request without court approval. A trial court agreed with the parents, but the Missouri Supreme Court reversed the ruling. The Cruzans obtained certiorari from the U.S. Supreme Court, which heard oral argument on December 6, 1989.

When Robert Presson, assistant attorney general of Missouri, was addressing the Court, Justice Blackmun asked,

"Have you ever seen a person in a persistent vegetative state?"
"I have seen Nancy Cruzan herself," Mr. Presson responded.
This was obviously not the answer that Mr. Blackmun expected.
"You have seen Nancy? Have you seen any others?" he asked. (*New York Times*, December 7, 1989, pp. A1, B26)

In June 1990, the Court ruled that the Fourteenth Amendment protects a person's right to refuse life-sustaining treatment when that person manifests this refusal through such means as a "living will," but upheld the state's power to require continuing treatment for Cruzan. The five-justice majority on the second point (a group that did not include Justice Blackmun) distanced themselves, implicitly or explicitly, from Nancy Cruzan. Chief Justice William H. Rehnquist's opinion for the Court said, "[T]he question is simply and starkly whether the United States Constitution prohibits Missouri from choosing the rule of decision which it did." Justice Sandra Day O'Connor's concurring opinion pointed out that *Cruzan* did not resolve this "difficult and sensitive problem. Today we decide only that one state's solution does not violate the Constitution." Justice Antonin Scalia showed slightly more awareness of the quandary: "The various opinions in this case portray quite clearly the difficult, indeed agonizing, questions. . . . What I have said above is not meant to suggest that I would think it desirable, if we were sure that Nancy Cruzan wanted to die, to keep her alive by the means at issue here. I assert only that the Constitution has nothing to say about the subject" (*Cruzan v. Missouri*, 1990, p. A18).

What is relevant? What the Constitution provides, what Missouri did, and the reliability of the evidence of Nancy Cruzan's intentions. What is irrelevant? Difficulty, sensitivity, agony, Nancy Cruzan's condition, and her parents' relationship with her. The Court majority took pains to separate its decision from the concrete situation that produced the case. This rejection of the emotional, the experiential, and the individual in favor of the rational, the detached, and the generalizable is a common feature of legal thinking.

This set of priorities—rational over emotional, abstract over concrete, general over particular—has also been described as a common feature of *male* thinking.[2] Many scholars who would not accept any rejection of reason as inherently antifemale have nevertheless posited gender differences, whether inherent or acquired, in ways of thinking. Carol Gilligan's important work *In a Different Voice* (1982) asserts that women's moral reasoning differs from men's in being more rooted in the context of concrete experience and relationships. A decade earlier, Philip Slater characterized "rationalism" as "the inability to perceive wholes," as one of the "disconnector virtues" practiced and prized by men. Slater contrasted this kind of "icy pathology" with the warmth, nurturance, and awareness of "humanity's embeddedness in a larger organic system" associated with women (1974, pp. 26, 33, 155; 1970, ch. 3).

Legal reasoning is inevitably a variety of moral reasoning. However conscientiously a judge strives to keep his or her own morality out of a decision, most statutes that judges must interpret reflect some moral standard. Similarities also exist between legal reasoning and scientific reasoning. Both legal and scientific inquiry represent efforts to impose order on material. The assumption that "a political world can be constructed and controlled with words" (Harris, 1982, p. 34) is analogous to Francis Bacon's model of scientific research as a quest for mastery over nature (Keller, 1987, pp. 242–46).

Like "mainstream" moral philosophy, "mainstream" philosophy of science has been attacked as male biased. Some philosophers of science posit the existence of gender differences in scientific reasoning. Evelyn Fox Keller's study of Nobel prizewinner Barbara McClintock, for instance, contrasts McClintock's emphasis on "letting the material speak to you" with the attempts of her mostly male peers to "impose an order" on the material in the Baconian model (1987, p. 243; 1983). The idea of a contrast between "abstract, deductive" male reasoning and "concrete, contextualized" female reasoning has become a staple of contemporary feminist epistemology (Bartlett, 1990, p. 832; Binion, 1989; Sherry, 1986). The logical step from this dichotomy to the idea that philosophy, science, and law are "male" disciplines, antithetical to female ways of thinking and knowing, is a short one.

The overwhelming historical realities—that these disciplines were founded, were monopolized for centuries, and continue to be dominated by men—lend credence to this conclusion. So does the powerful emotional resonance that works like Gilligan's and Keller's have had for female scholars. An additional attraction of this kind of theory lies in the fact that control, whether of the natural or the political world, can become something more threatening. The graphic "gang rape" metaphor trenchantly describes a feeling that most women will recognize from their own dealings with men, both in public and in private. Consider, for example, these bits of dialogue: "Name one time when I———," with the response then followed by, "That was a special situation; you cannot generalize from it"; or, "You're contradicting yourself if you demand *both* equality of opportunity *and* maternity leaves"; or, "I challenge you to find support for *Roe v. Wade*, in the text of the Constitution, the intent of the framers, or any constitutional doctrine. Go on, convince me." I am sure that some women, somewhere, have used this ploy. But suppose we encountered statements like these in a novel, as part of a lengthy passage in which the author expects the reader to know, without being told, which character is speaking. Would any reader have trouble guessing whether the speaker was male or female?

The technique is familiar: Reason enables "A" to set a trap for "B." Once B is trapped, A is free to discount B's demands, grievances, or opinions. But is it reason that oppresses, or power? Do we find this familiar technique of trap setting as oppressive when attempted by students, or on the frequent occasions when young children try it? Even when they set logical traps for us, they cannot make us change our behavior to accommodate their wishes.

The problem with reason when used by men against women in the above examples is twofold. First, the men have the power to refuse to change their behavior, whether the context is personal or public. Second, the men have preset the agenda; the concept of equality in the second example, and the constitutional doctrine in the third, result from the priorities that men have chosen in activities on which they have had a monopoly. It is the uses to which reasoning is put—not the reasoning itself—that is coercive.

Most feminist scholars refuse to equate reasoning with instrumental reasoning or with any particular technique thereof (Hawkesworth, 1989, p. 553; Jaggar, 1983, p. 115). One feminist analysis of legal reasoning asserts that it combines techniques in ways that undermine existing notions of a male/female dichotomy: "This process unfolds, not in a linear, sequential, or strictly logical manner, but rather in a pragmatic and interactive manner. Facts determine which rules are appropriate, and rules determine which facts are relevant" (Bartlett, 1990, p. 836).

Yet another powerful objection to a feminist rejection of philosophy, science, or law as male emerges if we recall an emotional, intuitive response at least as potent as that evoked by contemporary theories of gender difference: the intense attraction that these disciplines have had for unnumbered women over the centuries. To be sure, the life of the mind has appealed and been accessible to only a tiny minority of women, but that is also true of men. Women have pursued learning so passionately that they fought to get into universities and graduate schools and into the professions. Once there, women have delighted in their intellectual work—probably not in the first year of law school or during the Ph.D. qualifying examinations, but in approaching mastery of their disciplines.

The obstacles confronting these women have consisted not in the lack of fit between their minds and male-oriented scholarship, but in sexist prejudice and in conflicts between professional work and socially imposed domestic responsibilities. Yet, despite these barriers, women have produced philosophy, science, and jurisprudence every bit as good as that done by men. Men may think in ways that cut off women's demands, but thinking has been something that women do very well indeed.

And Constitutional Feeling

Analysis—that is, using one's reason in an effort to examine one's emotional response to radical feminist critiques of reason—suggests that any effort to characterize reason as nonfemale or emotion as nonmale is contradicted by the facts of everyday experience, in constitutional interpretation as elsewhere. Traditionally, female activities *do* include thinking, and traditional male activities *do* include feeling— whether or not these faculties are recognized as such in the contexts in which they appear.

Sara Ruddick's article "Maternal Thinking" (1983) demonstrates that reason is a tool women use to realize their goals in childcare and childrearing—activities so typically female that everyone knows what we mean when we label them "mothering." Asking questions, establishing criteria by which to assess answers, and acting on findings are intellectual—*not* emotional—activities. Maternal thinking does not drive out feeling; it is unlikely that excluding emotion in favor of thought is one of the "characteristic errors" (1983, p. 214) of the discipline in which the mother engages. The point is, rather, that this activity, commonly seen as an expression of warm nurturing "femininity," is also an intellectual activity. In mothering—of all places!—the dichotomy between thought and feeling does not hold.

Now, consider constitutional thinking. The separation between thought and feeling, theory and experience, doctrine and opinion, represented by *Cruzan* has often been a goal for constitutional interpreters. The same Justice Blackmun who seemed to be searching to combine the two halves into a whole during oral argument in that case has scrupulously separated them elsewhere. Dissenting in the 1972 death penalty case *Furman v. Georgia*, Blackmun explained why he voted to uphold capital punishment despite "my distaste, antipathy, and, indeed, abhorrence" for the practice. "Our task . . . is to pass upon the constitutionality of legislation that has been enacted and that is challenged. That is the sole task for judges. We should not allow our personal preferences as to the wisdom of legislative and congressional action, or our distaste for such action, to guide our judicial decisions in cases such as these" (pp. 405, 411).

If Blackmun had substituted "dictate" for "guide" in that last sentence, few readers would have any trouble agreeing with the statement. My criticism of *Cruzan*, for instance, was not meant to suggest that what the justices should have done was to arrange a trip to a Washington hospital, spend a day at the bedside of a patient in a condition similar to Nancy Cruzan's, and vote solely on the basis of the emotions that this experience evoked. But contact with such a patient might have guided and improved the judicial search through the texts for the relevant principles. Feelings serve a purpose, and, in most decision making, we ignore experience and emotion at our peril.

What is troubling about *Cruzan* is not the justices' refusal to lead with their feelings, but their apparent insistence on making a decision in isolation from feeling and experience. Abe Fortas's remark about his argument before the Supreme Court in *Gideon v. Wainwright* (1963) is apposite: "What I'd like to have said was, 'Let's not talk, let's go down and watch one of these fellows try to defend himself' " (Lewis, 1964, p. 120). If the integration of reason and emotion is essentially female, then women have much to bring to constitutional interpretation.

The difficulty with that statement is that calling for such an integration implies that emotion is not already there. This implication is false. More than a few examples exist of opinions that partake of the emotional, the individual, and the concrete. Justice William J. Brennan's dissent in *Cruzan*, for example, pointed out that "Nancy Cruzan has dwelt in that twilight zone for six years. She is oblivious to her surroundings and will remain so" (1990, p. A18). Or recall Felix Frankfurter's statement in *Rochin v. California:* "This is conduct that shocks the conscience" (1952, p. 172), compared with Hugo Black's and William Douglas's insistence on literal readings of the Fourth and Fifth Amendments. Between *Rochin* and *Cruzan* lie numerous examples of constitutional feeling, some of them not necessarily recognized as such by their authors.

One area in which judges often prefer to emote rather than to think is in cases concerning the family—especially the relationship of parents and children. The series of cases involving parental notification or consent before a minor's abortion contain examples of an idealized, uncritical view of family relationships. But an even clearer example comes from two 1979 cases upholding a parent's right to request that a minor child be committed to a state institution. One of the institutionalized children in *Parham v. J.R.* was a six-year-old boy whose mother and stepfather "were unable to control [him] to their satisfaction" (1979, p. 589). They got him admitted to a Georgia institution, and eventually relinquished custody of him. The plaintiffs in the companion case, *Secretary of Public Welfare v. Institutionalized Juveniles*, included children committed for such offenses as "making weird noises, refusing to do work, and talking back to teachers" (*Institutionalized Juveniles v. Secretary of Public Welfare*, 1978, p. 38).

Some detached, rational, typically "masculine" analysis of these facts would seem to require the thinker to question the relevance, at least, of conventional generalizations about parent–child relationships. But Chief Justice Warren Burger, writing for the majority, based his ruling on such traditional pieties as this: "[N]atural bonds of affection lead parents to act in the best interests of their children" (1979, p. 602). These opinions rest on an idealized concept of the family that does not seem to hold up in reality—especially when we remember that, in the commitment cases as well as in the abortion cases, the laws can only reach situations where the traditional bonds between parents and children have broken down. Opinions like *Parham* seriously weaken any claim that constitutional interpretation excludes emotional reaction in favor of reasoning. The ongoing presence of unquestioned emotional commitments in mainstream constitutional doctrine allows the feminist jurist to question any claim that feminist critiques of that doctrine are based on emotional reactions and are therefore invalid.

The discipline of constitutional interpretation does not maintain, in practice, a dichotomy between reason and emotion, between theory and experience, between the general and the individual. To reject reason as somehow "antifemale" would be to commit the same error that the familiar "male" opposite practice does: It assumes oppositions where none necessarily exist. The fact that, at least since Plato's *Republic*, people have constructed theories that organize the psyche in this oppositional way does not prove that the psyche so organizes itself, or that mental activity separates itself into these kinds of divisions. A feminist approach to constitutional law may perform the valuable service of discrediting those traditional dichotomies.

Constitutional Doing

Law is more than an academic discipline; it is also a manifestation of power. While "constitutional interpretation" can refer to abstract exegesis of portions of the text (see Peltason, 1988; Crosskey, 1953), the term more often means case adjudication or theorizing prompted by such adjudication. This kind of interpretation is a political activity, taking place in a political context that has its own rules, which are as important as the conventions of scholarship. A feminist approach to constitutional interpretation must deal with its political as well as its intellectual meaning.

Justice Scalia's conclusion in *Cruzan* that "the Constitution has nothing to say about the subject" arose not only from his reading of text and precedent, but also from his conviction that "the Federal courts have no business in this field" (1990, p. A18). Scalia was invoking a theme that runs through much of the literature on constitutional interpretation: the need for judicial self-restraint. The judge is admonished to forswear "a jurisprudence of idiosyncrasy" (Meese, 1985, p. 6) in favor of "self-conscious renunciation of power" (Bork, 1984, p. 11). Though these quotations come from judicial conservatives, the concern for judicial restraint has not been theirs alone. Jurists at all points on the ideological spectrum have insisted that judges do not constitute a "super-legislature" (*Griswold v. Connecticut*, 1965, p. 482), but must defer in ambiguous cases to public officials whose duty it is to enact and enforce law and who are elected by and directly accountable to the people (see Black, 1969; Hand, 1961).

Not all constitutionalists agree that "the counter-majoritarian difficulty" (Bickel, 1962, p. 16) requires judges to practice restraint; with equal plausibility, we can infer from the presence of a written constitution and of an appointed judiciary that majority rule is not the sole or primary organizing principle of American government (see Dworkin, 1977, ch. 5; Murphy et al., 1986, pp. 23–26). Nor has every jurist who preached self-restraint practiced it consistently (see, e.g., Hirsch, 1981, ch. 5; Murphy, 1982). But the important point is that deliberate refusal of power is one of the available rules that guide constitutional adjudication. The judge must hold back, must give others' desires priority over his or her own, must assume a secondary—if not a subordinate—role.[3]

This emphasis on "deference" and "renunciation of power" evokes demands that have been and continue to be made of women. The "feminine" role has historically involved a considerable amount of putting oneself second to others. Now, obviously, a judge is not going to act like a woman in a subordinate relationship to a man. But something is going on in this concept of the judicial role that is similar to certain influential concepts of women's roles. We can even think of other public and traditionally male roles in which this kind of self-subordination to the interests of others plays a part: lawyers in relation to their clients, for instance. And if the practice of judicial self-restraint is sometimes more apparent than real, that gap between appearance and reality hardly distinguishes the judicial from the feminine role.

Another aspect of the political context in which constitutional interpretation takes place is the need, at least for appellate judges, to convince other people of the validity of their position. Frankfurter's "shocks the conscience" language in *Rochin*, for example, may have been at least as much a product of his need to command a majority as of any shared judicial emotion. Studies of "judicial strategy" (Murphy, 1964), of particular roles (Danelski, 1960), and of specific instances of consensus building (e.g., Kluger, 1975, ch. 25; Ulmer, 1971), have shown that a classic description of presidential power (Neustadt, 1960, p. 32) applies as well to appellate judges: Theirs is "the power to persuade." This characterization may hold even more strongly for the judge than for the president, because judges have few, if any, ways to coerce their peers and must, therefore, rely on persuasion.

Analyses of judicial decision making that rely on biographical material rather than case votes suggest that successful persuasion appeals to a judge's feelings, to abstractions like collegiality, loyalty, or patriotism, or to a judge's ego and vanity, at least as often as it appeals to the intellect. We can appreciate this point by examining two classic examples of successful judicial persuasion: Felix Frankfurter's attempt to secure a unanimous vote in *Hirabayashi v. United States*, in 1943; and Earl Warren's similar accomplishment in the first *Brown v. Board of Education* case in the 1953–54 term.

The initial vote on *Hirabayashi* was 8:1 to uphold the curfew imposed by the military on all West Coast residents of Japanese dissent. Frankfurter's first effort to persuade the only dissenter invoked his colleague's "desire to do all that is humanly possible to maintain and enhance the *corporate* reputation of the Court." When this appeal to loyalty failed, Frankfurter adroitly touched the nerves of the justice's intellectual and social insecurities, appealing to his patriotism (in wartime). Frankfurter wrote a memorandum mentioning (but not specifying) the dissent's "internal contradictions," and characterized the dissent as an accusation that "everybody is out of step except Johnny," and that the majority was "playing into the hands of the enemy" (Murphy, 1964, pp. 46–47; emphasis in the original). The dissent became a concurrence.

Warren's quest for unanimity in *Brown* may have gotten some tacit help from Frankfurter; the published accounts contain no record of Frankfurter pressing an intellectual advantage in the way he often did or challenging Warren's implication in conference that a vote to uphold segregation was a vote for racism. Warren himself won some goodwill by personally delivering his draft opinion to a hospitalized justice.

With the final holdout, Warren appealed to unity and loyalty as Frankfurter had done a decade before: "You're all by yourself in this now. You've got to decide whether it's really the best thing for the country" (Kluger, 1975, pp. 683–99; Ulmer, 1971).

The behaviors that Frankfurter and Warren displayed—emotional appeals, personal favors, flattery, and knowing when to be quiet—involve social skills traditionally associated with conventional femininity. Just as Ruddick's analysis of maternal decision making (1983) showed that a "female" activity incorporates certain skills thought of as masculine, analysis of judicial decision making suggests that this "male" activity incorporates elements of feminine behavior. Dichotomies between masculine and feminine, rational and emotional, abstract and concrete, general and individual—which seem plausible in theory—tend to collapse when we begin examining practice.

If this kind of analysis were extended to other areas of human activity, we might discover that dichotomies like these do not describe reality in general, that most human activities combine "masculine" and "feminine" skills. At any rate, this analysis has challenged the notion that men have constructed law the way they have constructed many sports: as an activity whose practices and procedures reward male abilities. Men's historic monopoly on formalized constitutional interpretation has not turned the enterprise into something men can do better than women. But we have yet to discover whether and how this monopoly has turned constitutional doctrine into something hostile to women.

Constitutional Interpretation

Undergraduate constitutional law texts often include a section on what the authors variously label "modes of," "methods of," "techniques of," and "approaches to" constitutional interpretation (e.g., Mason and Stephenson, 1990, ch. 2; Murphy et al., 1986, ch. 2; Rossum and Tarr, 1987, ch. 1). These essays schematize and typologize the material differently, but they convey the shared message that there exists a variety of different ways to "do" constitutional interpretation, that the interpreter has several available sources to which to look for guides to adjudication. These guides include the constitutional text, the intent of the framers, precedent, existing constitutional doctrine, logic, and the effort to adapt constitutional purposes to changing conditions that has been labeled the "living Constitution" approach.[4]

None of these approaches is *necessarily* exclusive of any of the others. For example, the interpreter can combine a search for original meaning, a textual analysis of the relevant clause or clauses, and an effort to make interpretation responsive to change. The results of such syntheses have been called, inter alia, "purposive analysis," "teleological," "giving effect to fundamental values" (Murphy et al., 1986, pp. 297, 299), "identify[ing] the Constitution's ends or purposes" (Rossum and Tarr, 1987, p. 10), or "construing the document in terms of constitutional aspirations" (Barber, 1984, p. 35). But advocates of at least two familiar methods have argued that they should supplant all others. For Hugo Black (1969), textual analysis became a search for binding, absolute, literal meaning. More recently, the search for the "intent of the framers" became a call to "resurrect the original meaning of constitutional provisions and statutes as the only reliable guide for judgment" (Meese, 1985, p. 17). Some scholars who are not exclusively committed to one particular method do reject certain items on the list as illegitimate. Originalist jurisprudence has been countered by—and, to an extent, arose in response to—pleas to "let the framers sleep" (Perry, 1982, p. 75). My purpose here, however, is not to choose among modes of interpretation, but to analyze them from a feminist perspective.

"I am always amused," Alan Dershowitz has written, "by the fact that so many of those who so loudly proclaim a slavish obeisance to the narrow intent of the framers are so much like them in background" (1990, p. 12). Interpreters who look to original intent for guidance rather than for mandates must still be aware that reference to the sources of original meaning is, inevitably, reference to *male* words, *male* values, and *male* purposes. This male monopoly applies also to text, doctrine, and precedent. Women did not participate either in the drafting or in the adoption of the original Constitution; throughout most of American history, women were excluded from participation in amending the Constitution or applying it to cases. Any constitutional theorizing that women got to do—and there may have been more than we know about, as has been proven true for art and literature—did not survive for us. Therefore, several widely used modes of constitutional interpretation inevitably bias us in a male direction.

From a feminist perspective, the need for a "living Constitution" becomes imperative. Rather than producing "a formula for an end run around popular government" (Rehnquist, 1976, p. 706), efforts to adapt the text to the times become potential correctives for women's historic exclusion. But flexibility is not a sufficient condition for change. It can work as easily to reinforce male bias as to control it. And within a male-dominated enterprise, we can expect it to work this way. For feminists, the choice between modes of interpretation may be a Hobson's choice between the approaches that virtually ensure male bias and those that permit it.

Knowing what we know about the human mind, it is virtually impossible to believe that things would have been exactly the same if women had been equal partners from the beginning. Contemporary jurisprudence, epistemology, and feminist theory alike concede the impossibility of "unmediated truth" (Hawkesworth, 1989, p. 536), the inevitable connection between conclusion and what Benjamin Cardozo called the "stream of tendency, whether you call it philosophy or not, which gives coherence and direction to thought and action" (1921, p. 12; see also Baer, 1990a; Frank, 1949; Harding, 1986; Harding and O'Barr, 1987).

The search for neutral principles that has animated much constitutional doctrine (see Wechsler, 1961) does not render doctrine impartial. Experience demonstrates the truth of the observation that "neutral rules and procedures tend to drive underground the ideologies of the decisionmaker" (Bartlett, 1990, p. 862). Individuality affects decision making, however much single-method interpreters try to deny it; and individuality includes one's gender.

Since constitutional adjudication is a collegial enterprise, the impact of gender is collective as well as individual. This chapter began with a description of law as a language spoken by males. We need to appreciate the full import of that statement. Law has been spoken not only *by* males, but *to* them, and, usually, *about* them. This monopoly has been so extensive that a best-seller could describe the Supreme Court in the late 1970s as having "a men's-club atmosphere" (Woodward and Armstrong, 1979, p. 15). Constitutional history has been the history of men speaking to a male audience.

Constitutional interpretation is a discipline that offers ample opportunity to the creative individual mind. In fact, this freedom is what has troubled such diverse judges as Hugo Black and Robert Bork. What Roberto Unger wrote about a particularly relevant constitutional issue has general application: "The detailed structure of American equal protection doctrine cannot be derived from either the Constitution itself or all [its] general conceptions and commitments. No one who had mastered this intellectual structure together with the constitutional history of the United States and all relevant features of American

society and culture could have foreseen that equal protection doctrine
would have assumed its present form" (1986, p. 50).

So far, all this chapter has provided is an explanation of how doctrine
might have developed in male-biased ways. Will this theory stand up
in practice? A look at the "present form" that equal protection
doctrine has "assumed" is illustrative. Equal protection doctrine has
constructed the complex, cacophonous, even chaotic material of inequality as it is experienced in this country (or, if one prefers, has
distorted a simple reality) into the complex but more orderly concepts
of "discrimination" and "classification"—concepts that have subsets
like "suspect," "ordinary," "intermediate," "intentional," and so
forth. The legal concepts, in their turn, influence the ways in which we
perceive the reality, so that a black scholar may write of his children:
"They have been called names, have suffered slights and have experienced first hand the peculiar malevolence that racism brings out of
people. Yet they have never experienced racial discrimination"
(Steele, 1990, p. 46). Reality does not *demand* the making of these
distinctions; the vocabulary of legal doctrine has shaped the perception
even of nonlawyers like this father.

The same legal language, applied to sexual equality cases, also
affects women's sense of legitimate claims and distinctions. Application of these concepts to particular cases has resulted in some landmark judicial victories for women. But it has also led to results like the
following: Male-only draft registration is permissible, but veterans'
preference does not treat women unequally because it is not intentional
discrimination; women-only alimony is unconstitutional, but divorce
settlements that impoverish ex-wives are a constitutional nonissue; the
status of dragnet "fetal protection" policies that restrict women's
freedom is so unclear that legislatures just might give them a shot; and
the last Supreme Court equal protection case on sexual equality won
by a woman was decided in 1981.[5] All of these conclusions can be
made to make more or less sense within prevailing theory and practice.
But none of them was inevitable. Together, they tend to support rather
than to refute the following observation about the American legal
system: "No legal structure truly committed to equality for women
would end up with a scheme that offers extensive protection to the
right to bear arms or to sell violent pornography, but not to control
over our reproductive lives" (Rhode, 1990, p. 633).

The historic maleness of constitutional doctrine may help explain
why it is so difficult to construct plausible constitutional arguments to
support women's claims. The lack of fit between constitutional doc-

trine and freedom of choice, for example, may be due not to defects in the reasoning of *Roe v. Wade*, but to defects in the doctrine. The *apparent* contradiction between equal opportunity and maternity leaves may have similar roots. If women had been authoritative interpreters from the beginning, they might have constructed doctrine that included reproductive choice with no violence to history, theory, or logic (see Baer, 1990b). Or, women might not have needed to construct such a doctrine. After all, the law books are virtually barren of doctrine on the right to bear arms; this right exists because it was such a nonissue for so long that, once it became an issue, the people to whom this right mattered were strong enough to prevent the state from taking the right away.

Imagining what might have been is an exercise of limited value. We need to consider what could be: the possibilities for creating feminist constitutional doctrine, starting from where we are now. Is constitutional law inevitably male, or can women restructure it? A review of what this chapter has shown so far will help us to assess the potential of a woman-centered constitutional jurisprudence.[6]

Conclusion: Constitutional Recreating

What are women to law; and what is law, to women? Until recently, the only role women have played in large numbers is that of subject—the talked-about, the acted-upon, the dealt-with—by men talking to other men. Now, women are "doing law" as well as being "done-to" by it. Partly as a result of changes in the content of law, women are entering the profession of law in numbers approaching equality with men. Many of these women find law a hostile or indifferent habitat, a place where their needs and desires are ignored, trivialized, discounted, or brutalized, a country whose language is difficult for them to learn. An enterprise has begun in jurisprudence that is occurring as well in other disciplines: of "asking the woman question" (Bartlett, 1990), of evaluating the discipline's procedures, methods, and results from a feminist perspective.

A substantial body of feminist theory posits gender differences in knowing and reasoning that render virtually all male-constructed intellectual disciplines more difficult for women to practice. But even a brief analysis of the practice of constitutional interpretation suggests serious difficulties with this thesis as applied to law. Just as Sara Ruddick's analysis of maternal practice (1983) found that it incorporates abilities traditionally associated with men, my analysis of the theoretical and practical aspects of constitutional practice suggests that it incorporates capacities traditionally attributed to women. Law does not ask of women anything that they have not been doing elsewhere, while men, without necessarily realizing it, have been doing in law things that women are both expected to do and criticized for doing. Dichotomies between male and female skills have a way of disintegrating when we look at what people actually do.

The question of the existence of intellectual gender differences is far from settled. But analysis of actual practices suggests no reason to fear that constitutional interpretation is something women cannot do as well as men can. The content of existing theories of interpretation, however, does contain dangers for women; the different approaches urged on jurists either virtually ensure male-oriented results or invite them. A brief overview of the content of existing constitutional doctrine serves to vindicate this prediction. The doctrine allows some of men's claims to get constitutional status while some of women's equally important claims do not; there are also instances of women's interests *needing* protection when men's do not.

Unfortunately for the feminist jurist who would seek to change the doctrine, it also has a number of rules and conventions that are available to discredit such demands. A challenge to the rule that only deliberate discrimination can violate the equal protection clause approximates a demand for "result-oriented jurisprudence." The search for standards that would demand both equal employment rights and maternity leaves can be characterized as "inconsistent" and therefore "irrational." A jurisprudence that questions the exclusion of most divorce and child custody law from the scope of constitutional guarantees appears to question the principles of federalism and judicial restraint. A demand for recognition of the right to reproductive choice can be seen as substituting "asking the woman question" for "neutral principles." Any claim that cannot be rooted in prevailing doctrine can be rejected as substituting emotion for reason.

I submit that a feminist constitutional jurisprudence is free to reject these conceptual traps and to devise new approaches to constitutional reasoning. Conceding that the rules were not invented for the express purpose of frustrating claims to sexual equality, we can still raise the possibility that they serve that purpose. In Katharine Bartlett's words (1990), they "drive underground" ideologies. Since feminist ideology was not present to be driven underground when these rules were developed, feminists are justified in suspecting that they will frustrate women's claims.

This proposal is not so drastic as it may sound. I am not suggesting that feminists should declare constitutional rights by fiat. What I am suggesting is that feminists are justified in attempting to reason from preference to conclusion. How could such a process work? I have argued elsewhere that one way out of the doctrinal traps is to employ the mind's intuitive and imaginative faculties: to ask, for example, under what circumstances sexual equality could be compatible with the absence of a right to abortion (Baer, 1990b). Another possible approach for feminist constitutional scholars is to proceed from things we know as women that are not necessarily known to men, such as the ways in which society apportions the consequences of the absence of rights like reproductive choice. Other possible approaches have yet to be envisioned.

I am arguing for feminist jurists to give full creative license to the mind. The boundaries between reality and fantasy, between reason and emotion, between perceived and proven fact, are as conventional and artificial as the boundaries between neutral and result-oriented jurisprudence, between state and federal power, between consistency and inconsistency. Those rules served purposes that women had little if any part in articulating. A central task of feminist jurisprudence is a willingness to break the rules.

Notes

The author thanks the Henry M. Phillips Foundation and the American Council of Learned Societies for their financial support for this research.

1. Respectively, compare Flexner, 1970, ch. 10, with *Congressional Globe*, 1866; *Muller v. Oregon*, 1908, pp. 421–23; *Michael M v. Superior Court of Sonoma County*, 1981, p. 483.

2. The fact that Justice O'Connor joined the majority opinion does not defeat this argument. Although some feminist scholars (e.g., Sherry, 1986) have found a "feminine" orientation in her opinions, I reject any notion that the possibility of a feminist jurisprudence must stand or fall on doctrinal differences between the only woman ever to sit on the Supreme Court and her male peers. O'Connor is, after all, a product of the same legal training that they underwent.

3. It is not clear to what extent this rule applies to judges who are elected,

confirmed, or subject to removal by the voters, as most state judges are. So far, American theories of constitutional interpretation have taken the federal courts—all of whose judges are appointed with permanent tenure—as their reference point. These theories may be in need of serious revision if they are to apply to all appellate judges.

4. These typical conceptualizations do not present an exhaustive list of possible approaches. Modern texts do not recommend that a judge search for "natural law" principles, although the authors of the Fourteenth Amendment and the abolitionist leaders who had powerfully influenced several of them thought the Constitution incorporated such principles (see Baer, 1983, chs. 3, 4). Some approaches now on everyone's "list" would not necessarily always have been included; original intent, for instance, was not a common mode of interpretation in the nineteenth century.

5. The draft registration case is *Rostker v. Goldberg*, 1981; the veterans' preference case is *Personnel Administrator v. Feeney*, 1979; and the alimony case is *Orr v. Orr*, 1979. On divorce, see, e.g., Arendell, 1986; Weitzman, 1986. On fetal protection, see Dorris, 1989; Pollitt, 1990; *United Automobile Workers v. Johnson Controls*, 1991. The 1981 case is *Kirchberg v. Feenstra*. I have dealt with these issues at greater length elsewhere (Baer, 1989b).

6. In order to facilitate unfettered thought, I shall assume in the next section that constitutional interpreters are scholars, not judges. I am not concerned at this point with persuading majorities or with the limits of judicial power, but with constitutional doctrine as an abstract intellectual exercise. I have no expectations that any of my suggestions will be put into practice anytime soon; therefore, I have chosen not to restrict this analysis to what is realistic in the present political context.

Cases

Brown v. Board of Education, I. 1954. 347 U.S. 483.

Cruzan v. Missouri. 1990. 110 S.Ct. 2841. See transcript in *New York Times*, June 26, 1990, p. A18.

Furman v. Georgia. 1972. 408 U.S. 238.

Gideon v. Wainwright. 1963. 372 U.S. 335.

Griswold v. Connecticut. 1965. 381 U.S. 479.

Hirabayashi v. United States. 1943. 320 U.S. 81.

Institutionalized Juveniles v. Secretary of Public Welfare. 1978. 459 F. Supp. 30. E.D. Pennsylvania.

Kirchberg v. Feenstra. 1981. 450 U.S. 455.

Marbury v. Madison. 1803. 1 Cranch 137.

Michael M v. Superior Court of Sonoma County. 1981. 450 U.S. 464.

Muller v. Oregon. 1908. 208 U.S. 412.

Orr v. Orr. 1979. 440 U.S. 268.

Parham v. J.R. 1979. 442 U.S. 584.

Personnel Administrator v. Feeney. 1979. 442 U.S. 256.

Rochin v. California. 1952. 342 U.S. 165.

Roe v. Wade. 1973. 410 U.S. 113.

Rostker v. Goldberg. 1981. 453 U.S. 57.

Secretary of Public Welfare v. Institutionalized Juveniles. 1979. 442 U.S. 640.

United Automobile Workers v. Johnson Controls, Inc. 1991. 111 S.Ct. 1196.

References

Arendell, Terry. 1986. *Mothers and Divorce*. Berkeley: University of California Press.

Baer, Judith A. 1978. *The Chains of Protection*. Westport, CT: Greenwood Press.

———. 1983. *Equality under the Constitution*. Ithaca, NY: Cornell University Press.

———. 1989a. "The Fruitless Search for Original Intent." In Michael W. McCann and Gerald L. Houseman, eds., *Judging the Constitution*. New York: Little, Brown. Pp. 49–71.

———. 1989b. "The Limits of Constitutional Doctrine in Women's Rights." Prepared for delivery at the 1989 interim meeting of the International Political Science Association Committee on Comparative Judicial Research, Lund University, Sweden, August 21–23.

———. 1990a. "Reading the Fourteenth Amendment: The Inevitability of Noninterpretivism." In National Center for the Public Interest, *Politics and the Constitution: The Nature and Extent of Interpretation*. Washington, DC: American Studies Center. Pp. 69–82.

———. 1990b. "What We Know as Women: A New Look at *Roe v. Wade*." *NWSA Journal*, 2 (Fall): 558–82.

Barber, Sotirios A. 1984. *On What the Constitution Means*. Baltimore: Johns Hopkins University Press.

Bartlett, Katharine T. 1990. "Feminist Legal Methods." *Harvard Law Review*, 103 (February): 829–88.

Bickel, Alexander M. 1962. *The Least Dangerous Branch*. Indianapolis: Bobbs-Merrill.

Binion, Gayle. 1989. "Feminism and Law: Toward an Integration of Theory and Experience.'' Prepared for delivery at the 1989 interim meeting of the International Political Science Association Committee on Comparative Judicial Research, Lund University, Sweden, August 21–23.

Black, Hugo L. 1969. *A Constitutional Faith.* New York: Alfred A. Knopf.

Bork, Robert H. 1984. *Tradition and Morality in Constitutional Law.* Washington, DC: American Enterprise Institute.

Brennan, William J., Jr. 1985. ''The Constitution of the United States: Contemporary Ratification.'' Delivered at Text and Teaching Symposium, Georgetown University, Washington, DC, October 12.

Cardozo, Benjamin N. 1921. *The Nature of the Judicial Process.* New Haven, CT: Yale University Press.

Carter, Lief. 1988. *Reason in Law.* Third edition. Glenview, IL: Scott, Foresman.

Congressional Globe, 1866.

Crosskey, William W. 1953 (1978). *Politics and the Constitution in the History of the United States.* Chicago: University of Chicago Press.

Daly, Mary. 1973. *Beyond God the Father.* Boston: Beacon Press.

Danelski, David J. 1960 (1986). ''The Influence of the Chief Justice in the Decisional Process.'' In Walter F. Murphy and C. Herman Pritchett, eds., *Courts, Judges, and Politics.* Fourth edition. New York: Random House. Pp. 568–77.

Dershowitz, Alan M. 1990. ''The Sovereignty of Process: The Limits of Original Intention.'' In National Center for the Public Interest, *Politics and the Constitution: The Nature and Extent of Interpretation.* Washington, DC: American Studies Center. Pp. 11–16.

Dorris, Michael. 1989. *The Broken Cord.* New York: Harper & Row.

Dworkin, Ronald. 1977. *Taking Rights Seriously.* Cambridge, MA: Harvard University Press.

''Feminist Discourse, Moral Values, and the Law—A Conversation.'' 1985. *Buffalo Law Review,* 34 (Fall): 11–87.

Finley, Lucinda. 1986. ''Transcending Equality Theory: A Way out of the Maternity and the Workplace Debate.'' *Columbia Law Review,* 86 (October): 1118–82.

Flexner, Eleanor. 1970. *Century of Struggle.* Revised edition. Cambridge, MA: Belknap Press of Harvard University.

Frank, Jerome. 1949. *Courts on Trial.* Princeton, NJ: Princeton University Press.

Gilligan, Carol. 1982. *In a Different Voice.* Cambridge, MA: Harvard University Press.

Griffin, Susan. 1978. *Woman and Nature: The Roaring inside Her.* New York: Harper & Row.

Hand, Learned. 1961 (1974). *The Bill of Rights.* New York: Atheneum.

Harding, Sandra. 1986. *The Science Question in Feminism.* Ithaca, NY: Cornell University Press.

Harding, Sandra, and Jean F. O'Barr, eds. 1987. *Sex and Scientific Inquiry.* Chicago: University of Chicago Press.

Harris, William F. II. 1982. "Bonding Word and Polity: The Logic of American Constitutionalism." *American Political Science Review*, 76 (March): 34–45.

Hawkesworth, Mary E. 1989. "Knowers, Knowing, Known: Feminist Theory and Claims of Truth." *Signs*, 14 (Spring): 533–57.

Hirsch, H. N. 1981. *The Enigma of Felix Frankfurter.* New York: Basic Books.

Holmes, Oliver Wendell. 1897 (1986). "The Path of the Law." In Walter F. Murphy and C. Herman Pritchett, eds., *Courts, Judges, and Politics.* Fourth edition. New York: Random House. Pp. 20–24.

Jaggar, Alison M. 1983. *Feminist Politics and Human Nature.* Totowa, NJ: Rowman & Allanheld.

Kanowitz, Leo. 1969. *Women and the Law: The Unfinished Revolution.* Revised edition. Albuquerque: University of New Mexico Press.

Keller, Evelyn Fox. 1983. *A Feeling for the Organism: The Life and Work of Barbara McClintock.* San Francisco: W. H. Freeman.

———. 1987. "Feminism and Science." In Sandra Harding and Jean F. O'Barr, eds., *Sex and Scientific Inquiry.* Chicago: University of Chicago Press. Pp. 232–46.

Kluger, Richard. 1975. *Simple Justice.* New York: Vintage Books.

Law, Sylvia A. 1984. "Rethinking Sex and the Constitution." *University of Pennsylvania Law Review*, 132 (June): 955–1040.

Levi, Edward H. 1949. *An Introduction to Legal Reasoning.* Chicago: University of Chicago Press.

Lewis, Anthony. 1964. *Gideon's Trumpet.* New York: Vintage Books.

MacKinnon, Catharine A. 1987. *Feminism Unmodified.* Cambridge, MA: Harvard University Press.

———. 1989. *Toward a Feminist Theory of the State.* Cambridge, MA: Harvard University Press.

Mason, Alpheus Thomas, and Donald Grier Stephenson, Jr. 1990. *American Constitutional Law.* Ninth edition. Englewood Cliffs, NJ: Prentice-Hall.

Meese, Edwin III. 1985. "Toward a Jurisprudence of Original Intention." Address to the American Bar Association, Chicago, July 9.

Murphy, Bruce Allen. 1982. *The Brandeis–Frankfurter Connection*. New York: Oxford University Press.

Murphy, Walter F. 1964. *Elements of Judicial Strategy*. Chicago: University of Chicago Press.

Murphy, Walter F., James E. Fleming, and William F. Harris II. 1986. *American Constitutional Interpretation*. Mineola, NY: Foundation Press.

Murray, Pauli, and Mary Eastwood. 1965. "Jane Crow and the Law; Sex Discrimination and Title VII." *George Washington Law Review*, 34 (December): 232–56.

Neustadt, Richard E. 1960. *Presidential Power*. New York: John Wiley.

Ong, Walter. 1972. "Review of Brian Vickers's *Classical Rhetoric in English Poetry*." *College English*, 33 (February): 612–16.

Peltason, Jack W. 1988. *Corwin and Peltason's "Understanding the Constitution."* Eleventh edition. New York: Holt, Rinehart & Winston.

Perry, Michael. 1982. *The Constitution, the Courts, and Human Rights*. New Haven, CT: Yale University Press.

Pollitt, Katha. 1990. " 'Fetal Rights': A New Assault on Feminism." *Nation*, 250 (March 26): 409–18.

Rehnquist, William H. 1976. "The Notion of a Living Constitution." *Texas Law Review*, 54 (May): 693–706.

Rhode, Deborah L. 1989. "Equal Protection and Gender Justice." In Michael W. McCann and Gerald L. Houseman, eds., *Judging the Constitution*. New York: Little, Brown. Pp. 265–86.

———. 1990. "Feminist Critical Theories." *Stanford Law Review*, 42 (February): 617–38.

Rossum, Ralph A., and G. Alan Tarr. 1987. *American Constitutional Law*. Second edition. New York: St. Martin's Press.

Ruddick, Sara. 1983. "Maternal Thinking." In Joyce Trebilcot, ed., *Mothering: Essays in Feminist Theory*. Totowa, NJ: Rowman & Allanheld.

Sachs, Albie, and Joan Hoff Wilson. 1979. *Sexism and the Law*. New York: Free Press.

Scales, Ann M. 1986. "The Emergence of Feminist Jurisprudence: An Essay." *Yale Law Journal*, 95 (June): 1373–1403.

Schattschneider, E. E. 1960. *The Semisovereign People*. New York: Holt, Rinehart & Winston.

Schneider, Elizabeth. 1986. "The Dialectic of Rights and Liberties: Perspectives from the Women's Movement." *New York University Law Review*, 61 (October): 589–652.

Sherry, Suzanna. 1986. "Civic Virtue and the Feminine Voice in Constitutional Adjudication." *Virginia Law Review*, 72 (April): 543–616.

Slater, Philip. 1970. *The Pursuit of Loneliness*. Boston: Beacon Press.

——. 1974. *Earthwalk*. New York: Anchor Books.

Steele, Shelby. 1990. "A Negative Vote on Affirmative Action." *New York Times*, May 13: 46–49, 73–75.

Taub, Nadine, and Elizabeth M. Schneider. 1982. "Perspectives on Women's Subordination and the Role of Law." In David Kairys, ed., *The Politics of Law*. New York: Pantheon. Pp. 117–39.

Ulmer, S. Sidney. 1971. "Earl Warren and the *Brown* Decision." *Journal of Politics*, 33 (August): 689–702.

Unger, Roberto Mangabeira. 1986. *The Critical Legal Studies Movement*. Cambridge, MA: Harvard University Press.

Wechsler, Herbert. 1961. *Principles, Politics, and Fundamental Law*. Cambridge, MA: Harvard University Press.

Weitzman, Lenore. 1986. *The Divorce Revolution*. New York: Free Press.

West, Robin. 1988. "Jurisprudence and Gender." *University of Chicago Law Review*, 55 (Winter): 1–72.

Woodward, Bob, and Scott Armstrong. 1979. *The Brethren*. New York: Simon & Schuster.

6

Interpreting Abortion

Mark A. Graber

In *Feminism Unmodified*, Catharine MacKinnon declares that abortion law has "largely not been discussed in the terms I will use" (1987, p. 94). The standard understanding of abortion as a privacy right, she argues, reifies male ideology. In her view, feminists must "recast the abortion issue toward a new legal approach and political strategy: sex equality" (p. 250 n. 21). Elsewhere, MacKinnon (1989, p. 189) rejects as "gender neutral" liberal feminist claims that women need the right to control their reproductive activities so they may participate as equals in public life. When radical feminists speak of abortion rights as necessary for sex equality, she asserts, they recognize the rapelike quality of much sexual intercourse in a society whose "women are gendered and unequal" (pp. 185–86).

MacKinnon's writings are only the most recent of many efforts to rewrite *Roe v. Wade*.[1] Donald Regan, for example, previously suggested that "the most promising argument in support of the result of *Roe* has not yet been made" (1979, p. 1569). "Abortion," he claimed, presents "a problem in what we might call 'the law of samaritanism,' that is, the law concerning obligations imposed on certain individuals to give aid to others" (ibid.). Indeed, similar efforts to reconceptualize social practices other than abortion characterize much contemporary academic law. The seminal work of postwar American jurisprudence, Herbert Wechsler's "Neutral Principles of Constitutional Law" (1959, pp. 33–34), maintained that school segregation policies should be understood as raising freedom of association issues rather than equal protection issues.

These efforts to offer new understandings of abortion and other issues raise questions that legal scholarship rarely explores. Most works on constitutional theory offer interpretive strategies designed to elucidate the meaning of various constitutional provisions. Typical analyses of *Roe v. Wade* conclude that, properly interpreted, the Fourteenth Amendment does or does not protect abortion rights. MacKinnon, Regan, and Wechsler, by comparison, are interpreting a social practice. The former two scholars conclude that, properly interpreted, abortion is a Fourteenth Amendment right. Their interpretive activities focus on the texts, history, and values underlying public policies restricting abortion rather than on the text, history, and values underlying the equal protection clause. MacKinnon and Regan do interpret the Fourteenth Amendment. Such traditional exercises of constitutional theorizing, however, do not exhaust their arguments. These scholars seek to convince their readers both that the equal protection clause forbids certain kinds of state action and that restrictions on abortion are one kind of state action forbidden by the equal protection clause.

Although MacKinnon, Regan, Wechsler, and other legal scholars frequently advance new conceptions of social practices under constitutional attack, few works explicitly state or discuss the interpretive principles that should govern this activity. Contemporary constitutional theorists generally spend their energies debating the constitutional standards by which social practices should be judged and do not consider the constitutional standards by which social practices should be interpreted. Every assertion that a given social practice is or is not constitutional, however, requires some interpretation of that practice. For example, whether persons have a constitutional right to burn the flag depends on how flag burning and any restrictions on that activity are understood. *Texas v. Johnson*[2] might not have raised First Amendment issues if persons routinely interpreted flag burning as an attempt to release dangerous carcinogens (only present in flags) into the atmosphere, and any statutory bans on that practice as environmental protection measures.[3] Similarly, scholars cannot consider whether restrictions on abortion are constitutional until they have a theory about what abortion restrictions are.

This chapter is a preliminary effort to develop constitutional standards for interpreting social practices.[4] Rather than explore whether particular constitutional provisions should be interpreted as recognizing or granting women the right to terminate their pregnancies, my analysis examines how restrictions on abortion should be constitutionally interpreted. The first section below discusses how most academic lawyers interpret abortion. Law professors, I argue, consistently adopt apolitical perspectives when analyzing *Roe v. Wade*. Legal scholars interested in demonstrating timeless constitutional truths rarely consider information about contemporary political events when interpreting contemporary reproductive policies.[5] The second section interprets restrictions on abortion from a political perspective and suggests that the ways such policies have actually been implemented, justified, and politically maintained in the late twentieth century raise constitutional issues that are too often overlooked in legal writing. The third section below discusses the constitutional standards that should govern the interpretation of abortion (or any other social practice). Although apolitical perspectives are valuable for determining national identity and aspirations, constitutional values will be best promoted if persons charged with remedying constitutional violations place greater emphasis on the theoretical implications of the actual political events that give rise to constitutional controversies. The chapter concludes by suggesting that equal choice arguments based on actual late-twentieth-century abortion policies may provide better legal, political, and constitutional grounds for supporting the result in *Roe* than are provided by more abstract pro-choice arguments.[6]

The analysis below assumes that the proper interpretation of abortion is as much a question of constitutional theory as is the proper interpretation of the Fourteenth Amendment. Thus, scholars need not develop extraconstitutional standards for interpreting a social practice before considering whether that social practice is constitutional. The constitutional problems inherent in interpreting abortion, however, cannot be resolved through methodologies developed for interpreting various provisions of the constitutional text (however that text may be defined).[7] Rather, as the third section below argues, efforts to develop standards for interpreting abortion require understandings of what the constitution is, why it should be interpreted, and who should do the interpreting.

Apolitical Interpretations of Abortion

The contemporary legal academy seemingly offers a dizzying array of perspectives on American public life. Liberals, republicans, feminists, conservatives, critical legal theorists, critical race theorists, literary theorists, and economic theorists are all well represented, if not in the law professorate at large, then at least in the most prominent law reviews. There has recently been a groundswell of additional "new voices" in legal scholarship, each purporting to advance distinct and

valuable interpretations of various social and political practices in the
United States (see e.g., Delgado 1990; Matsuda 1988; Menkel-Meadow
1987).

Nevertheless, there is a surprising degree of consensus among the
disparate voices of the legal academy. Contemporary academic lawyers typically interpret social practices apolitically. Just as the dominant practitioners of recent ethical and political theory exhibit little
interest in actual political events and circumstances (I. Shapiro 1989,
1990), so law professors—even those who profess to believe that law is
politics—generally ignore empirical facts about the actual implementation, justification, or political maintenance of public policies.[8] Owen
Fiss (1982, p. 754) suggests that judges (and constitutional commentators) should imagine themselves as under a veil of ignorance—a philosophical construct developed by John Rawls (1971, pp. 136–42) to
prevent hypothetical founders from being aware of the particular
conditions of the society they will form. Although other legal scholars
are not so explicit, rarely do legal analyses consider those contingencies of political life that Rawls would exclude from the original position.

This apolitical perspective structures the way that virtually all contemporary legal scholars interpret the law, values, and politics of
American public policies. First, academic lawyers emphasize the constitutionality of law on the books, rather than law in action.[9] Law, in
recent constitutional theory, is what legal texts say state officials will
do about disputes—not what they actually do. Second, academic
lawyers normally discuss the constitutional status of any values they
believe should be considered when determining whether a particular
social practice is just, and not only those values that actually were
considered in debates over the establishment and maintenance of that
practice. Legal scholars place no special weight on the reasons that
motivate political activists to support or oppose various public policies.
Third, academic lawyers rely on the above understandings of the law
and values when determining the constitutional adequacy of the political process that enacted the legislation under constitutional attack.
The nature of the political forces that support a social practice, in their
works, can be derived from the content of the law on the books and
the philosophical justification of those laws.

This apolitical manner of interpreting public policy contributes to
the timeless quality of much constitutional debate. Oblivious to the
contingencies of their era, scholars write as if their arguments were
sufficient to resolve the constitutionality of any instance of a particular

social practice. For example, constitutional commentators typically discuss the constitutionality of any flag-burning restriction rather than the constitutionality of flag-burning restrictions as that policy exists in late-twentieth-century politics. Thus, constitutional theorists assume that, if a particular statute is presently unconstitutional, then that statute must always have been unconstitutional and, barring constitutional amendment,[10] always will be unconstitutional. The constitutionality of a given practice, to the legal mind, is relatively unaffected by any change in its underlying politics.[11]

John Hart Ely's and Catharine MacKinnon's critiques of *Roe v. Wade* illustrate the pervasiveness and perversities of these interpretive practices. Ely and MacKinnon articulate fundamentally different visions of both the constitution[12] and abortion. Ely, a leading proponent of democratic process models of the constitution and judicial function (see Ely 1980), considers abortion to be a practice that favors the liberty interests of pregnant women over the life interests of fetuses. MacKinnon, a prominent radical feminist (see MacKinnon 1987, 1989), regards abortion as a practice that exacerbates the evils of forced sex in a society that structurally discriminates against women. Each commentator, however, relies on a remarkably similar apolitical approach to abortion rights and restrictions in order to reach these distinct understandings of that social practice. In particular, neither Ely nor MacKinnon think that the constitutional status or interpretation of abortion is significantly influenced by facts about how restrictions on abortion have been implemented, justified, or politically maintained in contemporary American politics.

John Hart Ely's scathing attack on *Roe v. Wade*, published the year that decision was handed down, established the general framework within which most legal scholars analyze the holding of that case. In "The Wages of Crying Wolf" (1973), Ely maintains there is no legitimate line of legal argument that can justify the Supreme Court's declaration that most state restrictions on abortion are unconstitutional. "What is frightening about *Roe*," he asserts, is that the right to an abortion "is not inferable from the language of the Constitution, the framers' thinking respecting the specific problem in issue, any general value derivable from the provisions they included, or the nation's governmental structure. Nor is it explainable in terms of the unusual political impotence of the group judicially protected vis-à-vis the interest that legislatively prevailed over it" (pp. 935–36). For these reasons, Ely concludes that *Roe* "is bad because it is bad constitutional law, or rather because it is not constitutional law and gives almost no sense of trying to be" (p. 947).

Ely's assertion that the constitution does not protect abortion rights is based on a clear, albeit tacit, apolitical interpretation of abortion. The relevant law of abortion (or any other subject), Ely indicates, can be found in legislative enactments and judicial decisions. His essay treats abortion as normally illegal before 1973 because most states had statutes that made abortion a criminal offense (except in certain narrowly defined circumstances), and as legal afterward (except in certain narrowly defined circumstances) because the *Roe* plurality held that abortion restrictions interfere with the exercise of constitutional rights. More generally, he notes that there are "laws prohibiting the use of 'soft' drugs" because a social consensus exists that has been sufficient "to get [these] laws passed and keep them on the books" (Ely 1973, p. 923). In a similar vein, what Ely finds "most troubling" about abortion restrictions is the "disparity among state laws regulating abortion" that enabled persons who could afford the expense to travel to other states to terminate their pregnancies (p. 936 n. 94). Those states with more liberal statutory policies respecting abortion, he thinks, must also have been those states in which persons could most easily procure abortions (ibid.). Ely does admit that "a law that has been neither legislatively considered nor enforced for decades" might present a more problematic case (p. 935 n. 89); but as long as state statutes and judicial decisions have had some effect on abortion practices, he regards them as the sole sources of abortion law (ibid.).

Ely looks to moral philosophy for the relevant values or interests that judges (and commentators) should consider when determining whether abortion restrictions are constitutional. He begins his analysis by noting that "the moral issue" posed by efforts to balance the interests of the fetus and mother "is as fiendish as any philosopher's hypothetical" (Ely 1973, p. 927). Because these are the ethical values at stake in abortion debate, Ely maintains that the possible constitutional values at stake are also the liberty rights of women and the life rights of embryos. Ely does insist that courts should not resolve controversies the way a moral philosopher would.[13] Rather, he proclaims that judges should determine the constitutional weight of the various arguments that philosophers use to support or oppose restrictions on abortion. If the constitution gives special protection to values that support abortion rights and does not give similarly strong protection to values that support restrictive policies, then women have a constitutional right to terminate their pregnancies. States can freely regulate abortion, however, if the constitution gives equal weight to values that might be raised by either side of the abortion debate. Ely concludes that *Roe v. Wade* was wrongly decided because the constitution does not protect either the liberty interest of the woman or the life interest of the fetus. The majority's opinions, he declares, failed to associate "either side of the balance with a value inferable from the Constitution" (p. 933).

This understanding of abortion law and debate provides the foundation for Ely's claim that the abortion restrictions struck down in *Roe* were established and maintained in accordance with the democratic principles found in the constitution. The very existence of law on the books, Ely assumes, demonstrates that restrictions on abortion satisfy the constitutional requirement that majorities generally rule. Restrictions on abortion exist, he states, because "there exists a societal consensus that the behavior involved is . . . immoral" (Ely 1973, pp. 923–24). This "consensus," he admits, "is not universal but it is sufficient, and this is what is counted crucial to get the laws passed and keep them on the books" (ibid.). Ely recognizes that a majority of citizens may not favor abortion restrictions. Coalition politics, however, are not unconstitutional. "There is nothing unusual, and I was not aware there was anything wrong," Ely argues, "with an intense minority's compromising on issues about which it feels less strongly in order to gain support on those it cares most passionately about" (p. 935 n. 89).

Ely confesses that abortion policies may be unconstitutional if local legislatures refuse to treat with respect the concerns of those groups that advocate abortion rights. The Supreme Court, he argues, should strike down legislative restrictions on abortion if the values supporting abortion rights did not "receive adequate consideration in the political process" because they primarily advanced "the interests of 'discrete and insular minorities' unable to form effective political alliances" (Ely 1973, p. 933).[14] On the basis of his examination of the philosophical arguments for and against abortion, however, Ely concludes there is nothing prejudicial about the political forces that support the passage and maintenance of the statutes struck down in *Roe*. Judicial second-guessing of legislative balances, he maintains, should "be reserved for those interests which, as compared with the interests to which they have been subordinated, constitute minorities unusually incapable of protecting themselves." This is not the case with restrictions on abortion because such policies favor the interests of fetuses over those of women. Although Ely notes that, when "compared with men, women may constitute such a 'minority,' " he observes that "compared with the unborn, they do not" (pp. 934–35).

Ely assumes that restrictions on abortion pit men (as protectors of fetuses) against women because he believes that philosophical analysis of abortion demonstrates a conflict between the interests of women and the interests of fetuses. In other words, his work tacitly deduces facts about the politics of abortion from an analysis of the morality of abortion. Ely never thinks to examine actual political behavior to test the validity of this claim. Indeed, at no point in his analysis does Ely consider the interpretation or constitutionality of restrictions on abortion to be influenced by the way in which abortion laws actually function, the actual arguments persons make in favor of or against different abortion policies, or the actual nature of abortion politics.

Many scholars subsequently challenged Ely's interpretation of the Fourteenth Amendment. Some proponents of abortion rights assert that a constitutional right of privacy exists that encompasses a woman's decision whether to bring a fetus to term (see, e.g., Heymann and Barzelay 1973). Others, following a line of argument first developed by the moral philosopher Judith Jarvis Thomson (1971), assert that all persons have a right not to have their body inhabited by an unwanted, albeit innocent, invader (see Regan 1979; West 1988, pp. 59–60, 66). These "liberal" defenses or rewritings of *Roe*, however, do not challenge Ely's interpretation of abortion. Rather, virtually every contemporary defense of constitutional abortion rights seeks to prove that restrictions on abortion necessarily violate the constitution. Because all instances of abortion necessarily involve decisions whether to bring a fetus to term or whether one's body will be occupied by an unwanted entity, such arguments permit legal commentators to debate the constitutionality of abortion while remaining legally oblivious to the politics of abortion.[15] Indeed, because law professors treat as constitutionally irrelevant the actual political arguments that are used to attack or defend abortion restrictions, they find nothing peculiar about demands that the Supreme Court uphold or strike down a variety of state statutes on the basis of assertions only made in one law review article, a legal brief, or in the justices' chambers.

Catharine MacKinnon's defense of abortion rights superficially appears to be an exception to the apolitical character of mainstream constitutional theory. MacKinnon insists that her "feminist jurisprudence . . . is accountable to women's concrete conditions and to changing them" (1989, p. 249). Her works, she claims, are about "what is, the meaning of what is, and the way what is, is enforced"

(p. xii). MacKinnon's attack on the doctrinal basis of *Roe v. Wade* is grounded in what she believes was that decision's disregard of actual social circumstances. "Abstract privacy," she declares, "protects abstract autonomy, without inquiring into whose freedom of action is being sanctioned, at whose expense" (p. 193). In her view, abortion law can be meaningfully analyzed only when scholars "talk about sex, specifically about intercourse in relation to rape in relation to conception" (ibid.). "Abortion policy," MacKinnon concludes, must be "explicitly approached in the context of how women get pregnant; that is, as a consequence of intercourse under conditions of gender inequality" (1984, pp. 47–48).

Attention to the concrete realities women face, MacKinnon asserts, reveals that abortion is "an issue of forced sex." She maintains that "feminist investigations" indicate that "sexual intercourse . . . cannot simply be presumed coequally determined" (MacKinnon 1984, pp. 46–48). Contrary to popular beliefs, "men control sexuality," and contemporary debate over abortion rights merely "frames the ways men arrange among themselves to control the reproductive consequences of intercourse" (MacKinnon 1989, p. 188). In support of this assertion, MacKinnon emphasizes sociological studies demonstrating that many women do not consistently use contraception, even though they have both the financial resources and knowledge necessary to practice effective birth control (see, e.g., Luker 1975, esp. p. 23). "I wonder," she states,

if a woman can be presumed to control access to her sexuality if she feels unable to interrupt intercourse to insert a diaphragm; or worse, cannot even want to, aware that she risks a pregnancy she knows she does not want. Do you think she would stop the man for any other reason, such as, for instance, the real taboo—lack of desire? If not, how is sex, hence its consequences, meaningfully voluntary for women? . . . Sex doesn't look a whole lot like freedom when it appears normatively less costly for women to risk an undesired, often painful, traumatic, dangerous, sometimes illegal, and potentially life-threatening procedure, than it is to protect oneself in advance. (MacKinnon 1984, p. 47)

MacKinnon emphasizes that this failure to use contraception is not simply one consequence of social taboos about intercourse that have resulted in "women's repressive socialization to passivity or coolness" (1989, p. 188). Liberal, Freudian interpretations of abortion rights as freeing women to have "sex with men on the same terms as promised to men—that is 'without consequences,' " she argues, merely free "male sexual aggression" by removing "the one remaining legitimizing reason that women have had for refusing sex besides the headache" (MacKinnon 1984, p. 50). Feminists, MacKinnon concludes, must "rethink[] the problems of sexuality, from the repression of drives by civilization to the oppression of women by men" (p. 51).

Although she condemns the abstractions of "liberal" theory, MacKinnon tacitly adopts the same political understandings of abortion law, debate, and politics that characterize mainstream legal scholarship. Abortion law, in MacKinnon's writings, is law on the books. Her analysis focuses entirely on the texts of state statutes and the decisions handed down by the Supreme Court (MacKinnon 1989, pp. 186–87). The law prevents poor women from having abortions, she declares, because in *Harris v. McRae*[16] the Supreme Court upheld a federal statute barring the use of federal funds for that purpose (p. 192). That this Hyde Amendment has had no significant effect on the total number of legal abortions is, apparently, uninteresting (see Rosenberg 1991, p. 187). The values that MacKinnon maintains are at stake in the constitutional debate over abortion are those she believes should be considered in political debates over abortion and are not those that have actually been expressed in the abortion debate. Indeed, she thinks that "women have not been able to risk thinking about these issues" in terms of forced sex (MacKinnon 1989, p. 186). Finally, MacKinnon derives her understanding of the political forces maintaining and establishing abortion policies from her philosophical belief that the framework within which abortion has been debated discriminates against women. Abortion policies are dominated by men, she believes, because current policy serves what she sees as male interests. The privacy "right of men . . . to oppress women one at a time," MacKinnon asserts, "has a lot to do with why we can't organize women on the abortion issue" (MacKinnon 1987, p. 102). As was the case with Ely and other jurists whom she disparages as too abstract, MacKinnon never considers any study of how restrictions on abortion are implemented, justified, or politically maintained to be relevant to either the constitutional status or the interpretation of abortion.

MacKinnon's writings are more political than other works on abortion rights in one important sense. Her work, she claims, must be partially understood as a consciousness-raising exercise. Female (and male) consciousness needs to be raised, MacKinnon believes, because people do not recognize or are not free to articulate publicly the real nature of the sexist structures that underlie such social practices as contemporary restrictions on abortion or the granting of limited abortion rights. Her interpretation of abortion is, in her view, not based on abstractions, both because it is based on the realities women actually face and because persons exposed to her arguments in environments where they are free to consider and endorse them will recognize that abortion is a matter of forced sex (see generally MacKinnon 1989, pp. 83–105).

Unfortunately, MacKinnon presents no study of "concrete reality" to support her assertions. In particular, MacKinnon does not offer any research, feminist or otherwise, in support of her claim that a significant number of unwanted pregnancies result from sexual intercourse women were compelled to have (however "compelled" is defined).[17] The only feminist investigation MacKinnon's discussions of abortion cite is Kristin Luker's *Taking Chances: Abortion and the Decision Not to Contracept* (1975; see MacKinnon 1989, p. 299 n. 3).[18] Although Luker concludes that contraceptive risk taking cannot be explained without reference to social policies and attitudes that harm women, her research does not support and frequently belies many of the "concrete realities" that ostensibly ground MacKinnon's interpretation of abortion.[19]

Luker's study of 500 women who took contraceptive risks never even considers the desire to avoid intercourse as a factor in decisions not to use birth control. Although *Taking Chances* presents frequent excerpts from Luker's interviews with contraceptive risk takers, in only two cases did these women indicate that they did not consent to sexual relations (Luker 1975, p. 57).[20] Rather, Luker maintains that women often take contraceptive risks because of the "biological and medical side-effects" of birth control, including the desire not to interrupt intercourse to take precautions because that interfered with the pleasure of the activity (pp. 59–60), and because birth control "socially proclaims the user to be a sexually active woman, a 'cold-blooded' planner, a hard-eyed realist with no romance in her soul, and a woman who is perhaps too sexually active to be a lady" (pp. 49–50).[21]

MacKinnon notes that sexual double standards have deleterious effects on contraceptive risk taking. "Women," she claims, "feel compelled to preserve the appearance . . . of male direction of sexual expression, as if it were male initiative that women want, as if it were that which women find arousing. Men enforce this" (MacKinnon 1989, pp. 184–85). Luker, however, never considers this desire "to preserve the appearance of male initiative" to be a cause of contraceptive risk taking. None of the male or female subjects quoted in *Taking Chances* give that explanation of their failure to use birth control. Many of the women she interviewed indicate that male attitudes influenced their decision not to contracept, but what they most emphasize is either male ignorance or passive toleration of their contraceptive risk taking (Luker 1975, pp. 56–59).[22] Whereas MacKinnon asserts that "a good user of contraception can be presumed sexually available and, among other consequences, raped with relative impunity" (1989, p. 185), Luker finds that many women avoid ongoing use of contraception because, by giving indications that they are "frankly expecting sex" (1975, p. 51), they fear they may "not be courted on the same terms as a woman whose sexual availability is more ambiguous" (p. 49).

MacKinnon also presents no evidence supporting her claim that women and men will recognize abortion as being a matter of forced sex once their consciousness is raised. Indeed, contrary to Mac-Kinnon's bald assertions, Luker's study suggests that contraceptive risk taking is more likely to occur when women have some desire to be pregnant and, hence, want sex.[23] Women who fail to use birth control, Luker repeatedly points out, are "attempting to achieve more diffuse goals than simply preventing pregnancy (1975, p. 32, and see pp. 16, 138–39). Thus, Luker concludes that many women take contraceptive risks because, in part, they believe that if they become pregnant they will have established their fertility and femininity, will force lovers and significant others to redefine their relationship, and will be more eligible to receive psychological counseling (pp. 66–76).[24] These women, after consciousness raising, may question their reasons for engaging in unprotected sex, but they are not likely to rethink whether they consented to that activity.

MacKinnon's manner of interpreting "concrete reality" typifies the quality of empirical factfinding in much contemporary legal scholarship. Academic lawyers routinely make blithe statements of political fact that are belied by social science research. Despite clear evidence to the contrary, opponents of *Roe* frequently accuse the courts of inhibiting public debate on abortion (see Glendon 1987, p. 2; Perry 1988, p. 177; Epstein 1974, p. 168),[25] and proponents of constitutional abortion rights condemn pro-life activists for engaging in single-issue politics (see Dworkin 1989, p. 50; Tribe 1990b, p. A13).[26] Such claims are best understood as conclusions derived from theories about politics, rather than as evidence that independently supports such theories.[27] MacKinnon is more controversial than most constitutional theorists only because her conclusions are more radical. Her method of interpreting political life is that of a mainstream late-twentieth-century legal scholar.

Thus, MacKinnon offers the same relatively timeless interpretation of abortion that characterizes most legal writing on that subject. Historians and social scientists point out that the politics of abortion have changed throughout American history. Many groups active on one side of the abortion debate in the late nineteenth century are differently placed in the late twentieth century. Feminists, for example, were not major participants in post–Civil War abortion debates, and those that were involved seem to have favored abortion restrictions (see Ginsburg 1989, pp. 29, 31). Moreover, the decision not to contracept, which plays a vital role in MacKinnon's arguments, has been significantly influenced by mid-twentieth-century social and technological developments (see Luker 1975, pp. 114, 123, 127).[28] Nevertheless, neither MacKinnon nor Ely nor any other academic lawyer treats these political and social changes as relevant to constitutional debate. In Ely's work, abortion seems always to have been a question of the life interests of the fetus as opposed to the liberty interests of the mother. In MacKinnon's work, abortion seems always to have been a matter of forced sex. MacKinnon (1987, p. 93) implies that, when the millennium of gender equality comes, political or constitutional controversy over abortion will disappear because this matter becomes controversial only in a society that oppresses women.

A Political Interpretation of Abortion

Social practices do not necessarily raise different constitutional issues when interpreted from apolitical and political perspectives. The law in action may fairly reflect the law on the books. Public debate over an issue may mirror philosophical debate. The political history of a social practice may be accurately ascertained from the law on the books and philosophical debate. When interpreted politically, however, abortion law, debate, and politics do not correspond to their apolitical depiction in legal writing. The ways in which abortion restrictions have been implemented, justified, and politically maintained raise a very different set of constitutional concerns from those routinely considered by academic lawyers.

The Law of Abortion

Statutory restrictions on abortion never accurately described the legal obstacles that women faced when they sought to terminate their pregnancies. Although scholars estimate that approximately one out of every three or four pregnancies was aborted throughout the first 75 years of the twentieth century, women who had abortions and those who performed them were rarely prosecuted. The few prosecutions that were instituted had to confront jurors who were frequently unwilling to convict abortionists (see Rubin 1987, pp. 18, 36; Faux 1988, p. 88; Luker 1984, p. 53; Tribe 1990a, p. 35). Thus, persons seeking or performing abortions could normally predict that they would not suffer the statutorily authorized penalty for their conduct, particularly if they did not call public attention to their actions.[29]

Licensed physicians, who successfully fought in the late nineteenth century for the power to control abortion (see Luker 1984, pp. 32–35; Mohr 1978, pp. 147–70), were particularly immune to legal scrutiny.[30] Doctors rarely experienced any official inquiry about their decision whether an abortion was "medically necessary," however that term was defined by the appropriate statute or judicial decision. Theodore Lidz, a prominent physician, observes that "it is virtually unknown for an abortion performed in a hospital under proper jurisdiction to be questioned" (Rodman, Sarvis, and Bonar 1987, pp. 190–91). More generally, Kristin Luker's study of abortion policies concludes that— no matter what the particular statutory definition of a legitimate abortion—physicians agreed that, "if the characteristics of the practitioner and the conditions of the practice were 'reputable,' then the abortion was 'justifiable' " (1984, p. 85). According to her reading of the historical evidence, "if a reasonably plausible medical indication for abortion could be presented to a sympathetic physician, neither the medical society nor any other authority was likely to intervene" (p. 36). Indeed, many of the early participants in the abortion reform movement were motivated by their desire to make the law on the books conform to the law in practice. Doctors, in particular, wanted more assurance that public authorities would continue not to interfere with their abortion decisions (pp. 78, 82; see Rodman, Sarvis, and Bonar 1987, pp. 89–90; Rubin 1987, pp. 28–29).

Although neither legally sanctioned physicians nor unsanctioned abortionists were prosecuted when they violated statutory restrictions on abortion, those restrictions had important effects on the distribution of both safe and sanctioned abortions.[31] The complete withdrawal of state scrutiny significantly enhanced the power of the medical profession. The unregulated monopoly physicians enjoyed on the legal right to terminate pregnancies resulted in substantial variations in both the frequency and circumstances under which abortions were performed.

Because state officials did not interfere with medical abortion decisions (particularly if doctors did not perform abortions indiscriminately), the willingness of physicians to terminate pregnancies typically depended on their personal attitudes toward abortion or those of the relevant hospital administration. These attitudes varied considerably from place to place and from doctor to doctor. Some doctors performed abortions in circumstances that, at best, stretched statutory exceptions. Others were rarely willing to grant abortions even when circumstances clearly indicated that the procedure would be legal. Studies suggest that some clinics or hospitals were 55 times more likely than others to perform abortions (see Rodman, Sarvis, and Bonar 1987, pp. 166–67; Luker 1984, pp. 45–46).

Although luck played an important role in determining who received medical assistance, sanctioned abortions were not randomly distributed across the population. Studies of abortion practice before *Roe* demonstrate that physicians were far more likely to terminate the pregnancies of affluent white women than of their poor or black counterparts. The former had both the connections and the experience necessary to locate doctors willing to perform abortions, and the financial resources to pay them (see Rodman, Sarvis, and Bonar 1987, pp. 149–50). Although even wealthy women sometimes experienced problems, Luker suggests that "the upper-income woman who knew her family doctor quite well, who had some semblance of a physical reason to avoid childbirth, and whose motivation for abortion did not fundamentally offend the values of the physician may have had little difficulty in obtaining an abortion" (Luker 1984, p. 36; see Ginsburg 1989, p. 33). These inequities were only exacerbated by the implementation of abortion review boards in the 1950s and 1960s—which "tended to become market systems, in which women with wealth, information, and medical connections were far more likely to be granted abortions than their poorer, less well-informed, and less well-connected peers" (Luker 1984, p. 57; see Ginsburg 1989, p. 266 n. 21).

Black women inevitably faced additional difficulties obtaining abortions from an overwhelmingly white profession that shared the prejudices of the general population. A study of Georgia practices concluded that in 1970 single white women were 24 times more likely to be granted a "legal" abortion than single black women (Rodman, Sarvis, and Bonar 1987, pp. 149–50). Moreover, physicians used their control over abortion to affect the conditions under which poorly connected women received abortion. Hyman Rodman, Betty Sarvis, and Joy Walker Bonar point out that "some women were presented with a 'package deal'—the physician would agree to do the abortion if the women agreed to be sterilized" (p. 151). Needless to say, black women were particularly victimized by this practice (ibid.).

The distribution of safe unsanctioned abortions before *Roe* was also characterized by randomness and discrimination. Wealth, race, and medical connections proved as important in securing a so-called criminal abortion on the black market as they were in securing a "therapeutic abortion" in a hospital. Perhaps more important, these factors (as well as luck) greatly affected a woman's chance of receiving a competent (and sympathetic) abortion from an unsanctioned practitioner.[32] Because they lacked the resources to discover and pay for adequate care, poor women suffered and died more frequently from botched abortions than did more affluent women. Racial prejudice played a similar role in the distribution of safe unsanctioned abortions. Studies suggest that between 1940 and 1970 the mortality rate of blacks after "criminal abortion" was 2.4 to 9 times higher than that of whites (Luker 1984, pp. 74–75; Rodman, Sarvis, and Bonar 1987, p. 150).[33]

Roe v. Wade did not eliminate these problems. Rodman, Sarvis, and Bonar note that, "as with access to medical services generally, those who are young, poor, and members of minority groups do not have equal access to legally induced abortions" (1987, p. 83). Persons who live in conservative states or rural areas are also less likely to be able to exercise this constitutional right because there rarely are facilities in their neighborhoods that perform abortions (ibid.; see Ginsburg 1989, pp. 80, 267 n. 24). However, scholars suggest that *Roe*, while not substantially increasing the number of abortions, has "decreased discrimination against indigent women who previously had less access to 'medical' abortions than more affluent women" (Rodman, Sarvis, and Bonar 1987, p. 19). Moreover, as Kristin Luker argues, there is no reason to think judicial reversal of *Roe* would result in anything other than the resumption of those practices that characterized abortion prior to 1973. In this "Prohibition-type situation," she asserts,

abortions would be nominally illegal, but those with the right combinations of money and information would be able to get them. (And the combination would be important: a rich person in the heartland of Iowa would probably have a harder time than a middle-income person in New York with feminist connections.) Well-to-do people in general would get better abortions, and the poor would get worse ones. Every physician would have to interpret the law individually, and great variation would result. States like California would almost surely be liberal in interpreting the new law, and states like Mississippi most surely would not. (Luker 1984, p. 242)

Abortion rights activists are well aware of the wealth and race discriminations that have characterized the implementation of twentieth-century restrictions on abortion. Many admit that their efforts to legalize abortion are primarily motivated by their belief that women of lower socioeconomic status and nonwhite pigmentation should have the right to enjoy the same access to safe and sanctioned abortions to which wealthy white women have historically been privileged. Proponents of abortion rights have been particularly concerned with eradicating the evils associated with black-market abortions (see Tribe 1990a, pp. 43–44, 47–48; Rubin 1987, pp. 28–29). Indeed, anecdotal evidence suggests that pro-choice attorneys emphasize right-to-privacy issues in the courtroom only because experience shows such claims are more likely to be successful than the equal protection issues that actually inspired their attacks on state restrictions of abortion. Thus, in a similar vein, the chairperson of Planned Parenthood declared that this organization sponsored the litigation that led to *Griswold v. Connecticut*[34] (which actually concerned constitutional birth control rights) "only to extend the right of family planning to couples of limited income who do not have access to private physicians" (Carpenter 1989, p. 34).[35]

The Values at Stake in Abortion

Scholarly investigations of the pro-life and pro-choice movements suggest that the issues motivating political activists are not the issues that law professors consider when exploring whether abortion is a constitutional right. Kristin Luker's (1984) and Faye Ginsburg's (1989) studies of abortion politics in California and North Dakota, respectively, conclude that such issues as when life begins, whether persons have an obligation to be Good Samaritans, or whether unwanted pregnancies frequently result from forced sex are either not discussed by abortion activists or subordinated to what these political actors perceive as more fundamental issues.[36] At bottom, their studies maintain, contemporary abortion debate is over the place of women in American society. Luker maintains that "beliefs about the rightness or wrongness of abortion both represent and illuminate our most cherished beliefs about the world, about motherhood, and about what it means to be human" (1984, p. 10). Ginsburg sees abortion conflict as "a struggle taking place over the meaning attached to reproduction and its place in American culture" (1989, p. 7).[37] Contrary to some legal speculation, this debate is over the meaning of sex equality rather than over whether women's interests should be subordinated to men's. "Grass-roots pro-life and pro-choice women alike," Ginsburg declares, "envision their work as a full-scale social crusade to enhance rather than diminish women's position" (p. 218; see Klatch 1990, p. 542).

Proponents of abortion rights maintain that women can secure political and economic equality only if they have the rights necessary to control their reproductive capacities. In their view, the law should not convert the biological fact that only women can become pregnant into a social handicap for those women who wish to participate in the public arena. Feminists began demanding abortion rights, Luker claims, because they realized that "women could not get equal work until they could challenge the assumption that their work activities were, or ought to be, or might be subordinated to family plans" (1984, p. 118; see Ginsburg 1989, pp. 6–7).

An unwanted pregnancy, pro-choice activists point out, can significantly hamper female efforts to obtain professionally and financially rewarding work. They also recognize that, without abortion rights, women may be denied public opportunities for fear that an unwanted pregnancy might force them to drop out or significantly curtail their activities in the workforce. Career women can avoid pregnancy by remaining celibate or being sterilized, but proponents of abortion rights insist that women should not be required to abjure such a profoundly intimate activity as amative sex (intercourse for reasons other than procreation) or forever renounce parenthood in order to advance professionally, particularly when men are not obligated to make such sacrifices (see Luker 1984, pp. 176–78).

As the above comments suggest, pro-choice activists believe that women are as well suited as men to the public world of work and politics. In their view, the traditional role of woman as wife and mother is an antiquated cultural artifact, and not a natural condition. Luker maintains that proponents of abortion rights see men and women as "substantially similar" (1984, p. 176). Ginsburg (1989, p. 169), by comparison, finds that the abortion activists she surveyed think there are significant differences between the sexes, but these differences support their belief that women should have the rights necessary to participate as equals in the public world. Pro-choice activists, she claims, see abortion rights as not simply a means of economically and politically empowering individual women, but as necessary to remove the obstacles preventing social life from being infused with "female cultural values" that reflect women's experience and nature (ibid.).

Pro-life activists also frequently assert that women should have the rights necessary to participate in public life as equals. Most believe that women should have the legal right to pursue the same careers and enjoy the same salaries as men. Indeed, many of the abortion opponents Ginsburg interviewed regard themselves as feminists, and bitterly resent charges that they are antiwomen (1989, pp. 84, 126, 177, 191–93; see Luker 1984, pp. 160–61, 205).[38] Abortion restrictions, they insist, do not inhibit women from pursuing "fame, money, and worldly success" (Luker 1984, p. 171). Proponents of these policies, however, demand that a choice must be made between career and family, that "women who choose to be in the public world of work should eschew the role of wife and mother" (p. 169; see Ginsburg 1989, p. 188).[39] Celibacy, pro-lifers maintain, is not an onerous price to pay for avoiding unwanted pregnancies, because they believe that procreation is the major purpose of sex (Luker 1984, pp. 164–65, 208, 210; Ginsburg 1989, p. 9).

Although pro-life activists regard men and women as equals, by this they mean that "women are as valuable in their own sphere as men are in theirs" (Luker 1984, p. 205). Proponents of restrictions on abortion, Ginsburg declares, "accept difference, but not necessarily hierarchy, in the social and biological roles of men and women" (1989, p. 7). They believe that "men are best suited to the public world of work, and women are best suited to rear children, manage homes, and love and care for husbands" (Luker 1984, pp. 160–61). Equality, from this perspective, primarily requires that social policies place the same value on male and female activities. Policies that permit abortion are wrong, opponents argue, because they weaken social support for the domestic sphere of women.

Abortion on demand, pro-life activists charge, promotes male values and interpretations of sexuality. By divorcing "sexual pleasure and individual ambition . . . from procreation and social bonds of caretaking," abortion encourages women to act in "culturally male terms" (Ginsburg 1989, pp. 216–17). In particular, abortion permits persons—especially women—to subordinate feminine values of nurturance to male values of achievement (Luker 1984, pp. 168–71). By treating fertility as a social handicap rather than as a social resource, abortion rights denigrate distinctly female characteristics (Ginsburg 1989, p. 84).

Proponents of abortion restrictions further believe that abortion rights adversely affect most women. Such decisions as *Roe* encourage men's lust to the detriment of their sexual partners and children by substantially decreasing the probability that males who engage in intercourse will have to assume the social and legal obligations of fatherhood. Furthermore, social recognition of abortion rights is likely to decrease the support that men and society give to childbearing and childraising activities, since both activities can be understood as completely voluntary (p. 251, and see pp. 10, 190, 214–15; see also Luker 1984, p. 163). Finally, and more concretely, abortion increases the power of the resources held by better educated pro-choice women at the expense of the interests of pro-life women (Luker 1984, p. 217). In particular, abortion on demand decreases the value of monogamous sex as an inducement to marriage and increases the marital bargaining power of financial resources (p. 162).

This political perspective on the abortion debate suggests that the constitutional status of abortion cannot be resolved by demonstrations that the equal protection clause prohibits discrimination against women. Both sides to the abortion debate endorse sex equality.[40] Where pro-choice and pro-life activists differ is in their understanding of the meaning of constitutional equality. Thus, interpreted politically, the abortion debate raises three related constitutional issues. First, assuming that women are the constitutional equals of men, does the constitution consider women to be substantially similar to men? Second, if the constitution does not consider women and men to be substantially similar, does the equal protection clause nevertheless provide that women shall have the opportunity to compete with men as equals in all spheres of social existence, or does that clause mean only that social policy must value the feminine sphere of home and family as much as the masculine sphere of work and politics? Third, if the constitution does bar laws that prevent women from participating as equals in public life, are amative sexual relations of such importance to human existence that woman cannot be forced to remain celibate as a condition of such participation?

Abortion Politics

The above analysis of abortion law and political debate challenges legal understandings of the political forces that establish and maintain abortion restrictions. Studies of the implementation of abortion laws, for example, cast doubt on Ely's unsupported assertion that the formal existence of state restrictions on abortion proves that a majority of state citizens opposes abortion on demand. When political interests recognize, perhaps subconsciously, that they are not subject to the penalties prescribed by law on the books, they may be unmotivated to invest resources in attempts to repeal laws they oppose on philosophical grounds. This observation may partially explain the survey research that shows upper-income citizens are both inclined to favor abortion rights and support the major party most opposed to abortion rights (Luker 1984, p. 194; Tribe 1990a, p. 238). Of course, this apparent contradiction may simply reflect the willingness of affluent Americans to tolerate Republican abortion policies in order to obtain what they believe to be the superior benefits of Republican economic policies. Wealthy citizens, however, have not been forced to make this tragic choice because the enactment or maintenance of restrictions on abortion does not affect their ability to secure safe, if not sanctioned, abortions. As Laurence Tribe notes, during the 1970s and 1980s, "economically and politically powerful groups not gravely burdened by abortion regulations chose to spend their energies on what, to them, were more pressing concerns" (1990a, p. 51, see Luker 1984, p. 44). Thus, there is good reason to think that abortion restrictions on the books are neither reflective of majoritarian sentiment nor the product of legitimate coalition politics.[41]

The actual distribution of safe and sanctioned abortions in the United States may have had a similar effect on statutory abortion policies. Americans have historically recognized that equal enforcement of the law is one of the most essential elements of the republican institutions established by the constitution. James Madison thought that Americans would be protected "from oppressive measures" because their officials "can make no law which will not have its full impact on themselves and their friends" (Hamilton, Madison, and Jay 1961, p. 352). "Nothing," Justice Robert Jackson warned 150 years later, "opens the door to arbitrary action so effectively as to allow those officials to pick and choose only a few to whom they will apply legislation and thus to escape the political retribution that might be visited upon them if larger numbers were effected."[42] Unfortunately, political officials have not been subject to this vital check when considering restrictions on abortion. Because of their wealth and status, most American legislators, executives, and judges can enact, administer, and uphold abortion restrictions without considering whether such measures will force the significant women in their lives to carry every pregnancy to term. Moreover, pro-life elected officials may discount fears that they will be politically punished for their actions by affluent pro-choice voters because the policies they support will not significantly affect the lives of their most prominent campaign contributors.[43]

Although survey evidence supports claims that wealth and race discrimination affect the passage of laws restricting abortion, empirical research suggests that such restrictions would not be repealed if women were proportionately represented in state and federal legislatures.[44] Public opinion polls and field research have shown that men are as likely as women to favor abortion rights (Rodman, Sarvis, and Bonar 1987, pp. 140–43; see Luker 1984, p. 238). Indeed, at least at the grass-roots level, the anti-abortion movement is composed almost entirely of women (Ginsburg 1989, pp. 6, 134–35; Luker 1984, pp. 8, 194). Hence, there is no reason to think that abortion laws would be different if the political power of women increased, so long as such increases did not disproportionately benefit relatively affluent women who are more inclined to favor abortion rights than their less fortunate counterparts.

Such a redistribution of political power might have one important effect on abortion politics. In the contemporary New Deal party system, abortion has been a crosscutting issue that many mainstream politicians have sought to avoid (see Sundquist 1983, pp. 315–412; Rubin 1987, p. 84). While Reagan and Bush administration officials publicly condemned *Roe v. Wade*, James Sundquist has observed that, "in order to get on with his pressing economic agenda," President Reagan "had to avoid, postpone, and subordinate divisive conflicts over the social and moral measures of the New Right" (1983, p. 442). Similarly George Bush declared that he has no idea how his first Supreme Court nominees, David Souter and Clarence Thomas, feel about the constitutional status of abortion. As women gain more political power, politicians may be forced to pay more attention to those issues that women feel strongly about. Hence, a sexually equal party system might be as divided over abortion as the New Deal system is (was?) over federal economic policy.

Constitutional Interpretations of Abortion

The American constitution is simultaneously a statement of national aspirations, a collection of legal rules that limit and structure the exercise of governmental powers, an institution for ordering political rhetoric, and a series of compromises that have so far permitted people of very different visions of the good society to share the same national space (see Graber 1989). Because there is no single correct way of interpreting these many constitutions, there can be no single correct way of constitutionally interpreting abortion. When resolving any particular problem of constitutional theory, scholars must determine whether they should consider the constitution as aspiration, as law, as institution, as compromise, or as some combination of these multiple levels of constitutional existence. How one interprets abortion thus depends on the context in which abortion is being interpreted.

Considered in the light of our constitutional aspirations, the central issue abortion raises is whether the constitution contemplates a society whose democratic majorities determine the extent to which women are allowed to terminate their pregnancies. The status of abortion in the constitution's vision of the good society depends on whether there are any constitutional means of implementing, justifying, and politically maintaining abortion restrictions. Scholars may engage in this inquiry without examining the contingent features of contemporary abortion politics because the particular constitutional defects of one system of abortion regulations do not establish the unconstitutionality of all such regulations. Hence, from the perspective of the constitution as aspiration, abortion should be interpreted apolitically.

Although scholarly attempts to articulate constitutional aspirations require apolitical interpretations of social practices, efforts to elucidate national ideals clearly have important practical political implications. As Sotirios Barber (1984) points out, constitutional ideals should control how governments exercise their constitutional powers. On a more personal level, American identification is and should be influenced, if not determined, by attitudes toward this country's national aspirations as they are articulated in the constitution (see Levinson 1988). Some persons may find a nation not committed to protecting abortion rights (or, on the other hand, not committed to restricting abortions) to be unworthy of their loyalty and patriotism. Their rejection of the country's constitutional aspirations thus presents such persons with the difficult choice between subverting the constitution,[45] emigrating to another country, or retiring from political life. Those persons who accept or adopt an American identity, by comparison, may have a duty to help fulfill the constitutional promises of American life. If the constitution visualizes an order where all persons have equal access to abortions, persons committed to constitutional values may have an obligation to use their personal resources in ways that further, or at least do not obstruct, the achievement of this ideal. Good citizens, in this view, may not only be constitutionally required to support elected officials who are working to make abortions available to all women; they may have obligations—if they are lawyers—to serve as advocates for persons denied abortions or—if they are constitutional theorists—to write articles supporting equal abortion rights.

Considered in the light of constitutional law, however, the central issue abortion raises is whether contemporary majorities have constitutionally determined the extent to which women are currently able to terminate their pregnancies. Whether contemporary restrictions on abortion are constitutional exercises of governmental power depends on how those policies have actually been implemented, justified, and politically maintained. Scholars cannot engage in that inquiry without examining the contingencies of late-twentieth-century politics, unless they can establish that any system of abortion regulations necessarily abridges constitutionally protected rights. Apolitical demonstrations that some system of abortion regulation satisfies constitutional requirements do not establish the constitutionality of current policy. Thus, even if the constitution as aspiration envisions a nation whose democratic majorities are free to limit access to abortion, the constitution as law may not countenance abortion policies that primarily distribute both safe and sanctioned abortions on the basis of wealth and race. Similarly, even if the constitution's guarantee of republican government is not necessarily violated by legislation that restricts access to abortion, abortion policies may be unconstitutional if they are being politically maintained only because they do not actually affect the ability of state officials and affluent voters to secure safe and sanctioned abortions. Hence, from the perspective of the constitution as law, abortion should normally be interpreted politically.

Scholars who interpret social practices politically need not refrain from proposing new understandings of abortion rights and restrictions. The constitution clearly grants all persons the right to persuade their fellow citizens that a social practice should be interpreted in a particular way. Consciousness raising is both a legitimate and praiseworthy constitutional activity. Hence, there is nothing problematic about MacKinnon's method[46] of interpreting abortion if her work is understood only as an attempt to convince her fellow citizens that there are important relationships between forced sex and unwanted pregnancies. Such efforts to reconceptualize social practices, however, should not be advanced as authoritative grounds for present constitutional decision making. For a number of reasons, constitutional decisions should be made only on the basis of values shared by a significant number (though not necessarily a majority) of citizens.

The implementation and dominant political justification of most social practices are interrelated. The justification of any policy inevitably influences the way that policy is implemented. A teacher who believes that black students are inferior to white students is likely to treat them as such; a society that interprets abortion as a privacy right may deny funding to indigent women. Moreover, public justifications of social practices frequently create self-fulfilling prophecies. Segregation contributed to feelings of racial superiority and inferiority in part because white supremacists' arguments provided the political justification for Jim Crow institutions. If abortion restrictions are publicly understood as signifying a social belief that women should be content to be wives and mothers, then they may create an environment in which women are less likely to desire economic and political power.

Recent scholarly discussions of who should interpret the constitution further support political interpretations of the values that should be considered in constitutional abortion debate. Many political scientists (and a few academic lawyers) have claimed that, as a matter of history and theory, the Supreme Court has not had and should not have a monopoly on constitutional interpretation. Sanford Levinson has called for a more "protestant" understanding of constitutional authority—one that emphasizes "the community joined together in basically egalitarian discussion of the meaning (and demands)" of constitutional scripture (1988, p. 44; see Agresto 1984; Barber 1984; Fisher 1988; Murphy 1986). If average citizens are to be understood as constitutional interpreters, however, what they believe must influence constitutional decision making. When judges and other political officials make decisions relying on arguments that have no resonance in public discourse, civilian control of constitutional interpretation becomes limited to the power to influence who will be these ultimate constitutional interpreters.[47]

When social practices are interpreted politically, their constitutionality may vary from place to place and from time to time. Abortion restrictions that are constitutional in late-nineteenth-century Maine may not be constitutional in either late-nineteenth-century Nebraska or late-twentieth-century Maine. For this reason, constitutional authorities who determine that some social practice has not been constitutionally implemented, justified, or politically maintained need not declare that democratic majorities may never reenact such policies.

Rather, these constitutional authorities must insist only that future proponents of such measures demonstrate there is a strong probability they will pursue their goals in a constitutional manner. The test of any effort to remedy a constitutional wrong, from a political perspective, is only whether the probable consequences of the remedy would improve American politics from a constitutional perspective. On this ground, the result in *Roe* can be defended if analyses of the politics of abortion demonstrate that constitutional rules and rights were not respected when contemporary abortion policies were made, and that forbidding state regulations of abortion in the near future would make the United States a constitutionally superior society. Just as the constitutionality of abortion restrictions in the late twentieth century depends on the politics of abortion in that era, so the constitutionality of future efforts to reinstitute abortion restrictions should depend on how our descendants implement, justify, and politically maintain such policies.

The different status of abortion policies in different jurisdictions does not present a major problem for the political interpretation of social practices. Just as some people behave better than others, so some states have constitutional abortion politics and others do not. Constitutional problems arise only if constitutional authorities feel obligated either to strike down abortion restrictions in all states or none. Constitutional commentators do not face this problem, and neither do state officials. However, national officials—particularly national judicial officials—may conclude that they cannot politically declare that only ten particular states can restrict abortion.[48] Nevertheless, even these decisions can be guided by constitutional standards. If the choice is all or nothing, the crucial question is whether the United States would be a constitutionally superior nation if all manifestation of a social practice were forbidden in the near future, even if that meant voiding a few scattered constitutional instances of those practices. As part of the consequence of living in a national state, persons may have to accept some limitations on their democratic powers when a significant number of their fellow citizens have abused theirs.

From Pro- to Equal Choice

Political interpretations of social practices under constitutional attack may have one last virtue. By interpreting social practices politically, constitutional theorists might produce scholarship that discusses the constitutional adequacy of the reasons actually motivating judicial decisions. Political scientists believe, with good reason, that justices rarely decide cases for the reasons they give in their opinions (see, e.g., M. Shapiro 1978, pp. 195–200). Judicial output, however, may not be explained solely in terms of gut feelings or prior commitment to particular interest groups. Rather, what may consciously or subconsciously be moving the justices are political perceptions that, for reasons of legal style, cannot be mentioned in their opinions. As scholars have pointed out (see Cover 1982; Lusky 1942), many Vinson Court cases ostensibly holding that state officials violated the due process rights of black criminal suspects seem to have been decided actually on the basis of a judicial belief that the guilty law officials would never have treated a white suspect in that way. Similarly, although there is no concrete evidence to support this assertion, many of the justices in the *Roe* majority may have been more influenced by their knowledge of abortion politics than by their belief in the so-called right to privacy.

Scholars who interpret social practices politically would be more inclined to praise the virtues of Charles Black's (1960) assertion that school segregation was a product of racial discrimination than Herbert Wechsler's (1959) meanderings about the right of association. Black's discussion of *Brown v. Board of Education* advanced a simple argument. That case, he insisted, should not have been interpreted "in terms of what might be called the metaphysics of sociology: 'Must Segregation Amount to Discrimination' " (Black 1960, p. 427). In his view, "our question is whether discrimination inheres in that segregation which is imposed by law in the twentieth century in certain specific states in the American Union" (ibid.). The answer to this question was obvious. "Segregation," Black pointed out, "is historically and contemporaneously associated in a functioning complex with practices which are indisputably and grossly discriminatory" (p. 425).

> First, a certain group of people is "segregated." Second, at about the same time, the very same group of people, down to the last man and woman, is barred, or sought to be barred, from the common political life of the community—from all political power. Then we are solemnly told that segregation is not intended to harm the segregated race, or to stamp it with the mark of inferiority. How long must we keep a straight face? (Black 1960, p. 425)

For various reasons, this approach of legal argument has gone out of style. This chapter hopes to encourage scholars to make and consider the following argument:

First, the state passes various restrictions on abortion. Secondly, state officials permit physicians to perform abortions whenever their affluent friends wish to terminate their pregnancies, voice no objection when affluent women visit other states to have abortions, and wink at criminal abortions that maim and kill less affluent women. Then we are solemnly told that abortion restrictions are designed to protect the state's interest in (potential) human life. How long must we keep a straight face?

Notes

1. *Roe v. Wade*, 410 U.S. 113 (1973).
2. *Texas v. Johnson*, 491 U.S. 397 (1989).
3. Thus, polluters normally claim that regulations violate their constitutional property rights.
4. As a preliminary work, this piece is primarily designed to raise questions rather than offer answers. Readers interested in a thorough analysis of the theoretical and empirical literature on abortion should refer to my forthcoming *Equal Choice: A Political/Constitutional Interpretation of Abortion*.
5. By a restriction on abortion, I mean a law that limits, by design or effect, the availability of safe or sanctioned abortions.
6. This analysis obviously has significant implications for substantive debate over abortion rights. These implications are not discussed in this chapter, however, in order to highlight the preliminary questions inherent in efforts to interpret abortion. Needless to say, these substantive issues are important, and will be taken up in *Equal Choice* (see note 4 above).
7. For claims that the constitution consists of more than the document, see Murphy, Fleming, and Harris 1986; Levinson 1988; Ackerman 1989. I have not fully considered whether the claims made in this chapter depend on any particular interpretation of what texts constitute the constitution.
8. This relative unanimity is not coincidental. Virtually every modern constitutional theorist works within the framework of process jurisprudence as articulated by Lon Fuller. See especially Fuller 1940, 1978. I suspect that even critical legal theorists have more in common with Fuller than with the legal realists they claim as their intellectual forebears. Many legal radicals, unfortunately, obscure their relationship with their legal past by misinterpreting legal realism and offering what can most charitably be described as a parody of process jurisprudence. For a particularly grotesque example, see Peller 1988.
9. Pound 1910 is this classic statement of the distinction between "law in books" and "law in action." See also Llewellyn 1930. As these references to Pound and Llewellyn indicate, this tendency to interpret social practices apolitically is only characteristic of contemporary American law, and not of American law generally.
10. A number of scholars have suggested that the constitution can be and

has been amended by procedures other than those specified in Article V. See Ackerman 1989, 1984; Levinson, 1990. For reasons mentioned in note 7 above, this chapter takes no position on what constitutes a constitutional amendment.

11. There is a legal literature on the unconstitutionality of laws as applied. This literature, however, is rarely considered relevant to grand constitutional theory, and has played virtually no role in legal debates over the constitutionality of abortion restrictions.

12. For my use of lowercase with the word *constitution*, see notes 7 and 10 above.

13. I have elsewhere argued that Ely and virtually all other constitutional theorists maintain that courts should resolve issues exactly the way a moral philosopher would. See Graber 1989.

14. This, with much modification, later became the basis of Ely's representative-reinforcement model of the judicial function. See Ely 1980.

15. Laurence Tribe's recent book *Abortion: The Clash of Absolutes* epitomizes the place of empirical political research in contemporary constitutional theory. The first part of his work provides readers with a lengthy summary of the history of abortion politics in the United States. In the subsequent chapters on the constitutionality of abortion laws, however, Tribe does not treat as constitutionally relevant any matter discussed in the earlier chapters on the politics of abortion. See Tribe 1990a, esp. pp. 27–51, 77–112.

16. *Harris v. McRae*, 448 U.S. 297 (1980).

17. MacKinnon correctly asserts that persons can be compelled to have sex in the absence of violent threats, and has presented evidence that forced sex in these circumstances is a social problem. I suspect, however, that we would disagree over the precise definition of "forced sex."

18. For Luker's credentials as a feminist, see MacKinnon 1989, p. xv.

19. At one point, MacKinnon cites the Luker study immediately after asserting that "women who repeatedly seek abortions . . . when asked why, say something like, 'The sex just happened.' Like every night for two and a half years" (1987, p. 95). She does not state that *Taking Chances* supports her interpretation of the reasons why women take contraceptive risks.

Although the Luker study does not provide empirical support for MacKinnon's particular equal protection argument, Luker does, as the text suggests, provide evidence supportive of other claims that abortion restrictions discriminate against women.

20. I should note that in these two cases the lack of consent seems clear.

21. Two-thirds of Luker's subjects had been told that they would have difficulty becoming pregnant. This information apparently encouraged contraceptive risk taking both by tempting women to see if they were fertile and by decreasing their estimation of the probability that they would become pregnant if they failed to use birth control. Luker 1975, pp. 63, 68–69.

22. A few women did indicate that their lovers did not want them to use contraception, but most thought this was due to philosophical opposition to birth control. Luker 1975, p. 57.

23. As this suggests, women (and men) may want sex for reasons other than arousal.

24. Significantly, MacKinnon and Luker offer very different interpretations of how common such activities are, as a failure to use birth control. Whereas MacKinnon implies that contraceptive risk taking is an abnormal behavior— MacKinnon 1984, p. 47 (excerpted above in the text)—Luker characterizes as "unscientifically misogynist" those persons who treat "women who fail to protect themselves contraceptively as qualitatively different from people who fail to protect life or health in other ways." Luker 1975, p. 29, and see pp. 140–41.

25. Social science research uniformly concludes that *Roe v. Wade* was largely responsible for the development of the right-to-life movement and the insertion of abortion into electoral politics. See Luker 1975, pp. 125–26, 137; Ginsburg 1989, pp. 43, 72; Rubin 1987, pp. 186–88; Faux 1988, p. 179.

26. As will be noted in the next section, studies of pro-life activists conclude that they are not single-issue voters in any simple sense of the word.

27. Most social scientists recognize that empirical facts are rarely independent of the theories they support. Some even claim that theories predetermine the results of empirical investigation. Most academic lawyers, however, rarely bother looking at any empirical evidence when making claims about political life.

28. For a general discussion of technological change and abortion, see Luker 1984, p. 55.

29. Significantly, had Sherri Finkbine in 1964 not publicized her reasons for seeking to terminate her pregnancy, her scheduled abortion for a fetus deformed by thalidomide would not have been canceled and the ensuing public controversy would not have taken place.

30. Only one doctor in the twentieth century has been convicted for performing an abortion, and that conviction was reversed by the Supreme Court. Tribe 1990a, p. 38.

31. This chapter distinguishes between sanctioned abortions (those performed by a doctor statutorily authorized to perform abortions in certain circumstances) and unsanctioned abortions (those performed by a person not statutorily authorized to perform abortions). The standard terminological distinction between "therapeutic" and "criminal" abortions is problematic for two reasons. "Therapeutic abortions" done in circumstances where they were clearly not necessary to save the life of the pregnant women (however life is defined) were, in some sense, "criminal abortions." See Rodman, Sarvis, and Bonar 1987, p. 89. Similarly, seen from a political perspective, the label *criminal* hardly seems appropriate to describe an abortion the authorities have no intention to prosecute.

32. I assume without evidence that most sanctioned abortions were relatively safe. Indeed, that was probably the main reason why they were so desirable.

33. In addition to inequities in access and service, the black market is also typically characterized by inequities in regulation. Because state officials normally look the other way when such activities are carried out, persons are typically prosecuted for violating the law only when the state has other reasons for wishing to punish them. Luker 1984, p. 75.

34. *Griswold v. Connecticut*, 381 U.S. 479 (1965).

35. Constitutional theorists do assert that restrictions on state and federal funding of abortion unconstitutionally discriminate on the basis of wealth. See Perry 1988. This claim, however, is that the state must provide indigent persons with the resources necessary to exercise their constitutional abortion rights, particularly if the state also pays for analogous medical procedures. Thus, the wealth discrimination claims asserted in such cases as *Harris v. McRae* (see note 16 above and the relevant text) presuppose that there are other grounds for thinking that women have a right to an abortion. Interpreted politically, the abortion restrictions considered in *Roe* presented equal protection issues because they were implemented in ways that only limited the access of poor persons to safe and sanctioned abortion. As such, this claim does not depend on there being an independent constitutional right to privacy.

36. See especially Ginsburg 1989, pp. 41, 259 n. 28 (noting differences between the right to privacy and feminist arguments for abortion rights).

37. As these comments suggest, both scholars recognize that abortion activists are not engaging in single-issue politics.

38. The California pro-life activists surveyed by Luker were far more socially conservative than their North Dakota counterparts that Ginsburg surveyed.

39. Many of the pro-life activists surveyed by Luker opposed birth control (other than natural family planning). North Dakota abortion opponents seemed more tolerant of contraceptives. Although Ginsburg did not discuss the matter, I suspect these activists would be more willing to permit "career women" to lead active sex lives, though on the condition that the women accept the consequences of an unwanted pregnancy.

40. Although many pro-life activists oppose the Equal Rights Amendment, they do so because they believe that its likely interpretation will adversely affect women. See Luker 1984, p. 205.

41. Scholars have also suggested that until *Webster v. Reproductive Health Services*, 492 U.S. 490 (1989), many proponents of abortion rights were unmotivated to spend significant resources in political battles over abortion because they believed that the Supreme Court would declare unconstitutional any significant abortion restrictions. See Stewart and Nicholson 1979, p. 165.

42. *Railway Express Agency v. New York*, 336 U.S. 106, 112–13 (1949) (Jackson, J., concurring).

43. This is not to say that pro-life elected officials may never be punished for their actions—an assertion belied by post-*Webster* politics. My claim is only that the actual implementation of abortion policies is likely to affect the

intensity with which many affluent supporters of abortion rights pursue that end in electoral politics.

44. Abortion restrictions may violate the equal protection rights of women even if women's rights were not violated in the process by which such measures were passed.

45. Efforts to subvert a constitution are not necessarily evil. Where there is no alternative, bad constitutions should be subverted.

46. See notes 25–27 and the relevant text.

47. The constitution as compromise may also require political interpretations of social practices. From that perspective, the central issue abortion raises is whether there is a constitutional abortion policy acceptable to people who have very different beliefs about the morality of abortion. Thus understood, the constitutionality of abortion restrictions depends on whether the vast majority of Americans will be willing to support a country that enacts such policies, even if they personally favor alternatives. Such considerations clearly require examination of the beliefs and values actually held by American citizens. Constitutional decisions that are based on principles most Americans do not accept, thus, undermine the constitution as compromise.

I have not fully thought out how abortion should be interpreted from the perspective of the constitution as institution.

48. Notice, though, that both congressional legislation and federal judicial decisions have barred only some states and localities from adopting certain voting procedures. *Rome v. United States*, 446 U.S. 156 (1980); *South Carolina v. Katzenbach*, 383 U.S. 301 (1966); *Katzenbach v. Morgan*, 384 U.S. 641 (1966); *Rogers v. Lodge*, 458 U.S. 613 (1982).

References

Ackerman, Bruce. 1989. "Constitutional Politics/Constitutional Law." 99 *Yale Law Journal* 453.

———. 1984. "The Storrs Lectures: Discovering the Constitution." 93 *Yale Law Journal* 1013.

Agresto, John. 1984. *The Supreme Court and Constitutional Democracy*. Ithaca, N.Y.: Cornell University Press.

Barber, Sotirios A. 1984. *On What the Constitution Means*. Baltimore and London: Johns Hopkins University Press.

Black, Charles J., Jr. 1960. "The Lawfulness of the Segregation Decisions." 69 *Yale Law Journal* 421.

Carpenter, Dale Allen. 1989. "Revisiting *Griswold:* An Exploration of Its Political, Social, and Legal Origins." Unpublished senior essay, Yale College, April 16.

Cover, Robert M. 1982. "The Origins of Judicial Activism in the Protection of Minorities." 91 *Yale Law Journal* 1287.

Delgado, Richard. 1990. "When a Story Is Just a Story: Does Voice Really Matter?" 76 *Virginia Law Review* 95.

Dworkin, Ronald. 1989. "The Future of Abortion." 36 *New York Review of Books* 47 (September 28).

Ely, John Hart. 1980. *Democracy and Distrust: A Theory of Judicial Review.* Cambridge, Mass., and London, England: Harvard University Press.

———. 1973. "The Wages of Crying Wolf: A Comment on *Roe v. Wade.*" 82 *Yale Law Journal* 920.

Epstein, Richard A. 1974. "Substantive Due Process by Any Other Name: The Abortion Cases." In Philip Kurland, ed., *The Supreme Court Review, 1973* (Chicago: University of Chicago Press, 1974), p. 159.

Faux, Marian. 1988. Roe v. Wade: *The Untold Story of the Landmark Supreme Court Decision That Made Abortion Legal.* New York: New American Library.

Fisher, Louis. 1988. *Constitutional Dialogues: Interpretation as a Political Process.* Princeton, N.J.: Princeton University Press.

Fiss, Owen M. 1982. "Objectivity and Interpretation." 34 *Stanford Law Review* 739.

Fuller, Lon L. 1978. "The Forms and Limits of Adjudication." 92 *Harvard Law Review* 353.

———. 1940. *The Law in Quest of Itself.* Chicago: Foundation Press.

Ginsburg, Faye D. 1989. *Contested Lives: The Abortion Debate in an American Community.* Berkeley: University of California Press.

Glendon, Mary Ann. 1987. *Abortion and Divorce in Western Law: American Failures, European Challenges.* Cambridge, Mass.: Harvard University Press.

Graber, Mark A. 1989. "Our (Im)Perfect Constitution." 51 *Review of Politics* 86.

Hamilton, Alexander, Madison, James, and Jay, John. 1961. *The Federalist Papers.* New York and Scarborough, Ontario, Canada: New American Library.

Heymann, Philip B., and Barzelay, Douglas E. 1973. "The Forest and the Trees: *Roe v. Wade* and Its Critics." 53 *Boston University Law Review* 765.

Klatch, Rebecca. 1990. "The Two Worlds of Women of the New Right." In *Women, Politics, and Change,* edited by Louise A. Tilly and Patricia Gurin. New York: Russell Sage Foundation.

Levinson, Sanford. 1990. "A Multiple Choice Test: How Many Times Has the United States Constitution Been Amended? (a) 14; (b) 26; (c) 420 + 100; (d) all of the above." Paper presented at the meeting of the American Political Science Association, San Francisco.

———. 1988. *Constitutional Faith*. Princeton, N.J.: Princeton University Press.

Llewellyn, Karl N. 1930. "A Realistic Jurisprudence—The Next Step." 30 *Columbia Law Review* 431.

Luker, Kristin. 1984. *Abortion and the Politics of Motherhood*. Berkeley, Los Angeles, and London: University of California Press.

———. 1975. *Taking Chances: Abortion and the Decision Not to Contracept*. Berkeley: University of California Press.

Lusky, Louis. 1942. "Minority Rights and the Public Interest." 52 *Yale Law Journal* 1.

MacKinnon, Catharine A. 1989. *Toward a Feminist Theory of the State*. Cambridge, Mass.: Harvard University Press.

———. 1987. *Feminism Unmodified: Discourses on Life and Law*. Cambridge, Mass.: Harvard University Press.

———. 1984. *"Roe v. Wade:* A Study in Male Ideology." In *Abortion: Moral and Legal Perspectives*, edited by Jay L. Garfield and Patricia Hennessey. Amherst: University of Massachusetts Press.

Matsuda, Mari. 1988. "Affirmative Action and Legal Knowledge: Planting Seeds in Plowed-up Ground." 11 *Harvard Women's Law Journal* 1.

Menkel-Meadow, Carrie. 1987. "Excluded Voices: New Voices in the Legal Academy Making New Voices in the Law." 42 *University of Miami Law Review* 29.

Mohr, James C. 1978. *Abortion in America: The Origins and Evolution of National Policy*. New York: Oxford University Press.

Murphy, Walter F. 1986. "Who Shall Interpret? The Quest for the Ultimate Constitutional Interpreter." 48 *Review of Politics* 424.

Murphy, Walter F., Fleming, James E., and Harris, William F. 1986. *American Constitutional Interpretation*. Mineola, N.Y.: Foundation Press.

Peller, Gary. 1988. "Neutral Principles in the 1950's." 21 *Michigan Journal of Law Reform* 561.

Perry, Michael J. 1988. *Morality, Politics, and Law*. New York: Oxford University Press.

Pound, Roscoe. 1910. "Law in Books and Law in Action." 44 *American Law Review* 12.

Rawls, John. 1971. *A Theory of Justice*. Cambridge, Mass.: Harvard University Press.

Regan, Donald H. 1979. "Rewriting *Roe v. Wade*." 77 *Michigan Law Review* 1569.

Rodman, Hyman, Sarvis, Betty, and Bonar, Joy Walker. 1987. *The Abortion Question*. New York: Columbia University Press.

Rosenberg, Gerald N. 1991. *The Hollow Hope: Can Courts Bring About Social Change?* Chicago: University of Chicago Press.

Rubin, Eva R. 1987. *Abortion, Politics, and the Courts:* Roe v. Wade *and Its Aftermath*, revised edition. New York, Westport, Conn., and London: Greenwood Press.

Shapiro, Ian. 1990. "The Nature of Contemporary Political Science: A Roundtable Discussion." 23 *Political Science & Politics* 34.

———. 1989. "Gross Concepts in Political Argument." 17 *Political Theory* 51.

Shapiro, Martin. 1978. "The Supreme Court: From Warren to Burger." In *The New American Political System*, edited by Anthony King. Washington, D.C.: American Enterprise Institute for Public Policy Research.

Stewart, Debra W., and Nicholson, Jeanne Bell. 1979. "Abortion Policy in 1978." 9 *Publius* 161.

Sundquist, James L. 1983. *Dynamics of the Party System: Alignment and Realignment of Political Parties in the United States*, revised edition. Washington, D.C.: Brookings Institution.

Thomson, Judith Jarvis. 1971. "A Defense of Abortion." 1 *Philosophy and Public Affairs* 47.

Tribe, Laurence H. 1990a. *Abortion: The Clash of Absolutes*. New York: W. W. Norton.

———. 1990b. "A Nation Held Hostage." *New York Times*, July 2, p. A13.

Wechsler, Herbert. 1959. "Toward Neutral Principles of Constitutional Law." 73 *Harvard Law Review* 1.

West, Robin. 1988. "Jurisprudence and Gender," 55 *University of Chicago Law Review* 1.

7

Unsettling "Woman": Competing Subjectivities in No-fault Divorce and Divorce Mediation

Lisa C. Bower

Contemporary developments in several areas of the law suggest that, as Catharine MacKinnon observes, "[t]he initial transmutation of the feminist impulse into law [has] lost a lot in translation" (1991:1285). Writing within the context of current doctrinal assaults on *Roe v. Wade,*[1] MacKinnon's observation points to an issue that has become a central focus of current feminist legal scholarship: how to regain the ground that has been lost by the doctrinal erosion of early feminist victories in the legal arena.

An emerging body of scholarship has addressed this question by describing the limits of formal equality and by attempting to renegotiate the relationship between "equality" and the interests of women. For example, recent criticisms of formal equality (Becker 1987; Fineman 1991), no-fault divorce (Weitzman 1985; Kay 1990a), and gender-neutral child custody awards (Fineman 1988; Woods 1985; Germane 1985) discuss the limits of the equality standard and suggest a rethinking of the theoretical assumptions that underlie feminist strategies. And as questions of sexual difference—suppressed by the earlier feminist focus on formal equality—have emerged, the equality versus difference debate, which was instigated in its contemporary form by several Supreme Court decisions in the 1970s related to pregnancy leave, has become a site for the rethinking of feminist strategy.

Feminists' current engagement with the law is thus marked by a certain degree of circumspection. This caution has been engendered by, as Carol Smart describes it, "a growing awareness of the paucity of gains for women arising out of the pursuit of law reform" (1986:109).

Feminists' initial belief that the changes leading to equality for women, or the valorization of difference, would occur in a linear fashion has been replaced by a different characterization of law—one that recognizes its uneven development. This description of law sees it less "as a unity which simply progresses, regresses," and more as a structure and discourse that "operates on a number of dimensions" (Smart 1986:117).

An implicit question underlies this description of the limits of legal reform: How does the transformation of feminist interests occur in the legal field? In the following, I suggest that an exploration of how transformation in law occurs will require a focus on the processes whereby unevenness *and* continuity in the development of law and feminism are discursively produced. In other words, how has the illusion of continuity—a feature of both legal and feminist discourse—been fostered in a context where the terms of argumentation (which are themselves already indeterminate) are continually being contested, undermined, and redeployed? One way to expore these questions is to utilize a conception of both law and feminism as sites of struggle in which identities are constructed.

The notion of law as an arena of struggle in which subjectivities are contested has recently been advanced by a number of scholars (Coombe 1988; Silbey and Sarat 1989; Hartog 1987; Poovey 1988). According to Coombe, "law concludes or limits everyday struggles, authoritatively determines the qualities of individuals or groups, the social identities which people can lay claim to, and the ways in which personhood and experiences of self can be legitimately represented (1988:1). Law also accords legitimacy to particular representations of self while suppressing alternative conceptions.[2] Similarly, as some feminist scholars increasingly argue, feminism can be fruitfully examined as a contested site where notions of subjectivity are fashioned.

For example, feminism, according to Nancy Cott, has always been "full of double aims" (1987:50)—defining "woman" as both nurturing subject and as rights-bearing citizen. At the same time, paradoxically, feminism's political program has depended on the articulation of a unified conception of identity.[3] Feminist discourse can be aptly described as "presum[ing] upon the unity of its object of inquiry (women) *even* when it is at pains to demonstrate the differences within this admittedly generalizing and imprecise category" (Fuss 1990:2; emphasis original). What purposes have motivated this seeming contradiction? Why have feminists developed unitary conceptions of "woman" while simultaneously redefining this term as a site of contested meaning?

One obvious answer is that, historically, women have been invisible, unrepresented, or misrepresented in a variety of institutional settings, and in culture more generally. A primary goal of recent feminist scholarship has been to render women more visible. What is at stake is not mere visibility, but the fashioning of a category of subjectivity that can be represented in political and legal terms. In other words, feminists have used unitary definitions of "woman" to meet the requirements of representational politics, thereby eliding the ambiguity of the term. As a result, Judith Butler has observed, "the subject of feminism turns out to be discursively constituted by the very political system that is supposed to facilitate its emancipation" (1990:2).

Feminism itself is similarly shaped by its interaction with the discourses of law. As legal scholars have argued, law is a site of struggle over differing normative traditions and values, and legal doctrine is riddled with examples of competing precedents, alternative interpretations, and divergent views of social life (Trubek 1990:72; Kennedy 1975/76, 1986). I suggest that it is specifically the coexistence of competing rhetorical modes in law—such as classical individualism with its "insistence on defining and achieving objectives without help from others," and altruist protectionism, which "enjoins us to make sacrifices, to share and to be merciful" (Kennedy 1975/76:1713, 1717)—that supports the feminist construction of conceptions of woman as simultaneously nurturing subject and rights-bearing citizen. When feminists, like anyone, engage with the law, they utilize bits and pieces of law's contradictory rhetorical structure to advance a specific project.

While feminists' goal has always been at least rhetorically motivated by a desire to empower women, "speaking from the margin" has often necessitated appropriating the authority of particular representations of woman that have been used to oppress women. At least since *Muller v. Oregon*,[4] the altruist protectionism of law has been evoked by feminists with trepidation because it embodies a conception of woman as dependent, in need of protection, and radically different from, rather than equal to, man. Because feminists' control over the terms of representation and definitions of subjectivity have been limited "by the way in which the female sex is defined and positioned" (Poovey, 1988:23), they have needed to act in contradictory ways. This has included making woman a site of contested meaning by "evoking,

while at the same time confounding, the same arguments and definitions of subjectivity which have operated to exclude women."[5]

The use, often unconscious, of a nonunified and multiple conception
of woman has historically created tension and instability in feminist
discourse(s), and in the law. Internal contradictions in the law facilitate
the construction of multiple conceptions of woman. Feminists construct and confound definitions of woman for strategic purposes, and
thereby destabilize the term. However, cultural divisions and contradictions implicit in the meaning of identity, agency, gender, and sexual
difference are reflected in both law and feminism. These divisions limit
the destabilization of the unitary identity that has traditionally been
assigned to women.

In fact, feminisms' use of "woman" as a multiple term, rather than
as a unitary concept, has highlighted instability in legal discourse. The
legal response, informed by deeper social conflict over the meaning of
sexual difference and woman's identity, has been to reground female
subjectivity by assigning it a "new" unitary meaning. This has instigated feminists' bringing into the foreground yet another single definition of woman, for strategic purposes—while continuing to invoke
multiple subjectivities. In other words, legal categories help to define
feminists' articulation of subjectivity while at the same time feminists'
changing conceptualizations of woman alter legal discourse. And as
legal views of woman alter, feminists' views of subjectivity are transformed. This process accounts both for unevenness in the development
of feminism and for the uneven character of the law in relation to
changing the status of women.[6]

This view of law and feminism invites a number of questions: What
are the consequences when legal discourses intersect with other types
of subject-constituting discourses such as feminism? What is the manner in which various feminisms construct subjectivity? How do legal
definitions of "parent," "mother," and "marriage" contribute to the
scope of feminism's (or feminisms') construction of subjectivity by
delimiting and expanding it?

I suggest answers to some of these questions by examining debates
surrounding two related sites of struggle within both feminism and the
"legal field":[7] no-fault divorce, and divorce mediation. These two
issues demonstrate the manner in which divorce continues to be an
arena of conflict for feminisms.[8] They are also indicative of changes
within family law, signaling the degree to which this legal subfield is in
the process of redefinition.

In the next section, I shall examine no-fault divorce as a site of struggle within both feminism and the law. The passage of no-fault divorce in California in 1968 clearly laid the groundwork for subsequent changes in family law, such as divorce mediation and the current preference for joint custody. However, the debates surrounding the passage of no-fault divorce were fueled by contradictory arguments based on competing definitions of "marriage," "parenting" and "women's subjectivity." Next I discuss legal and feminist constructions of subjectivity and their interrelationship with feminist criticisms of divorce mediation.

Competing Subjectivities I: No-fault Divorce

An example of the paradoxical utilization of competing definitions of subjectivity can be seen in the development of no-fault divorce, a site of contention in law and feminism from the late 1960s on.[9] The passage of no-fault divorce suggested a dramatic shift in the legal and social theory of domestic relations, and brought into question the meaning of marriage and the description of divorce as pathological.

Setting the Terms

The implicit foundations of marriage prior to the 1960s were the nuclear family and traditional sex roles. Divorce was seen as a process that terminated the relationship between spouses—almost always because of fault on the part of one or the other—and that continued an unproblematic understanding of sex roles. The underlying assumption was that men and women in a marriage relationship had discrete and gender-specific functions to fulfill. This view of sex roles was reflected in divorce proceedings. Mothers generally retained custody of children under the "tender years doctrine," which supported maternal preference in custody cases; and fathers continued their "traditional" role of providing economic support.

In the late 1960s, feminists and some family lawyers helped to create an alternative vision of marriage that was influenced by several factors including the growing emphasis on individual rights, and the popularization of therapy, due to the increased jurisdiction of the "psy" professions. Different conceptions of gender identity were developing. And feminist criticisms of traditional marriage, coupled with the promotion of shared parenting as the key to changing gender relations, also contributed to a new vision of marriage and the family.[10] Marriage signified imprisonment; no-fault divorce connoted freedom. After California's passage of no-fault divorce in 1968, divorce would be viewed as a specific type of liberating experience—one that was a legitimate and often necessary step in achieving self-actualization and personal growth.

No-fault divorce helped to construct these developments, and validated the idea that individuals could terminate unhappy and unfulfilling marriages without constructing fictitious scenarios about a spouse's unfaithfulness or abusive behavior. Paradoxically, what emerged from the no-fault period were revitalized societal and legal conceptions of marriage, family, and self: The postdivorce family became a conventional life-style. Because divorce was viewed as restructuring the family and relationships within the family, the key element of the new family structure was the development of a viable, cooperative, and continuing relationship between parents that would cushion children from the deleterious effects of a "family breakup." Coparenting and joint custody became the preferred arrangements, and mediation a popular procedure for effecting these goals. Taken as a whole, these changes removed the edge that the previous maternal preference standard had provided for women with children, and reconfirmed the value of the institution of marriage and the image of the family, albeit radically restructured (Girdner 1986:167–70).

Of course, this view of the marital relationship proved to be a fantasy, suggesting that marriage and family are not "experienced in their own right, but essentially in relation to other circumstances and pressures" (Demos 1979:59). No-fault divorce facilitated the creation of a fiction many people wanted to believe was true: that men and women have equal interests in parenting and abilities to parent; that relationships never have to end acrimoniously, but can always be worked out; and that men and women are, in economic and symbolic terms, equal.

Establishing the Paradox

Feminist arguments for equality and critiques of "traditional" marriage—exemplified by the writings of Herma Hill Kay (1968, 1972), one of the early supporters of no-fault divorce—were part of the rhetoric surrounding no-fault divorce and were integral to establishing a new subjectivity for women. But, at least in the case of Kay, the defense of equality for women was always coupled with arguments about the need to protect the mothering role, even as it was being redefined. To effect emancipation, Kay played on individualist notions of rights; and to protect the mothering role, she invoked a protectionist, altruistic idea of social intervention in her concept of the "Family Court," which would use informal processes.

Writing in 1972, four years after the passage of no-fault divorce in California, Kay described joint responsibility for parenting as the only way for mothers to be freed from the "excessive demands of motherhood" and to become independent subjects (1972:1696). Divorce, in this view, was a potentially liberating experience, freeing women from their traditional role as mother and nurturing subject, and enabling them to compete equally as wage earners. Kay believed that it was only by achieving equality that women could achieve independence; traditional marriage, she argued, was a questionable institution because it resulted in loss of identity for women. Restructuring the institution of marriage—an effect of the new divorce laws—would benefit men and women by fostering and accommodating equalitarian relationships.

Kay saw law as a powerful force in the construction of self. Because she believed that law has an influence on how women perceive themselves, she wanted to change the divorce laws. As she stated, when

> the wife begins to share the burden of family support, she will be able to insist that her work is as important and valuable as her husband's. Until then she will continue merely to supplement family income, rather than be an integral part of a team. . . . This will require a surrender of the luxury [*sic*] and limitations of wifely dependence in exchange for the challenge and freedom of womanly independence. (Kay 1972:1695)

Kay's arguments about equality and women's role in marriage were derived from the work of her contemporaries. By the early 1960s—well before the passage of no-fault divorce—there was already a substantial and growing body of feminist work available,[11] which she used to develop her position. Writing against several decades of mother-blaming discourse,[12] American feminists beginning in 1963 with the publication of Betty Friedan's *The Feminist Mystique* launched a sustained attack on notions of traditional marriage and mother-centered childrearing. Their goal was to accelerate the demise of the nuclear family and traditional conceptions of marriage. Kay's arguments thus relied on theoretical perpectives on marriage, motherhood, and individual self-development that predated the 1970s, and that were, in fact, part of the discourse not only of Kay, but also of other feminists such as Jessie Bernard (1977) and Alice Rossi (1964).

It would be a mistake, however, to view feminist positions surrounding no-fault as addressing only equality. On the contrary, Kay—as a key actor in the legislative hearings in California—argued for the adoption of a separate Family Court as an integral part of no-fault divorce (Kay 1968:1205). Her central argument for the Family Court was that an alternative court procedure could protect some women against economic hardship at the time of divorce, especially when extended family ties and social support were unavailable.

Kay's ideas about the informal Family Court as a procedural alternative to formal court proceedings were strongly influenced by Laura Nader, a legal anthropologist and Kay's colleague at the University of California, Berkeley (Kay 1990b). Kay's thinking was particularly affected by an article titled "Conflict Resolution in Two Mexican Communities," written by Laura Nader and Duane Metzger in 1963. Kay was intrigued with the fact that in the Mexican communities Nader studied there were available a "wide range of remedy agents" to which both men and women could appeal for resolution of marital conflict (Nader & Metzger 1963:585). The exact choice of legal agent was influenced, however, by (among other things) the "sex of the parties" (ibid). In one region—Oaxaca—women utilized the court system more consistently than men as a means of correcting husbands' behaviors. In Nader's view, this was because "women [could] find no other authority to which their husbands [were] accountable" (p. 590). Because the specific social and familial structure of Oaxaca—which had "lost or abandoned" (p. 591) its responsibility for marriage—made it difficult for women to support themselves without a husband, the community court was one of the few remaining places where women could seek protection against abandonment and future economic hardship.

Kay's views on the Family Court were supported by a conception of woman that recognized the battle for women's equality had not been won. "The economic position of women is not," Kay wrote, "despite years of effort and the provisions against sex-based discrimination in employment contained in the Civil Rights Act of 1964, equal to men" (1968:1233). The Family Court idea died in the California Assembly in 1969—but not before Kay had pointed out that, under the new divorce arrangements, women might need ongoing assistance in terms of property division and spousal support. Part of the reason the Family

Court had such importance for Kay was the assurance it gave that alimony and child support orders would be available and enforced for women who had custody of children or who could support themselves adequately after divorce (pp. 1234–35). As Kay saw it, incorporating the Family Court idea into the no-fault legislation could prevent some of the financial problems that would inevitably result from women's economic inequality—problems well documented by feminists after the passage of no-fault divorce.[13]

In any case, the proposal for a Family Court was dropped from the final legislation for budgetary reasons, much to Kay's chagrin (Kay 1990b). It had been her hope that the Family Court would provide a useful division of labor between lawyers and divorce counselors; the former would then be freed from their role as "amateur family therapists," and the latter could help divorcing couples "look at their situation constructively" (1968:1227). In contrast to her later (1972) view of marriage as a generally oppressive relationship and of divorce as a means of facilitating the development of independent subjectivity, her discussion of the Family Court (1968) revealed a more precise understanding: that the divorce process, when guided by therapeutic intervention, could be an opportunity for couples to unlearn "disastrous patterns" so as to avoid repeating them in new relationships. According to Kay, then, divorce counseling could be important as a means of saving the institution of marriage (1968:1228).

Kay recognized that not all women fit her reformulated understanding of female subjectivity. She also realized that the institution of marriage could be salvaged, at least for some, as an arena in which egalitarian relationships could find their full expression, especially when combined with a therapeutically assisted commitment to behavioral change. The logic of Kay's position thus suggests that she was actually struggling with competing views of female subjectivity and contradictory views of marriage. In fact, the entire debate surrounding no-fault divorce was articulated in terms that centered not only on equality, but also on shifts in feminist discourse about the meaning of woman as mother and as equal subject.

Well-known commentators on the no-fault debates, such as Lenore Weitzman (1985) and Herb Jacob (1988) have consistently argued that neither feminists nor feminism had a significant role in these debates. They have, however, highlighted the degree to which the rhetoric of equality permeated the no-fault debates. As Weitzman describes it, this rhetoric was used first by male reformers[14] and subsequently by "lawyers and judges as a mandate for 'equal treatment' with a vengeance" (1985:366).

Weitzman and others have described the use of equality rhetoric by men as "male backlash." But they have overlooked the fact that feminist arguments about marriage, parenting, and a reconstructed meaning of woman's subjectivity were in circulation concurrently with the no-fault debates. Male appropriation of this discourse clearly reflects the fact that equality rhetoric, particularly in the legal field, can be utilized for contrary and often competing purposes. To describe the appropriation of feminist arguments for equality simply as male backlash obscures the complex process whereby the destabilization of female identity posed threats to male identity. Destabilization occurred through the assertion that "woman" was not merely defined by the mothering role and, therefore, in need of protection. However, once woman is refigured as a plural subject, as more than wife and mother, the limits of destabilization are reached, and societal and legal pressure is exerted to reinscribe "woman" as a homogeneous category.

Feminist equality discourse, which generated a questioning of the "dominant fictions" about marriage and traditional gender roles, created a "loss of belief in male adequacy" (Silverman 1990:114). On the one hand, male identity as defined by wage-earning capacity was threatened; on the other, dual conceptions of woman threatened to undermine the cultural inscription of woman as occupying the space of a negative term, as "lack"—the bedrock underlying dominant notions of male identity and sexual difference.[15] In less abstract terms, women's claims to freedom and independence from a restrictive marital identity implied real changes in men's identity, with unanticipated consequences for both men and women.[16] The appropriation of equality rhetoric by male reformers for purposes other than those intended by feminists can be viewed then as an attempt to restabilize male and female identity, to halt the breakdown of the male/female binary—a breakdown that the no-fault debates symbolically and practically represented.

Although feminists in the no-fault debates maintained competing views of women's subjectivity, one specific representation of self—woman as equal subject—emerged as central. The ramifications of this are captured in the following quotation, demonstrating how feminists struggled to make sense of the legal changes that followed the passage of no-fault divorce:

> To the degree that the mother works and otherwise functions outside the home, i.e. takes her place in the larger community on the egalitarian basis

to which women's rights proponents are committed—she jeopardizes the judgment that she is the preeminent psychological parent.[17] . . . The Victorian system of sex role assignment that produced the presumption in favor of maternal custody collides with contemporary female needs and self-image; but surrender of the edge proffered by the presumption provides no assurance that Victorian assumptions will not persist, to their [i.e., women's] disadvantage, in a gender-neutral setting. (Sheppard 1982:233)

It is not surprising that subsequent debates among legal feminists in the 1980s centered on the earlier displacement and redefinition of the mothering role. In the following section, I shall consider how the mothering role and the concepts of nurture and care that have been historically aligned with this role are repositioned in contemporary feminist critiques of divorce mediation and the legal field. Feminist critics of mediation are concerned with a conception of woman as nurturing subject. They unsettle this subject position, however, by contextualizing the mothering role and arguing for a return to formal legal procedures.

Competing Subjectivities II: Feminist Critiques of Divorce Mediation, or Repositioning Mother

Divorce mediation is in many respects the logical outgrowth of no-fault divorce. Once the meanings of family and parenting and marriage were redefined by the passage of no-fault, the procedures associated with the adversary system of divorce seemed inadequate. No-fault divorce "dictated the evolution of new procedures consonant with the spirit of the legislation," enabling "the family lawyer, finally, to perform the role that no-fault divorce permit[ted] and encourage[d]" (Winks 1980/81:615, 653).

If divorce were to be an emancipatory event based on cooperative relationships between individuals, then a procedure commensurate with this goal would have to be developed. Under the adversary system, divorce proceedings had been defined by a winner-take-all mentality. Spouses were encouraged to scour the past for evidence of immoral, licentious, or cruel behavior on the part of their spouses, and lawyers were forced to provide simple—and often fabricated—resolutions to complex problems involving interpersonal relationships. By contrast, divorce mediation seemed appealing; it could be both future oriented and responsive to the individual situation—ideas that were supported by the reconfiguration of marriage and female subjectivity provided by no-fault divorce.

Feminist arguments for equality, and their subsequent appropriation by judges in divorce and child custody cases, promoted the idea of mediated divorce as a more effective way of creating the new family in which parenting would be shared and equalitarian relationships between men and women realized. The equality standard also energized feminist notions of shared parenting and arguments for joint custody. However, as I have suggested, there were coexisting and contradictory feminist arguments in circulation at the time of the no-fault debates. These arguments were exemplified by Kay's belief that the Family Court, which resonated with the altruistic protectionism of the law, would provide protection for women—particularly mothers—because it was a "therapeutic" alternative to the adversary process.

One way feminists critical of divorce mediation advance the conception of woman as mother and nurturing subject is by arguing that mothers need protection during the divorce process and in child custody hearings—a linkage to Kay's earlier argument. However, in contrast to Kay, who believed that an alternative forum—the Family Court—could protect mothers by providing therapeutic assistance, some feminists see mediated divorce as the problem to be solved, and argue that women are better served and protected by formal adjudication and the discourse of the law (see Sheppard 1982; Lerman 1984; Fineman 1988; Woods 1985; Lefcourt 1984; and Bottomley 1985).

In her arguments for the Family Court, Kay failed to anticipate the occupation of the mediation process by the social work profession. As Martha Fineman (1988) and others (Germane 1985; Sheppard 1982:32; Lerman 1984:61; Bottomly 1985:168, Leitch 1986/87:170) have argued, social workers—once assigned a relatively minor role in the divorce process, which was primarily controlled by legal dictates under fault divorce—have redefined divorce as an emotional crisis. Billing themselves as experts in therapeutic reconciliation, social work professionals have dramatically changed the divorce process. In particular, they have been key actors in redefining the standard of child custody from the "best interest of the child" to a decided preference for joint custody. Divorce—once a potentially emancipatory event for women because it terminated oppressive marital relationships—now often becomes a condition of dependency for women because of the demand that ongoing relationships be retained between divorcing couples.

Fineman couples her critique of the rhetoric of social workers with a plea for attention to the concrete reality of women's lives; as she notes, "whether or not custodial mothers exist as a legal category, they exist as a practical reality experienced by many children of divorce and their mothers" (1988:733). This contextualization of the mothering role implies an attention to the social and political environment that constructs women's lives. Rather than rely on theoretical arguments about the position of women in society, critics like Fineman show how mediation and no-fault divorce foster fantasies about marriage and mothering that do not comport with women's experience of the mothering role. What has been lost—suppressed by arguments for woman as equal subject, and by the discourse of social workers that aggrandizes sharing, caring, and ongoing relationships—is "the voice of the mother" (p. 730).

Of course, arguments that focus on the mothering role reinstate the subject position *woman as nurturing subject* that some feminists, such as Kay, sought to escape by claiming the position of woman as equal subject. The tension between these two subject positions is embodied in contemporary feminist arguments that retain a commitment to formal equality while arguing that substantive equality for woman is still not a reality (see Uviller 1978).

The documentation of women's economic problems after divorce has provided feminists with a vocabulary with which to describe the experience of divorcing women.[18] Reluctant to abandon the idea of equality, some feminists have resolved the tension between conceptions of woman as equal subject and woman as nurturing subject by emphasizing women's dependency status while simultaneously asserting the importance of rights-based discourse and individualist legal formality. Lefcourt, for example, noted,

> The fundamental premise which must be understood in order to analyze the impact of the use of mediation in family law is that women are less powerful than men in this society. (Lefcourt 1984:267)

As she also observed, though,

> The growing use of mediation is coming at a time when new laws have provided women with additional legal rights. . . . [E]fforts should be made to restore and expand women's access to the court system. (Lefcourt, 1984:267, 269)

I suggest that it is the assertion of women's dependency, based on their role as nurturers, simultaneously with arguments for formal legal rights that both supports and unsettles the idea of woman as nurturing subject. Feminist critiques of mediation are characterized by descriptive arguments highlighting women's dependence. Paradoxically, feminists turn to the legal system—which historically has both created and codified this dependence—because the law also provides a discourse of rights as well as a formidable arsenal of regulations, both to protect and to change conditions of dependence. While feminist arguments that contextualize the mothering role do not necessarily question the principle of dependency, they enable the construction of what Mary Poovey (1988) describes as the "wronged woman"[19]—a position with considerable resonance in the law.

Feminists advance the concept of "wronged woman in need of protection" to subvert the traditional male "defender role"—one that has long characterized the law's relation to women (Poovey 1988:69). This feminist position is adopted not to reinforce notions of dependency based on women's essential maternal nature, but to show in a variety of ways how social position and inequalities in power govern the concerns of women in the divorce process.

Feminists' descriptions of women's social, political, and legal situation in the wake of no-fault divorce, and their criticisms of subsequent developments such as divorce mediation, allow them to claim the role of defender for their own purposes. When coupled with the assertion of rights claims, notions of woman's unitary identity as nurturing subject and as dependent are further unsettled.[20] Unlike certain earlier historical uses of the defender role by women in the nineteenth century that did not make questions of equality and rights a central issue,[21] some feminists critical of mediation argue that the language of rights (Woods 1985; Sheppard 1982; Lerman 1984; Bottomley 1985) and of formal legal procedures (Fineman 1988) is precisely what divorcing women need. Legal discourse provides important bargaining chips that can be used to consolidate and advance women's victories in the legal arena (Woods 1985) and to keep "private" issues in the public domain (Bottomley 1985:185), thereby creating an opportunity for collective empowerment. The assertion of rights by feminists also brings into question the essentialized categories that describe men as public subjects, holders of rights, and women as private subjects, sites of nurturance. At the same time, though, rights discourse makes it difficult both to invoke the idea of protectionism and to utilize it for the benefit of divorcing women.

Arguably, the limits of feminists' destabilization of a unitary definition of woman are reached when, as in the no-fault divorce debates, competing subjectivities begin to imperil notions of sexual difference embodied in the law. While feminists destabilize the maternal role ultimately to protect it, unsettling this conception of woman creates the possibility for others to appropriate it for their own purposes (e.g., fathers' rights groups). This shows that the advancing of rights claims is a hazardous undertaking. As Carol Smart notes, "opposing rights claims can only produce a contest in which more and more evidence is built up on each side" (1989:156). Furthermore, male appropriation of the maternal role may include the desire to usurp women's procreative function, to become "the mother." In an age in which the meanings of "mothering" and "parenting" are remarkably confused, it is thus possible that men may respond to feminist demands for shared childrearing practices in such a way as to make women more marginal than ever (Modelski 1988:80).

Conclusion

By examining how competing subjectivities function in the law, in feminism, and in the relationship established between the two, I have described a process whereby conceptions of woman are produced and restrained by structures and institutions, such as the law, through which emancipation of the subject is sought. While, as Judith Butler (1990) has argued, particular political practices may create the demand for a unitary conception of identity, the case of the legal system is more complex. Law is neither a hegemonic discourse nor an immovable structure. Rather, it is a contradictory set of practices, formal and informal procedures, and competing rhetorical modes. Legal discourses create the opportunity for formulating claims in a variety of ways, thereby making the "legal constitution of social relations multilayered and complex" (Sarat 1990:372).

However, law reflects and reinforces ideologies and dominant fictions—including the intractability of sexual difference—that emanate from numerous sources in society and culture. Ideologies that embody identity and agency are figured in society and language, and reinforced in legal discourse. To the degree that law becomes a nexus for and a means of disseminating these ideologies, it limits the expression of a nonunitary notion of woman.

The indeterminacy of law also creates limits and imposes other barriers. For example, both in the no-fault debates and in feminist critiques of divorce mediation, the terms for constructing and destabilizing woman's subjectivity—equality rhetoric, "informality" (i.e., the

Family Court), the language of rights, altruistic protectionism, and classical individualism—are drawn from the legal system and used by feminists to construct notions of female subjectivity. These same tools are easily appropriated by groups and individuals with competing claims and different agendas.

While feminists' construction of "woman" affects legal discourse, subsequent changes in the law may be at odds with the desired outcome. From feminists' perspective, this produces unevenness in the law regarding the status of women. Law then becomes the site for another round of competition over the meaning of "woman," and feminists scan the legal field for arguments that will support their counterclaims. The result is unevenness in the development of feminist discourse, as well, as it tacks between competing notions of woman and differing rhetorical modes within the legal field.

By examining competing subjectivities at work in the legal field, I have shown how multiple conceptions of woman are produced, unsettled, and unsettling—suggesting that legal discourse both facilitates and limits changes in the meaning of "woman" and the status of women. Because there are limits to articulating notions of multiple subjectivity, feminists are forced to choose strategically between different notions of self. Yet, neither the conception of woman as nurturing subject nor the conception of woman as full subject of classical individualism is adequate. Law, it appears, is limited as an arena for accommodating differences within "woman." Although this reflects deeper and more complex problems and contradictions within both law and feminism, it does not necessarily erase the potential of the legal field as an arena of struggle. It does, however, suggest that a reconsideration of the strategic devices and terms of representation that have historically been used to change women's position before the law is now in order.

Notes

1. *Roe v. Wade*, 410 U.S. 113 (1973).
2. Of course, as Michel Foucault suggests in "Power and Strategies" (1980), law is not a "seamless web" of domination. On the contrary, what attracts many contemporary sociolegal scholars to Foucault's work is the way in which discursive representations of subjectivity are integrated into a theory of social power that pays detailed attention to the institutional effects of discourse and their role in the constitution of subjects. Law is a particularly fruitful site for examining how subjectivities are produced as the effects of

"disciplinary power," and as the result of the performative capacity of legal language and its universalizing and neutralizing capacities.

3. Nancy Cott (1987) has described how the nineteenth-century "woman movement" depended on a number of representations of woman. The strand of feminist argumentation that focuses on women's nurturing qualities as a means of changing social and legal arrangements has, historically, been expressed simultaneously with feminist claims for individual rights and equal treatment. As Cott notes,

> Nineteenth-century feminists could (and did) argue on egalitarian grounds for equal opportunity in education and employment and for equal rights in property, law and political representation, while also maintaining that women could bring their special benefits to public life by virtue of their particular interests and capacities. (Cott 1987:20)

Also see Karen Offen's "Defining Feminism: A Comparative Historical Approach" (1988:134–50), where she captures the same idea in her discussion of the "relational" and "individualist" modes of feminist discourse.

4. *Muller v. Oregon,* 208 U.S. 412 (1908).

5. This quote is an excerpt from a presentation given by Joan W. Scott on the influence of poststructuralist theory on legal scholarship, as part of the Institute for Legal Studies Colloquia Series, University of Wisconsin Law School, Madison. A similar point is made by Martha Minow in "The Supreme Court 1986 Term—Foreword: Justice Engendered" (1987:19–20).

6. As Carol Smart notes in "Feminism and Law: Some Problems of Analysis and Strategy," "The idea of uneven development of law is an important one. . . . To analyze law this way creates the possibility of seeing law both as a means of liberation and, at the same time, as a means of the reproduction of an oppressive social order" (1986:117).

See also Mary Poovey's *Uneven Developments: The Ideological Work of Gender in Mid-Victorian England* (1988), where she uses the concept of unevenness to explain how representations of gender were constructed, contested, and deployed for different—and often competing—goals in a number of institutionalized settings in mid-Victorian England.

7. The concept *field* is a key element in the work of Pierre Bourdieu, a French sociologist and social theorist. A field is "an area of structured, socially patterned activity or 'practice.' " Understood metaphorically, it is like a "magnet," exerting a force on all those who come within its range. However, those who experience its pull are often not aware of the source (Bourdieu 1987: 805–6). I use the term *legal field,* instead of *law,* to highlight the ideas of struggle, power, and resistance that are implicit in Bourdieu's use of "field."

8. See Mary Shanley, " 'One Must Ride Behind': Married Women's Rights and the Divorce Act of 1857" (1982), and Mary Poovey, "Covered but Not Bound: Caroline Norton and the 1857 Matrimonial Causes Act," in *Uneven Developments* (1988:55–88), for discussions of nineteenth-century British divorce law and women—discussions that parallel my analysis of contemporary divorce reform and feminism.

9. This is not the standard view of the no-fault debates. Lenore Weitzman and Herb Jacob, both of whom have written comprehensively on the emergence of no-fault divorce, have argued that feminism had a limited—indeed nonexistent—role to play in the development of no-fault divorce. See Weitzman, *The Divorce Revolution* (1985:487); Herb Jacob, *The Silent Revolution* (1988:173).

10. Nancy Chodorow's *The Reproduction of Mothering* (1978) and Dorothy Dinnerstein's *The Mermaid and the Minotaur* (1976) are the classic statements of the importance, and potential benefits, of shared parenting.

11. Examples could include Jessie Bernard, "Introduction," in Chapman and Gates, *Women into Wives: The Legal and Economic Impact of Marriage* (1977); Alice Rossi, "Equality between the Sexes: An Immodest Proposal" (1964); Betty Friedan, *The Feminine Mystique* (1963); Kate Millett, *Sexual Politics* (1969); and Simone deBeauvoir, *The Second Sex* (1952).

12. A well-known and widely read document that blamed the ills of the nation on "mom" was Philip Wylie's *Generation of Vipers* published in 1942.

13. After the passage of no-fault divorce in the late 1960s, some feminists highlighted Kay's early concern about women harmed by the divorce process, by noting that, "if both parents were equally eligible for child custody and support, . . . joint custody would be used as a tool to reduce child support payments which many women desperately needed for their children and themselves" (Jacob 1988:139).

14. In 1969 James Hayes, who was chair of the Judiciary Committee of the California Assembly, authored a report declaring the legislative intent of the No-fault Divorce Act's financial provisions. Hayes pointed out that there was a new consideration involved: the approaching equality between men and women (Kay 1987:300). The full passage from the report reads thus:

> When our divorce law was originally drawn, woman's role in society was almost totally that of mother and homemaker. She could not even vote. Today, increasing numbers of married women are employed even in the professions. In addition, they have long been accorded full civil rights. Their approaching equality with the male should be reflected in the law governing marriage dissolution and in the decision of the courts with respect to matters incident to dissolution. (quoted in Kay 1987:300 and Weitzman 1985:211)

At a later date, Hayes cited this passage in seeking the termination of a court order that required him to support his former wife (Kay 1987:300). For a description of the Hayes divorce and the application of Hayes's views of equality, see Weitzman 1985:211–12 and Eisler 1977:24–32.

15. According to the French psychoanalyst and social theorist Jacques Lacan, woman functions both as a "total object of fantasy . . . , elevated into the place of the Other and made to stand for its truth" and "as an absolute category . . . which serves to guarantee [an imaginary unity] on the side of the man" (Mitchell and Rose 1982:50, 47).

16. An analogous discussion is found in Jane Silverman Van Buren's description (1989) of the unsettling effects of change as America moved into a

"secular, urban and technological era" in the mid-nineteenth century. She notes that "the structures and principles which had guaranteed the organization, control and containment of emotions became more tentative, even obsolete," as "new ideals (such as democratic ideology) thinly masked the terrors of the experience of living out Utopian dreams of freedom and equality" (Silverman Van Buren 1989:66).

17. The term *psychological parent* was first used by Joseph Goldstein, Anna Freud, and Albert Solnit in *Beyond the Best Interest of the Child:* "[T]he role of psychological parent can be fulfilled either by a biological parent of a child or by an adoptive parent or by any caring adult—but never by an absent, inactive adult, whatever his biological or legal relationship to the child may be" (1973:19).

As the decision in the 1976 case of *Simmons v. Simmons* (576 P. 2d 589, 1978) demonstrated, when the idea of parenting is uncoupled from gender it often works to women's disadvantage. In *Simmons,* the court ordered that custody be changed from the mother to the father, based on the father's remarriage and the mother's obtaining employment (see Polikoff 1982:240).

18. Lenore Weitzman's book *The Divorce Revolution* (1985) has been a crucial resource for some feminists because it provides statistical evidence regarding the position of women before and after divorce, and outlines the deleterious effects of no-fault divorce.

19. See Mary Poovey's discussion of Caroline Norton and the 1857 Matrimonial Causes Act in *Uneven Developments* (1988:51–88).

20. While the "rights question" has become a complicated issue in legal and feminist scholarship, for the purposes of my discussion I see rights discourse as important because it is part of the process of shifting notions of women's identity.

21. See Hendrik Hartog's discussion of the remarkable Mrs. Packard's battles to obtain custody of her children in "Mrs. Packard on Dependency" (1988), as well as Mary Poovey's discussion of Caroline Norton in *Uneven Developments* (1988:51–88).

References

Becker, Mary. 1987. "Prince Charming: Abstract Equality." In *Supreme Court Review,* edited by Philip Kurland, pp. 201–48. Chicago: University of Chicago Press.

Bernard, Jessie. 1977. "Introduction." In *Women into Wives: The Legal and Economic Impact of Marriage,* edited by Jane Roberts Chapman and Margaret Gates, pp. 9–14. Beverly Hills, Calif.: Sage.

Bottomley, Anne. 1985. "What Is Happening to Family Law? A Feminist Critique of Conciliation." In *Women in Law,* edited by Julia Brophy and Carol Smart, pp. 162–87. London: Routledge & Kegan Paul.

Bourdieu, Pierre. 1987. "The Force of Law: Toward a Sociology of the Juridical Field." *Hastings Law Journal* 38:805–53.

Butler, Judith. 1990. *Gender Trouble: Feminism and the Subversion of Identity.* New York: Routledge.

Chodorow, Nancy. 1978. *The Reproduction of Mothering: Psychoanalysis and the Sociology of Gender.* Berkeley: California.

Coombe, Rosemary. 1988. "Contesting the Self: Negotiating Subjectivities in Nineteenth Century Ontario Defamation Trials." Paper presented at the Law and Society Association Annual Meeting, June 9–12, at Vail, Colorado.

Cott, Nancy. 1987. *The Grounding of Modern Feminism.* New Haven, Conn.: Yale.

DeBeauvoir, Simone. 1952. *The Second Sex.* New York: Vintage.

Demos, John. 1979. "Images of the American Family, Then and Now." In *Changing Images of the Family,* edited by Virginia Tufte and Barbara Myerhoff, pp. 43–60. New Haven, Conn.: Yale.

Dinnerstein, Dorothy. 1976. *The Mermaid and the Minotaur: Sexual Arrangements and Human Malaise.* New York: Harper & Row.

Eisler, Riane. 1977. *Dissolution: No Fault Divorce, Marriage and the Future of Women.* New York: McGraw-Hill.

Fineman, Martha. 1988. "Dominant Discourse, Professional Language and Legal Change in Child Custody Decisionmaking." *Harvard Law Review* 101:727–74.

———. 1991. *The Illusion of Equality.* Chicago: University of Chicago.

Foucault, Michel. 1980. "Power and Strategies." In *Power/Knowledge,* edited by Colin Gordon, pp. 134–45. New York: Pantheon.

Friedan, Betty. 1963. *The Feminine Mystique.* New York: Dell.

Fuss, Diana. 1990. *Essentially Speaking.* New York: Routledge.

Germane, Charlotte, Margaret Johnson, and Nancy Lemon. 1985. "Mandatory Custody Mediation and Joint Custody Orders in California." *Berkeley Women's Law Journal* 1:175–200.

Girdner, Linda. 1986. "Child Custody Determination: Ideological Dimensions of a Social Problem." In *Redefining Social Problems,* edited by Edward Seidman and Julian Rappaport, pp. 165–83. New York: Plenum.

Goldstein, Joseph, Anna Freud, and Albert Solnit. 1973. *Beyond the Best Interest of the Child.* New York: Free Press.

Hartog, Hendrik. 1987. "The Constitution of Aspiration and 'The Rights That Belong to Us All.' " *Journal of American History* 74:1013–33.

———. 1988. "Mrs. Packard on Dependency." *Yale Journal of Law and Humanities* 1:79–103.

Jacob, Herb. 1988. *The Silent Revolution: The Transformation of Divorce Law in the United States.* Chicago: University of Chicago.

Kay, Herma Hill. 1968. "A Family Court: An Immodest Proposal." *California Law Review* 56:1205–48.

———. 1972. "Making Marriage and Divorce Safe for Women." *California Law Review* 60:1683–1700.

———. 1987. "An Appraisal of California's No-fault Divorce Law." *California Law Review* 75:291–319.

———. 1990a. "Beyond No-fault: New Directions in Divorce Reform." In *Divorce Reform at the Crossroads,* edited by Herma Hill Kay and David Sugarman. New Haven, Conn.: Yale University Press.

———. 1990b. Interview with author. Chicago. March 23.

Kennedy, Duncan. 1975/76. "Form and Substance in Private Law Adjudication." *Harvard Law Review* 89:1685–1750.

———. 1986. "Freedom and Constraint in Adjudication: A Critical Phenomenology." *Journal of Legal Education* 36:518–62.

Lefcourt, Carol. 1984. "Women, Mediation and Family Law." *Clearinghouse Review* 18:266–69.

Leitch, M. Laurie. 1986/87. "The Politics of Compromise: A Feminist Perspective on Mediation." *Mediation Quarterly* 14/15:163–75.

Lerman, Lisa. 1984. "Mediation of Wife Abuse Cases: The Adverse Impact of Informal Dispute Resolution on Women." *Harvard Women's Law Review* 7:57–113.

MacKinnon, Catharine. 1991. "Reflections on Sex Equality under Law." *Yale Law Journal* 100:1281–1328.

Millett, Kate. 1969. *Sexual Politics.* New York: Ballantine.

Minow, Martha. 1987. "The Supreme Court 1986 Term—Foreword: Justice Engendered." *Harvard Law Review* 101:10–95.

Mitchell, Juliet, and Jacqueline Rose, eds. 1982. *Feminine Sexuality: Jacques Lacan and the Ecole Freudienne.* New York: Norton.

Modelski, Tania. 1988. "Three Men and Baby M." *Camera Obscura* 17:69–82.

Nader, Laura, and Duane Metzger. 1963. "Conflict Resolution in Two Mexican Communities." *American Anthropologist* 65:584–92.

Offen, Karen. 1988. "Defining Feminism: A Comparative Historical Approach." *Signs* 14:119–57.

Polikoff, Nancy. 1982. "Why Are Mothers Losing? A Brief Analysis of the Criteria Used in Child Custody Determinations." *Women's Rights Law Reporter* 7:235–43.

Poovey, Mary. 1988. *Uneven Developments: The Ideological Work of Gender in Mid-Victorian England.* Chicago: University of Chicago.

Rossi, Alice. 1964. "Equality between the Sexes: An Immodest Proposal." *Daedalus* 98:607–52.

Sarat, Austin. 1990. " '. . . The Law Is All Over': Power, Resistance and the Legal Consciousness of the Welfare Poor." *Yale Journal of Law and the Humanities* 2:343–79.

Scott, Joan W. 1990. Presentation at the Institute for Legal Studies, University of Wisconsin–Madison Law School. March.

Shanley, Mary. 1982. " 'One Must Ride Behind': Married Women's Rights and the Divorce Act of 1857." *Victorian Studies* 25:355–76.

Sheppard, Annamay. 1982. "Unspoken Premises in Custody Litigation." *Women's Rights Law Reporter* 7:229–34.

Silbey, Susan, and Austin Sarat. 1989. "Dispute Processing in Law and Legal Scholarship: From Institutional Critique to the Reconstruction of the Juridical Subject." *Denver University Law Review* 66:437–98.

Silverman, Kaja. 1990. "Historical Trauma and Male Subjectivity." In *Psychoanalysis and Cinema,* edited by E. Ann Kaplan, pp. 128–42. New York: Routledge.

Silverman Van Buren, Jane. 1989. *The Modernist Madonna: Semiotics of the Maternal Metaphor.* Bloomington: Indiana.

Smart, Carol. 1986. "Feminism and Law: Some Problems of Analysis and Strategy." *International Journal of the Sociology of Law* 14:109–23.

———. 1989. *Feminism and the Power of Law.* New York: Routledge.

Trubek, David. 1990. "Back to the Future: The Short, Happy Life of the Law and Society Movement." Institute for Legal Studies, Working Paper Series 4, University of Wisconsin–Madison Law School.

Uviller, Rena. 1978. "Fathers' Rights and Feminism: The Maternal Presumption Revisited." *Harvard Women's Law Journal* 1:107–30.

Weitzman, Lenore. 1985. *The Divorce Revolution.* New York: Free Press.

Winks, Patricia. 1980/81. "Divorce Mediation: A Nonadversary Procedure for the No-fault Divorce." *Journal of Family Law* 19:615–53.

Woods, Laurie. 1985. "Mediation: A Backlash to Women's Progress on Family Law Issues." *Clearinghouse Review* 19:431–35.

Wylie, Philip. 1942. *Generation of Vipers.* New York: Rinehart.

8

Fetal Rights and Feminism

Joseph Losco

In 1989 Kimberly Hardy, a "crack"-addicted mother, was arrested in Michigan on charges of delivering drugs to her newborn through the umbilical cord. Hardy admitted that she had been using drugs up to the night before she gave birth to her son. Areanis was born jaundiced, constipated, and unable to keep formula down. He had a small head and soon developed a mysterious infection. After an emergency court hearing was held, the boy was removed from Hardy's custody and entrusted to foster care. Her subsequent conviction was overturned by the Michigan Court of Appeals (Mann, 1991).

A Superior Court judge in Washington, D.C., sentenced Brenda Vaughan to jail in a check-forging case in which she pled guilty in April 1988. The judge noted that the jail sentence he gave her for a first-time offense was primarily intended to protect her fetus from the 30-year-old pregnant woman's drug addiction (Sherman, 1988).

On October 3, 1987, Jennifer Clarisse Johnson gave birth to a girl with traces of cocaine in her bloodstream. She told the attending paramedics—who had arrived in response to a call about an overdose—that she had consumed more than $200 worth of crack earlier in the evening and was concerned about the effects of the drug on her unborn child. She was prosecuted under a Florida law designed to punish drug dealers who administer drugs to children under 18. The state court of appeals upheld her conviction and she was sentenced to 14 years of probation and participation in a drug rehabilitation program (*New York Times,* April 19, 1991).

In February 1987 a judge in a San Diego court heard a case against Pamela Stewart Monson, who had ignored her doctor's warnings about her behavior's potential effects on the fetus she carried. The doctor had warned her to refrain from street drugs and from sex and to seek immediate medical care in the event of vaginal bleeding. Prosecutors charged that, on the day she delivered, she took amphetamines, had sex with her husband, and did not call paramedics until 12 hours after bleeding began. Her son was born brain-dead, with amphetamines in his system. Though the case was dismissed, it is generally recognized as the first in which criminal charges, on behalf of a fetus, were brought against its pregnant mother (Chambers, 1987).

In 1986 a California court responded favorably to a father's request that his brain-dead pregnant wife be kept alive until such time as their baby could be taken by caesarean section, over the objections of the woman's family (Sherman, 1988).

These are just a few of the many recent cases dealing with "fetal abuse" and "fetal rights" that have elicited so much attention on the part of pro-life and pro-choice forces alike. About 50 such cases involve women drug addicts who have allegedly endangered their fetuses at various stages of pregnancy. These cases have stirred intense debate among civil libertarians, jurists, scholars, bioethicists, the general public, and most notably feminists who see this sort of prose-cution as an assault on the gains women have made in the matter of reproductive choice.

One perhaps obvious point should be noted at the outset, however. The type of potential conflict discussed here is actually rare. The overwhelming number of pregnant women are anxious to ensure, often at great risk to themselves, that the fetus they carry develops into a healthy and secure newborn. This is why cases like these are by nature "hard cases." They deal with behaviors that, both on the part of individuals and of government agencies, appear out of the norm. Their discussion is complicated by rhetoric on all sides that generalizes across cases and from hard cases to standard uncomplicated ones. Yet the implications of the debate are so enormous that rhetorical excesses may sometimes seem justified. Discussion of these issues within our own analytical context, however, must progress with the utmost caution.

This chapter will review some of the concerns raised by feminists in recent times concerning this growing area of controversy. I will first review the legal context in which the debate has arisen. Then I will distinguish between two kinds of feminist arguments that have taken different approaches in dealing with this matter. Because liberal femi-nists have mounted the most detailed attack on the trend toward fetal rights from within the legal tradition in which it has arisen, I will concentrate my analysis here, trying to assess the state of the issues to date. Finally, I will address public health policy issues, and then the possible future of the fetal rights debate.

The Legal Context

Three types of court action characterize the current debate over fetal rights and abuse: court-ordered intervention, criminal prosecution, and tort action.

Court-ordered Interventions

Some of the most tragic and well publicized cases involving fetal rights have occurred in the area of court-ordered interventions where medical or legal authorities, seeking to assert their recommendations over the objections of the pregnant woman, have ordered a seizure of the fetus through forced caesarean section. In 1987 Angela Carder, a cancer patient who had become pregnant, was advised by her doctors that she was nearing death. She agreed to undergo life-extending treatment in the hope that the fetus would survive long enough to become viable. She also agreed with the doctors' recommendation of caesarean delivery. A court-appointed counsel for Carder and the fetus and counsel for the District of Columbia were allowed to intervene when she reconsidered her earlier decision. Despite protests by her family members, the court allowed the surgery to proceed. Within two days, both the newly delivered daughter and the mother were dead. (For details, see Merrick, 1990.) There are other examples, however, where—despite a court order—the woman was able to avoid surgery and give successful vaginal delivery (e.g., *Jefferson v. Griffin Spaulding County Hospital*, 1981).

These cases are fraught with legal and ethical problems. Should the views of the medical community be allowed to take precedence over those of the pregnant woman? Does court action in this area violate due process? Are the interests of the state sufficient to overcome other legal and civil liberty concerns raised in overriding the right to bodily integrity?

Some advocates of fetal rights like Jeffrey Parness (1985), Patricia King (1979), and Margery Shaw (1984) would allow medical interventions if necessary to bring about a healthy birth. In citing precedent for forced medical intervention, they point to cases like *Strunk v.*

Strunk (1969), which authorized a forced kidney transplant to a sibling from a Kentucky man who had been declared "feeble-minded," and to *Raleigh Fitkin–Paul Morgan Memorial Hospital v. Anderson* (1964) in which blood transfusions were ordered for several Jehovah's Witnesses. Yet these decisions may not be completely comparable since they are complicated by questions of gross incompetence and unrelated religious issues (see e.g. Gallagher, 1987:26–28, 34–35).

Other supporters of some type of fetal rights indicate nonetheless that medical interventions, while perhaps warranted by the medical needs of the fetus, cannot meet the test of due process and thus should be abandoned. For example, John Robertson (1989:265) acknowledges that the hospital setting in which women confront doctors and attorneys (often without extensive consultation with their own counsel) cannot meet the demands of due process, especially given the intrusive and violative nature of the procedures proposed. Thus, fetal rights advocates like Robertson back away from medical intervention—with rare exception—while acknowledging a role for criminal law in prosecutions after birth. Fortunately, the number of forced interventions of the type described here is small. Janet Gallagher (1987:11) estimated that there have been fewer than a dozen known cases.

Criminal Law

Most criminal prosecutions have been brought against pregnant women on the basis of laws not specifically intended to deal with a fetus. For example, Pamela Monson (discussed above) was charged on the basis of an 1872 law intended to force absent fathers to pay child support. The law had been amended in 1986, however, to include a provision in which parents are held culpable for acts that endanger the potential lives of their unborn. But it was because this law had not been originally intended to apply to pregnant women that the San Diego judge, E. Mac Amos, threw the case out of court.

Seventeen states have criminal codes that apply to the murder of an unborn child. Thirteen of these states require that the fetus be viable. Two states have expanded their definition of common law homicide to include viable fetuses. Arizona and Indiana impose criminal liability for causing the death of a fetus at *any* stage (Johnson, 1990:51). Yet, problems remain in prosecuting under these statutes due to the questionable legal status of the fetus. (For a discussion of philosophic and legal problems associated with the ascription of personhood status to a fetus, see Losco, 1989.) As a result, prosecutors have increasingly taken to the courts only after a live birth.

In *People v. Bolar* (1982), the defendant was accused and convicted of reckless homicide after being involved in an auto accident in which she was found to be drunk. Her baby was delivered by caesarean section and lived for approximately two minutes. The court held that the newborn, having been "born alive," was a person for purposes of prosecuting the mother. State prosecutors also relied on the born-alive rule in the case of Melanie Green, who in 1989 was charged with involuntary manslaughter and delivering a controlled substance to a minor, following the birth of her daughter who lived for two days. Pathologists asserted that maternal use of cocaine had caused the placenta to rupture prematurely, thus resulting in oxygen deprivation, brain swelling, and eventually death. The grand jury declined to bring an indictment.

In the Michigan case described at the beginning of this chapter, Kim Hardy was tried on a standard charge of drug transmission. The prosecution did not make the case that the fetus per se was harmed or that it must be protected before birth. Rather, Hardy was charged with transmitting the drug to a live child in the minute or so after birth just before the umbilical cord was severed. Jennifer Johnson, also discussed above, was convicted under prosecution of the same type of born-alive drug transmission statute.

In fact, more and more "fetal rights" cases are being brought to the courts on the "born-alive" rule. Nineteen states now have laws that allow child abuse charges to be made against women who give birth to a child with illegal drugs in his or her bloodstream. This approach bypasses the thicket of interpretations dealing with the legal status of the fetus, since the death of a live child—and not a fetus—thus constitutes the crime. The postbirth approach also deflects much of the criticism that liberal feminists have leveled at fetal rights supporters who make personhood claims for the fetus. Fetal rights advocate John Robertson (1989) has made the born-alive provision a vital part of the doctrine he proposes. According to Robertson, government action should be limited to postbirth prosecution since, first, the legal status of the fetus is then not in question and, second, the woman could have exercised her civil liberty to abort within the *Roe* framework (see also Robertson, 1983). If she engages in an action that egregiously endangers the fetus and decides nevertheless to carry it to term, she is legally culpable for adversely affecting the interests of the newborn.[1]

Federal action that would encourage postbirth prosecutions has indeed been under consideration. In July 1989 Sen. Pete Wilson (R–Calif.) introduced the Child Abuse during Pregnancy Prevention Act of 1989. According to this bill, in order to be eligible for program grants a state would have to certify that it is a crime in that state for a woman to give birth to an infant who is addicted or impaired by a substance abused by its mother during pregnancy. And the state must attach to this crime a three-year minimum sentence of incarceration in a custodial rehabilitation center. The bill applies both to women who take illegal drugs and to those who ingest excessive amounts of legal substances like alcohol that lead to the impairment of the newborn. Presently, three states (Illinois, Minnesota, and Delaware) have legislation imposing special penalties on pregnant women who abuse controlled substances.

Tort Law

Through the system of torts, the court attempts to balance one party's security interests with another's interest in freedom of action. Tort law involving the fetus is fairly well developed. Section 869 of the *Second Restatement of Torts* (1979), for example, holds that one who tortiously causes harm to an unborn child is subject to liability for harm if the child is born alive. The provision goes on to say that, since our knowledge of factors affecting birth is not perfect, a court may require more in the way of convincing evidence of causation when the injury is claimed to have occurred early in pregnancy.

Tort cases involving fetuses have largely involved third parties like doctors or medical firms whose actions have led to wrongful death or wrongful life (i.e., a suit brought by an affected child who claims that he or she was allowed to come to term in some adverse condition as a result of negligence or abuse by others). One example of a successfully prosecuted wrongful life case is *Curlender v. Bio-Science Laboratories* (1980), in which the court recognized the standing of an infant plaintiff to recover from pain and suffering endured because of a laboratory's misinformation about the chances of contracting Tay Sachs disease. In *Bonbrest v. Kotz* (1946), the plaintiff was an infant who had been harmed when a doctor removed him from the mother's womb in a negligent manner. The court held that the fetus was a distinct legal entity to whom duty of care was owed. In states where wrongful life cases are permitted, the courts have moved from a position in which life—no matter what the condition of the newborn—was not recognized as an injury subject to tort action, to the acknowledgment of a tort claim with recoverable damages, given verifiable injury. At least three states (California, New Jersey, and Washington) recognize the rights of infants with birth defects to claim damages under wrongful life torts. Some states have taken action to protect against such claims (Minnesota, South Dakota, and Utah).

While tort actions are usually directed by custodians (parents) of the child against third parties for pain and suffering and can result in money damages that allow the parents to raise the child with his or her consequent defects, tort claims are increasingly being made against pregnant women. For example, a Michigan court in *Grodin v. Grodin* (1980) allowed a child to sue his mother for taking an antibiotic that caused prenatal injuries, and an Illinois court in *Stallman v. Youngquist* (1987) allowed a five-year-old girl to sue her mother for damages to her intestinal tract that were caused by an auto accident in which the woman was allegedly driving under the influence of alcohol. Elements of a prima facie tort case include the existence of a standard of care that has been violated, recognition of a duty, and evidence of breach of duty, injury, and proximate cause (Smith, 1986:186). Each of these points remains contentious in the current debate over fetal rights.

Feminist Viewpoints

While the term *feminism* is used to apply to viewpoints that emphasize power, status, and control by women, feminism actually reflects a variety of philosophic positions, all of which are not necessarily compatible. Alison Jaggar (1983) discerns at least four types of feminist doctrine, from liberal to Marxist. Susan Behuniak-Long (1990) divides feminist viewpoints into two broad categories on the basis of response to reproductive issues and the use of new reproductive technologies, and labels them "liberal feminism" and "radical feminism." While, as she notes, there are important elements of overlap between these categories and while these are but two variants in a much wider spectrum of feminist positions, concentrating on these two can give us a useful indication of important differences within the scope of feminist views dealing with reproductive issues.

Behuniak-Long notes that feminism in the early 1960s seemed fairly unified so far as reproductive issues were concerned. Reproductive technology meant the freedom to choose. Advances in birth control and contraception gave more control over reproduction to women.

With medical advances in the 1970s and 1980s like in vitro fertilization, fetal surgery, and the ability to sustain life outside the womb at earlier stages of gestation, liberal and radical feminist views tended to diverge. While the former argued in favor of technological knowledge and change so long as decisions about whether to "use or refuse" remained individual and unconstrained, radical feminists—seeing reproductive technology as an extension of patriarchal control—called for restrictive laws. As Behuniak-Long summarizes, "Therefore the present reproduction demands of liberal and radical feminists appear to be contradictory; the liberals demanding the freedom to choose, and radicals insisting on the necessity of protective legislation" (1990:42).

Liberal feminists emphasize long-standing liberal tenets regarding individuals as rational actors who should be free to make their own decisions, especially in private matters like reproduction. The battle for sexual equality has been largely the battle to demonstrate that women are rational agents on a par with men, capable of the same degree of autonomy in action as men, and as entitled to a full complement of rights (see e.g. Okin, 1989). Sexual inequality, being the result of unjust discriminatory laws and sex-role socialization, can be largely eradicated by the introduction of gender-neutral laws. The goal is to create a legal environment where women are genuinely free to make their own decisions—especially regarding reproduction.

In contrast, the radical feminists' position is implicitly contextual and social (Petchesky, 1990:331). It is informed by a perspective that Rosalind Petchesky calls "moral praxis," in which individual decisions are based on the real relationships and needs of actual women rather than on an abstract notion like rights. Radical feminists have rejected the rhetoric of "choice" in favor of "control." They question whether women living in a patriarchal society can avoid being exploited and manipulated by medical researchers and practitioners, and call for a thoroughgoing social change in which the very terms of the reproductive debate and the definitions of "maternity," "childbearing," and "motherhood" are recast. Like some liberal feminists (but perhaps more vigorously), they express distrust of the medical establishment, often noting the adverse effects pregnant women have suffered by conforming to trends in medical science (e.g., thalidomide, DES, outmoded weight-gain prescriptions, etc.; see e.g. Rothman, 1989: esp. 159–68; Atwood, 1986).

With regard to the emerging issue of fetal rights, the vast majority of feminists apparently agree in rejecting the validity of any claims in favor of the fetus over the woman carrying it.[2] However, the reasons why liberal feminists and radical feminists maintain this position are quite different. And at stake in this feminist debate is the very nature of the maternal–fetal relationship.

Liberal feminism emphasizes the notion that a fetus is part of a woman's own body. Thus, decisions about the welfare of the fetus are hers alone, since these are ultimately decisions about how she treats her own body. Allowing the government to intervene on the part of the fetus is tantamount to invading her constitutional rights to privacy and autonomy of action. Such intervention, if unchecked, would enable the "government virtually to dictate how pregnant women must live their lives" (Johnsen, 1989:180). This position was in great part validated in *Roe v. Wade* (1973) and in subsequent decisions contributing to a woman's "right to choose." Yet the position is also fraught with some dangers. As gestation progresses, the fetus becomes increasingly differentiated from the pregnant woman. Genetically, of course, it is distinct from the mother at conception. But from the standpoint of mobility, ability to live outside the womb, and ability to develop independently of the woman's body, the fetus develops greater distinction in the later stages of pregnancy up to birth. The moral and legal importance of this differentiation is not lost on liberal feminists who recognize that claims on behalf of a late-term fetus complicate the legal picture (e.g. Nolan, 1990:16). Yet the essence of the liberal feminist position remains that the fetus is part of the woman's body and, for all intents and purposes, only she can make decisions about her body and the potential life she carries within it.

Radical feminists adopt a more complex position with regard to the status of the fetus. Petchesky (1990), for example, claims that the fetus is not medically a part of the woman's body at all:

> On the level of "biology alone," the dependence [of the fetus on its host] is one-way—the fetus is a parasite. Not only is it not part of the woman's body but it contributes nothing to her sustenance. It only draws from her; nutrients, immunological defenses, hormonal secretions, blood, digestive functions, energy. (Petchesky, 1990:350)

Radical feminists emphasize the notion of relationship with the fetus over the rights-bearing nature of either woman or fetus. The fetus draws its identity from the woman in the relationship that develops during and after pregnancy. This is a relationship that the woman can foster or terminate. If the woman desires the child, she will nurture it and allow a mutual dependence to grow, creating a social and moral bond. It is her "attentive consciousness" in providing conditions of nurturance or allowing these to go unmet that determines the personhood status of the fetus. Questions of moral personhood cannot arise independent of the woman's desire to build such a status for the entity she carries, since, as Petchesky argues, personhood involves consciousness and sociability—conditions that are not even met after livebirth and that depend on constant nurturing to emerge. As Petchesky notes, "the fetus is never viable insofar as it remains utterly dependent for its survival on the mother or another human caretaker until long after birth" (1990:350).

Other radical feminists agree that the moral agency of the fetus grows out of a relationship the woman must choose to enter and to continue, but take a view more akin to the liberal position that the fetus is part of the woman's own body. For example, Barbara Katz Rothman (1989) argues that the fetus is a part of the woman's body that gradually becomes another person if the woman enters into a nurturing relationship with it.[3] Yet, like Petchesky, Rothman eschews the language of rights and argues that viability should not place limits on a woman's decision to abort, since hers is the decision to create or "not to create" (p. 123). Only the woman who is the primary caretaker can decide whether her resources are enough to allow the fetus to come to term. For some women, even a late-term abortion will be only a minor inconvenience; for others, it is an occasion of great sorrow. Only the individual woman can decide her course on the basis of the real-life situation in which she finds herself (pp. 123–24).

For radical feminists, the notion of fetal rights is inappropriate since they reject the idea that the fetus could ever have interests separate from the woman who bears it. Further, radical feminists reject the individualistic philosophic base on which the rhetoric of individual rights and the rhetoric of a right to choose are predicated. Choices are never fully free in our society since they are constrained by social expectations shaped by male dominance and class structure. What often masquerades as choice is nothing more than an offering of male-determined alternatives. In rejecting the rhetoric of choice, radical feminists often affirm limitations on what some consider "rights," in the interest of furthering long-term feminist goals. Thus, for example, some feminists argue that viewing or publishing pornographic material or, in the sphere of reproductive rights, using sex-selection technologies ought to be prohibited. These are false liberties and are opposed to the long-term interests of women. Radical feminists replace the vision of individual rights with a view toward control, in which women come to dictate the terms of reproduction. In regard to care for the fetus, the woman decides whether to continue or end the relationship she enters into, making this decision on the basis of a number of unique factors that can only be understood contextually. A choice-based view is rejected since it implies that rights to choose are conferred by others. Women need no permission to make decisions regarding the potential lives they carry.[4]

Thus, radical feminists reject the very terms with which liberal feminists carry on the dialogue over maternal interests under the law. As Petchesky notes,

We must . . . take a moral stance that is also a political stance: to refuse the terms of the dilemma, to reject being caught between unviable "choices." This is very different from demanding the "right to choose." We are saying that we reject the choices. . . . [M]aking authentic moral judgments about abortion and having choices that are real involve changing the world. (Petchesky, 1990:360)

The radical feminist position defines away the legal and ethical questions that have arisen in regard to fetal rights controversies. While radical feminists oppose fetal rights no less strongly than liberal feminists, they remain above the fray of the legal battles fought in the trenches by liberal feminists. Radical feminism calls for political action in transforming society, in reforming perceptions and the terms of political discourse. But because most of the current controversy over fetal rights has taken place within the context of the liberal legal doctrine embraced by liberal feminists, and since it is these mainstream arguments that are most likely to shape the immediate future for women faced with such legal dilemmas, it is to a discussion of liberal feminist arguments that we now move.

Liberal Feminism and the Law

Liberal feminist reliance on the legal concept of rights has placed the thrust of their debate in the legal arena. Radical feminists would argue that change must be political, initiated from political sources, and not played out within the framework of already existing patriarchal legal codes. This is not to say that feminists of all varieties have not employed both legal and political means at some time. It is just that the thrust of their arguments forces them to confront different arenas for the primary resolution of grievances. Below I will review some of the legal challenges made by liberal feminists to the notion of fetal rights and will try to assess the current state of law in each area.

Fundamental Rights

The cornerstone of the feminist legal argument against the concept of fetal abuse is the notion of "fundamental rights." Fundamental rights are those singled out for special protective status free from unwarranted government interference and not easily overridden when the rights of claimants collide. Among the fundamental rights recognized by the courts are the right to privacy in matters relating to "marriage, procreation, contraception, family relationships, and child rearing and education," as delineated in the Supreme Court case *Whalen v. Roe* (1977). *Roe v. Wade* (1973) recognized the right to privacy with respect to abortion within a trimester framework where the woman retains relative autonomy in abortion decisions during the first two trimesters. Together, these are the rights generally implied when feminists speak of the "right to choose." Of course, the right to choose (i.e., the right to privacy) does not mean a woman can choose to engage in illegal behavior with impunity. For example, no woman (pregnant or otherwise) has the right to abuse drugs, even if this affects her interests alone. Autonomy rights are always constrained by societal norms and laws. Even fundamental rights can be circumscribed when they collide with the fundamental rights of others or come into conflict with "compelling state interests." For example, the right to bear arms does not mean the state cannot limit their availability or use for the sake of public safety and health. Nevertheless, feminists argue that the right to privacy established by the Supreme Court in the 1970s protects pregnant women from government interference in the choices they make regarding the conduct and continuance of pregnancy.

Three questions of preeminent importance for the feminist legal position may be outlined as follows:

1. What constitutes a compelling state interest sufficient to override the fundamental right to privacy in matters of procreation?
2. When does such a compelling interest arise?
3. How does one balance fundamental rights against compelling state interest?

We will consider these questions (though not in this order) below. Additional questions regarding potential duties and their fundamental fairness will be addressed afterward.

When Does Compelling State Interest Arise?

The second question in the list above is easier to answer than the first. The Court in *Roe* effected a compromise between the alleged compelling interest of the state and the right of a woman to control decisions affecting her unique ability to bear children. The *Roe* compromise consisted in dividing pregnancy into trimesters in which the state has an increasing interest as the fetus develops toward birth. The state has no justification for interfering in the first trimester, can intrude only to the point of specifying operational procedures for abortion in the second trimester, and can set more stringent standards in the third trimester, to the point of prohibiting abortions with the exception of those that are necessary to protect the life and health of the pregnant woman. Judged, then, from the standpoint of *Roe* and subsequent decisions, a woman's actions with regard to childbearing cannot be coerced by the state during the first two trimesters.

While the trimester framework has been declared problematic,[5] feminists correctly point out that, with regard to abortion, women have quickly adapted their decision making to the framework the Court imposed. The overwhelming number of abortions occur well before the third trimester. Nan Hunter reports, "Since abortions became legal nationwide, women have been able to make their abortion decisions earlier and earlier in pregnancy. Today, 99 percent of all abortions are performed in the first 20 weeks of pregnancy; after 24 weeks, the period in which viability becomes possible, only 0.01 percent are performed" (1989:130). Late abortions are usually most common among teens who have waited too long as a result of greater impediments in obtaining abortions and among those who have had to wait for the results of amniocentesis or other screening tests that are performed well along in pregnancy to determine genetic abnormalities. Still, some feminists (e.g. Hunter, 1989; Gallagher, 1987; Johnsen, 1989) argue that the state has no compelling interest in controlling the actions (including abortions) of pregnant women even beyond the end of the second trimester. The tenability of this position hinges in part on what constitutes "compelling interest" in the first place.

What Constitutes Compelling Interest?

Many liberal feminists assert that government interference in a pregnant woman's decisions about the treatment of her own body implies the existence of a rights status for an entity that has not yet come into being. Conferring rights status on the fetus sufficient to justify the state's compelling interest in protecting those rights places the rights of a hypothetical entity above those of a live rights-bearer (the woman herself). Compelling interest could only be asserted were the courts to recognize the fetus as a rights-holder worthy of protection. As Lynn Paltrow notes, "the Supreme Court has held that at no stage of development is a fetus a 'person' with rights separate from the woman. Neither legally nor biologically are fetuses independent parties with rights enforceable against the woman" (1990:44). While some feminists admit that a late-term fetus may be entitled to greater ethical concern than a previable fetus (e.g. Nolan, 1990:20), they argue nonetheless that conferring legal rights to the fetus is not warranted and unnecessarily places the interests of woman and fetus in potential conflict.

Paltrow is correct, of course, about the Supreme Court's unwillingness to rule on the constitutional status of the fetus, per se. However, she skims over the Court's position that the state may establish a compelling interest in the "potential life" of the fetus, especially in the late stages of gestation. In fact, even those members of the Court who were most sympathetic to the appellees in the recent case *Webster v. Reproductive Health Services* (1989) reiterated the validity of this right and seemed to indicate that the closer the fetus comes to full gestation, the more compelling is the state's interest in its potential life. For example, Justice Sandra Day O'Connor—concurring with the majority—wrote,

> No decision of this court has held that the state may not directly promote its interests in potential life when viability is possible. Quite to the contrary. (*Webster*, 109 S.Ct. at 528)

Justice Harry A. Blackmun—who strongly dissented in *Webster*—nevertheless opined that

> the viability standard takes into account the undeniable fact that as the fetus evolves into its postnatal form, and as it loses its dependence on the uterine environment, the state's interests [*sic*] in the fetus' potential human life, and in fostering a regard for human life, becomes compelling. (*Webster*, 109 S.Ct. at 553)

And dissenting Justice John P. Stevens wrote,

As a secular matter, there is an obvious difference between the state interest in protecting the freshly fertilized egg and the state interest in protecting a nine month gestated, fully sentient fetus on the eve of birth. There can be no interest in protecting the newly fertilized egg from pain or mental anguish because the capacity for such suffering does not yet exist; respecting a developed fetus, however, that interest is valid. (*Webster*, 109 S.Ct. at 564)

Thus, it is clear that even those members of the Court who have been most supportive of a woman's right to choose are willing to grant a compelling state interest late in pregnancy (sometime postviability) in which the woman's fundamental right to privacy may be circumscribed by the potential life of the fetus.

The case for total individual autonomy is also compromised by the health and welfare duties of the state, though this is less often discussed. The cost of treating a "cocaine baby," for example, is estimated at $1,000 per day for neonatal intensive care. Extended treatment can cost as much as $35,000 to $150,000 per child (Zucchino, 1990). These are costs that are borne by society either through private insurance or, as is more likely in the case of indigent patients, through public support. The National Association for Perinatal Addiction estimates that about one out of every ten newborns is exposed in the womb to one or more illicit drugs, cocaine being the most frequent (reported in *Time,* May 13, 1991: 57). In some locales as many as 15 percent of newborns have been shown to suffer some damage resulting from the mother's use of illicit chemicals during pregnancy (Chasnoff et al., 1989). If future studies confirm these findings, the scope of the problem may well make the state's case even more compelling.

Balancing Interests

Even if grave interests are acknowledged, however, at what point do they become so compelling as to override fundamental rights? What standards must the state meet in establishing compelling interests? Some have maintained that the state need only present a "rational basis" standard. Since activities like illegal drug use are not protected as fundamental rights, the court need only be persuaded that it is rational public policy to prohibit such activities to protect the fetus. However, liberal feminists argue that, since the prosecution of pregnant women challenges the fundamental right to privacy, the more difficult test of strict scrutiny must be met in establishing compelling interest. Accordingly, the state must establish that its actions are narrowly tailored to meet the needs it asserts and that the means it uses are the least burdensome to fundamental rights of any means available. Dawn Johnsen (1989) asserts that a host of worthy state goals have not met this lofty standard in proving compelling interest when pitted against fundamental rights. For example, the courts have not found sufficient compelling need to protect victims of sex abuse when this interest confronts the Sixth Amendment rights of the accused (p. 206). Johnsen speculates that the courts are especially unlikely to establish compelling interest when the methods employed for meeting this interest include intrusive procedures that violate the bodily integrity of the pregnant woman.

However, in criticizing the liberal feminist position, John Robertson points out that the courts have allowed forced seizures for compelling need in "civil commitment, prison sentences, capital punishment, the draft, forced treatment of adults for the sake of minor children and blood tests and surgery to recover evidence of a crime" (1989:265). Robertson further asserts that state action can be narrowly tailored to fit those cases where the actions of the woman are most egregious (e.g., wanton disregard through drug abuse despite repeated warnings) and where the goal of prosecution is to force rehabilitation after the birth of the child. As an additional protection, Robertson notes that the woman retains the freedom to terminate the pregnancy under the terms of *Roe*. It is only if she voluntarily gives up this right and continues with the pregnancy and the behavior detrimental to the fetus that state action would be warranted (Robertson, 1983).

It should also be remembered that the current prosecutorial strategy of prosecuting only if "born-alive" avoids many of the pitfalls that liberal feminists identify. Since the action is then taken in response to deleterious effects on a living being and since it does not involve violating bodily integrity, the rational basis test may be sufficient for conviction (Logli, 1990). The prosecution need only show that the woman violated some rational standard of care in adversely affecting the newborn. Thus, while liberal feminists appear to be on strong legal ground in cases involving forced seizures, the strength of their arguments in born-alive prosecutions continues to be tested with mixed results (e.g., Kim Hardy's conviction was overturned, but Jennifer Johnson's was not; see the beginning of this chapter).

However, even if one were to accept Robertson's formulation regarding the permissibility of prosecution (and liberal feminists do not), one would still be confronted with a host of related issues concerning the duty of the pregnant woman and the state's interest in "potential life."

What is the quality of life that the state has a compelling interest to advance? Does the mother have a duty to provide conditions conducive to this state?

Quality of Life

Barbara Katz Rothman (1989) has written that recent biological findings have altered the nature of myths concerning the womb. While once the womb was seen to be a protective fortress housing precious cargo, now it is being seen as a vulnerable and dangerous environment—one that not even women can be trusted to keep secure (Rothman, 1989:159). While both myths may perpetuate the stereotype of woman as fetal container, the latter may be more disturbing since it opens the womb to control by others. Clearly, medical science has altered our view of the fetal environment. New data are generated daily regarding the nature of fetal development in relation to a host of intrauterine and external environmental factors. The effects of workplace hazards (Blank, 1991), chemicals (Nolan, 1990), genetic transmission (Nelson, 1979), infectious diseases (Auger et al., 1988), and other factors raise questions about the duty of a woman—and others—to monitor and control the fetal environment.

In light of our increasing knowledge, some legal commentators advocate a fetal right to begin life with a sound mind and body. Margery Shaw (1984), for example, holds that women could be held legally negligent if they knowingly and wittingly pass on deleterious genes, if they furnish alcohol to minors by drinking during pregnancy, or if they engage in a number of activities shown to be deleterious to the fetus. Both parents—but particularly mothers, in the case of actions taken while pregnant—should consider the quality of life of the offspring they cause to enter the world. At the other end of the spectrum are those commentators who assert that even the ingestion of illegal drugs like cocaine cannot be considered cause for action against pregnant women. There is insufficient evidence, they say, showing the assured adverse effects of drugs on the newborn. Wendy Mariner, Leonard Glantz, and George Annas (1990), for example, say that cocaine's precise contribution to newborn maladies is uncertain since studies concentrate on women in lower socioeconomic levels who are exposed to other simultaneous risks that cannot be individually factored. Since the precise effects of drug abuse cannot be estimated, there can be no legal duty on the part of the pregnant woman to refrain.

Some liberal feminists recognize the moral dilemmas posed by new medical knowledge, such as it is. Dawn Johnsen (1989:199), for example, a staunch supporter of women's rights against claims on behalf of the fetus, admits that it is sometimes difficult to hold free from culpability the actions of a drug user in a late-term pregnancy. Nevertheless, Johnsen holds courts to a strict level of accountability in justifying the invasion of privacy rights in such cases. Other liberal feminists (e.g. Nolan, 1990) admit of a moral responsibility to avoid those substances that are likely to be deleterious, but question whether the state has any legal recourse in pursuing a say in the matter. Women are solely responsible, it is argued, for both the beneficial and harmful consequences of their actions on the fetus, and they are the ones who must live with the results of their behavior.

Liberal feminists appear to be on solid ground when they argue that no woman can be expected to provide an ideal fetal environment. There are so many environmental, congenital, and other potential sources of harm that it is almost impossible for a woman to be aware of all the dangers. Most harmful exposures occur early in pregnancy, before even the woman herself knows she is pregnant. The proposed standard of avoiding anything and everything that affects soundness of body and mind is thus wildly unrealistic. Yet we need not accept the opposite position, either—that there are no applicable standards of acceptable conduct, at all.

Standards of Care

While it is impossible to hold women to an idyllic standard of care, some advocates of fetal rights support the less stringent criterion that pregnant women be required to do no harm (see Feinberg, 1984). Most feminists oppose the institution of any standards of either care or harm avoidance, however, arguing that this opens the door for the medical regimentation of pregnancy—the "slippery slope argument," as it is called. Feminists fear restrictions against the use of alcohol, against driving, and infringement on a number of freedoms. They cite, for instance, the *Stallman v. Youngquist* case (discussed earlier in the chapter), which managed to exert a chilling effect despite the fact that it was reversed on appeal. Such cases illustrate, it is charged, the nature of the slippery slope toward which we are headed if legal standards of care are applied to women. The specter of "pregnancy police" has been raised—of society's agents enforcing standards on pregnant woman and violating their right to private action ("Pregnancy Police," 1988). Further, it is argued that many of the sources of potential harm are simply out of the control of women (see Mariner et al., 1990). These include unhealthy environments, air pollution, poor socioeconomic conditions. Since there is no community standard to provide a healthful environment for pregnant women, it is folly to hold women to a protective stance they can only minimally effect.

Critics of the liberal feminist position have responded that the slippery-slope fears are unwarranted. They point out, for instance, that child abuse laws have not led to a full-scale invasion of the family, to "child abuse police" (Robertson, 1989). Rather, these laws have attempted to balance the rights of parents with the societal need to protect children, in a manner analogous to the case of fetal abuse.

Some policy specialists—while acknowledging the difficulties associated with establishing a "standard of care" for pregnant women—do not despair of forging rational yet flexible guidelines. For example, Robert Blank (1986) argues that establishment of such standards would involve not just biological knowledge, but an understanding of what the community considers to be reasonably prudent. In any such effort, the public must be brought into a meaningful dialogue on the matter. And minimally, a determination must be made of the foreseeable degree of risk that maternal actions entail. Carol Ann Simon (1978) offers the suggestion of applying a "prudent parent standard" that would presume a minimum level of knowledge about the requirements of care, based on what is commonly known in the community, that is, on what the community considers reasonable or unreasonable. Yet, even such standards would have to be balanced against the rights and needs of the pregnant woman.

While it as difficult to protect from all harms as it is to provide an ideal environment, this does not preclude a duty to avoid preventable likely harm. The use of illicit drugs, it is true, does not in all cases result in serious harm. Yet it is hard to dispute that there is increasing information about the long- and short-term deleterious effects on infants of persistent drug abuse. Babies born to drug-addicted mothers generally have a low birth weight and developmental problems. It is not unusual for them to suffer retinal damage as well as seizures. In the most serious cases, they are stillborn (Hoffman, 1990). While the long-term effects are still being studied, there is evidence that babies born to cocaine-addicted mothers may suffer from severe physical deformities, behavioral aberrations including impulsiveness and mood-iness that may be linked to lesions found in their brains, learning disabilities, and impaired motor and social skills including a difficulty in distinguishing between mothers and strangers (*Time,* May 13, 1991: 56–60). Even were it not for the evidence of harm to the potential life of the fetus, the argument that women are the best judges of what is best for themselves and their future children is compromised in the case of a drug abuser who may not be capable of discerning rational conduct while under its influence.

Yet, a woman is not alone in providing a standard of care for the fetus. Male partners, medical personnel, and others share responsibil-ity for limiting harm. Third parties can be held criminally liable (as, e.g., in Arizona and Indiana, which have feticide laws that impose jail sentences on those who cause the death of a fetus at *any* stage of gestation) or sued (as in *Curlender v. Bio-Science Laboratories* [1980], discussed earlier) for causing harm to a fetus. Doctors and medical personnel are especially vulnerable to suit for negligence. If these other persons share responsibility for harm avoidance to the fetus, what actions are permissible on their part in regulating the actions of pregnant women who come under their care or jurisdiction? In this regard the recent *Automobile Workers v. Johnson Controls* (1991) decision may prove ironically troublesome for liberal feminists.

The *Johnson Controls* case has been hailed as a victory for women over the discriminatory hiring policies of business. In this case, a unanimous Supreme Court ruled that barring fertile women from well-paying high risk jobs violates Section 703(e)(I) of Title VII of the Civil Rights Act.[6] Exclusion from employment can only occur when there is a "bona fide occupational qualification" that an employee cannot meet. The Court said that women at Johnson Controls are as capable of doing their jobs as their male counterparts and may not be forced to choose between having a child and having a job. Thus, an employer cannot bar women from a job simply because of workplace hazards. In this case, the most troublesome workplace hazard was lead, a sub-stance that has been shown to have significant adverse effects on the life chances of fetuses (see e.g. Blank, 1991). While some legal experts hold that the protection given by the *Johnson Controls* ruling should now allay employer fears about being sued for harm to fetuses, it is unlikely that the assurances of these experts will prevent any such suits from materializing. In fact, Justice Byron White—while concur-ring—noted this potential problem: "Common sense tells us that it is part of the normal operation of business concerns to avoid causing injury to third parties, as well as to employees, if for no other reason than to avoid tort liability and its substantial costs'' (*Automobile Workers v. Johnson Controls,* 111 S.Ct. at 1210). White goes on to say that, since the laws of all states permit children to bring lawsuits for prenatal injuries, employers should take this potential liability into account.

As for Johnson Controls itself, after the Supreme Court's ruling, officials for the company said they would probably return to the practice of warning women of hazards and having them sign waivers relieving the company of liability (*New York Times,* March 21, 1991). This amounts to transferring liability from the company to the individual woman in decisions regarding what types of exposure to which she is willing to submit herself. Consequently, in the instance of a pregnant woman and the care of her fetus, it lets third parties off the hook. If the practice of limiting liability by the use of waivers turns out to be effective, it is not unreasonable to speculate that physicians, hospitals, medical providers, insurance companies, and so on will use such devices to limit their own liabilities in cases where there is reason to believe that the woman may not comply with a reasonable standard of care. This could force women (or, at best, both parents) to face alone the costs of raising an impaired child without benefit of suit to recover damages from the third parties involved. The *Johnson Controls* ruling could have the effect of substantially increasing the liability of pregnant women in the long run.

Discriminatory Impact

Liberal feminists argue that fetal rights action illegally discriminates against pregnant women by singling them out as a class for special treatment. They also suggest that fetal rights prosecutions discriminate against minorities and those in lower socioeconomic classes.

Clearly, pregnant women *are* the primary targets in this type of legal action, for obvious biological reasons. The question that must be raised, critics of liberal feminism contend, is whether or not this is justifiable. For policy reasons, certain classes of individuals have been allowed to be treated differently. For example, men are assigned primary combat responsibility in the military for policy reasons—be they wise or misguided. But are women being prosecuted for being pregnant, as some feminists (e.g. Paltrow, 1990) claim?

Mariner, Glantz, and Annas (1990) argue that pregnant women who use drugs are being prosecuted solely for being pregnant, since the *use* of drugs itself is not ordinarily a criminal offense, but (usually) only its possession or sale, and since pregnancy, unlike driving a car, is not an activity regulated by the state through licensure. Their reasoning seems tortured, however. It is not drug use or pregnancy that is at issue in fetal abuse cases, but the endangerment or transmission of illicit substances to a party the state may (subject to all the caveats discussed above) have compelling reason to protect.

But there is no reason why pregnant women should be singled out for actions they may not have committed alone. For example, in the Monson case described at the beginning of the chapter, there seems to have been good reason for prosecuting the child's father, as well, since he contributed to the fetal harm by having sex with his wife despite her doctor's warnings. There is also evidence that he procured the drugs she took and took them along with her (Johnsen, 1989). Since many women in the late stages of pregnancy are dependent on their husband's income for support, there seems also to be good reason for holding the men accountable for the welfare of the fetus if they fail to contribute proper financial support. Numerous other instances of male liability could be cited as well. For example, Lori Andrews (1989a:376–77) supports bringing suits against sperm donors who conceal information about their genetically or otherwise transmissible infectious diseases. To this, we might add the likelihood of potential suits against males who transmit these diseases through sexual intercourse, as well. Legal action in all of these cases does not seem unwarranted if the goal is to protect "potential life." The fact that such actions are not normally prosecuted seems to confirm the feminist charge of sexual bias. More research is needed to determine the degree to which genetic material contributed by males results in genetic defects in newborns. For example, there appears to be good evidence that genetic diseases can be transmitted by men who have experienced even low-level exposure to toxic metals (according to Dr. Ellen Silbergeld, as reported in *Time,* November 26, 1990:90). Ann Aschengrau and Richard Monson reported in the *American Journal of Public Health* that children of men who served in Vietnam were almost 2 percent more likely to suffer from serious malformations ranging from clubfoot to heart disease. Even more dramatic are the findings of researchers Ricardo Yazigi, Randall Odem, and Kenneth Polakoski, who reported in 1991 the discovery that cocaine readily attaches to sperm, which might carry the drug into the egg at the time of conception (Yazigi et al., 1991). Such findings, if confirmed, implicate male behavior in the transmission of preventable health risks to the fetus and raise important questions about the culpability of males who knowingly transmit such hazards.

Liberal feminists also argue that prosecutions tend to single out minority and poor women in a discriminatory manner. And in fact, most of the notable cases discussed in the literature have been confined to this group. Yet several studies show the incidence of illegal substance use to be greater in white women. In the first comprehensive study of its sort, Ira Chasnoff and his coauthors (1989) found the rate of positive drug tests to be 15.4 percent among white women and 14.1 percent among black women, although black women showed a much higher rate of cocaine addiction. Yet, as one study in Florida showed, black women were 9.56 times more likely than white women to be reported for their substance abuse (Sherman, 1989:28). The reasons are familiar. Minority and poor women are more likely to attend public hospitals and clinics where reporting is required. White women are more likely to attend private physicians and to secure private treatment. It is probably no accident that—with regard to two cases discussed early in the chapter—the conviction of Kim Hardy, a white attorney, was overturned while that of Jennifer Johnson, a poor black woman, was not. Of course, such figures on the discriminatory impact of prosecutions do not on their own justify the abandonment of prosecution. They do, however, serve to emphasize the nature of problems endemic to law enforcement in the United States—a subject that deserves separate treatment.

Public Health Issues

Liberal and radical feminists alike argue that public policy should focus on prevention of prenatal injury, rather than punishment. Women who drink excessively or who abuse drugs while pregnant, they argue, are caught up in a social system in which they have no control. Many of these women are themselves victims of sexual abuse or come from homes in which drugs were abused routinely. They are often desperate, without education and without the means to secure adequate care for themselves or for the fetuses they carry. In addition, drug treatment for poor pregnant women is virtually nonexistent. Most drug treatment facilities are not open to pregnant women. One study of New York drug clinics showed that 54 percent categorically excluded pregnant women and 67 percent excluded pregnant women on Medicaid who are addicted to crack (Chavkin, 1990). Jennifer Johnson, convicted in the Florida case discussed earlier, was one of those who sought help but was turned away. Those treatment programs that do allow pregnant women are often geared toward males and result in poor success rates among women in general. There are some model programs designed specifically for pregnant women that do show success—for example, Hutchinson Place in Philadelphia (as reported in the *Indianapolis Star,* November 4, 1990), and the Women and Infants Clinic in Boston and at Daytop Village in New York (as reported in *Time,* May 13, 1991)— but these are expensive and still in the early stages of study and development.

The threat of punishment, it is also argued, will have the result of keeping pregnant women away from health care and drug treatment programs in the first place. Women who fear that their doctors will turn them in for having abused substances or for not following a particular medical regimen will simply stay away from health care services. This is the position taken, for example, by the National Association of Perinatal Drug Addiction and Research (Paltrow, 1990:47 n. 39). While this point makes a good deal of sense, the evidence for it is largely anecdotal. And there is anecdotal evidence as well that some pregnant women may not seek drug treatment or health care unless faced with the threat of legal action—for example, loss of custody, or imprisonment (as reported in *Time,* May 13, 1991). Obviously this is an area that needs more intensive study.

It is admitted by even fetal rights advocates (e.g. Robertson, 1989) that imprisoning pregnant women is no solution if the intent is to improve the life chances of the fetus. Prisons simply do not have the facilities necessary to attend to the needs of pregnant women. However, equally punitive measures are already widespread, though less frequently discussed. In many states, hospitals routinely test for the presence of drugs in the urine of a newborn. A positive test is often sufficient to trigger the removal of the infant from the custody of the mother (Sherman, 1989). It might be argued that, in some cases, this is justified. "Addicted" babies are often moody, and addicted mothers may have difficulty handling the demands of such newborns. Yet, a judgment as to the fitness of a parent can hardly be made on the results of a single test, and the harm that can come from the child's spending time away from its mother in an impersonal holding facility has been demonstrated (Greene, 1989). Decisions about how to treat such cases of alleged fetal or child abuse cannot be made with sweeping a priori solutions. They demand careful analysis of individual cases to determine how best to balance maternal and child interests.

There is one point about which there tends to be almost universal agreement on the part of feminists of all stripes, on the part of prosecutors (Logli, 1990), and even on the part of right-to-life groups (Sherman, 1988). Namely, prosecutions must not be the primary means of dealing with the broader social problem of prenatal health care. For example, organizations from quite disparate political viewpoints came together to lobby against Sen. Pete Wilson's Child Abuse during Pregnancy Prevention Act of 1989. The National Abortion Rights Action League, Planned Parenthood, the National Right to Life Committee, and the U.S. Catholic Conference all agreed that, with regard to improving the health of babies, "special punitive measures against pregnant women do not accomplish this . . . goal" (Johnsen, 1989:212). Liberal and radical feminists must build on this unlikely coalition, despite its admittedly large potential for conflict over control of the health care agenda.

Still, even if government were to make prenatal health its highest priority, difficult cases of the sort discussed here would not be likely to go away.[7] In fact, were substantial investments made on behalf of this group as a class, the potential for conflict over the liability of pregnant women might even increase.

Conclusion and Future Concerns

Feminists seem to have been successful in slowing the number of court-ordered medical interventions by arguing forcefully for bodily integrity and by raising sufficient questions about the legal status of the fetus to alter the course of prosecutions during pregnancy. Of course, continuing advances in prenatal surgery and care may alter the course of prosecutions further. Supporters of fetal rights, however, have managed to hold a number of pregnant women accountable for harm to the fetus through the "born-alive" strategy; and there is no indication that the number of tort cases involving the maternal–fetal conflict will dwindle soon.

The Board of Trustees of the American Medical Association (AMA) has issued guidelines that will no doubt become the focus for continued debate. The board recommends against judicial intervention except in exceptional cases "where the treatment poses an insignificant or no health risk to the woman, the procedure entails a minimal invasion of her bodily integrity, and would clearly prevent substantial and irreversible harm to her fetus." It also recommends against criminal sanctions or civil liability for harmful behavior by the pregnant woman toward her fetus. Yet, while noting that it is difficult to imagine circumstances that might warrant legal action, the board points out that "absolutely prohibiting legal penalties for all potentially harmful actions by pregnant women may seem extreme. . . . [I]t seems incongruous to suggest that society should have no legal recourse for such behavior." It finds permissible the removing of custody of children born to addicts, though warns against the abuse of this practice. Finally, it calls for greater prevention through education and access to rehabilitative treatment (AMA Board of Trustees, 1990:2670). While this set of guidelines is designed to "balance" the interests of woman and fetus, debate will continue to focus on hard cases. Radical feminists who are distrustful of the medical establishment will find little in its policy statement to recommend a continued reliance on medical judgment regarding health risks, and liberal feminists will object to the continued possibility of legal action—especially when the AMA admits that it cannot conceive of instances when such action might be warranted. Nevertheless, the guidelines will serve to focus continued debate.

As law in this area becomes a bit more settled and predictable, it is likely that the health care perspective focusing on prevention will deservedly receive more attention. Yet, the likelihood of success in gaining greater access to health care and drug treatment for pregnant women is not bright in an era of tight budgets.

The most serious challenge to the feminist position is likely to come from the high court. There exists the real possibility that a newly constituted Supreme Court will revisit *Roe* in the near future and that *Roe* may be overturned.[8] What happens to the fetal rights argument if the fundamental right of a woman to choose is taken away?

If the Court allows the state to set limits on abortion and even to determine that the state has a compelling interest in the future life of the fetus from conception onward, the slippery slope feared by feminists may become reality. Women will not be free to control reproduction for any period, since the viability standard will be dismantled. Women will be required to take to term fetuses that they may not want and that may suffer serious defects. In a health care system already constrained by high costs and the need to ration medicine, it is possible that health care providers will wind up placing greater burdens on women at earlier times in pregnancy in order to limit liability and public expense. This will likely increase the number of prosecutions against women, the number of infants with serious maladies, and the likelihood of deaths among women seeking illegal abortions.

Ironically, however, the revocation of *Roe* would take away one of the strongest arguments of those who advocate some type of legal culpability for pregnant women who act in a negligent manner: the argument that a woman is free to choose whether to continue the pregnancy and risk prosecution or to terminate it. The freedom of a woman to exercise this right is seen as an important safeguard against wrongful prosecution since it allows her to weigh rationally the life chances of her offspring against life-style choices in the continuance of her pregnancy. Without the safeguard of *Roe,* it can be argued, decision making is taken away from the woman and so also is culpability. Kathleen Nolan expresses the moral perspective that informs this logic:

A woman's claim to act as she chooses (based on the principle of autonomy) appears to be legitimately constrained (morally) by her relation to a fetus in an ongoing pregnancy, although it is important to note that this constraint is based on her freely choosing to be in relationship to a dependent other. If women are unable to choose not to conceive or not to remain pregnant, then, the involuntary nature of their relationship changes its moral character. Women whose sexual partners refuse to use contraception or women who are unable to contracept or abort because of their financial status, may stand in a different moral relationship to their offspring than women who can freely choose to become pregnant and care for a child. (Nolan, 1990:18)

Flawed as it may be, *Roe* has become a means for adjudicating claims against the most egregious abuses perpetrated on both women and fetuses. It has provided a middle ground sufficiently broad to reduce the number of genuine conflicts between the needs of the woman and concern for the fetus to (for the most part) only the most difficult and traumatic cases. Without *Roe,* the middle ground is lost.

Notes

1. Feminists oppose Robertson's prescription (1989) on the grounds that this stance would penalize women who bring a fetus to term, relative to those who abort if they are doubtful about the way in which their behavior has contributed to the health of the fetus. It would, in effect, impose abortion in order to avoid prosecution—an action violative of fundamental privacy rights.

2. Differences in philosophic outlook and reasoning do not dilute the apparent solidarity among many feminist scholars who write on this subject regarding opposition to "fetal rights."

3. In a confusing set of passages, Rothman seems to waiver on this position. At one point, she seems to equate the differences between a late-term fetus and an early-term fetus with the differences between "our old selves, our aging selves," and "our young selves" that have yet to "become something very different" (1989:161).

4. There is a potentially deeper division between radical and liberal feminists regarding the nature of sexual equality. Some radical feminists appear willing to entertain the possibility of genuine sexual differences with regard to orientation and personality (e.g. Gilligan, 1982; Rothman, 1989). Many liberal feminists point out the inherent dangers in this position and warn that it can undercut the demand for political equality and fundamental rights by raising questions about the psychological prerequisites of rights-bearing agents (see e.g. Andrews, 1989b).

5. The Court majority raised substantial and explicit questions about the ongoing relevance of the trimester framework in *Webster v. Reproductive Health Services* (1989).

6. Public Law 88-352 (July 2, 1964), as amended.

7. John Condon (1986) has documented examples of "fetal abuse" by women that may not be easily remedied by education or availability of treatment. Condon argues that these women are "at risk" for fetal abuse since they may have been abused themselves or may live in an abusive environment. He describes cases of conscious abuse of late-term fetuses (physically or through ingestion of harmful substances) in which the women refuse to abort. He recommends that health care officials be alerted to the signs of such abuse and intervene early to foster greater commitment on the part of both parents (where possible) to the pregnancy.

8. On April 22, 1992, the Supreme Court heard oral arguments in the case *Planned Parenthood of Southeast Pennsylvania v. Casey*. Both Planned Parenthood and the U.S. Justice Department asked that the case be used to revisit the *Roe* decision in order to make a final determination either upholding the principles established in that case or nullifying them. [With this manuscript in press, on June 30, 1992, the Court reaffirmed its commitment to the core holding of *Roe* by a 5–4 vote.—Ed. note.] The Court will likely have several additional opportunities in the next few years, however, to readdress that issue. Given the Court's propensity to rule on narrow grounds, it is most likely that, in the short run, the high court will simply chip away at *Roe* by granting greater powers to the states to regulate abortion. If this occurs, the framework of *Roe* may stand in those states with liberal abortion statutes and fall in those where legislatures are more inclined toward restriction. The net effect will be a practical diminution of the right to choose, signaling, in the words of Justice Blackmun, an abandonment of *Roe* "not with a bang but a whimper" (*New*

York Times, July 4, 1989, p. A-13). Still, this might be preferable to an outright reversal of *Roe* in a political environment where abortion rights are not universally supported.

References

AMA (American Medical Association) Board of Trustees. 1990. "Legal Interventions during Pregnancy." *Journal of the American Medical Association* 264(20):2663–70.

Andrews, L. 1989a. "Alternative Modes of Reproduction." In *Reproductive Laws for the 1990's,* N. Taub and S. Cohen, eds. Clifton, N.J.: Humana Press, pp. 361–403.

———. 1989b. *Between Strangers.* New York: Harper & Row.

Aschengrau, A., Monson, R. 1990. "Paternal Military Service in Vietnam and Risk of Late Adverse Pregnancy Outcomes." *American Journal of Public Health* 80 (October): 1218–24.

Atwood, M. 1986. *The Handmaiden's Tale.* Boston: Houghton-Mifflin.

Auger, I., Thomas, P., DeGruttola, V., Morse, D., Moore, D., Williams, R., Truman, B., Lawrence, C. 1988. "Incubation Periods for Pediatric AIDS Patients." *Nature* 336(8):575–77.

Automobile Workers (International Union, United Auto, Aerospace and Agricultural Workers of America, UAW, et al.) v. Johnson Controls Inc., 111 S.Ct. 1196; 498 U.S.— (March 20, 1991).

Behuniak-Long, S. 1990. "Radical Conceptions: Reproductive Technologies and Feminist Theories." *Women and Politics* 10(3):39–64.

Blank, R. 1991. "Fetal Protection Policies in the Workplace." Paper delivered at the annual meeting of the Midwest Political Science Association, Chicago, April 18–20.

———. 1986. "Judicial Decision Making and Biological Fact: *Roe v. Wade* and the Unresolved Question of Fetal Viability." *Western Political Quarterly* 37, 4 (December): 584–602.

Bonbrest v. Kotz, 65 F. Supp. 138 (D.C. 1946).

Buss, E. 1986. "Getting beyond Discrimination: A Regulatory Solution to Problems of Fetal Hazards in the Workplace." *Yale Law Journal* 95:577–98.

Chambers, M. 1987. "Charges against Mother in Death of Baby Are Thrown Out." *New York Times,* February 27, I-25, col. 1.

Chasnoff, I., Griffith, D., MacGregor, S., Dirkes, K., Burns, K. 1989. "Temporal Patterns of Cocaine Use in Pregnancy." *Journal of the American Medical Association* 261, 12:1741–45.

Chavkin, W. 1990. "Drug Addiction and Pregnancy." *American Journal of Public Health* 80:483–87.

Condon, J. 1986. "The Spectrum of Fetal Abuse in Pregnant Women." *Journal of Nervous and Mental Disease* 174(9):509–16.

Curlender v. Bio-Science Laboratories, 106 Cal.App.3d 811, 165 Cal.Rptr. 477 (1980).

Feinberg, J. 1984. *Harm to Others.* New York: Oxford University Press.

Gallagher, J. 1987. "Prenatal Invasions and Interventions: What's Wrong with Fetal Rights." *Harvard Women's Law Journal* 10:9–58.

Gilligan, Carol. 1982. *In a Different Voice.* Cambridge, Mass.: Harvard University Press.

Greene, M.S. 1989. "Boarder Babies Linger in Hospitals." *Washington Post,* September 11, pp. A-1, A-7.

Grodin v. Grodin, 102 Mich.App. 396, 301 N.W.2d 869 (1980).

Hoffman, J. 1990. "Pregnant, Addicted and Guilty?" *New York Times Magazine,* August 19, pp. 32–35, 44, 53, 55, 57.

Hunter, N. 1989. "Time Limits on Abortion." In *Reproductive Laws for the 1990's,* N. Taub and S. Cohen, eds. Clifton, N.J.: Humana Press, pp. 129–54.

Jaggar, A. 1983. *Feminist Politics and Human Nature.* Sussex, England: Rowman and Allanheld.

Jefferson v. Griffin Spaulding County Hospital, 247 Ga. 86, 274 S.E.2d 457 (1981).

Johnsen, D. 1989. "From Driving to Drugs: Governmental Regulation of Pregnant Women's Lives after *Webster.*" *University of Pennsylvania Law Review* 138:179–215.

Johnson, P. 1990. "The ACLU Philosophy and the Right to Abuse the Unborn." *Criminal Justice Ethics* (Winter/Spring): 48–51.

King, P. 1979. "The Judicial Status of the Fetus: A Proposal for Legal Protection of the Unborn." *Michigan Law Review* 77:1647–87.

Logli, P. 1990. "Drugs in the Womb: The Newest Battlefield in the War on Drugs." *Criminal Justice Ethics* (Winter/Spring): 23–29.

Losco, J. 1989. "Fetal Abuse: An Exploration of Emerging Philosophic, Legal and Policy Issues." *Western Political Quarterly* 42(2):265–86.

Mann, J. 1991. "Cure an Addict, Save a Child." *Washington Post,* April 5, p. C-3.

Mariner, W., Glantz, L., Annas, G. 1990. "Pregnancy, Drugs and the Perils of Prosecution." *Criminal Justice Ethics* (Winter/Spring): 30–41.

Merrick, J. 1990. "Maternal–Fetal Conflict: Adversaries or Allies?" Paper presented at the annual meeting of the American Political Science Association, San Francisco, August 30–September 2.

Nelson, W. 1979. *Textbook of Pediatrics*, 11th ed. Philadelphia: Saunders, esp. pp. 352–55.

Nolan, K. 1990. "Protecting Fetuses from Prenatal Hazards: Whose Crimes? What Punishment?" *Criminal Justice Ethics* (Winter/Spring): 13–23.

Okin, S. M. 1989. *Justice, Gender and Family*. New York: Basic Books.

Paltrow, L. 1990. "When Becoming Pregnant Is a Crime." *Criminal Justice Ethics* (Winter/Spring): 41–47.

Parness, J. 1985. "Crimes against the Unborn." *Harvard Journal on Legislation* 22:97–172.

People v. Bolar, 109 Ill.App.3d 384, 440 N.E.2d 639 (1982).

Petchesky, R. 1990. *Abortion and Woman's Choice: The State, Sexuality and Reproductive Freedom*. Boston: Northeastern University Press.

"Pregnancy Police: The Health Policy and Legal Implications of Punishing Pregnant Women for Harm to Their Fetuses." 1988. *NYU Review of Law and Social Change* 277:292–309.

Raleigh Fitkin–Paul Morgan Memorial Hospital v. Anderson, 42 N.J. 421, 201 A.2d 537, cert. denied, 377 U.S. 985 (1964).

Robertson, J. 1989. "Reconciling Offspring and Maternal Interests during Pregnancy." In *Reproductive Laws for the 1990's*, N. Taub and S. Cohen, eds. Clifton, N.J.: Humana Press, pp. 259–74.

———. 1983. "Procreative Liberty and the Control of Conception, Pregnancy, and Childbirth." *Virginia Law Review* 69:405–64.

Roe v. Wade, 410 U.S. 113 (1973).

Rothman, B. K. 1989. *Recreating Motherhood*. New York: Norton.

Shaw, M. 1984. "Conditional Prospective Rights of the Fetus." *Journal of Legal Medicine* 63:63–116.

Sherman, R. 1989. "Keeping Babies Free of Drugs." *National Law Journal*, October 16, pp. 1, 28–29.

———. 1988. "Keeping Baby Safe from Mom." *National Law Journal*, October 3, pp. 24–25.

Simon, C. A. 1978. "Perinatal Liability for Prenatal Injury." *Columbia Journal of Law and Social Problems* 14:47–81.

Smith, D. C. 1986. "Wrongful Birth, Wrongful Life: Emerging Theories of Liability." In *Abortion, Medicine, and the Law*, 3rd ed., J. D. Butler and D. F. Walbert, eds. New York: Facts on File, pp. 178–94.

Stallman v. Youngquist, 52 Ill.App.3d 683, 504 N.E.2d 920 (1987).

Strunk v. Strunk, 445 S.W.2d 145 (1969).

Webster v. Reproductive Health Services, 109 S.Ct. 3040 (1989).

Whalen v. Roe, 429 U.S. 589 (1977).

Yazigi, R., Odem, R., Polakoski, K. 1991. "Demonstration of Specific Bonding of Cocaine to Human Spermatozoa." *Journal of the American Medical Association* 266, 14 (October 9): 1956–59.

Zucchino, D. 1990. "Philly Program Targets Drug-addicted Pregnant Women." *Indianapolis Star*, November 4, p. D-2.

9
Afterword: Sexual Difference and Equality

Mary Lyndon Shanley and Richard Battistoni

The essays that make up the chapters of this volume contribute to a growing body of work on feminist jurisprudence that makes clear both the excitement and frustration of trying to use lawsuits to achieve greater equality between women and men. They also reveal the profoundly gendered nature of both the workplace and the home, and of the interlocking nature of the gender hierarchies found in each. Unjust in and of themselves, these gender hierarchies also account to some extent for the shockingly low level of public support our society gives to families and to children—its most vulnerable members. The "difference that difference makes" is so great, in fact, that neither a sex-blind approach nor one based on recognition of male–female differences is, by itself, adequate for securing either justice for women and men or the well-being of their children. The collective lesson of these quite diverse essays is that promoting equitable treatment for individuals, genuinely reciprocal and interdependent relationships between adults, and stable relationships with caring adults for children will require a massive social and political commitment and a restructuring of both the public and domestic worlds. The actions required to achieve full gender justice will move us beyond strategies focused on jurisprudence and the courts into those based in democratic politics, workplace restructuring, and greater equality in the American household.

The preceding chapters reveal the multiple ways in which the law fails to protect both women and children from economic vulnerability. Mark Graber's analysis in Chapter 6 of the ways in which access to abortion is limited by class and race could be extended to a wide range of social and medical services that are unavailable to poor women and their children. In Chapter 8, Joseph Losco gives chilling accounts of women being charged with criminal offenses when their children are born with problems traceable to lack of proper prenatal care. He concludes from these cases that women must retain the right to choose to have an abortion if they are going to be held liable for birth defects. We would draw another lesson: In case after case, the negligence is not that of the woman alone, or even primarily, but that of society. It is profoundly misguided to hold a pregnant woman responsible for drug-related birth defects when she has been denied access to drug-rehabilitation programs; or to make a woman but not her partner culpable for irresponsible sexual behavior; or to remove children from a woman's custody because she is too poor to provide for them, rather than providing her a job or a child allowance.

Lisa Bower shows in Chapter 7 how, after divorce, women and children are frequently thrust into poverty because the ex-wife does not have earning power comparable to that of her husband. The low level of child support awards, exacerbated by the low level of compliance with whatever awards are made, means that children as well as women suffer from the sex-role division of labor that simultaneously makes women responsible for the day-to-day care of children and economically vulnerable. No-fault divorce and the subsequent changes in family law have thus become "equal treatment with a vengeance."[1]

Can we arrive at a feminist theory of legal equality that will address the specific problems of economic and political vulnerability faced by women and, by extension, by those children in their care? The essays by Judith Baer (Chapter 5), Mary Becker (Chapter 4), Leslie Goldstein (Chapter 2), and Joan Williams (Chapter 3) seek to answer this question by looking at one of the dominant issues in feminist jurisprudence over the past decade: the "sameness" versus "difference" debate. That debate centers around the question of whether women's interests are better served by arguing that women and men deserve the *same* treatment under the law, or that the law should take account of significant *differences* between women and men in order to achieve lived equality.

At first glance, the sameness or "equal treatment" approach appears straightforward, and in the 1970s it informed many of the legal reforms achieved by feminists. The idea of an unbiased, universal legal norm of equality that would rule out all forms of gender discrimination is consonant with American individualistic ideology and traditions of procedural justice. Equal treatment has been effective, historically, in eliminating discriminatory laws that were based on women's presumed weakness or inferiority to men.

The problem with equal treatment arguments is that they adopt an unspoken and often unacknowledged male standard under the guise of neutrality. While the demand for equal treatment can effectively knock down employment barriers based on sex, it gains for women only what men already have, and only for those women whose life situations match that male standard. For example, the Supreme Court ruled that there was no discrimination based on pregnancy involved when the State of Missouri refused to pay unemployment benefits to a woman who lost her job when her employer would not rehire her after she attempted to return to work from a maternity leave.[2] The Court held that denying unemployment compensation to women who lose their jobs because they give birth is not discrimination due to pregnancy, because the state also denies unemployment benefits to others who leave work for reasons "unrelated to work or to the employer."[3] Strict equal treatment arguments are therefore not particularly helpful when female workers seek to protect their income or jobs when they become mothers, since men do not interrupt their work to become parents, and employers are reticent to expand their leave policies in sex-neutral ways.

The effort to counteract the implicit male standard in much of the law has led many legal theorists to argue that women's differences from men—whether stemming from biology or culture—should inform certain laws. Maternity leaves, statutory rape laws, a male-only draft, and affirmative action policies are acceptable on this argument because they do not require that women be regarded as or act like men in order to receive legal protections or benefits. "Special treatment" accommodates gender differences where appropriate and thereby gives voice to women's specific experiences and needs.

Despite the attractiveness of this attention to women's concrete experiences, when this attention occurs in the context of pervasive gender hierarchy, it carries with it the implication of superiority and inferiority, better and worse, normal and deviant. Even a narrow accommodation of the sex differences associated with pregnancy may be damaging to the long-term equality interests of women. Wendy Williams argues that legislation granting women maternity benefits evokes the "protective" labor laws passed at the turn of this century, and carries with it a number of substantial costs:

> First, it makes women who are likely to become pregnant less desirable employees and thus increases the incentive to discriminate against women

of the "vulnerable" age and marital status. Second, special treatment can shift attention from the fact that the employer has a generally inadequate sick leave policy to the fact that some employees have special privileges. Energies which might constructively be directed toward improved working conditions are diverted into hostility toward fellow workers, specifically women who become pregnant and have children. Last and certainly not least, the legislation perpetuates an outmoded ideology—woman as unique and separate, with a special reproductive role in which the state has sufficient interest to single her out for special treatment.[4]

Adjudication based on difference can also enhance the status quo; arguments for maternal preference in custody disputes, for example, seem to protect women's interests in keeping their children with them, but run the danger of reinforcing the notion that mothers rather than fathers not only *do* perform more parenting functions but *should* do so.

As it turns out, both sides in the difference debate play into the hands of a male-referenced legal system. As Catharine MacKinnon trenchantly observes,

> Concealed [in the debate] is the substantive way in which man has become the measure of all things. Under the sameness standard, women are measured according to our correspondence with man, our equality judged by our proximity to his measure. Under the difference standard, we are measured according to our lack of correspondence with him, our womanhood judged by our distance from his measure. Gender neutrality is thus simply the male standard, and the special protection rule is simply the female standard, but do not be deceived: masculinity or maleness, is the referent for both.[5]

To break the hold of the male standard underlying the difference debate, analysis must focus on the *relationship* between female and male experiences. That is, the relevant "difference" is not located in women's (or men's) nature, but in the socially and institutionally structured relationship between them that makes their differences matter. Analysis must focus not on difference itself, but on "the difference that difference makes" in women's and men's lives and opportunities. Jurisprudential and political strategies must work to free women, men, and children from destructively rigid gender dualisms, allowing them to express and alleviate genuine differences and at the same time live together in community.

Joan Williams and Leslie Goldstein suggest in this book that the law could move away from attributing difference to one sex or the other through enacting gender-specific but sex-neutral legislation. Such laws could recognize the particular needs of those who perform traditional "women's" roles without implying that their work is exclusively or naturally women's work. For example, a rule that awarded custody to the person who has been a child's "primary caretaker" would be preferable to a presumption favoring either the mother or joint custody. The sex-specific "maternal preference" assumes that women are, and should be, the parents responsible for the day-to-day care of children and does nothing to foster fathers' responsibility for their children. A legal preference for joint custody, by contrast, treats women and men, mothers and fathers, equally, but slights the fact that often one parent (usually the mother) gives more time and energy to childrearing than the other parent. Rather than automatically favoring mothers on the one hand or treating unalikes equally on the other, a primary caregiver rule would acknowledge the stronger claims created by the parent who has been providing greater and more sustained care.

Similarly, sex-neutral leave or other workplace policies could supplant traditional maternity leave policies and allow workers to take time off to care for others and yet maintain job security. One example of this kind of inclusive workplace leave policy is the Family and Medical Leave Act (proposed and passed by Congress but vetoed by President George Bush). The act would have required employers with large workforces to grant up to 12 weeks of unpaid leave to workers to care for new children or ill relatives or for their own medical problems.

In the immediate future, the suggestion that legislatures enact and courts apply rules that are sex blind but gender specific is probably the best one can hope for in combating some of the disabilities created by both sex-based discrimination and a lack of accommodation to the needs of women or those who take on women's traditional roles. Gender justice and the needs of children seem to us to demand more radical changes in the long run, however. For example, the primary caregiver rule in custody cases and a sex-neutral parental leave policy do nothing by themselves to change the gender structures that result in one parent's assuming the bulk of the care of a family's children. Most two-parent families are forced to consider a number of factors in choosing a primary caregiver for young children. It is likely that one parent working full-time will earn more than both working part-time; part-time jobs rarely carry medical and pension benefits; and continuity of employment is necessary for benefits, job retention and promotion, and future work options. Because the man can usually earn more than the woman, there are economic reasons for his becoming the family's primary wage-earner, and the woman the primary care-giver (even when the woman also works outside the home), in two-parent heterosexual families. But this does not mean that such an arrangement is the best possible one for each parent, or for their child, nor that it is the one they would choose if different options were available; it is simply their choice under the constraints of present circumstances. Some policy changes would make the choice of primary caregiver for a couple's children more meaningful. For example, equal pay for work of "comparable" worth would make women and men more equal competitors on the job market, and not automatically confer the breadwinner role on the male. But even this would not allow both parents to be involved equally with childcare and paid labor either by sharing the effort on a daily basis or by rotating duties year by year.

There are a number of considerations that suggest the desirability not simply of equalizing the economic opportunities of women and men, but of reordering social roles to create greater uniformity in the kinds of tasks that women and men perform. Mary Becker notes in this book that feminists are torn between creating a world in which women's traditional roles are less binding on women so that women can move into better paying, more prestigious "men's" jobs, and one in which women's roles and traits are highly valued and thus compensated directly or given legal protection (as with alimony). Yet this conundrum arises in part because the problem presents itself as a choice between moving women out of the home or protecting them when they remain within it. The alternative of having men take on what have traditionally been women's responsibilities for home and children is less often put forward; the fact that its realization appears remote does not make it less just or desirable.

Giving men greater responsibility for the care of household, children, and other dependents would enable women to take on expanded roles as earners and citizens. Joan Williams points out here that only a change in roles will put women and men in more equal economic bargaining positions. When gender roles become more fluid, the sharp (but false) distinction between what is private and what is subject to public deliberation and decision making will break down. This should increase women's voice in politics. As theorists from Aristotle to Thomas Jefferson to John Rawls have asserted, civic participation is essential to full adult life in a democratic polity. (The fact that Aristotle and Jefferson would have excluded women from citizenship does not alter the fact that they thought participation in the life of the polity is essential to the highest form of human activity.) Women in a democratic polity both need and deserve access to public economic and political activity.

These goals for women might seem to be purchased at the expense of men. The implicit but still driving assumption of the business world that workers have wives at home makes it hard to see what benefits men would get from gender equality. Men's increased involvement in and responsibility for domestic life would decrease their ability to dominate the world of wage labor and political deliberation. This would, in turn, diminish men's relative power in the family. Also, some women who might be happier if single or living in a same-sex household would be freed from current economic pressures to live with a man.[6] Still, despite the loss of economic and social dominance, a more even distribution of power might well bring some benefits to men. John Stuart Mill was one of the few political theorists who addressed this issue, and he believed that male dominance is ultimately as harmful to men as to women.[7] Drawing on Hegel's discussion of the mutual corruption of the master–slave relationship, Mill argued that sexual inequality has led to a stunting of human capacities and prevented the development of full self-consciousness and self-knowledge. He was convinced that the development of individual men, and of the human species, necessitates mutuality, reciprocity, and friendship that can only flourish under conditions of equality. According to Mill, then, relinquishing privilege (by reason of race, class, and sexual orientation as well as of sex, we would add) is not only required by justice, but beneficial to the formerly dominant person as well.

Men would also benefit from increased contact and interaction with children. Aristotle portrayed the tasks involved in raising very young children as work of "mere necessity"—repetitive chores that do not engage the higher human capacities—but his distinction between work that engages us as animals and as humans is falsely dichotomous. Susan Okin has argued that there is not such a sharp distinction between the habits of the parent/homeworker and those of the citizen, and that public policy will benefit from greater role-sharing between women and men.[8] "[T]he experience of being nurturers, throughout a significant portion of our lives, . . . seems likely to result in an increase in empathy, and in the combination of personal moral capacities, fusing feelings with reason, that just citizens need."[9] Judith Baer asserts in this book that since one problem with "male" constitutional jurisprudence is its tendency to ignore feelings and experience or to drive them underground amid formal rules, if such role sharing were to promote a greater attention to concrete experience, it might even improve the quality of constitutional interpretation.

Greater flexibility and similarity in female/male tasks would certainly seem likely to benefit children. Currently, the sex-role division of labor makes children economically vulnerable if they do not live in a household with an adult male, because women's earning power is so low, and fathers so frequently fail to pay child support. Almost one-quarter (24.2%) of children in the United States lives in single-parent households headed by women, and almost half (44.5%) of these households is below the poverty level.[10] We should hope that the rate of default on child support payments would decrease for noncustodial parents who had been closely involved in their children's daily lives before the divorce. In two-parent families, children would benefit from having both parents attuned to the children's emotional and developmental needs. And if both men and women worked in the public and domestic worlds, children would not have their aspirations and senses of self bound by their own sex, but would see before them women and men who were both deeply involved in the work of citizen and parent.

It is clear that litigation about female and male differences or sameness—while important—will not by itself achieve the long-term goals of giving women greater economic and political power and men greater domestic responsibility. Equality jurisprudence has taken the first steps toward breaking down the barriers—those of class, race, and sexual orientation as well as gender—that have been used to deny citizens the power individually and collectively to shape their lives. But jurisprudential solutions, feminist or otherwise, are inherently limited. Courts must wait for cases to be brought to them before acting, they tend to rule on the narrowest of legal grounds, they defer to legislatures and other governmental institutions, and they are disinclined to initiate major social changes. Moreover, legal arguments must be framed in the language of the current male-dominated legal tongue in order to win rights or affirmation. In this sense, legal discourse may more often silence than encourage the voices of women and others who have been historically excluded from American law.

The essays in this book suggest that gender equality requires us to move beyond the limits of litigation to empower women's voices. A broadened political discourse would enable people to see and address needs in context, not simply as framed by current legal argumentation. For example, the problems Joseph Losco addresses here must be confronted in a political setting, where citizens could deliberate over the issues of sex education and birth control, pre- and post-natal care, drug rehabilitation for pregnant addicts, better support for poor mothers, as well as abortion and fetal rights. This would advance the discussion from the adversarial conflict between women's rights and fetal rights in a way that would enhance the lives (and rights) of both women and children. The sweeping changes in the organization of the workplace that Joan Williams sees as necessary if wage labor is to take account of reproduction and family responsibilities will require extensive debate and struggle in both the political and business arenas. As Mary Becker contends, a responsive, democratic political process allows citizens to make all kinds of arguments about what should be done to meet their needs. Only such broad and unconstrained debate gives us any hope of figuring out and implementing measures that will increase lived equality between women and men.

The fate of the sameness/difference debate is important not only to feminist jurisprudence, but to democratic theory as well. The feminist critiques of "malestream" jurisprudence represented in these essays demonstrate that in our present democratic discussions not all are equal in their ability to speak. Nor do others feel obligated to listen to the voices of the less powerful. It is crucial to democratic politics that the polyphony of citizen voices speak and be heard. A democratic polity must effectively pluralize difference, exposing the problems of legal distinctions and the pain suffered by those excluded from legal categories and judgments because of their differences. This implies not only talk but, in Patricia Williams's words, "listening at a very deep level to the uncensored voices of others."[11] Or as Martha Minow says, "It is not even enough to imagine the perspective of the other; we must also try to share deliberations with the other person."[12] For pluralist democracy to survive, we must be able to "constitute ourselves as members of conflicting communities with enough reciprocal regard to talk across differences."[13]

The sameness and difference debates that have been at the center of feminist jurisprudence for the past decade have laid bare the deep and destructive impact of gender divisions on women and men as individuals, as family members, and as citizens, as well as on their children. As the essays in this book make clear, neither gender-neutral standards nor rules based on gender differences can by themselves work the transformations of economic, political, social, and familial life that are necessary if women and men are to meet as equals in our society. And until such time, their associations—both public and private—will fall short of the ideal of mutuality and reciprocity that must be part of any democratic vision or practice.

The transformations suggested here will not obliterate all differences; this is neither possible nor desirable in a pluralistic society. Nor is there a single road ahead that will bring us to the land of sexual equality. Feminists must fight for equal rights when they are denied, but with the constant awareness that "rights" always exist within specific historical configurations of institutional and social practices. When procuring "equal rights" would simply mean laying claim to equal treatment within a structurally unsound or unfair status quo, people who are female, poor, members of a racial minority, gay, or lesbian must fight for the recognition and accommodation of their particular or "different" needs in law and new social arrangements. Feminists must also take steps to ensure that their own discourse is pluralistic, that it listens carefully to the variety of voices that articulate women's experiences. As Minow cautions, "Current feminists need more, not less, attention to relationships (as do rights theorists) to remind us to consult, debate, and explore—with people we think different from ourselves—the hidden assumptions about unstated norms that we retain."[14] All of this will require much hard work—in courts of law, in corporate boardrooms, in trade union halls, in innumerable organizations from political parties to block associations, and around family dinner tables. That work is essential if we are to secure both justice and democracy for all women and men, and for their children who, after all, are the parents and citizens of our common future.

Notes

1. Lenore Weitzman, *The Divorce Revolution* (New York: Free Press, 1985), p. 366.
2. *Wimberly v. Labor and Industrial Relations Commission of Missouri*, 479 U.S. 511 (1987).
3. Ibid. at 517.
4. Wendy Williams, "Equality's Riddle: Pregnancy and the Equal Treatment/Special Treatment Debate," 13 *NYU Review of Law and Social Change* 325 (1984/85):371.
5. Catharine MacKinnon, *Feminism Unmodified* (Cambridge, Mass.: Harvard University Press, 1987), p. 34.
6. Christine Littleton, "Women's Experience and the Problem of Transition: Perspectives on Male Battering of Women," *University of Chicago Legal Forum* (1989):23–57.

7. John Stuart Mill, "The Subjection of Women," in Alice Rossi, ed., *Essays on Sex Equality* (Chicago: University of Chicago Press, 1971).

8. Susan Okin, *Justice, Gender and the Family* (New York: Basic Books, 1989).

9. Ibid., p. 186.

10. U.S. Department of Commerce, Bureau of the Census, *Household and Family Characteristics*, Current Population Reports, Series P-20, No. 424 (Washington, D.C.: Government Printing Office, March 1991).

11. Patricia Williams, "Alchemical Notes: Reconstructing Ideals from Deconstructed Rights," 22 *Harvard Civil Rights–Civil Liberties Law Review* 402 (1987):411.

12. Martha Minow, *Making All the Difference* (Ithaca, N.Y.: Cornell University Press, 1990), p. 383.

13. Ibid., p. 390.

14. Ibid., p. 382.

Index

abortion, 5–6, 8, 18–20, 35, 173–207, 238–45, 258–59, 270; disparate access to by geography, 188–89; disparate access to by race, 187, 188, 189, 194, 196, 264; disparate access to by wealth, 6, 178, 187, 188, 189, 193, 194, 196, 200, 264; governmental funding for, 19–20, 197, 203; in relation to fetal protection, 7, 235, 246, 256–57, 264; infrequency of prosecutions for, 186–87; legal restrictions of, 178, 179, 180, 182, 185–89, 196, 197, 198, 200, 203; legalization of, 19; parental consent for, 155–56; see also fetal protection; pro-choice movement; pro-life movement; Roe v. Wade

ACLU, 22, 133, 136, 142; Women's Rights Project, 22, 34, 37, 100, 116, 145

affirmative action, 4, 100–102, 104, 106, 108, 120, 126, 127–30, 133–34, 144, 145, 265; see also Johnson v. Transportation Agency

alimony, 4, 8, 36, 59, 109, 110–13, 138, 139, 140, 162, 166, 217, 226, 268; see also Orr v. Orr; Otis v. Otis

AMA, fetal protection guidelines, 255–56, 259

American Booksellers Association v. Hudnut, 32

American Medical Association. See AMA

Aristotle, 103, 135, 268, 269

Arizona Governing Committee v. Norris, 37

Autoworkers v. Johnson Controls. See United Auto Workers v. Johnson Controls

Bacon, Francis, 152

Baer, Judith, 4, 5, 39, 147–71, 264, 269

Barber, Sotirios, 160, 167, 195, 204

Bartlett, Katharine, 149, 152, 153, 161, 163, 164, 167

battered women syndrome, 15, 33

Battistoni, Richard, 1, 263–73

Bayh, Birch, 22

Beal v. Doe, 35

Becker, Mary E., 3, 4, 14, 27, 32, 34, 39, 99–145, 209, 227, 264, 268, 271

Behuniak-Long, Susan, 7, 10, 237, 238, 259

Bender, Leslie, 15, 32, 38, 39

Bernard, Jessie, 216, 226, 227

Bickel, Alexander, 157, 167

Binion, Gayle, 39, 152, 167

Black, Hugo, 155, 157, 160, 161, 168

Blackmun, Harry, 148, 150, 154, 244, 258

blacks. See race

Bonbrest v. Kotz, 236, 259

Bordieu, Pierre, 225, 228

275

Wald, Patricia, 61
Walker, Lenore, 15, 33
Warren, Earl, 158–59
Wasserstrom, Richard, 75
Weber. See Steelworkers v. Weber
*Webster v. Reproductive Health
    Services*, 203, 244, 245, 258, 262
Wechsler, Herbert, 173, 174, 199, 207
Weitzman, Lenore, 2, 21, 24, 25, 30,
    36, 38, 88, 89, 96, 137, 138, 140,
    166, 171, 209, 217, 218, 226, 227,
    230, 272
West, Robin, 14, 15, 32, 33, 34, 38,
    39, 50, 74, 76, 80, 81, 149, 171,
    207
Whalen v. Roe, 242, 262
White, Byron, 133, 134, 250
wife-battering, 3, 15, 20, 23, 29, 33
Williams, Joan, 3, 4, 14, 15, 25, 26,
    32, 33, 34, 36, 38, 39, 41–98, 264,
    267, 271

Williams, Patricia, 271, 273
Williams, Wendy, 14, 15, 22, 25, 26,
    32, 33, 37, 38, 39, 96, 120, 136,
    137, 141, 265, 272
Wilson, Joan Hoff, 148, 170
Wilson, Pete, 236, 255
Wimberly, Linda. *See Wimberly v.
    Labor and Industrial Relations
    Commission of Missouri*
*Wimberly v. Labor and Industrial
    Relations Commission of Mis-
    souri*, 99, 115, 133, 141, 272
Wittgenstein, Ludwig, 15, 46–47
Wolgast, Elizabeth, 50, 75, 76, 81,
    97, 133, 142
women's clubs, 113
women's culture. *See* domesticity,
    ideology of
work, devaluation of women's, 2, 23

Yudof, Marlene, 75, 77, 142

Contributors and Acknowledgments

Judith A. Baer is associate professor of political science at Texas A&M University. She has published articles in the *Western Political Quarterly, Law and Policy Quarterly, Women and Politics, Law and Social Inquiry,* and *NWSA Journal.* Her most recent book is *Women in American Law* (New York: Holmes & Meier, 1991).

Richard Battistoni is associate professor of political science at Baylor University. He is the author of a number of books and articles, including *Constitutional Government: The American Experience* (St. Paul, Minn.: West, 1989) and *Public Schooling and the Education of Democratic Citizens* (University: University Press of Mississippi, 1986). He is currently working on a book dealing with the changing nature of equality in the American constitutional experience.

Mary E. Becker is professor of law at the University of Chicago School of Law, where she teaches feminist theory, family law, trusts and estates, and employment discrimination. She has published articles on these subjects as well as on Social Security, the Constitution, and religion; and is currently at work (with coauthors Morrison Torrey and Cynthia Bowman) on a casebook in feminist jurisprudence. Her chapter, "Prince Charming," originally appeared as an article in *The Supreme Court Review* (ed. Philip Kurland; Chicago: University of Chicago Press, 1987), whose permission to reprint it is gratefully acknowledged; some editorial changes have been made.

Lisa C. Bower is assistant professor of political science at Arizona State University. Currently, she is working on a book about the transformation of feminist and legal feminist arguments and strategies in the legal field.

Leslie Friedman Goldstein is professor of political science at the University of Delaware. She is the author of *In Defense of the Text* (Lanham, Md.: Rowman & Littlefield, 1991), *The Constitutional*

Rights of Women (Madison: University of Wisconsin Press, 1988), and numerous articles on the subjects of political theory and constitutional law.

Mark A. Graber is an assistant professor of government at the University of Texas at Austin. He is the author of *Transforming Free Speech* (Berkeley: University of California, 1991), *Equal Choice: A Political/Constitutional Interpretation of Abortion* (forthcoming), and several articles on American constitutional politics.

Joseph Losco is professor of political science at Ball State University. He has published in the area of bioethics and political theory, including most recently *Political Theory: Classic Writings, Contemporary Views* (with coauthor Leonard Williams; New York: St. Martin's Press, 1992). He currently serves on the Executive Board of the Association for Politics and Life Sciences.

Mary Lyndon Shanley is professor of political science on the Margaret Stiles Halleck Chair at Vassar College. She is the author of *Feminism, Marriage and the Law in Victorian England* (Princeton, N.J.: Princeton University Press, 1989) and coeditor of *Feminist Interpretations and Political Theory* (with Carole Pateman; University Park: Penn State University Press, 1990). She is currently at work on a book on ethical issues in contemporary family law, and during 1991–92 served as a scholar-in-residence at the Princeton University Center for Human Values.

Joan C. Williams is currently a professor at The American University, Washington College of Law, and during 1991–92 was visiting professor at the University of Virginia Law School. Her work has appeared in a variety of journals dealing with history, philosophy, and law, including *Nomos*, the *Journal of Women's History,* and the law reviews of Duke, Michigan, Virginia, Harvard, NYU, and Texas. She specializes in the law of property and local government, and feminist and nonfoundationalist jurisprudence. Her chapter "Deconstructing Gender" originally was published as an article in 87 *Michigan Law Review* 797 (1989), whose permission to reprint it is gratefully acknowledged; some editorial changes have been made, and a number of notes deleted.

Copyediting was done by Pat Merrill and indexing by Martha Ross, both of whose excellent assistance is gratefully acknowledged.